UNDERSTANDING
CROSS-CULTURAL MANAGEMENT

We work with leading authors to develop the strongest educational materials in business and management, bringing cutting-edge thinking and best learning practice to a global market.

Under a range of well-known imprints, including Financial Times Prentice Hall, we craft high quality print and electronic publications which help readers to understand and apply their content, whether studying or at work.

To find out more about the complete range of our publishing, please visit us on the World Wide Web at: **www.pearsoned.co.uk**

UNDERSTANDING
CROSS-CULTURAL MANAGEMENT

Marie-Joëlle Browaeys and Roger Price
Nyenrode Business University

Prentice Hall
FINANCIAL TIMES

An imprint of **Pearson Education**

Harlow, England • London • New York • Boston • San Francisco • Toronto • Sydney • Singapore • Hong Kong
Tokyo • Seoul • Taipei • New Delhi • Cape Town • Madrid • Mexico City • Amsterdam • Munich • Paris • Milan

Pearson Education Limited

Edinburgh Gate
Harlow
Essex CM20 2JE
England

and Associated Companies throughout the world

Visit us on the World Wide Web at:
www.pearsoned.co.uk

_____

First published 2008

ISBN: 978-0-273-70336-5

British Library Cataloguing-in-Publication Data
A catalogue record for this book is available from the British Library

Library of Congress Cataloging-in-Publication Data
Browaeys, Marie-Joëlle.
  Understanding cross-cultural management / Marie-Joëlle Browaeys and
Roger Price.
     p. cm.
Includes bibliographical references and index.
  ISBN 978-0-273-70336-5
  1. Diversity in the workplace—Management.   I. Price, Roger, 1946-   II. Title.
HF5549.5.M5B75 2008
  658.3008—dc22

                                                                        2008010056

10 9 8 7 6 5 4 3
11 10

Typeset in 10/12.5 pt Minion by 73.
Printed by Ashford Colour Press Ltd, Gosport.

Contents

Preface
Learning about cross-cultural management

Knowing is not enough; we must apply.
Willing is not enough; we must do.

Johann Wolfgang von Goethe

Preparing for global business

Given the globalization of business and increasing diversity within the workforce of so many industries and organizations, a cross-cultural component in management education and training can no longer be considered as a useful 'add-on' merely for those who might consider venturing abroad to pursue their career. Nowadays, more and more managers are required to work effectively across cultural borders. Even if they are confined to their offices, they are more and more likely to interact with people from other cultures. Awareness, education and training in cross-cultural management has therefore become a 'must', whatever the type of business education concerned, whether it be for aspiring graduates at the start of their career or for those senior managers who wish to increase their effectiveness in their present positions or their employability in the international market.

The approach of this book

This book is the result of our experiences in educating executives and postgraduate students in the areas of cross-cultural management and cross-cultural business communication. It reflects the need we felt for a practical, hands-on approach to study in this area which:

- offers a broad, if selective, view of current thinking on culture linked to management, organization and communication. So it would not be just one particular (theoretical) approach to cross-cultural studies or an encyclopaedic survey of the theories involved;
- allows the theories and ideas mentioned to be applied to practice through the inclusion of examples and brief case studies from the business world, as well as activities that require some of the theories outlined to be applied to business situations and to the reader's own work situation.

Combining a concise overview of cross-cultural concepts and learning-by-doing activities is an approach to cross-cultural management we have found to be effective for both instructors and students, trainers and trainees. Students are exposed to approaches to cross-cultural aspects of business rather than being overwhelmed with detail about countries and their cultural 'profiles' based on one theoretical framework. At the same time, they are asked to apply these approaches in a practical and relevant manner to a number of case studies, many of which are taken from the business media. When doing so, students are expected not only to use the concepts, but also to apply their own intuitive insights and cross-cultural experience. This can be a rewarding experience for those concerned because the learning-by-doing activities themselves can reveal cultural assumptions and attitudes of those undergoing the learning process.

The instructor will, it is hoped, appreciate the concise overview of theories and concepts relating to cross-cultural management while being provided with activities to *facilitate learning*. Moreover, the material enables the instructor to make maximum use of the environment in which the learning is taking place. As a facilitator in the process, the instructor helps the students not only to 'construct' their own understanding based on their knowledge and experience, but also to take advantage of the informal learning process through those activities, which encourages interaction between trainees. Having said that, however, we believe that this book is also a valuable resource for self-study because it enables readers to extend and to deepen their cross-cultural awareness.

This approach to learning reflects a concern we had when preparing a book that deals with culture: knowledge of oneself is as important as the knowledge of theory.

The structure of the book

The book is divided into three parts:

- **Part One: Culture and management** deals with the concept of culture, its facets and the levels at which culture operates. It explores cultural dimensions in the business context and examines the cultural dilemmas that arise for managers in making decisions. It finally presents a model of culture based on cultural value orientations that affect managerial activities.

- **Part Two: Culture and organizations** considers the influence of culture on aspects of organizations, including structures, corporate cultures and the role of leadership. The cultural factors involved in strategy and strategic alliances come to the fore as well as in fundamental organizational change. Culture and marketing, along with the question of cultural diversity in organizations, are also addressed.

- **Part Three: Culture and communication** examines how culture affects the process of communication both within and between cultures. Various cross-cultural contexts are dealt with, including negotiations and international teams. Cross-cultural conflict is given particular attention as are the skills required to be an intercultural communicator.

Each of these parts is made up of six chapters. Each chapter in turn contains one or two **cross-cultural concepts**, which each contain the main ideas and theories relating to a particular subject-area as well as examples related to the theory, and at least one **activity**. Each part concludes with two **final activities**.

The cross-cultural concepts are compilations of ideas and theories developed by researchers in the area of cross-cultural management, as well as overviews that we have developed. Those students who wish to read more detailed accounts, or who wish to read other articles on the areas in question, are given a list of references at the end of each chapter.

The activities in each chapter relate explicitly to the concepts presented. The activities allow the learner to apply these concepts through exercises of various kinds, including case analysis. Case studies play a prominent role in the activities because they have proved to be an effective learning tool. Confronted with a dilemma described in each case, students are forced to consider their potential behaviour in the context described and learn from the choices they make. Interaction with their peers and instructor when accounting for their choices compels them to *talk about their experiences* and feelings, as well as the insights they have gained from reading the cross-cultural concepts in the book. The cases deal with many cultural contexts, so students are confronted with different ways of thinking, thereby helping them to develop transcultural competence.

The **final activities** at the end of each part pull the strings together. Being more extended in nature and incorporating the elements of each part, they are intended to provide a broader perspective of the area in question.

Flexibility of approach

The arrangement of material is such that it allows flexibility in the sequence to be followed. Although we would suggest that Part One be the starting point for any programme of study, the sequence of chapters in Part Two and Part Three, as given below, need not be followed slavishly. The chapters may be re-arranged according to the priorities of the instructor and/or student. For example, if Chapters 8 and 18 are studied one after another, then the cultural aspects of leadership can be examined in terms of the communicative skills considered appropriate and effective in different national/organizational cultures. A further example: Chapters 9 and 15 can be studied together and so allow the issue of company takeovers and mergers to be combined with the negotiating process involved.

Part One Culture and management	Part Two Culture and organizations	Part Three Culture and communication
1 Determinants of culture	7 Culture and corporate structures	13 Cross-cultural business communication
2 Dimensions of culture in business	8 Culture and leadership	14 Barriers to intercultural communication
3 Western business cultures	9 Culture and strategy	15 Negotiating internationally
4 Business cultures in the East	10 Cultural change in organizations	16 Working with international teams
5 Cultural dimensions and dilemmas	11 Culture and marketing	17 Conflicts and cultural differences
6 Cultures and management styles	12 Cultural diversity in organizations	18 Developing intercultural relationships

Instructor's website

The website (**www.pearsoned.co.uk/browaeys**) dedicated to the book, offers additional teaching resources which allow instructors to use the book more efficiently and effectively. This site contains extra materials which essentially consist of an audio-visual recording of PowerPoint slides, as well as suggested answers to questions relating to the activities.

Acknowledgements

We would like to thank, first and foremost, Nyenrode Business University for allowing us to prepare this book. We are particularly indebted to our colleagues in the university library who, through their patient dedication and efficiency, have allowed us to draw upon a considerable number of information sources.

We are also grateful to the editorial team at Pearson Education, for their unstinting professional support, and to the *Financial Times*, whose coverage of international business has proved to be an inspirational source of case studies for the book.

Our thanks also go out to the numerous contributors to the book. The contributions made by Fons Trompenaars and alumni from our university deserve particular mention.

Last, but by no means least, we would like to thank our friends for their advice and ideas, and our families for their patience and encouragement during the time-absorbing process of writing this book.

Publisher's acknowledgements

We are grateful to the following for permission to reproduce copyright material:

Figure I.2 from Schneider, S.C. and Barsoux, J.L. (2003) *Managing Across Cultures*, 2nd edition, p. 21, Prentice Hall; Table I.1 Bodley, J.H., *Cultural Anthropology: Tribes, States and the Global System*, 1994, Mayfield Publishing Co. The material is reproduced with permission from McGraw-Hill Companies; Figures 3.1, 3.2, 4.1 and Table 2.3 from *Culture Leadership and Organizations: The Global Study of 62 Societies* by House, R.J. et al (eds). Copyright 2004 by Sage Publications Inc. Table 8.1 reprinted with permission of The Free Press, a Division of Simon & Schuster Adult Publishing Group, from A Force for: How Leadership Differs From Management by John P. Kotter. Copyright@ 1990 by John P. Kotter, Inc. All rights reserved; Figure 9.1 from *Breaking through Culture Shock* by Marx, E., Nicholas Brealey Publishers. Copyright 2001; Table 10.1 from Schein, E.H. (1989) 'Organisational culture: what it is and how to change it', in Evans, P., Doz. Y. and Laurent, A. (eds) *Human Resource Management in International Firms*, p. 66, Palgrave Macmillan; Figure 11.1 from Hoecklin, L. (1995) *Managing Cultural Differences: Strategies for Competitive Advantage*, p. 101, Addison Wesley; Figure 15.2 from Weiss, S.E. (1994) 'Negotiating with Romans: Part 1', *Sloan Management Review*, 35(2), pp. 51–61, Massachusetts Institute of Technology; Table 16.1 from Robbins, S.P. (2000) *Essentials of Organizational Behaviour*, 6th edition, p. 106, Prentice Hall; Figure 17.2 from *Handbook of International and Intercultural Communication* by Ting-Toomey, S. & Oetze, J-G.I. Copyright 2001 by Sage Publications Inc Books. Reproduced with permission of Sage Publications Inc.; Figure 18.2 from *International Journal of intercultural Relations*, 23(1), Casrnir, F.L. foundations for the study of intercultural communication based on a third-culture building model, pp. 91–116, copyright (1999), with permission form Elsevier.

Extract from Adler. *International Dimensions of Organizational Behavior*, 4E. © 2002 South-Western, a part of Cengage Learning, Inc. Reproduced by permission. www.cengage.com/permissions; Extract from McSweeney, B. (2002) 'Hofstede's model of national cultural differences and their consequences', *Human Relations*, 55(1), pp. 89–118, Sage Publications; Extract from Hickson, D.J. and Pugh, D.S. (2001) *Management Worldwide*, Penguin Books; Extract from Hoecklin, L. (1995) *Managing Cultural Differences: Strategies for Comparative Advantage*, p. 37, Addison-Wesley; Extract from Morden, T., *Six country comparisons in Cross Cultural Management: An International Journal*, Vol.2, No.4, 1995, pp. 15–23. Copyright Sage Publications; Extract from Walvogel, J., *Email and workplace communication*, 2001, p. 7–8, School of Linguistics and Applied Language Studies, University of Wellington: New Zealand; Extract from www.worldwidewords.org, Michael Quinion World Wide Words; Extract from Barouktakis, M., Unleash the Power of the Hispanic market, on Quirk's Marketing Research Review, April 2000; Extract from *Conflict Management in the Asia Pacific: Assumptions and Approaches in Diverse Cultures*. Copyright 1999 Kwok Leung and Dean Tjosvold. Reproduced with permission of John Wiley & Sons, Asia, Extract from Casse, P. (1981) pp. 143–145 *Training for the Cross-Cultural Mind*, 2nd edn.

We are grateful to the Financial Times Limited for permission to reprint the following material:

Chapter 2 'Fake news', © *Financial Times*, 15 December 2006; Chapter 3 'Why financial scandals differ in the US and Europe', © *Financial Times*, 13 April 2005; Chapter 3 'South America unity still a distant dream', © *Financial Times*, 9 December 2004; Chapter 4 'A tale of two Russian factories', © *Financial Times*, 7 July 2006; Chapter 4 'South Korea tries to clip wings of the chaebol', © FT.com, 5 February 2007; Chapter 4 'A new generation of family firm', © *Financial Times*, 10 March 2007; Chapter 4 'A different breed of foot soldier', © *Financial Times*, 18 May 2005; Chapter 8 'Le patron, der Chef and the boss', © *Financial Times*, 9 January 2006; Chapter 9 'Marriage after a century of cohabitation', © *Financial Times*, 28 June 2005; Chapter 10 'Brussels launches probe into secret accounts', © *FT.com*, 17 July 2003; Chapter 13 'Straight-talking, English-speaking culture brings communication problems', © *Financial Times*, 9 November 2006; Chapter 13 'Why English is de rigueur in many French boardrooms', © *FT.com*, 25 March 2006; Chapter 14 'Germans aim to spring a World Cup surprise', © *Financial Times*, 22 May 2006; Chapter 16 'Virtual teams endeavour to build trust', © *Financial Times*, 9 September 2004; Chapter 16 'Virtual teams', © *Financial Times*, 12 May 2005; Chapter 18 'Ask the experts: business ethics', © FT.com, 21 August 2006; Chapter 18 'Third of companies think they have been hit by bribery', © *Financial Times*, 9 October 2006.

We are grateful to the following for permission to use copyright material:

Chapter 3 'Airbus and the damage done by economic patriotism', from The Financial Times Limited, 2 March 2007.

In some instances we have been unable to trace the owners of copyright material, and we would appreciate any information that would enable us to do so.

Part One

CULTURE AND MANAGEMENT

Introduction to Part One

Setting the scene

This introductory chapter will give an outline of the research in the field of culture and management, which in turn serves as a framework for Part One.

The concept of culture

Many experts in their fields have wracked their brains to come up with what they consider to be their concept of 'culture'. Those working in the field of cultural anthropology, alone, for example, have come up with a long list of definitions of the concept, based on their analysis of ethnological, social, psychological and linguistic data. The attempt made by Bodley (1994) to summarize these (Table I.1) gives an idea of all the facets of culture which need to be taken into account from an anthropological perspective.

Although acknowledging the multiplicity of culture, the authors of this book consider that the fundamental aspect of culture is that it is something all humans learn in one way or another. It is not something people inherit but rather a code of attitudes, norms and values, a way of thinking that is learnt within a social environment. Family, the social environment, school, friends, work – all these help to form this code and determine how people see themselves and the world. The national culture and the particular region people live in also help to shape a person's cultural profile.

Although culture is reflected in individual behaviour, it is a way of thinking shared by individuals in a particular society that makes culture what it is.

Table I.1 Diverse definitions of culture

Topical	Culture consists of everything on a list of topics, or categories, such as social organization, religion and economy
Historical	Culture is social heritage, or tradition, that is passed on to future generations
Behavioural	Culture is shared, learned human behaviour; a way of life
Normative	Culture is ideals, values, or rules for living
Functional	Culture is the way humans solve problems of adapting to the environment or living together
Mental	Culture is a complex of ideas, or learned habits, that inhibit impulses and distinguish people from animals
Structural	Culture consists of patterned and interrelated ideas, symbols, or behaviours
Symbolic	Culture is based on arbitrarily assigned meanings that are shared by a society

Source: Bodley (1994): 9.

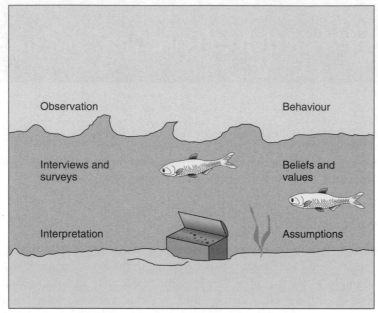

Figure I.1 Navigating the seas of international business
Source: Adapted from Schneider and Barsoux (2003): 21.

Culture operates on three levels

Culture operates on three levels, the first being on a level where it is observable and tangible. Here, **artefacts** and **attitudes** can be observed in terms of architecture, rituals, dress codes, making contact, contracts, language, eating and so on. Operating at a second level, culture is to do with norms and values. Beliefs – or **norms** – are statements of fact about the way things are. These are the cultural rules, as it were, which explain what is happening at level one and determine what is right or wrong. **Values** are to do with general preferences as to what is good or bad, how things should be. The third – and deepest level – has to do with **basic assumptions**. This level is difficult to explore and what lies there can only be construed through interpretation of what is happening at the other levels. Interpretation involves trying to explain why we act according to particular rules or in line with particular values. It is to do with the question 'Why?' and the attempt to answer it with more than just a 'Because!'

Figure I.1, based on one devised by Susan Schneider and Jean-Louis Barsoux, gives a visual interpretation of these levels of culture and the ways they can be investigated. Exploring culture can be compared with exploring the ocean. On the surface, artefacts, rituals and behaviour can be seen. These give an idea of what may be below. The underlying norms and values can be ascertained through interviews and surveys. The assumptions lying at the very bottom can only be inferred through interpretation.

Giving dimensions to culture

Assumptions in the exploration of culture – the key dimensions – come from the work of anthropologists, Kluckholn and Strodtbeck. In 1961, they developed a comparative model with six cultural orientations:

1. the nature of people;
2. the relationship to nature;
3. the relationship to other people;
4. the modality of human activity (doing and being);
5. the temporal focus of human activity (future, past, present);
6. the concept of space (private/public).

These cultural orientations have inspired researchers in culture and management, such as Schein, Adler, Hall, Hofstede and Trompenaars. These dimensions can help to define the cultural profile of people and discover the preferences that cultures have in relation to their environment.

Understanding culture and management

The researchers referred to in Figure I.2 have developed models relating to this area:

- Edgar Schein examined the effect of the organization on culture.
- Edward Hall was one of the first to study the role of communication in management.
- Nancy Adler pioneered the study of the influence of culture on organizational functions.
- Geert Hofstede and Fons Trompenaars both established dimensions to measure the impact of national culture on management.

Part One examines the effect of culture on management by examining the insights each of these researchers has developed. The approaches presented are intended not only to provide some understanding of culture and management in an international environment, but also to help develop the attitude and behaviour desirable in a specific cross-cultural context.

The **concepts** in each chapter are followed by one or more **activities** and **points for reflection**. The activities allow the reader to apply what has been learned from the preceding concepts to a scenario. A number of (edited) articles, many of them from the *Financial Times*, appear throughout the text, as do short case studies taken from business life. These require analysis by means of questions posed afterwards. Finally, there are points for reflection, which are intended to consolidate your learning. This same structure will be used in Part Two and Part Three.

Chapter and concept overview

Chapter 1 Determinants of culture

Chapter 1 examines the very concept of culture, its facets as well as the role of norms and values. The levels at which culture operates – from family through organization to society – are also described. The chapter is divided into two concepts:

- **Concept 1.1 Facets of culture.** After giving a short definition of the word 'culture' and its various 'layers', the concept will analyse the meaning of value systems for societies.
- **Concept 1.2 Levels of cultures.** This concept considers the national cultures of organizational cultures and those elements that define them.

Schein
Relationship with nature
Human activity
Human nature
Relationships with people
Time
Truth and reality

Trompenaars
Relationship with nature
Relationships with people
Universalism versus particularism
Individualism versus collectivism
Affectivity
Diffuse versus specific
Achievement versus ascription
Relationship with time

Kluckholn and Strodtbeck
Relationship with time
Human activity
Human nature
Relationships with people
Time

Adler
Human nature
Relationship with nature
Individualist/collectivist
Human activity (being/doing)
Space (private/public)
Time (past/present/future)

Hall
Space: personal/physical
Time: monochronic/polychronic
Language: high context/low context
Friendships

Hofstede
Uncertainty avoidance
Power distance
Individualism/collectivism
Masculinity/femininity

Figure I.2 Dimensions of culture
Source: Schneider and Barsoux (2003): 34.

Chapter 2 Dimensions of culture in business

Chapter 2 explores cultural dimensions in the business context with particular reference to research by Geert Hofstede and GLOBE (Global Leadership and Organizational Behaviour Effectiveness), an ongoing research project. It also puts forward criticisms concerning the cultural dimension construct, particularly that devised by Hofstede.

The chapter is divided into two concepts:

- **Concept 2.1 National cultural dimensions in the business context.** The five dimensions developed by Hofstede are explained, and the extremes of each characterized in terms of management and business.

- **Concept 2.2 The influence of national culture on business culture.** The influence of national culture values on organizational values and practices is explored, with reference to the nine cultural practice dimensions devised by the GLOBE project. The extent to which employees of multinational companies (organizations which are not embedded in one particular culture) are themselves culture-bound is also examined.

Chapter 3 Western business cultures

This chapter, together with Chapter 4, gives an overview of business cultures in the world, using a metaconfiguration devised by House *et al.* (2004) of culture clusters. Elements in particular countries belonging to each of ten clusters are highlighted. Western business cultures are surveyed in cluster terms, and some similarities and differences between component countries noted. The countries covered include those in Western Europe and Latin America. The examination of the Anglo cluster includes comments on North America and Australasia.

Chapter 4 Business cultures in the East

Five Eastern clusters are examined next, in terms of certain similarities that set them apart from Western business cultures. An Eastern Europe cluster is considered, as well as two clusters in Asia, the one influenced by Confucianism, the other by Hinduism. The importance of tribal identification among sub-Sahara countries in African is touched upon, together with the cultural diversity of one economically important country, South Africa. Finally, an outline is given of the cultural elements shared by Arab countries in the Middle East.

The chapter is divided into five parts in accordance with the five clusters being discussed: Eastern Europe, Confucian Asia, Southern Asia, Sub-Sahara Africa and the Middle East.

Chapter 5 Cultural dimensions and dilemmas

Chapter 5 explores further cultural dimensions, particularly those from the work of Fons Trompenaars, and highlight the dilemmas these raise in management decision-making.

The chapter is divided into two concepts:

- **Concept 5.1 Values orientations and dimensions.** This concept returns to the sources that inspired researchers in cross-cultural management. Particular attention is given to the Trompenaars' dimensions, which can be useful for the analysis of cultural differences in management. Hofstede's review of these dimensions is outlined, together with the reaction given by Hampden-Turner and Trompenaars to Hofstede's comments.

- **Concept 5.2 Reconciling cultural dilemmas.** This concept explains the method devised by Trompenaars and Hampden-Turner for finding a way to resolve dilemmas when doing business with different cultures.

Chapter 6 Cultures and styles of management

This chapter proposes value orientations drawn from those presented in Chapters 1 to 5, as well as other value orientations taken from the work of Edward Hall, among others.

The chapter is divided into two concepts:

- **Concept 6.1 Management tasks and cultural values.** This concept presents a model of culture based on cultural value orientations and examines their influence on managerial activities.

- **Concept 6.2 Other views on cultural values.** This concept briefly examines approaches to value-based cross-cultural theories, approaches that reflect the globalization of business.

Final activities

Part One contains two extra activities:

1. **Three steps for developing cross-cultural effectiveness.** The chapters of Part One are followed by a final activity in which readers draw up their own cultural profile. Using this profile, readers are asked to outline strategies to enable them to operate effectively in a particular country.

2. **The Galderma case study.** This, subtitled 'An empirical study of cross-cultural relations between French, German and British Managers in an international company', investigates how managers of three European cultures cope with cultural differences when they are working together.

What you will gain

After working through Part One you will gain more insight into:

- understanding the link between culture and management;
- determining the effect of culture on the management of business;
- exploring ways in which cross-cultural effectiveness can be developed.

References

Bodley, J.H. (1994) *Cultural Anthropology: Tribes, states and the global system,* Mountain View, CA: Mayfield.

House, R.J., Hanges, P.J., Javidan, M., Dorfman, P.W. and Gupta, V. (eds) (2004) *Leadership, Culture and Organizations: The GLOBE study of 62 societies,* Thousand Oaks, CA: Sage.

Kluckholn, F. and Strodtbeck, F. (1961) *Variations in Value Orientations,* Evanston, IL: Peterson Row.

Schneider, S.C. and Barsoux, J.L. (2003) *Managing Across Cultures,* 2nd edn, Harlow: FT Prentice Hall.

Chapter 1

Determinants of culture

Culture is an integral part of all human societies. With the advent of globalization, the notion of culture has taken on a broader meaning and has come to be an important element of organizations. These two aspects of culture will be developed in this chapter.

Concept 1.1 will explore the notion of culture in society, while Concept 1.2 will consider the influence of culture on socio-economic realities such as the management of companies.

Learning outcomes

After reading this chapter, you will gain an understanding of:

● the concept of culture and the role of norms and values in determining culture;

● the relationship between culture, organizations and management;

● the concept of culture at various levels, both national and organizational.

Concept 1.1   Facets of culture

According to Fleury (2002), a society is an organized group of individuals who share functional relations. The complexity of present-day societies is increasing the roles for an individual and is, at the same time, diversifying the ways these roles can be interpreted. These roles are determined by culture. Each society defines its own norms and the ways in which they are realized. It can therefore be said that culture is a structure that gives form to behaviour and fixes the framework of exchanges between the people of this group. The function of culture is integration, adaptation, communication and expression. Societies are organized politically into nations, but within this national unity subcultures may exist with specific cultural characteristics. These groups use the society in which they are embedded as their framework of reference, and share their nationality, language and institutions, while being delineated by their socio-economic, historic or geographic characteristics.

What does culture really mean?

One can never use the word 'culture' without being obliged to give a range of definitions that contradict each other! Even if this term had only one meaning, irrespective of whether it was aesthetic, philosophical, national, organizational or managerial, it would only be a form of individual or collective representation. Genelot (1998: 195) stresses that 'men are products of their culture: their representations, their visions of what is good and what is wrong, their behaviour at work, their concepts of organizations are the fruit of the representations carried by their ancestors'. Can one therefore state that a change of culture would only be a change in representations? Anthropologists, sociologists, historians and philosophers have all put forward their definitions, but none of them seems to be sufficiently precise or inclusive.

Rather than look for an exact definition, it may be preferable to look for a meaning that is blurred but which somehow addresses the rather abstract idea of culture. Hofstede (1980: 25) refers to culture as 'the collective programming of the mind which distinguishes the members of one human group from another'. When elaborating on his definition, he says: 'Culture, in this sense, includes systems of values; and values are among the building blocks of culture.' This definition is frequently referred to in cross-cultural literature, probably because it is blurry enough to encompass other definitions, but sharp enough to reflect key elements of a culture.

Consider the implications of Hofstede's definition. Collective programming of the mind implies that members of a group are programmed by that group to perceive the world in a certain way, themselves and others included. In other words, the group shares meanings that hold them together. Furthermore, this definition implies that the group's culture is somehow learned rather than being innate. It is passed down from generation to generation and is the basis of the socialization process in childhood when the norms of behaviour and the values on which these norms are based are learned. Finally, culture is to be seen as relative: no cultural group is 'better' in any absolute sense. There is no cultural standard whereby one group's perception of the world is intrinsically superior to another's.

The building blocks referred to earlier need to be examined more closely: the values which cultural groupings share and the resulting norms of behaviour.

Norms and values

Each culture can be seen as having three layers. The *first*, outer layer is the 'behavioural' or 'explicit' level. It is what you notice immediately when you go abroad for the first time: the language, the food, the architecture, the houses, the buildings and so on. But it is also the communication style: Latin cultures, for example, use exuberant body language and facial expressions. Other, less exuberant cultures, such as those in Nordic Europe consider this sort of behaviour to be 'over the top', but it is really just a matter of comparing the communication styles of one culture with those of another.

The *second* layer contains the 'norms and values'. Every culture has its own system of norms and values. Together, these form the national characteristics of a culture, and act as its framework of reference. Although norms and values are generally presented as a unit, a distinction must be made between the two. Norms are the rules of a society, determining what is good or bad with regard to behaviour. People are, however, allowed a certain individual freedom of choice between what 'you should always do' and what 'you should never do'. Norms are the written and unwritten rules of a society. Values are what is considered important or unimportant, beautiful or not beautiful, right or wrong. A value is something experienced inwardly and which is not up for discussion. The preference or aversion it contains is taken for granted by its bearers.

The *third* and innermost layer, and which lies at the core of 'culture' contains its assumptions and beliefs. These are difficult to describe or explain. When you are asked to justify why you do this or say that, the answer is often: 'I don't know.' Why, for example, do people eat with a knife and fork or with chopsticks? Well, that's the way people eat. . . .

The system of values and norms not only varies from culture to culture, but also from one part of a society to another. Not every individual 'operates' from the same basis, nor do sub-cultures within a society. Moreover, a culture is never static, because norms and values are always changing. However, since every culture is so deep-rooted, the changes are never sudden or extreme and a certain constancy is maintained.

Sociologists who have compared the value systems of countries in terms of the way in which norms and values have developed in society, have concluded that there are four categories (Ruano-Borbalan, 2002: 339):

1. Traditional society, in which religion plays an important role . . . large families are encouraged, conformity is rewarded and individualism rejected. This is, for example, the case in many Arab countries;

2. Rational society, in which the interests of the individual come first, birth control is encouraged and the authority of the state is recognised. Germany . . . is a typical example;

3. A society in which survival is the primary concern, where the people are not happy and rather intolerant, where equality between the sexes has little chance . . . where materialism is predominant . . . This is often the situation in ex-communist countries;

4. Post-modern society . . . tolerant and democratic, such as those in Scandinavia and the Netherlands.

Politics and norms and values

The influence of politics on norms and values is obvious when it comes to bringing global unity to humanitarian norms and values. These are formally laid down in the 'Universal Declaration of Human Rights'. In a number of countries, however, politics also has a say in education, dress, manners and many other aspects of daily life. Recent reports from Iran, for example, show the degree of political interference in people's lives there. Students from Iranian universities heavily criticized their highest political leaders and the government's vice squad for persistently prescribing how Iranians should dress, how they should do their hair and how they should enjoy themselves.

Conversely, there are degrees of acceptance with regard to what politicians in each country may or may not do; what constitutes a scandal – and what does not. In Nordic Europe, for example, it is acknowledged that there is corruption in political life now and again, but in no way is it regarded as acceptable. If caught out, a politician must resign. In southern Europe, however, involvement in a corruption scandal does not necessarily mean the end of a politician's career. A politician may be involved for several years in corruption proceedings but stay in his/her post, despite being investigated for embezzlement for example. In Surinam, where corruption is regarded as an unavoidable evil, certain limits are nevertheless placed on wayward behaviour. Anyone who attempts to launch a coup d'état there, for example, will be severely punished.

The freedoms a politician may enjoy in his or her private life are also different according to country. When an affair came to light between a US president and an intern working in the White House, there was a call for him to be impeached because he had lied about his relationship with the intern during a formal investigation. The impeachment process stumbled in the Senate and the president was allowed to complete his term of office. In France, however, sex scandals of this nature do not happen. 'Insiders' may have been aware of the double life being led by the country's president (an illegitimate daughter of his eventually emerged at his funeral) but, at the time, his extramarital relationship was regarded as a private matter. Homosexual politicians may not be accepted in many countries, but in the Netherlands, for example, a country where marriage between homosexuals is allowed by law, their sexual orientation is again regarded as a private matter.

Where a certain degree of economic, political and social integration is taking place between countries, can one talk of a movement towards a shared system of norms and values? Referring to the possibility of European countries sharing such a system, the French philosopher Edgar Morin (1987), declared that the creation of a European culture had nothing to do with dominant basic ideas (such as Christianity, humanism, rationalism, or science). It had to do instead with the opposition between ideas. Put another way, what is important in the forming process of European culture is the meeting of diversity, of opposite poles, the complementarity of ideas. This is what Morin calls 'dialogique': the union of two forms of logic, of two different principles, without their duality being lost. The association of contradictory terms or concepts can form one complex phenomenon. He takes mankind as an example: a human is both entirely determined biologically as well as culturally. This 'dialogique' can be found in every culture, but is particularly intensive within the European culture where there is an enormous amount of interaction and interference within areas to do with values, e.g. religion/rationality, mythical thought/critical thought, and humanism/science.

Cultural assumptions in management

After social norms and values comes the third layer of culture: assumptions. This layer is also referred to by Schein when identifying organizational culture. His work is a useful guide in the examination of cultural assumptions in a managerial context, and offers insights into the question of managing relationships. He defines culture as:

> a set of basic assumptions – shared solutions to universal problems of external adaptation (how to survive) and internal integration (how to stay together) – which have evolved over time and are handed down from one generation to the next.
>
> Schein, 2004: 14

In terms of external adaptation, this means, for example, asking: to what extent does management within a culture assume that it can control nature or to what extent is it controlled by nature? This question is allied to that of the nature of human activity: is doing more important than being, acting more important than reflecting? In terms of internal integration, this means asking a question such as: 'Are humans basically assumed to be good or evil' or trying to determine whether relationships at work are more important than the task itself.

The questions raised by Schein on cultural assumptions of organizations imply that management in an international context has not only to take account of the norms and values of the specific culture of a company, but also its cultural assumptions.

Concept 1.2 Levels of cultures

According to Schein (1999), a culture starts developing in a context where a group of people have a shared experience. Members of a family, for example, share a life together and develop a certain togetherness through undergoing experiences inside and outside the home. Small groups without blood relations can develop the same closeness through sharing a pastime, a hobby or occupation; the experience they share may be rich enough to allow a culture to be formed.

In a business context, culture can develop at different levels – within a department or at the various ranks of a hierarchy. A company or organization can develop its own culture, provided that it has what Schein calls 'sufficient shared history' (1999). This applies also for a collection of companies within a particular business or sector, or for organizations in, say, the public sector. This collective experience can be related to regions of a country, or regions across countries, or a grouping of nations themselves when they share a common experience, be it language, religion, ethnic origins or a shared historical experience in their development. In this concept we will try to distinguish levels at which cultures develop.

Culture and nation

When cross-cultural matters are under discussion, the terms 'culture' and 'nation' should be carefully distinguished, as Tayeb (2003) makes clear. She takes as an example the Kurds. Although they are a people with a distinctive cultural identity, they nevertheless live in three nation states – Turkey, Iraq and Iran. This is an obvious example of one culture straddling the political boundaries of two or more nation states.

This culture/nation distinction can, as Tayeb points out, have a bearing on the way organizations operate. If 'culture' is defined as a set of historically evolved, learned and shared values, attitudes and meanings, then this has an influence on organizations at both macro and micro level.

At the macro level, the nation, in terms of its laws and economic institutions, must be considered by organizations going about their business. They have to take account of the measures taken by the state to protect its interests and those of its inhabitants. These can range from specific employment laws and safety legislation to general economic and social policies. These macro-level considerations are not only subject to change through political changes in government, but also through the desire of the nation's rulers to share legislation at social and economic level with other nations within some kind of association.

At the micro level, the organization is influenced by cultural elements relating to employer–employee relationships and to behaviour among employees. Those wishing to introduce any changes with a view to improving management effectiveness or increasing productivity must take account of these elements when implementing such changes.

National culture

Although cultural make-up has many facets reflecting experience in life and membership of different groupings at different times in various environments, there is, as Tayeb (2003: 13) says, 'a constant thread . . . through our lives which makes us distinguishable from others, especially those in other countries: this thread is our national culture'. This national culture may be heterogeneous in nature, but it will contain enough elements which together enable a national culture to be created.

Tayeb (2003) gives a list of these elements and considers their effect at both micro and macro level. She starts with two elements that contribute to the building of a nation and the creation of a national culture:

- the physical environment;
- the history the nation has undergone.

She then refers to 'institutions' that contribute to the establishment of a national culture:

a) *Family.* The basic social unit where 'acculturation' takes place, where the culture of a particular environment is instilled in a human from infancy.

b) *Religion.* Religious beliefs can have a significant effect on a person's view of the world. This does not mean that people need to 'believe', but religion has helped in all sorts of direct and indirect ways to shape the environment in which people live.

c) *Education.* The value system on which education is based and the choices it makes in terms of the curriculum both help in the formation of a culture, particularly where educational institutions are well developed. At the micro level, the teaching approach used and the manner of learning can also affect future learning. This, in turn, can determine the quality and versatility of human resources in the labour market.

d) *Mass communication media.* Tayeb pays particular attention to the effect of recent advances in communication on the development of culture. The ever-increasing presence of mass media has given a new meaning to shared experience: newspapers, magazines, television and radio, 'bring people closer together irrespective of their geographical locations, but also in terms of spreading values, attitudes, tastes, meanings and vocabulary – in short, culture' (Tayeb, 2003: 20). She does not, however, regard this as being a threat to the distinctive cultural characteristics of a nation. Instead, the mass media have created a new common dimension in which people can share experiences if they choose to.

e) *The multinational company.* This is a powerful culture-building institution, whose products and services can influence the way people live, whose operations can affect how and where they work. However, the multinational is also influenced by the preferences at national level with regard to product taste and form and the promotion of its goods and services.

Organizational culture

Edgar Schein (1999) refers to the *power* of culture on account of the extent to which it determines our behaviour individually and collectively. In organizational terms he remarks on how cultural elements affect the way strategy is determined, goals are established and how the organization operates. Furthermore, the key personnel involved are influenced by their own cultural backgrounds and shared experience since these have helped shape their own values and perceptions.

Schein (1990: 111) develops his definition of culture when defining organizational culture:

(a) a pattern of basic assumptions, (b) invented, discovered, or developed by a given group, (c) as it learns to cope with its problems of external adaptation and internal integration, (d) that has worked well enough to be considered valid and, therefore (e) is to be taught to new members as the (f) correct way to perceive, think, and feel in relation to chosen problems.

Drawing on this definition, organizational culture can be said to be the acceptance – in a tacit or formal way – of norms of specific behaviour by the members of an organization.

Corporate culture

The term 'corporate culture' takes the question of organizational culture a step further. As Meschi and Roger (1994) point out, if an organization develops into a multinational conglomerate, the culture at headquarters may influence that of subsidiaries abroad. In the same way, a firm involved in a joint venture with a company from another country may well find that the presence of the 'foreign' partners influences the underlying culture of the firm. What evolves over time in terms of 'corporate culture' can have as its basis the 'original' organizational culture, or the national/regional culture – or a combination of the two.

The extent of the influence of corporate culture is disputed among experts in the field. Some regard a clearly defined corporate culture as key to a (multi-)national company's success. Others consider a flexible culture to be the key to success because it can adapt to, and respond more effectively to, a local/national environment.

Although it is useful to know where the countries in question lie on the dimensions of national culture when working with other cultures, there are other factors at play, particularly the culture of the company itself. This is determined not just by external cultural factors such as the national and regional cultures, but also by internal cultural factors. The extent of cultural control, through company goals, manuals, instructions and the presence of long-standing employees, is important. The nature of the line of business the company is in may have an important influence on the culture as well as the professional culture attached to key positions within the organization.

Professional culture

This is essentially to do with the set of values shared by people working together professionally. Schein (1996: 237) talks of three professional cultures in management. First, there are the 'operators' who are directly involved in production of goods or the provision of services. Second, there are the 'engineers', the people who design and monitor the technology behind the production and/or provision of services. Those who share this culture tend to show a preference for solutions where systems rather than people are involved. Third, there are the 'executives', the senior managers who share tacit assumptions regarding 'the daily realities of their status and role'.

The question of how these professional cultures co-exist within an organization preoccupies many scholars. How do the executives handle the 'operators' and 'engineers'? How best to manage conflict constructively? To what extent is delegation and empowerment desirable? What styles of management are appropriate?

Culture and management

At the foundation of all the cultures mentioned lies the individual's culture. It is individuals who ultimately form the culture of an organization. The values they embody as members of an organization are formed partially through the family, social and national environment, and partially through the professional, organizational and corporate culture.

It is up to management to take into account the diversity of people in an organization and to manage their cultural differences. In an international context, however, what does cross-cultural management mean?

Nancy Adler (2002: 11) gives a definition of what cross-cultural management is about:

> Cross-cultural management explains the behavior of people in organizations around the world and shows people how to work in organizations with employees and client populations from many different cultures. Cross-cultural management *describes* organizational behavior within countries and cultures; *compares* organizational behavior across countries and cultures: and, perhaps most important, seeks to understand and improve the *interaction* of co-workers, managers, executives, clients, suppliers, and alliance partners from countries and cultures around the world.

The importance of cross-cultural management is evident in a world where all kinds of co-operation between companies in many countries is on the increase. Whether these are mergers, takeovers, partnerships or strategic alliances, they all need to be analysed in cultural terms, not only to determine where benefit can be gained but also where difficulties may be encountered when companies are working together.

This chapter has given a brief overview of the levels at which culture operates. These will be dealt with in more detail in Chapter 2, particularly in Concept 2.2, which examines the influence of national culture on organizational culture. The question of business culture will be addressed in Chapters 3 and 4.

ACTIVITY 1.1

Defining an organizational culture

Schein's definition of organizational culture, as quoted in Concept 1.2, is as follows:

(a) a pattern of basic assumptions, (b) invented, discovered, or developed by a given group, (c) as it learns to cope with its problems of external adaptation and internal integration, (d) that has worked well enough to be considered valid and, therefore (e) is to be taught to new members as the (f) correct way to perceive, think, and feel in relation to chosen problems.

Schein, 1990: 111

Using Schein's definitions, do the following tasks.

Task 1

Select an organization you are familiar with (i.e. one where you have worked or where you would like to work). If you have access to the Internet, you could examine the annual report of a company, its mission statement, its directors and possibly the way it is organized, to try and answer the following questions.

a) What are the basic assumptions within the organization?

b) Where do you think these assumptions come from?

c) To what extent could the national culture have an influence on the organizational behaviour of this company?

Examples

- If you look at the website of **Marks & Spencer**, for example (**www.marksandspencer.com**), you can click on 'The Company' section for the annual report, as well as the company's corporate social responsibility (CSR) report.

- **Shell** is another example. If you look at its home page (**www.shell.com**), you can click on 'About Shell', then 'who we are' to discover the company's vision, values and leadership. Shell also has websites for its national operations. By choosing a country on the home page you can find out if any aspect of the company receives particular emphasis. For example, Shell's Kenya site gives an account of the group's business principles, just as the other national sites do. However, it also has a page devoted to compliance with these principles.

Task 2

Compare your findings with those of your peers.

Conclusion

Chapter 1 has shown how difficult it is to give a definition of the word 'culture'. Apart from the multitude of definitions, culture can also be considered at various levels, the deepest of which, according to Edgar Schein contains 'cultural assumptions'. This level, according to Schein, can also be found in the culture of an organization.

This chapter also shows that the individuals in a group form a culture that can be national, organizational or professional. This implies that cross-cultural management has to take into account all of these contexts, not only within organizations but also in relations with companies of different countries.

Points for reflection

1. The word 'culture' is used in many ways, such as when people talk about 'political culture', 'national culture', 'organizational culture', or 'youth culture'.

   Does the word 'culture' always have the same meaning? Moreover, can the same definition be used to describe different notions?

2. Managing an organization also involves managing human resources. These resources are not static: employees can move to another position, or leave an organization, or be replaced. Ideally, any newcomers will adapt to the culture of the company or at least respect it.

Can a corporate culture be managed? If so, explain what can be done for it to be managed. If not, explain why.

Further reading

Schneider, S.C. and Barsoux, J.-L. (2003) *Managing Across Cultures*, **Pearson Education, FT Prentice Hall.** This book develops understanding of how culture influences management practice and also guides teams and organizations as to how to be more effective in international business. Theoretical foundations are linked to practical applications.

References

Adler, N.J. (2002) *International Dimensions of Organizational Behavior*, 4th edn, Ohio: South-Western, Thomson Learning.

Fleury, J. (2002) *La culture,* Paris: Editions Bréa.

Genelot, D. (1998) *Manager dans la complexité*, 2nd edn, Paris: INSEP Editions.

Hofstede, G. (1980) *Culture's Consequences,* London: Sage.

Meschi, P.-X. and Roger, A. (1994) 'Cultural context and social effectiveness in international joint-ventures', *Management International Review,* 34 (3): 197–215.

Morin, E. (1987) *Penser l'Europe*, Paris: Gallimard.

Ruano-Borbalan, J.-C. (2002) 'Valeurs et cultures: allons-nous devenir post-modernes?' in Journet, N. (ed), *La culture,* Auxerre: Sciences Humaines Editions: 335–342.

Schein, E.H. (1990) 'Organizational culture', *American Psychologist,* 42 (2): 109–119.

Schein, E.H. (1996) 'Culture: the missing concept in organization studies', *Administrative Science Quarterly,* 41 (2): 229–240.

Schein, E.H. (1999) *The Corporate Culture Survival Guide,* San Francisco, CA: Jossey-Bass.

Schein, E.H. (2004) *Organizational culture and leadership,* 3rd edn, San Francisco: Jossey-Bass.

Tayeb, M. (2003) *International Management,* Harlow: Pearson Education.

Chapter 2

Dimensions of culture in business

This chapter explores the conceptualisation of culture in terms of 'dimensions'. These are concepts that allow variations between the attributes of cultures to be quantified. Attention will be given to the reflection of these cultural dimensions in the business environment.

Concept 2.1 will first outline a model of value orientations drawn from social anthropology that has proved to be influential in the development of a dimensional approach to cross-cultural comparisons. It will then summarize the dimensions developed by Geert Hofstede, paying particular attention to the fifth dimension (short-term/long-term orientation). The concept will finally pinpoint some criticisms of Hofstede's model.

Concept 2.2 will consider the influence of national culture on business culture by first examining the relationship between values of national cultures and those of organizational cultures as reflected in organizational practices. This will lead to a more recent projection of cultural dimensions developed by the GLOBE project, as well as the methods used in the research to determine values and practices at both organizational and societal level. The concept ends with an account of research carried out into the perception of managers from different cultures towards their organization, particularly those working with multinationals.

Learning outcomes

After reading this chapter you will:

- understand the concept of cultural dimensions;
- be familiar, in particular, with the five-dimensional model developed by Hofstede as well as the culture construct definitions of more recent research by the GLOBE group;
- be acquainted with criticisms of Hofstede's concept;
- have some insight into the relationship between societal values and practices and the culture of organizations working within a society.

Concept 2.1 National cultural dimensions in the business context

One important hypothesis underlying much research into culture is the stability of a culture's characteristics. Although cultural groupings all undergo change over time according to the ways they deal with the challenges laid down by their environment, they each remain constant in the sense that they maintain certain notions about the world and attitudes towards their fellow humans.

The characteristics that define each cultural group can offer international managers considerable insights when it comes, for example, to co-operating with companies from other cultural backgrounds. If awareness of cultural differences is consciously raised, then the ability to analyse the effectiveness of employing business policies in differing cultural environments is considerably improved.

A model from social anthropology

Before examining cultural differences in the business context, it is worthwhile considering a comparative model developed in the early 1960s that has been influential in other, more recent models relating to cross-cultural management. Kluckholn and Strodtbeck (1961) devised a model based on responses to questions concerning the human condition. An adapted version of this is given in Table 2.1, together with the possible range of responses.

This model, drawn from the field of social anthropology, suggests that a particular cultural grouping will display a certain orientation to the world in response to the above questions. It does not claim, however, that all individuals within a particular grouping will respond in the same way. Moreover, it does not account for so-called sub-cultural groupings or for the way organizations in a particular cultural environment respond to the questions. Nevertheless, it does enable a comparison to be made along certain dimensions of different cultures. Moreover, the model has proved to be the source of inspiration for many other researchers into cross-cultural matters, including Trompenaars (see Chapter 5) and Hofstede.

Table 2.1 Variations in value orientations

Basic questions	Range of responses		
What is the character of human nature?	Good	A mixture of good and evil	Evil
What is man's relationship to nature?	Man dominates	Harmony between man and nature	Nature dominates
What is the time focus of human activity?	Past	Present	Future
What is the modality of human activity?	Spontaneous expression of desires	All-round development of self	Achieving measurable goals
What is the relationship of man to man	Hierarchical	Collectivist	Individualist

Source: adapted from Kluckholn and Strodtbeck (1961): 11-12.

Hofstede's dimensions

Geert Hofstede's research in the area of culture and management is known worldwide. His theories are not only frequently quoted and applied in cross-cultural research, but also used (often indiscriminately) in prescriptive works on dealing with other cultures. Despite, or maybe because of, its prominence, his work has provoked much criticism from theorists and practitioners alike, as we will see later. Nevertheless, consideration of Hofstede's work is indispensable to any study on culture and management.

Hofstede developed a dimensional approach to cross-cultural comparisons through his pioneering studies into how management is affected by differences between cultural groupings. He conducted extensive studies into national cultural differences, the first being across employees working in subsidiaries of a multinational corporation (IBM) in sixty-four countries. Hofstede, who had founded and managed the personnel research department of IBM Europe, took a database of scores resulting from attitude surveys among IBM employees worldwide and re-analysed the figures. The surveys had been developed as a management tool to examine issues relating to the work situation (determined beforehand through interviews with personnel). The original respondents in these surveys were matched groups (Hofstede, 1980) in seven occupational categories, five of them being non-managerial and two managerial.

The research set-up, as well as the statistical methods used by Hofstede, were applied by other researchers to other groups, including students in twenty-three countries, commercial airline pilots in twenty-three countries and civil service managers in fourteen countries. These studies together identified and validated the first four dimensions of national culture differences described in this concept. Hofstede later developed a fifth dimension to account for value orientations that emerged from research carried out from a Chinese perspective.

Hofstede used the results of his research to produce a comparison between cultures on four and eventually five dimensions:

- Power distance (high/low): attitudes to authority, the distance between individuals in a hierarchy.
- Uncertainty avoidance (high/low): the degree of tolerance for uncertainty or instability.
- Individual versus group orientation: independence and interdependence, the loyalty towards oneself and towards a group.
- Masculine versus feminine orientation: importance of work goals (earnings, advancement) compared with personal goals (co-operation, relationships).
- Short-term versus long-term orientation: fostering virtues related to the past and present or virtues related to the future.

It should be stressed that these dimensions form a general model and are not necessarily applicable in specific circumstances. They describe tendencies within a certain cultural grouping; they present orientations adopted by the majority of members of a cultural grouping in normal situations. They do not account for cultural differences in absolute terms but in relative terms.

In the second edition of his publication *Cultures and Organizations* (2005), which he wrote with his son, Hofstede examines differences between cultures not only at society level, but also in terms of the family, education and the workplace. When examining these cultural dimensions this book will focus on the workplace, i.e. the business context.

Table 2.2 Extremes of Hofstede's 'power distance' dimension

Low power distance	High power distance
There should be a minimum of inequality since it can exploit others	Inequality is unavoidable and everyone has the place they deserve
If there is a hierarchy in an organization it is only for the sake of convenience	Hierarchy in an organization reflects natural differences
People who are superiors or subordinates are all the same	Superiors or subordinates are different kinds of people
Everyone should enjoy the same privileges; there should be no status symbols	Power-holders are entitled to privileges and status-symbols
Subordinates should be consulted	Subordinates should be told what to do
Individuality is to be respected	Authority is to be respected
The manager should be a resourceful democrat	The manager should be a benevolent autocrat

Low/high power distance

'Power distance' refers to the extent to which members of a culture expect and accept that power is unequally distributed in society. It was developed by Hofstede on the basis of earlier research concerning preferences for power among different cultures and, in particular, on research identifying centralization as a characteristic of organizations (Pugh, 1976).

As the Hofstedes' book says: 'Power and inequality, of course, are fundamental facts of any society and anybody with some international experience will be aware that all societies are unequal, but some are more unequal than others' (Hofstede and Hofstede, 2005: 137). Essentially, this dimension reflects how a culture relates to authority of one form or another. In relational terms, the comparisons made between cultures on this dimension convey the extent to which subordinates are dependent on their bosses. The extremes of this cultural dimension are characterized in Table 2.2.

How subordinates view their superiors depends on a combination of factors, and this combination can vary considerably from one culture to another. In some cultures the status of superiors is important: their position in the hierarchy, their age, their family and their connections. In others, greater importance is attached to a person's competence and experience. In short, it may be that who you are is more important than what you do – or vice versa.

This leads to the question of how subordinates deal with their superiors, however they may be chosen. If they show great respect for status and life experience, they may be reluctant to show initiative and prefer to be given instructions instead, which are then accepted without question. If they consider their superior to be more of a first among equals, they will consider that person's judgements, decisions and instructions to be subject to discussion and may even challenge them.

In high power distance cultures, effective managers are essentially benevolent autocrats who are focused on the task. They are inaccessible and enjoy privileges their power gives them. If things go wrong, the subordinates – who are dependent on their superiors – are usually to blame. In low power distance cultures, on the other hand, effective managers are more oriented towards the people in an organization and allow them to participate more in making decisions. The relations between subordinates and superiors are more horizontal than vertical: superiors are accessible and try to make out they are less powerful than they are. If anything goes wrong, the system is more to blame rather than the individuals involved.

Table 2.3 Extremes of Hofstede's 'collectivist/individualist' dimension

Collectivist	Individualist
'We' mentality	'I' mentality
Identity is based on one's social group	Identity is based on the individual
Decisions are primarily made according to what is best for the group	Decisions are based primarily on individual needs
Relationships prevail over task	Tasks prevail over relationships
Focus is on belonging to an organization	Focus is on individual initiative and achievement
Values differ according to the group (particularism)	Value standards apply to all (universalism)

Individualism/collectivism

This dimension concerns itself with the relationship between the individual and the group. To what extent are individuals in society autonomous and to what extent are they embedded in the group? This particular construct, apparent in ancient civilizations and to be found at the heart of much philosophical thought about the nature of the state and the individual, continues to be given much attention in many disciplines, particularly sociology, anthropology and psychology. It was Hofstede who subjected this construct to empirical investigation on a large scale and eventually produced a ranking of societies in individualistic/collectivistic terms.

The extremes of this dimension are characterized in Table 2.3.

This dimension is essentially about the importance which a cultural grouping attaches to relationships. Some cultures place more importance on personal relationships rather than the task to be performed or the deal to be completed. These relationships may well be within an extended family, so that blood-ties guarantee trust and loyalty. Relations outside the family need to be built on face-to-face social encounters. Loyalty to those within the circle of relations and friends is considered essential and is rewarded in many ways. Collective achievement is the focus, rather than the attainment of individual goals and careers. Indeed, some form of personal sacrifice may be necessary for the sake of the common good. In individualist cultures, the focus is more on rights and the achievements of the individual. Individuals are expected to achieve their own goals and to do so are willing, if necessary, to undergo contractual obligations. Managers expect employees to fulfil the terms of a contract and vice versa. Close ties may develop between the two, but this does not diminish the value of the contractual arrangements. Within this sort of environment, competition between individuals is encouraged thus allowing individuals to meet their goals and needs, as long as these are in line with those of the organization within which the individual is working.

Masculinity/femininity

From his initial studies at IBM, Hofstede perceived a dimension whereby certain societies could be characterized as being essentially assertive and competitive (masculine in nature), whereas others could be considered to be more caring and therefore more feminine. Hofstede does stress rather traditional roles of the sexes: masculine values such as achievement and exercise of power are used to characterize cultures along this dimension as are feminine values: caring for others, being less self-centred. Nevertheless, when a culture is

Table 2.4 Extremes of the 'masculine/feminine' dimension

Masculinity	Femininity
Distinct gender roles	Fluid gender roles
Men are assertive, women are nurturing	Men and women in nurturing roles
Stress on competition and performance	Stress on co-operation and environmental awareness
Acquisition of wealth	Quality of life
Ambition motivates	Service motivates
Live to work	Work to live
Sympathy for successful achiever	Sympathy for the unfortunate
Independence ideal	Interdependence ideal
Managers are expected to be decisive and assertive	Managers use intuition and strive for consensus

examined in terms of the work environment, this dimension allows clear distinctions to be made between cultures in terms of their attitude to work. The characterization of the two extremes of this dimension show how dramatic these distinctions can be (Table 2.4).

Highly masculine cultures see work as a challenge, offering the possibility of high rewards and recognition. The stress is on performance, on competing with others to achieve goals. Highly feminine cultures give more attention to the broader picture, particularly to relationships with others in the workplace. Quality of life is a prime concern, not just in terms of how the work is performed but also in terms of what the work achieves.

This dimension is one that Hofstede (1998: 11) himself characterized as 'taboo' since he saw the 'duality of male versus female' as a problem always under discussion, and answers to which cause wide-ranging discussion. The taboo was greatest, he felt, amongst 'masculine' countries where there was considerable stress on political correctness and concern about sexual harassment. Perhaps the very explicit use of the term masculine/feminine exacerbated matters, as evidenced in the tendency of other researchers exploring the phenomenon to talk of 'gender egalitarianism' (House et al, 2004) or to incorporate features of this dimension into one relating to assertiveness.

Uncertainty avoidance

This fourth dimension measures the extent to which people in a certain culture avoid uncertainty. To what extent do they feel threatened by ambiguous, risky situations? To what extent do they prefer predictability in their lives, clearly prescribed rules and procedures in their work? Uncertainty-avoiding cultures perceive life as a battle against anxiety and stress. They may be willing to accept familiar risks but not the danger of the unknown. To that end they tend to resist innovation or anything that deviates from the known. They appreciate authorities who have the 'right' answers, who lay down rules to prevent ambiguities. Cultures with low uncertainty avoidance are not disconcerted by ambiguity, and tolerate differences generally. They perceive that there are not always answers to problems and that laws are not always effective or necessary in dealing with deviation – they may be changed if deemed ineffective.

The two extremes of this dimension are characterized in Table 2.5.

Table 2.5 Extremes for Hofstede's 'uncertainty avoidance' dimension

Low uncertainty avoidance	High uncertainty avoidance
Uncertainty in life is threatening and must be reduced	Uncertainty is a fact of life: take things as they come
Intolerant of deviant persons and ideas	Deviance is not a threat
Predictability and clarity are preferable	Ambiguity is tolerated
Concern about security	Readiness to take risks
Resistance to change	Toleration of innovation
Formal rules and regulations are necessary	The fewer rules there are the better
Consensus is better than conflict	Competition and conflict can be constructive
Belief in experts and their knowledge	Belief in generalists and common sense
There is an inner urge to work hard	Hard work as such is not a virtue

Managers in uncertainty-avoiding cultures would be expected to maintain the rules and regulations of an organization, to have precise answers to questions and to give exact instructions. Managers in cultures with low uncertainty avoidance would be expected to uphold or establish rules only as absolutely necessary (most problems can be resolved without strict rules anyway); managers cannot possibly be the source of all wisdom and may need to draw others into their decision-making who are more competent.

Hofstede's initial four dimensions have had an enormous influence on the development of management theories in many management areas, particularly those focusing on relations between the leader and the led. Two dimensions, power distance and uncertainty avoidance, are particularly important in this respect. As Hofstede himself says:

> Both dimensions help answer two fundamental questions:
>
> 1. Who should have the power to decide what?
> 2. What rules or procedures should be followed in order to attain the desired ends?
>
> Hofstede and Hofstede, 2005: 63

Table 2.6 (page 26) summarizes the influence of the four dimensions on issues of management and business.

The fifth dimension: short-term versus long-term orientation

The dimensions above were supplemented by this, fifth, dimension. Hofstede (2001) maintains that this dimension was not found in the data used to determine the original dimensions because the questions used in the surveys were designed by Westerners. Only when an investigation was made into values suggested by researchers with what Hofstede calls 'Eastern minds' did this additional dimension come to the fore.

This fifth dimension emerged from a survey, carried out around 1985, among students from twenty-three countries. This was initiated by Michael Bond and associates who were attempting to measure value orientations from a Chinese perspective. The instrument which they developed – the Chinese Values Survey (CVS) – contained an element called the Confucian dynamism scale, reflecting those values upheld by Confucius and his followers.

Confucius, born in 551 BC in the province of Lu, China, was a political figure, educator and philosopher. He lived during a time when China was divided into small states locked in

Table 2.6 The effect of Hofstede's four dimensions on issues in management and business

Power distance	Low	High
Organizational structure	Relatively flat	Hierarchical pyramid
Status symbols	Relatively unimportant	Very important
Importance of 'face'	Face-saving less important	Face-saving Important
Participative management	Possible	Not possible
Role of manager	Facilitator	Expert
Uncertainty avoidance	**Low**	**High**
Corporate plans	Seen as guidelines	Seen as important to follow
Competition	Seen as advantageous	Seen as damaging
Budgeting systems	Flexible	Inflexible
Control systems	Loose	Tight
Risk	Take	Avoid
Individualism	**Collectivist**	**Individualist**
Decision-making	Group consensus	Individual
Reward systems	Group-based	Individual/Based on merit
Ethics/values	Particularism	Universalism
Organizational concern	Look after employees	Employees look after selves
Masculinity/Femininity	**Masculine**	**Feminine**
Valued rewards	Money, performance	Quality of life
Networking	Important for performance	Important for relationships
Interpersonal focus	Getting the task done	Maintaining relationships
Basis for motivation	Ambition – getting ahead	Service to others

Source: http://homepage.psy.utexas.edu/homepage/class/Psy365M/Merritt/HOFcharts.html

endless conflict and power struggle. He spent many years travelling from state to state, speaking for peace and universal love among humankind. His teachings, preserved by his followers, form the basis of subsequent Chinese thought on how the ideal man should live and interact, as well as how society and government should be formed. Humans, Confucius believed, could eventually reach a state of perfectibility through learning from the Chinese past and attain a state of orderliness and peace by adopting the traditional values of their forefathers. It was these forefathers who had a perfect understanding of the order in heaven and on earth: by following their rituals, humans could create within themselves the same wisdom.

The principles of Confucian teaching are summarized by Hofstede (2001: 354) as follows:

1. The stability of society is based on unequal relationships between people.

2. The family is the prototype of all social organizations. A person is not primarily an individual; rather, he or she is a member of a family.

3. Virtuous behaviour towards others consists of not treating others as one would not like to be treated oneself (the Chinese golden rule is negatively phrased!).

4. Virtue with regard to one's tasks in life consists of trying to acquire skills and education, working hard, not spending more than necessary, being patient and persevering.

Table 2.7 Hofstede's fifth dimension

Short-term orientation	Long-term orientation
Need for achievement, self-determination	Need for accountability, self-discipline
Loyalty towards others can vary according to the needs of business	Develop and maintain lifelong personal networks
People should be rewarded according to their abilities	Large social and economic differences should not be tolerated
Stress is on short-term profits	Stress is on future market position
Managers and employees are in different camps	Owner-managers and workers share the same aspirations

The fifth dimension from Bond's studies is defined by Hofstede as the short-term versus long-term orientation. Although all the values to be found along the dimension are taken from the teachings of Confucius, those deemed short-term in nature are oriented towards the past and present and are more static; whereas those deemed to be long-term are oriented towards the future and are more dynamic. It should be noted that one end of the dimension is not to be considered better or worse than the other – they are simply orientations towards life.

A *short-term* orientation includes fostering virtues related to past and present, especially respect for tradition, preservation of face and fulfilling social obligations. A *long-term* orientation includes fostering virtues oriented towards the future, especially perseverance and thrift, ordering relationships by status, and having a sense of shame.

In relation to the business context, this dimension can be characterized as in Table 2.7.

In his study of overseas Chinese, Gordon Redding (1990) shows how Confucian dynamism works and how the values in this continuum are reflected in the way the Chinese run their businesses outside China. The companies are owned by the family and usually run by one dominant family member. They are kept small to enable this family control to persist since non-family employees are unlikely to have the necessary loyalty to the enterprise. If such companies decide to co-operate with other companies they do so through a network of personal relations based on (extended) family members, village, clan or ethnic group within the Chinese population. The Confucian virtues of thrift and persistence are evident in their cost-conscious approach and in their patient accumulation of wealth. The two virtues are combined in the way the Chinese move the Chinese capital round the world to take advantage of low risk and high profitability.

Bond (1988) chose to label these values as Confucian since they generally reflect the teachings of Confucius. Hofstede prefers not to use the Confucian label since, in his view, the majority of the countries where the fifth dimension was found are 'unfamiliar with Confucius's teachings, and anyway, *both* opposing poles of the dimension contain Confucian values' (2001: 315). Confucius nevertheless permeates the values of a number of countries in Asia, as Chapter 4 will show.

The fifth dimension may be less categorical than Hofstede's original four dimensions, yet it offers insight into values which the latter do not account for.

Criticism of Hofstede's model

The very simplicity of Hofstede's framework of analysis is seductive: he has come up with a minimum number of dimensions to enable cultural observers and analysts to pinpoint features to which they and their readers can relate. The fact that the results of replicated research often reflect those of Hofstede's original research has helped to increase his stature in the field.

However, since the publication in 1980 of his major work, *Culture's Consequences*, Hofstede has been subject to criticism from fellow researchers and from humble mortals who are wrestling with day-to-day problems arising from cross-cultural co-operation in an increasingly global world. As criticism has grown, so has the robustness of Hofstede's reactions to them, aided and abetted by the results of many follow-up research projects and the employment of facts and figures produced by economic institutions to back up his findings. Possibly tired of the occasional but persistent criticism of his work, Hofstede even lists a number of the reservations made about his work in the second edition of *Culture's Consequences* in 2001. These deal with the criticism that using surveys to measure culture is unsuitable, that using nations as units of analysis is not the most appropriate, that using only surveys at one company – IBM – as the basis of his research cannot yield information about entire national cultures. Finally, he responds to the reproach made that culture cannot be boiled down to so few dimensions.

Hofstede counters these criticisms with authority. Surveys are suitable, he maintains, but should not be the only method used. He agrees that nations are not always appropriate units of analysis, but they are the only sort of unit available. When it comes to the criticism concerning the use of data from IBM, he reminds his critics of the detailed and thorough research methods used, the well-matched samples obtained and the correlations with other data, including many replications of his research. As for the reproach made that his five dimensions cannot possibly tell the whole story, his reaction is, basically: if others can find more dimensions that are independent of those he has devised and which can be validated – fine. As he puts it: 'Candidates are welcome to apply' (Hofstede, 2001: 73).

Doubts remain, however, concerning a number of aspects of Hofstede's research in terms of reliability and validity. A number of critics point out that the respondents could not be called representative because they were taken from only one location in each country and from only one company (IBM) and its carefully selected employees. Hofstede, however, considered this to be an advantage to his research because the company is homogeneous in nature, and this allowed a comparison to be made of cultural values across the subsidiaries. By ensuring that respondents to his questionnaires shared one organizational culture as well as one occupational culture (if their responses were matched), Hofstede believed he had been able to isolate nationality:

> The only thing that can account for systematic and consistent differences between national groups within such a homogeneous multinational population is nationality itself . . .
> Hofstede, 1991: 252

To make the assumption that there is homogeneity within IBM is, for many critics, a questionable one, particularly if, as Hofstede maintains, you can separate its organizational and occupational cultures from the national cultures present. Can one really talk of one organizational culture at IBM? Hofstede had not investigated this question carefully and acknowledged in his later work that organizations could contain different types of organizational culture. Even if the idea is accepted of one organizational culture within IBM, is such a culture, as Hofstede maintains, to do with perceived common practices rather than the values of the employees concerned? (This issue is discussed further in Concept 2.2.) Even if Hofstede has matched the results of the survey at IBM on an occupational basis, can one talk of a homogeneic occupational culture in the company?

McSweeney is one of Hofstede's staunchest critics. Pursuing Hofstede's notion that 'occupational values . . . are learned through socialization at school or university' (Hofstede, 1991: 182), McSweeney wonders whether employees from different nations who share the same occupation can really be said to share uniformity of culture: courses purporting to deliver similar qualifications can differ considerably between countries as well as within a country. As for someone in marketing at IBM, McSweeney remarks that that person:

> . . . was just as likely to have studied zoology, or anthropology, or French, as 'marketing' itself . . .
>
> McSweeney, 2002: 98

As for cultural homogeneity, McSweeney argues that if it is important for there to be a sameness in organizational and occupational terms, then the national culture should display a similar homogeneity. However, the results of the surveys show considerable variation within the samples in each country. Therefore, according to McSweeney, rather than talking of cultural uniformity whereby each inhabitant of a nation embodies the same cultural values, Hofstede can only resort to using cultural average tendencies when comparing nations.

If we therefore add to this criticism the points made concerning the source of Hofstede's data, its representative nature and the questions around the homogeneity of organizational cultures, then McSweeney's words below are particularly pertinent:

> If somehow the average tendency of IBM responses are assumed to be nationally representative then, with equal plausibility, or rather equal implausibility, it must also be assumed that this would be the same as the average tendency in every other company, tennis club, knitting club, political party, massage parlour, socialist party and fascist party within the same country.
>
> McSweeney, 2002: 101

The dimensions Hofstede uses to delineate cultural differences have also undergone many critical reviews. Apart from questioning whether just five dimensions can really encapsulate all the complexities of a national culture, critics cast doubt on the independent nature of each of Hofstede's dimensions: how can we be sure, they argue, that these dimensions do not interact? There is also doubt expressed about the way Hofstede differentiates between cultures on each dimension according to their position on a continuum. Although this position reflects an 'average tendency', it does not account for which situations cause cultures to emphasize one extreme of a continuum rather than the other. McSweeney (2002) takes up this point and refers to the work of scholars who maintain that the opposite ends of any dimension – such as individualism and collectivism – co-exist in all of us. Situations cause one or the other end to come to the fore.

Finally, there are questions about Hofstede's notion that cultures are territorially bound. Even though Hofstede himself acknowledges that this unit of measurement is not perfect, objections continue to be raised about the validity of national cultural profiles, particularly in the light of recent world developments. What is the status of Hong Kong's profile now that it has become part of China? Is it now to be regarded as a sub-culture within a much larger entity? What about the cultural profile of (former) Yugoslavia? Do all the independent states that once comprised the country now 'deserve' separate full-blown cultural profiles? Then there is the question of Belgium. This very small country has recently received much attention within Europe because of the political tensions there. This is a country where Dutch-speaking Flemings, French-speaking Walloons and German-speaking Belgians live side-by-side with their distinct identities, languages, cultural bodies and

Exhibit 2.1

FT

Fake news

Belgium's public television broadcaster RTBF was in hot water yesterday after running a hoax news show declaring that the powerful Flemish region had declared independence, breaking up the nation. The 30-minute programme, in which a reporter outside the royal palace claimed the king had fled the country, fooled thousands of viewers, who besieged the French-language channel with phone calls.

But Guy Verhofstadt, the (Flemish) prime minister, was unamused, branding the show a bad joke. Some ambassadors were also said to have been fooled, sending news of the 'split' to their home countries. There were even comparisons to Orson Welles' *War of the Worlds* broadcasts. One frustrated official said: 'The frightening thing is that, with all the tension, things like this could become self-fulfilling prophecies.'

Source: *Financial Times*, 15 December 2006: 12.

regional parliaments, as well as one federal parliament. What is the value of a set of statistics that waters down crucial differences between the 'sub-cultures' of Belgium and presents itself as a cultural profile of 'Belgium'? What would happen to this cultural profile if Flanders (the Flemish region of Belgium) or Wallonia (the French-speaking region) actually declared independence from the rest of Belgium (see Exhibit 2.1)?

In short, the validity and applicability of Hofstede's model is called into question by a number of critics, not only by scholars but also by practitioners in the field of cross-cultural management training who feel uneasy when applying Hofstede's dimensions to 'the real world'.

We will return to criticism of Hofstede's work in Chapter 5 when comparing Hofstede's dimensions with those devised by Trompenaars.

Concept 2.2 The influence of national culture on business culture

Values and practices

The relationship between national culture and the culture of companies working within a national culture has undergone extensive and intensive investigation. Many internal factors are believed to influence a company's culture, such as company goals, manuals, rules and regulations, and particularly the presence of long-standing employees. However, it is the national culture in which an organization is embedded that has been found to be the main influence.

Organizational culture, or its equivalent in the US, corporate culture, is itself a construct and has therefore many definitions. Generally speaking, however, it is the perception of an organization shared by those working in it. This perception encompasses not only certain beliefs about the organization in terms of what it is, what it stands for and what its mission is, but also certain organizational values that those working in it acquire with regard to 'how things ought to be' (Mead, 1994: 139). These values are deep-rooted and not easily susceptible to change.

What is the status of these organizational values? Schein (2004) regards them as being the equivalent of national culture in terms of the influence they have on an organization. He sees them as a set of implicit assumptions about how to behave. The major difference, however, is that the values of national culture are acquired early on in life, whereas organizational values are likely to be learned much later on and in a conscious way. That very difference leads Hofstede (2001: 394) to reject any equivalence; the two types of culture are of different kinds and using the word 'culture' for both can be misleading. His own empirical research in this area led him to the conclusion that 'shared perceptions of daily practices should be considered the core of an organization's culture'. By 'practices' he means conventions, customs or habits acquired when working in the organization. This is at odds with many – mainly US – writers who talk of shared values as being at the heart of a company. Hofstede (2001: 394) argues that, although founders or leaders of companies may impress their values on a company's culture (see Chapter 8), the effect these may have on employees comes through shared practices. As he writes: 'Founders/leaders' values become members' practices.'

Many of Hofstede's findings have been confirmed by those of the Global Leadership and Organizational Behaviour Effectiveness research programme, in short, the GLOBE project. GLOBE is a long-term programme designed to conceptualize, operationalize, test and validate a cross-level integrated theory of the relationship between culture and societal, organizational and leadership effectiveness. The first two phases of the project are described in House et al (2004).

During the first phase of the project, the investigators developed additional dimensions of societal cultural variation, a number of which have their origins in those identified by Hofstede. These are given in Table 2.8. The dimensions were used to examine the practices/values construct at industrial, organizational and societal level.

As the examples in Table 2.8 indicate, the questions asked of the respondents were asked firstly in terms of 'is' and 'are', so that the responses would indicate actual practice, i.e. 'the way we do things'. They were later asked the same questions using 'should', to enable a response that indicated the value(s) held by each respondent (i.e. 'the ideal way of doing things').

When the researchers investigated the relationship between societal and organizational practices and societal and organizational values, the respondents used were all taken from medium to large companies operating in three industrial sectors in their home country. To ensure that respondents represented their own culture, multinational employees were not questioned. The results showed that organizational cultural practices varied among the societal systems being investigated, no matter which industrial sector the organizations were operating in (House et al, 2004). Moreover, the societal values and practices had a significant effect on organizational culture on all nine dimensions of organizational cultural practice.

Before moving on to the question of national values in multinationals, it is worthwhile noticing that, despite the praise given to the GLOBE project for the scale and thoroughness of its efforts, there has been criticism of the construct devised, criticism which echoes some of the doubts described earlier concerning Hofstede's model. Even Hofstede (2006) himself is critical of GLOBE's need to use nine dimensions. When re-analysing their scores he found a significant correlation between the dimensions. After using factor analysis, he was able to reduce their number to five.

Table 2.8 Culture construct definitions and sample questionnaire items

Culture construct definitions	Specific questionnaire item
Power distance: the degree to which members of a collective expect power to be distributed equally	Followers are (should be) expected to obey their leaders without question
Uncertainty avoidance: the extent to which a society, organization, or group relies on social norms, rules and procedures to alleviate the unpredictability of future events	Most people lead (should lead) highly structured lives with few unexpected events
Humane orientation: the degree to which a collective encourages and rewards individuals for being fair, altruistic, generous, caring and kind to others	People are generally (should be generally) very tolerant of mistakes
Collectivism 1 (institutional collectivism): the degree to which organizational and societal institutional practices encourage and reward collective distribution of resources and collective action	Leaders encourage (should encourage) group loyalty even if individual goals suffer
Collectivism 2 (in-group collectivism): the degree to which individuals express pride, loyalty and cohesiveness in their organizations or families	Employees feel (should feel) great loyalty towards this organization
Assertiveness: the degree to which individuals are assertive, confrontational and aggressive in their relationships with others	People are (should be) generally dominant in their relationships with each other
Gender egalitarianism: the degree to which a collective minimizes gender inequality	Boys are encouraged (should be encouraged) more than girls to attain a higher education (scored inversely)
Future orientation: the extent to which individuals engage in future-oriented behaviours such as delaying gratification, planning and investing in the future	More people live (should live) for the present rather than for the future (scored inversely)
Performance orientation: the degree to which a collective encourages and rewards group members for performance improvement and excellence	Students are encouraged (should be encouraged) to strive for continuously improved performance

Source: House et al (2004): 30.

National culture values in multinationals

Although the GLOBE research appears to confirm the predominance of national culture values over organizational culture values, the question can be raised as to whether national culture values prevail among those employees who were not questioned in the GLOBE project because they were not members of the societies into which the organizations were embedded.

André Laurent (1983) has carried out investigations into the attitudes of managers in several countries towards their organization. A series of studies he made concerning national differences in concepts of management produced interesting results. Over a period of two years, questions were put to experienced international managers attending executive programmes at an international business school. The findings showed clear differences between countries with regard to the perception of organizations as political, systems, authority systems, role-formalization systems and hierarchical relationship systems.

The study was replicated among much younger and less experienced MBA students and, in two multinational companies, one being a US-based chemical firm with subsidiaries in France, Germany and Great Britain, later in amended form in another multinational. The results from the replications were essentially the same as those from the first survey among executive programme participants. Although it might have been expected for those working in multinationals to have undergone some kind of homogenizing effect in terms of managerial concepts, the results showed a surprising stability. Moreover, the results from the first multinational surveyed showed respondents' concepts to be even more entrenched.

Laurent's conclusion – that the management process in the ten countries surveyed is as much culture-bound as their cooking – is echoed in the results of the GLOBE project's survey among company employees working in their own society. The national culture remains dominant within the organization. As Laurent explains, employees do not leave their national culture behind at the company entrance.

This concept has outlined dimensions of culture, giving particular attention to those devised by Hofstede. The deep-seated nature of the values embedded in these dimensions has also been illustrated in terms of the values inherent in organizational cultures: practices between companies may vary, but the values of those working in the company environment remain constant in the sense that they maintain certain notions about the world and attitudes towards their fellow-humans.

The characteristics defining each cultural group can offer international managers considerable insights when it comes, for example, to co-operating with companies from other cultural backgrounds. If awareness of cultural differences is consciously raised, then the ability to analyse the effectiveness of employing business policies in differing cultural environments is considerably improved.

ACTIVITY 2.1

The role of the manager

An example is given below of one of the statements to which respondents were asked to react by André Laurent when he was investigating the attitudes of managers in a number of countries towards their organization. This study was outlined at the end of Concept 2.2.

Examine the results and answer the question below the figure.

'It is important for a manager to have at hand precise answers to most of the questions that his subordinates may raise about their work.'

Figure 2.1 Agreement with statement: a manager should have precise answers
Source: based on figures in Laurent (1983: 86).

Question

Using these figures, how would you characterize the attitudes of Swedes, Germans and Japanese towards the role of the manager in an organization?

ACTIVITY 2.2

Read the case study and answer the questions below.

Pulling out all the stops

A Canadian packaging company wished to extend its activities in the area of convenience foods. It had pinpointed one particular area where it could supply pizza boxes to half a dozen chains of pizza restaurants which operated home delivery services. These chains relied on local suppliers for their pizza boxes and were unhappy with the products supplied, the irregular delivery and, above all, the cost.

Through intensive online research and consultation with the commercial section of the embassy of the People's Republic of China, the Canadians had managed to find a packaging manufacturer near Shanghai that could provide pizza boxes at a very reasonable price in line with the specifications and quantities required – and deliver them within the deadlines set.

Negotiations by email and phone had taken place and a deal seemed imminent. Before contracts could be signed, however, it was agreed that both the Chinese and Canadians should visit each other's headquarters and meet face-to-face to establish complete confidence in their venture and to settle final details. The Chinese were to visit Canada and the Canadians were to fly to China two weeks later.

The Canadian company decided to pull out all the stops to give their visitors a reception they would never forget. They arranged an elaborate welcome ceremony in a five-star hotel, to be followed by an authentic Chinese dinner. Considerable attention was paid to all the details involved – some of the ingredients for the meal had even been specially imported for the occasion.

Eventually the big day came and the Chinese guests were whisked by limousine to the hotel where they were greeted by the Canadian company's president and management team. Despite the lavish words of praise from the Canadians in front of the hundred guests present, and the bonhomie everyone tried to engender, the Chinese remained reticent and very formal in their behaviour. During the meal the Chinese did not seem to appreciate the effort put into the food they were served. Moreover, they said very little and the attempts by the Canadians to keep the social conversation going eventually ended in silence on both sides. Despite being promised an exotic Chinese floor-show after the dinner, the delegation made their excuses (they were tired after their journey) and quietly retired to their rooms. The Canadians were surprised and disappointed. What had gone wrong?

Questions

1. Why were the Canadian hosts surprised by the behaviour of the Chinese? How do you think the Canadians expected the Chinese to behave?

2. Why do you think the Chinese behaved the way they did?

3. Below is the analysis of the event as given by the author (Wei Xinjiang, from the People's Republic of China). Draw from the analysis the key preferences of the Chinese when it comes to doing business with Western cultures.

Author's analysis

The main reason for the Chinese guests leaving suddenly has to do with the culture differences between Canadians and Chinese. As we know, China is a very polite country and the Chinese are very hospitable. They like their own food and they enjoy eating Chinese food abroad.

However, if the Chinese are offered too much hospitality they are rather embarrassed. The Chinese businessmen are on what they consider to be a normal business visit to Canada, so they only expect a normal, ordinary welcome. If they are treated in what they consider to be an unusual way, they will be upset. This is particularly the case if the Chinese company in question intends to give its Canadian business partners a normal welcome when they visit China.

There exists a reciprocity principle in normal Chinese communication. If this reciprocity is not respected in normal business relations, the Chinese will suspect the motives of the other side and be unhappy, or even angry.

Modern China has a mixed culture, which comprises traditional culture, Marxism and Western culture. One of the consequences of this mix is that, although the Chinese prefer formality, they do not like it in an extreme form. If a situation is too formal, then the Chinese become inactive and lazy in their behaviour. They prefer doing business during dinner, which should be a friendly, fairly informal and comfortable event. If, after the formal welcoming ceremony, the Canadians had tried to arrange such a dinner during which both sides could have got down to business, then the Chinese would not have felt irritated and the results could have been very different.

How can you be successful when dealing with the Chinese? The most important thing to remember is that everything should have a proper degree. The Chinese dislike going to extremes: nothing should be too good or too bad. It is a question of trying to find a balance between good and bad. The Chinese expect others to treat them as they treat others. Extreme forms of behaviour only exist under extreme conditions. Otherwise there should only be moderation.

This can be seen in the way the Chinese deal with their friends. There are three kinds of friends in China: close friends, remote friends and common friends. If you treat a remote friend in the same way you treat a common friend, that friend will be embarrassed. A common friend will expect to be treated in a common way, in a way which is neither too polite nor impolite. The middle way is the right way.

4. If you had to choose a word to describe Chinese culture, what would that word be?

5. Read the information on the fifth dimension one more time. Try to explain the Chinese author's analysis by using the values described in Concept 2.1.

Conclusion

This chapter has explained the cultural dimensions of Hofstede and the relationship between national cultural values and those of organizational cultures. It has also outlined the many criticisms of Hofstede's research method, particularly the reliability and applicability of the findings. The chapter has also explained how the researchers involved in the GLOBE project have expanded this five-dimension model to eighteen and used a survey method which allows for a better understanding of the relations between organizational practices and social values. Their findings include confirmation of studies carried out by Laurent, which show the persistence of the national cultures of employees and managers in all organizations, including multinational companies.

The significance of Hofstede's fifth dimension – short-term and long-term orientation – has also been described. This dimension is of special significance bearing in mind the increasing importance in current business of the relations between the Western countries and those in the East, especially China.

Points for reflection

1. This chapter has described cultural dimensions that can give insight into differences between national cultures.

   What are the advantages and limitations when using these dimensions to describe organizational cultures?

2. Hofstede's cultural dimensions were characterized in this chapter in relation to the business environment.

   Which of these dimensions – and the others referred to in this chapter – do you consider to be most relevant to the study of culture in the business context? Explain your choice.

3. Hofstede supplemented his dimensions with a fifth one arising from research carried out by researchers with 'Eastern minds'.

   What added value does this extra dimension give to measuring the effect of culture in the business context?

4. One criticism of Hofstede's work is that the scores on each dimension reflect only an 'average tendency' of a particular country, and therefore inadequately reflect the wide range of responses given within a country to the survey, particularly from sub-cultures.

   Look up the profile of your country, as given on the Geert Hofstede website (www.geert-hofstede.com) and consider its analytical value, particularly with regard to any sub-cultures which you are aware of within your country.

Further reading

Burns, R. (1998) *Doing Business in Asia: A cultural perspective*, **Melbourne, Australia: Addison Wesley Longman.** This book provides a reference point for Western business people visiting Asian countries. Burns gives assistance in determining the nuances of cultural behaviour, expectations and values, and the affect of these issues on business activities.

Hofstede, G. and Hofstede, G.J. (2005), *Cultures and Organizations: Software of the Mind*, **2nd edn, London: McGraw-Hill.** The book describes and analyses Geert Hofstede's research. It has been completely rewritten. His co-author, his son Gert Jan, has hands-on experience teaching the subject to students and practitioners.

McSweeney, B. (2002) 'Hofstede's model of national cultural differences and their consequences: a triumph of faith – a failure of analysis', in *Human Relations* **55 (1): 89–118.** This article is a detailed and passionate critique of Hofstede's national culture research. McSweeney questions the assumptions underlying Hofstede's research method and findings, and contains many useful references to other critics of Hofstede's work. Hofstede responded to McSweeney in the following article:

Hofstede, G. (2002) 'Dimensions do not exist: a reply to Brendan McSweeney', *Human Relations* **55 (11): 1355–1361.**

McSweeney in turn reacted to Hofstede's response in the same edition of the journal:

'The essentials of scholarship: a reply to Geert Hofstede', *Human Relations*, **55 (11): 1363–1372.**

References

Bond, M.H. (1988) 'Finding dimensions of individual variation in multicultural studies of values: the Rokeach and Chinese value surveys', *Journal of Personality and Social Psychology,* 55 (6): 1009–1115.

Hofstede, G. (1980) *Culture's Consequences,* 1st edn, Beverly Hills: Sage.

Hofstede, G. (1991) *Cultures and Organizations: Software of the mind,* London: McGraw-Hill.

Hofstede, G. (1998) *Masculinity and Femininity: The taboo dimension of national cultures,* Thousand Oaks, CA: Sage.

Hofstede, G. (2001) *Culture's Consequences,* 2nd edn, Thousand Oaks, CA: Sage.

Hofstede, G. (2006) 'What did GLOBE really measure? Researchers' minds versus respondents' minds', *Journal of International Business Studies,* 37: 882–896.

Hofstede, G. and Hofstede G.J. (2005) *Cultures and Organizations: Software of the Mind,* 2nd edn, London: McGraw-Hill.

House, R.J., Hanges, P.J., Javidan, M., Dorfman, P.W. and Gupta, V. (eds) (2004) *Leadership, Culture and Organizations: The GLOBE study of 62 societies,* Thousand Oaks, CA: Sage.

Kluckholn, F. and Strodtbeck, F. (1961) *Variations in Value Orientations,* Evanston, IL: Row, Peterson.

Laurent, A. (1983) 'The cultural diversity of western conceptions of management', *International Studies of Management and Organization,* 13, 1–2: 75–96.

McSweeney, B. (2002) 'Hofstede's model of national cultural differences and their consequences: a triumph of faith – a failure of analysis', *Human Relations,* 55 (1): 89–118.

Mead, R. (1994) *International Management: Cross-cultural dimensions,* Cambridge, MA/Oxford: Blackwell Business.

Pugh, D.S. (1976) 'The "Aston" approach to the study of organisations' in Hofstede, G. and Kassem, M.S. (eds), *European Contributions to Organisation Theory,* Assen, The Netherlands: Van Gorcum: 62–78.

Redding, G. (1990) *The Spirit of Chinese Capitalism,* Berlin and New York: Gruyter.

Schein, E.H. (2004) *Organizational Culture and Leadership,* 3rd edn, San Francisco: Jossey-Bass.

Steers, R. and Sànchez-Runde, C. (2002) 'Culture, motivation, and work behaviour' in Gannon, M.J. and Newman, K.L. (eds), *Blackwell Handbook of Cross-Cultural Management,* Oxford: Blackwell: Chapter 10.

Chapter 3

Western business cultures

When faced with a cornucopia of cultures, it is natural to try and establish some sort of order that allows cultures to be clustered in terms of their similarities. Doing so enables those involved in multicultural operations to gain a perspective, be it a very general one, of similarities and differences between cultures.

Creating clusters of cultures has been attempted by authors such as Ronen and Shenkar (1985) and Hickson and Pugh (2001). House et al (2004) have taken the concept further and devised a 'metaconfiguration' (Figure 3.1). The findings from their own research using the nine dimensions referred to in Chapter 2 naturally play an important role, as do the results of previous empirical research projects. Religion, languages, geography and eth-nicity are considered relevant factors, as are work-related attitudes and values. Historical developments and economic similarities are also seen as playing a crucial role in the clus-tering. The result is a configuration on an East–West axis, with the clusters arranged according to calculations relating to the average distance in societal culture dimensions. The Anglo and Sub-Saharan clusters are placed in the centre since they show mid-level scores on the nine dimensions used. The countries in the clusters are given in Figure 3.2.

The metaconfiguration in Figure 3.1 will be the starting point for this chapter and Chapter 4. Each will take aspects of each cluster relating to history, religion and work-related values and practices, and will feature certain countries within each cluster (as in Figure 3.2). Chap-ter 3 will consider the four European clusters as well as Latin America, i.e. the left hemi-sphere of Figure 3.1.

Learning outcomes

After studying Chapter 3 you will:

● Become familiar with the idea of clustering cultures according to their similarities, par-ticularly the metaconfiguration of clusters devised by the GLOBE project.

● Discover which characteristics bring together countries in a number of clusters within the Western half of this metaconfiguration. Three of these clusters are within Europe: Latin European, Nordic European and Germanic Europe. A fourth cluster – Anglo – is to be found both within Europe and across the globe. The fifth cluster is Latin American.

● Gain awareness of some of the problems arising from cooperation between and within these clusters.

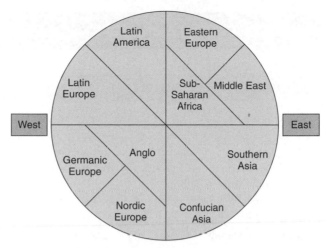

Figure 3.1 Clusters of cultures
Source: House et al (2004): 201.

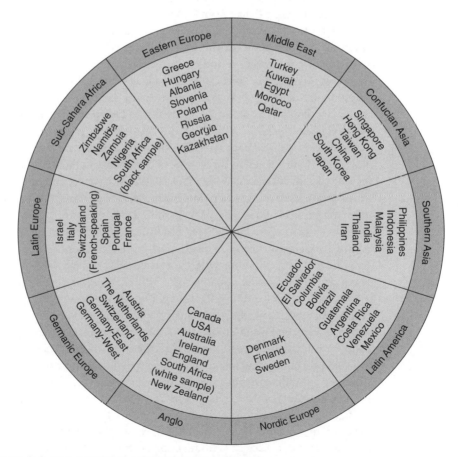

Figure 3.2 The countries composing each cluster
Source: House et al (2004): 190.

Concept 3.1 Western culture clusters

Europe's culture clusters

As the figures indicate, four of the five European clusters are in the western hemisphere and a fifth, Eastern Europe, has been firmly placed in the eastern hemisphere. This last cluster will be dealt with in Chapter 4, even though some of the countries it contains have explicitly chosen to belong economically and politically to organizations that bring the other European clusters together.

One such organization is the European Union, which is the latest in a line of attempts through the centuries to make Europe more than just a geographical phenomenon. Originating as a common economic market that allowed a number of (West) European countries to trade fairly, it has developed into a body with common institutions at economic, social and political levels to which the member countries have delegated some of their sovereignty.

The historical roots of the EU lie in the Second World War, as do those of a parallel institution, the Council of Europe. They were set up to bring peace and prosperity to a continent whose countries had been at war with each other. The aim of the Council of Europe is to establish and promote fundamental values such as human rights, the rule of law and democracy; to eradicate torture and inhuman and degrading treatment; to eliminate all forms of discrimination as well as to foster co-operation with other international and European organizations and institutions. The council has come to play a special role in the development of the EU by laying down economic, social and legal benchmarks for new applicant countries. By doing so it is creating a European identity based on common values and practices.

However, to what extent can one talk of a European culture based on such values and practices? There is certainly an increasing uniformity in the way affairs are organized and in the way people run their lives, particularly thanks to the effects of the EU. Nevertheless, this organization itself has a rather ambivalent attitude towards the concept of a European culture: while one EU body talks of its wish to develop a unified cultural entity, another talks of the need to preserve Europe's many cultures. Those who shout 'I am a European' may be essentially exclaiming an ideal based on a desire for European unity (or stating an obvious geographical fact); those denying the existence of Europe see nothing more than institutional structures binding a hotchpotch of different cultures (Exhibit 3.1).

Despite the domination of Rome and the predomination of Christianity over centuries, despite increased co-ordination and co-operation between European countries, despite shared representation and legislation, cultural differences between regions and countries have not been eradicated. Cultural values of a society are still being handed down from generation to generation in the same way as those of an individual. Some shifts may occur over time, but clear cultural differences still survive. Moreover, through continuing expansion of the EU, one could argue that the EU and its sister organizations are becoming more heterogeneous.

It could be argued that a much more united Europe existed in the early Middle Ages (from around the fifth to tenth centuries) when a number of its countries shared common features of a feudal society. With no strong central authority, political power was dispersed among lords who in turn granted vassals authority over particular lands. Those peasants who tended particular landholdings were obliged to supply the lord with labour and or

Exhibit 3.1

Establishing values among EU citizens

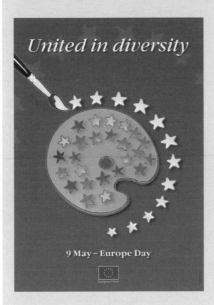

United in diversity

9 May – Europe Day

One of the thrusts of an EU project on 'Cultural identities, shared values and European citizenship' is the preparation of the 'Little blue book' on the core values underpinning European

citizenship. The aim of this book is to present to the general public the question of values and what kind of common or core values should be presented and exemplify these core values. It should also provide background reading and information as well as inspiration for the future citizens to whom it is addressed. A group of specialists from all over Europe is responsible for the preparation of this book. It is being developed around chapters on dialogues and case studies. The dialogues will focus on:

- Citizens and the state (protection of the state against arbitrary power).
- The clash of rights (freedom of the press, tradition v universalism).
- Dialogue on environmental rights.
- The right to live where you wish.
- Living in a divided community.
- A just war.
- The pursuit of truth and realpolitik.
- Is democracy enough?

Source: Council of Europe website: www.coe.int/t/e/cultural_co-operation/heritage/cultural_identities/Littlebluebook_EN.asp (accessed 16 April 2007).

part of the land's output. This was a system essentially based on man-to-man relations, the one depending on the other, in an agrarian economy with limited money exchange.

As Morin (1987) declares, the political and cultural Europe of today is the result of the disruption of this feudal system and the ensuing conflict. This, as well as its Greek, Roman and Judeo-Christian streams in its culture, is what makes Europe unique.

The regional differences mentioned earlier have a lot to do with the influences that events in history brought to daily life. The Roman Empire with its strict hierarchies and its codified system of laws was one; the invasion of the Vikings who maintained local, largely independent communities with their own laws and hierarchies was another. These two influences will be the starting-point of an overview of the differences between the various European clusters.

Latin Europe

Managing and organizing in societies characterized by Romance languages close to Latin, by Roman-style legal systems and strong Roman Catholic churches still differs from other societies where the Romans held little or no sway. The Roman Empire had the greatest effect on countries below the river Rhine. In Latin Europe, there is a more personal approach to managing and organizing. There may be a highly-developed bureaucracy present in Latin countries, but the layers of hierarchy and the procedures involved in getting things done are so formalized that working round them is quicker and in the end more efficient. That is why there is a reliance on family and personal relationships and connections to work around the system, to bend the rules.

Nevertheless, the boss is the boss, and the authority of that person rests on the need of a country's people for strong rule. There is often a tension between this dependency on and loyalty towards authoritarian figures and a distrust of authoritarian systems in general. Prominent figures may exploit this tension by showing their ability as leaders to impose their stamp, their will on unwieldy closed hierarchies.

As Boisot indicates (1993: 222) in his article on management in Spain:

> The need for a strong leader and a hierarchical leader, however, does not necessarily give the enterprise manager the kind of mandate that would allow him to play a proper co-ordinating role.

Managers lack the legitimacy to perform their role effectively and can be perceived as devious exploiters of the economic system. This problem of managerial legitimacy is one, he believes, prevalent in Latin culture because the economic dimension is perceived to be little more than an expression of the political culture.

In her book on Italian management, Vidal (1992) distinguishes two types of business leaders in Italy. A company is run by two people, a couple as it were, who share each other's confidence and complement each other. The one plays the role of leader and spends most of his time with external contacts in search of information that will allow him to adjust company objectives. While doing so, he keeps an eye on what is happening inside the company. The other assumes the role of manager in the traditional sense, focusing his attention on what is happening within the company while still keeping an eye on the world outside.

A leader in France, however, is alone at the top. Such power involves not only fulfilling contractual obligations, but also preserving the status of the position. If he is not moderate when enacting his power, if he lacks breadth of vision or is seen as mean-minded, then he is seen to belong to what Segal (d'Iribarne et al.: 1998) calls the category of 'little bosses'.

Unlike the other countries in Latin Europe, France was formed by a wide range of peoples, consisting at the start mainly of Celts (the Gauls), Romans and Germans (the Franks). The country came into being after the separation of Francia Occidentalis (the West Frankish kingdom, now France) from Francia Orientalis (the East Frankish kingdom, now Germany). In the eighteenth century, France became the model of European culture, not only through the dissemination of the universal values – liberty, equality and fraternity – proclaimed during the French Revolution, but also through its language. However, at the end of the century, its predominance in Europe waned as that of its main rival, England, flourished.

It is perhaps the historical role of France as the upholder of universal cultural values that has made it reluctant to envisage a plurality of cultures, or to talk of one culture for one people. This notion, which evolved in the equivalent of present-day Germany at the end of the eighteenth century, goes against the French idea of a universal culture or civilization. Nevertheless, the term 'culture' in France is applied to the description of customs relating to certain professional, social or regional categories. Even the French talk, for example, of 'French-style' bureaucracy when describing the friction between two professional categories within a state-owned enterprise.

In short, the French idea of universal culture and their concept of a unity of cultural communities within their society, contrasts strongly with the notion held in other European countries of a national culture essentially based on compromise (d'Iribarne et al, 1998).

Examined in terms of the cultural dimensions put forward by House et al (2004), the Latin European cluster is characterized as being low in terms of humane orientation practices, although humane orientation scores in terms of values more closely resemble those of other European clusters. This humane orientation construct addresses the degree of concern, tolerance and support extended to others. As a cluster with low humane orientation practices, self-interest is high, as is lack of consideration for others. However, in terms of consideration for family, the countries concerned are collectively inclined, showing greater loyalty and cohesiveness to their family. As will be seen later in this chapter, when looking at Latin America, the family concern is even more in evidence in the Latin countries of the New World.

Nordic Europe

The presence of the Vikings who swept down from Scandinavia and occupied parts of northern Europe is still felt. They helped to reinforce the contrast between the cultural characteristics of the Northerners and those of the Roman Empire. They had no overriding hierarchy, no elaborate systems of control. Instead, they maintained large independent communities, each with its own laws and governing bodies.

The Viking heritage of self-sufficiency, fairness, egalitarianism and democracy is reflected in the way Scandinavian business is run. In most companies, bosses are seen more as team leaders and group facilitators as opposed to being decision makers who delegate tasks to others. As such, employees are often encouraged to express their opinions freely at meetings and everyone's opinion is given consideration when making decisions. However, the final decision often lies in the hands of the group leader.

The countries of Nordic Europe share one distinctive feature – their approach to authority. Their inhabitants do not regard those in authority as remote persons whose word is to be accepted unquestioningly. They face up to them, question their decisions, and expect to be consulted on issues affecting them. Those managing and being managed are less far apart socially than in Latin Europe, with more emphasis put on the job being done than the position in the hierarchy. Managers are not expected to have all the answers but instead to make effective use of the expertise among their co-workers. These characterizations are reflected in the position of Nordic European countries on the cultural dimensions relating to power distance as devised by both Hofstede and House et al.

Germanic Europe

House et al (2004) admit that the cultural separation of Germanic and Nordic Europe is not as great as among other clusters. Along with the Nordic countries, Germanic countries show lower power distance than their other fellow Europeans. However, in terms of managing uncertainty, some societies – Germany, Austria – tend to adopt a longer-term perspective when making strategic decisions. They are also more concerned with getting the job done than with the work environment and family. On the assertiveness dimension, which corresponds in many ways to Hofstede's masculine/feminine dimension, there appears to be a contrast, however. Individual initiative, assertive behaviour, explicit communication, emphasis on results rather than relationships are much more a feature of Germanic countries.

A further reference to the Romans is worth making here. Romans conquered 'Germania' and trained its inhabitants to become loyal warriors in Rome's wars of expansion and even entrusted them with guarding the Roman emperor. However, it was one of these loyal warriors, Arminius, who organized a revolt against the Roman armies in the Teutoburg Forest as they were turning lower Germania into a Roman province. With the annihilation of three Roman legions, the empire recognised that it had reached its limit. The Rhine became the boundary rather than the Elbe. Result: Germania retained its distinctive culture and language and until the nineteenth century retained a collection of small principalities.

A number of authors, including Lendering (2003), argue that had Germania not asserted itself and so allowed the Romans to continue their occupation up to the North Sea coast, then the tribes would have eventually adopted Latin. They would have brought this language to Britain instead of the Germanic language which lies at the base of the English language. English might never have existed without the revolt of the Germanic tribes.

The Anglos

The term 'Anglo' is an abbreviation for 'Anglo-Saxon', which is used to describe people from the British Isles as well as those who emigrated to North America and Australasia. The latter will be dealt with once the Anglos have been characterized in the European context.

It was Anglo-Saxon tribes – the Angles, Saxons and Jutes – who, along with other tribes from Northern Europe, settled in large numbers in 'Britannia', the province that the Romans had established on the lowlands of the British mainland and later abandoned. With the eventual consolidation of the various settlements and kingdoms, this area became known as England. England eventually became the dominant part of a larger political entity, now known as the United Kingdom of Great Britain and Northern Ireland, which includes Wales, Scotland and Northern Ireland. The use of the term 'British' reflects the union of these peoples and the amalgam of elements that constitute their culture.

Using Hofstede's cultural dimensions, the British can be characterized as having less power distance and lower uncertainty avoidance than their European neighbours, while at the same time being more individualistic and more ambitious/aggressive than their counterparts on the continent.

The relaxed British approach to management contrasts strongly with the Latin and Nordic approach. Although bureaucracy is the most common form of organization, and instrumental in creating Britain's economic success in the nineteenth century, the British handle it in a very pragmatic way. As Hickson and Pugh (2001: 50) indicate:

> Characteristically, they balance its potential rigidities by day-to-day pragmatism, working things out as they go along, rather than taking bureaucratic prescription too far. They do not try to manage uncertainty by issuing regulations and declarations, of which they are sceptical. Hence it has been said that the British see an organization as a 'market' in which people negotiate what has to be done . . . .

This ties in with the very individualistic nature of the British. The job is a job, regarded as separate from one's personal life, a task to be performed impersonally. This can be seen in the way personnel are selected. Although the selection process may appear the same across European countries, the emphasis in Anglo-Saxon cultures, as Lisa Hoecklin (1995) notes, is on the extent to which the individual concerned can contribute to the tasks of the organization. That is why, according to her, it is normal for intelligence and skills to be measured and assessment centres to be employed.

Selecting employees

Some comparisons between the British and countries from the Latin and Germanic clusters are relevant here to highlight differences with regard to recruitment and employment generally. In Latin countries, more focus is placed during the selection process on the extent to which the applicant will fit into the group of employees concerned. The emphasis, therefore, is on interpersonal skills and tests of personality and communicative competence. Referring to a survey comparing French and UK methods of selection, Hoecklin (1995) points out the tendency for the French to use one-to-one interviews rather than panel interviews and to make use of references much less than the British. She contrasts the 'particularist' approach of the French, where the concern is not just about skills criteria but also about operating successfully within a 'web of relationships and hierarchies', with the 'universalist' approach of the British, where more reliance is placed on more objective criteria about applicants' intellect or technical skills to determine whether they fit into the organization.

In Germanic cultures, there is equal concern for the appropriate technical skills, but in a much broader and long-term context. As Hillmert (2002) indicates, the (potential) employer and employee are not just concerned with the present requirements of a company but also with the longer-term occupational career of a candidate. Whereas the occupation of a British employee is closely connected to the firm where he/she works, that of the German employee is considered more as a step in the development of a career that involves further (state-supported) vocational training and inter-firm mobility. The stability of careers in Germany contrasts strongly with the job-hopping tendencies and short-term perspectives of British employees who do not benefit from a co-ordinated training provision from the state, employers and trade unions.

Hillmert (2002: 682) depicts Britain as a deregulated liberal market economy where:

> British enterprises act under conditions of high-profit orientation and a relatively short-time horizon. They are, therefore, comparatively unwilling to invest in longer-term training. Moreover, in a highly flexible labour market, there is no particular requirement for training as a screening period for future long-term personnel.

Anglosaxonization

This Anglo-Saxon focus on short-term profit in a deregulated environment is deplored by many countries in present-day Europe. Political leaders of some EU countries often use the term 'Anglo-Saxon' when referring to the increasing commitment among the newer members of the EU to profits and free markets at the expense of social responsibility. These leaders are afraid that the social fabric of their countries will crumble through the increasing predominance of market forces. This anxiety reflects the wish of some of them for the EU to develop into a tight body of nations with a serious political commitment, rather than just being a sophisticated free trade area with an unambiguous legal and financial framework.

Such differences in policy involve questions of culture, explicitly or implicitly. To what extent, for example, can those countries that prefer state institutions to have significant influence on their economy work together with countries that prefer minimum state interference in the workings of the market? So-called rational arguments used in policy discussions are often based on the distinct preferences shared by the inhabitants of a country, preferences which may or may not be shared with other countries. This applies also to the future expansion of the EU. Fear has often been expressed of a 'watering down' of cultural identities as the

EU expands further east, and this in turn has raised the matter of whether Europe itself has a cultural identity that must be preserved or protected. The possible accession of Turkey to the EU, for example, is seen by some as a threat to the European way of life in some or all of its facets. Others see the inclusion of Turkey as an enrichment of the European community and a boost to the development of the EU's economic power.

Whatever agreements may be reached at economic or social level, co-operation of whatever sort can clearly only work if there is a willingness to do so at cultural level. Observers of the developments in Europe have noted this from the start, including one of the founders of the original European Community, Jean Monet. He was allegedly asked by a reporter what he would do differently if he had the chance to start over again with the development of the community. He was said to have replied: 'I would start with the culture.' These words resound as strongly nowadays as they did when first reported.

The concern about the 'anglosaxonization' of Europe is a suitable starting-point for examination of the Anglo approach to business outside Europe. The Anglo business culture will be reviewed in the US, Canada and Australasia areas of the world, where large numbers of immigrants from the British Isles (including Ireland) set up home and business.

The Anglos outside Europe

Anglo-Americans

The term White Anglo-Saxon Protestants or WASPs is the term often used in North America to describe the people who made up most of the population of the USA when the country was still in its infancy. The values which these people took along when they emigrated have had a significant influence on the shape of US culture.

The original settlers in North America brought with them what Max Weber referred to as the Protestant work ethic. In his influential book *The Protestant Ethic and the Spirit of Capitalism*, first published in 1905, Weber studied the psychological conditions underpinning the development of capitalist civilization. He argued that modern capitalism was born from the spirit of Christian asceticism in its specifically Protestant form. He saw a link between the self-denying ethos of the Protestant sects and the behaviour patterns associated with capitalism, above all those to do with hard work.

Although this work ethic is considered by some observers to be dying a slow death in Europe, it is still regarded as being a driving force within US business. The many immigrants who followed the early settlers were not all in any sense protestant in their religious beliefs, but they adopted the ethic. They too became intent on achievement and improvement, on realizing the 'American Dream' and doing so within the parameters laid down by the new country's first governments.

These parameters were consciously developed by the US founding fathers when they were deciding on how society was to be organized. Rejecting the privileges from which many of the immigrants had wished to escape, they adopted the principle of equality, as reflected in a number of institutions which checked and balanced each other. The president was to check the power of Congress and Congress to check the power of the president, and the Supreme Court to check the power of both by referring to the rule-book of the Constitution. These rules must also be applied in the same way to the drive for individual achievement, the competitive and aggressive will to succeed in business. The US constitution, as interpreted by the Supreme Court, guards the rights of the citizen, determines whether businesses are operating against the interests of the individual. As the reporter and broadcaster Alistair Cooke (1973: 145) pointed out:

> [The justices of the Supreme Court] . . . look at the old stately document and decide whether you can, say, run an undertaker's firm and also hold stock in an insurance company . . . whether a public bus company can compel you to listen to piped music . . .

Within companies themselves there are strict rules and procedures to be followed. The 'impersonal organization' is predominant, just as in other Anglo countries, with a clearly defined hierarchy. This is not to be seen as inflexible, however. Just as the constitution can be 'interpreted', so can the rules and regulations. A common sense, pragmatic approach is needed to deal with uncertainty. Hickson and Pugh (2001) refer to the US organization as a 'negotiated order'. There may be a clearly defined hierarchy with explicit responsibilities for all concerned, but those higher on the ladder can be addressed by those on the lower ranks and the rules questioned. After all, the overriding concern is the advancement of the company; without it, self-advancement is itself in danger.

A strong, shared commitment among a company's employees allows for considerable delegation and decentralization to be established more easily. This makes it easier for a company to contend with uncertainty and allows for an attitude towards the vicissitudes of the market that is more relaxed than in other 'Anglo' organizations. Thriving on competition is a feature: strong competition keeps a company on its toes and encourages innovation.

A vital indicator of success for US businesses is the 'bottom-line'. Although financial results are crucial to all Anglos, Americans are much more concerned about the bottom-line in the short-term. This attitude engenders considerable criticism, especially among those who believe that investments of whatever kind often need time to bear fruit. On the other hand, US companies are continually aware of the interests of shareholders. Money engenders money, and time is the key instrument. Time must be harnessed as effectively as possible to enable progress, advancement and continuing commitment to the company.

One clear difference that is frequently referred to when British and American businesses are being compared is the way they look at the future. The general optimism prevalent in US business concerning the future – and future success – is said to contrast strongly with the more nuanced view of British business about future developments.

The article in Exhibit 3.2 looks at differences between European and American companies with regard to financial controls.

Anglo-Canadians

Canada, originally the territory of the Indians and Inuit, was first explored by the French who set up their first colony around Quebec. The British also set up colonies and it was they who eventually took control of Canada through settlement and warfare.

Canada became independent in 1867, but still maintains within its borders clear French–Canadian and Anglo-Canadian identities. This has frequently led to political clashes between the two communities. Although French and English are the two official languages of Canada, the province of Quebec has the majority of French speakers and it is they who almost succeeded in getting the province separated from the rest of Canada in 1995.

Anglo-Canadian society, i.e. Canadians who are not French-speaking, comprises not only those of British origin, but also many continental Europeans and Asians, particularly Chinese. However, their ways are Anglo, including the way they manage. Despite what

Exhibit 3.2

FT

Why financial scandals differ in the US and Europe

By Michael Skapinker

'Does Europe hate us?' Thomas Friedman, the *New York Times* columnist, asked in a documentary on the Discovery Channel last week. The answer, he concluded after pottering around the Continent looking increasingly worried, was 'yes'.

From the war on terror to attitudes to maternity leave, Mr Friedman's film made it plain that Europeans inhabited a different world from Americans. When it came to business, he portrayed a Europe whose bureaucrats plotted endlessly to make life difficult for US companies. Brussels was banning pharmaceutical ingredients regarded as perfectly safe in the US. European competition authorities had stamped on the ambitions of US companies from Microsoft to Coca-Cola.

His narrative punctuated by the sort of menacing soundtrack film-makers reserve for those moments before dad opens the door to discover that his family has been murdered by machete-wielding maniacs, Mr Friedman asked: 'Is this the end of the west?'

Quite possibly – and it gets worse. According to a recent paper by John Coffee of Columbia law school, the US and Europe are so far apart that they even suffer from fundamentally different corporate scandals.[*]

Take two emblematic examples: Enron in the US and Parmalat in Europe. The Enron misdeeds were aimed at boosting and maintaining the energy trader's share price. At Parmalat, the diary group, by contrast, money appears to have been siphoned off for the benefit of particular individuals.

The divergence reflects underlying differences in the way US and European companies are organized, Prof Coffee argues. In the US, the typical company's shareholders are a widely dispersed group. Being too fragmented to exercise day-to-day control over executives, they attempted to align top managers' interests with theirs by granting them share options.

In 1990, the average chief executive of an S&P 500 Industrial company earned $1.25m (£660,000), of which 92 per cent was in cash and 8 per cent in equity. By 2001, the average chief executive was earning more than $6m, of which 66 per cent was in equity.

The prevalence of share options substantially changed US chief executives' attitudes to presentation of their companies' earnings. 'During early periods, US managements famously employed "rainy day reserves" to hold back the recognition of income that was in excess of the market's expectation in order to defer it until some later quarter when there had been a shortfall in expected earnings,' Prof Coffee writes.

'Managers engaged in income smoothing, rolling the peaks in one period over into the valley of the next period. This traditional form of earnings management was intended to mask the volatility of earnings and reassure investors who might have been alarmed by rapid fluctuations.'

By the late 1990s, chief executives, stuffed with share options, were doing something different: 'stealing' earnings from future periods to create an 'earnings spike' to meet market expectations and prevent the share price from taking a dive.

'Although such spikes may not be sustainable, corporate managers possess asymmetric information and, anticipating their inability to maintain earnings growth, they can exercise their options and bail out,' Prof Coffee writes. He cites studies demonstrating a relationship between how extensively companies use options and the likelihood of their falling victim to fraud.

European companies, on the other hand, often have controlling shareholders or groups of shareholders, who do not need indirect mechanisms such as share options to control management. They can simply tell them what to do. European chief executives have less freedom to manipulate their earnings. But they also have less incentive to do so.

Fraud still occurs in Europe, but it is a different sort of fraud and different people perpetrate it. Instead of executives manipulating earnings, dominant shareholders use their control to help themselves to the company's assets.

Because European and US companies are vulnerable to different types of fraud, they should adopt different ways of preventing it. While US corporate governance reforms have concentrated, for example, on ensuring that independent audit committees deal with the auditors, this might be less effective in Europe where the board struggles to escape the controlling shareholder's influence.

'Although diligent auditors could have presumably detected the fraud at Parmalat . . . one suspects that they would have likely been dismissed at the point at which they began to monitor earnestly,' Prof Coffee says.

He confesses he does not have a simple suggestion on how to prevent European-style frauds. Regulators could require auditors to report to minority shareholders, he says, but he appears to accept this is unlikely to have many takers.

A second objection to his argument that European fraud is different from the American variety is that there are prominent exceptions. What about Ahold and Vivendi? Were not these European companies whose scandals involved earnings manipulation? They were, Prof Coffee says, but that manipulation either happened in their US subsidiaries or in companies such as Vivendi that turned themselves into US-style conglomerates and therefore took an American form.

What of Tyco, a US company where the top managers allegedly appropriated assets for themselves? Prof Coffee acknowledges that the differences between US and European companies are overall tendencies rather than iron-clad rules.

In the polarised world described by Mr Friedman, I suppose we should take some comfort from the small number of Europeans and Americans imitating one another's misbehaviour.

*John Coffee, 'A theory of corporate scandals: why the US and Europe differ', http://papers.ssrn.com/sol3/papers.cfm?abstract_id=694581

Source: *Financial Times,* 13 April 2005: 12.

Question

Fraud seems to be a universal phenomenon. In this case, however, the author underlines the difference between committing fraud in the US and Europe. Can you explain how this difference comes about?

many Canadians consider to be the overbearing presence of the US their style of management is more British in the sense that it is less formalized, less driven by individual goals and more aware of society as a whole. This is particularly important in a country which is proud of being a 'mosaic', in which different cultural groups tend to be socially intact and maintain their cultural identities, rather than a 'melting-pot' as the US claims to be.

Two multicultural tests that Anglo-Canadian business people undergo relate to getting on with the neighbours. Dealing with French Canadians entails coming to terms with Latin attitudes to management, to a world where schedules, memos and agendas are less adhered to, where conviviality and connections are more important than time-planning and punctuality. When dealing with Americans, Canadians are only too aware of the need to stand their own ground, to counter the tendency of Americans to assume that Canadians are just like them, despite the fact that they speak the same language, have similar lifestyles and share a similar frame of reference.

Relations between the Anglo-US and Anglo-Canada have proved to be very fertile ground for many Canadian writers and commentators. One of the most famous, Northrop Frye, observes that:

> American students have been conditioned from infancy to think of themselves as citizens of one of the world's greatest powers. Canadians are conditioned from infancy to think of themselves as citizens of a country of uncertain identity, a confusing past and a hazardous future.   www.liveabroad.com/articles/canada.html

This comment reflects the contrast often made between the pushy, boastful, optimistic American and the low-key, modest and cautious Canadian. Pierre Trudeau, a former Canadian prime minister, spoke of another aspect of US–Canadian relations:

> Americans should never underestimate the constant pressure on Canada which the mere presence of the United States has produced. We're different people from you and we're different people because of you. Living next to you is in some ways like sleeping with an elephant. No matter how friendly and even-tempered is the beast, if I can call it that, one is effected [*sic*] by every twitch and grunt.
> http://www.cla.ca/issues/cla_buildingtheknowledgeeconomy_final.pdf

Exhibit 3.3

Love thy neighbour

The Canadian government website has a dialogue with its people on its foreign policy. Here is the advice it gives on Canada-US relations:

- The increase in American investment and the prevalence of American cultural products in Canada are a threat to Canadian identity. They lead Canadians to expect institutions and policies that replicate those of the US rather than being representative of Canada.
- Canada should avoid a 'holier than thou' approach to relations with the US and treat its relationship with the US with greater respect.
- Canada should be seeking common ground with the US. Working to maintain stable

relationship with the US is in Canada's economic and security interests.

- Canada should reduce its economic dependence on the US and stop using the US as a reference point in defining Canadian culture.
- The security of the Canada-US border should be maintained, but not at the expense of trade.
- US foreign policy positions are constantly evolving. Canadian policy toward the US should not be based solely on the realities of the current administration. Policies should be created with the long term in mind.

Source: www.foreign-policy-dialogue.ca/en/news/bulletin7.html

Anglo-Australians

Australia and New Zealand were both colonies of the UK. Britain claimed Australia as a colony in 1788 and New Zealand became a separate UK colony in 1840 after first being administered by the Australian state of New South Wales. The lives of the early inhabitants of this remote part of the world, the Australian Aborigines and the New Zealand Maoris, were irrevocably changed by the European settlers. In Australia these were first convicts from the UK and later free immigrants. In New Zealand these were predominantly UK whalers and traders.

When both countries became independent of the UK, they still retained their essential Anglo-Saxon identity. Further waves of British migrants were welcomed with open arms, while other Europeans of non-British origin were expected to shed their particular cultural identities and integrate with the host population. Australia, however, has been the first to acknowledge the increasing ethnic diversity created by more recent waves of immigration from other non-European countries, particularly from countries in South-East Asia. The country now sees multiculturalism as being at the heart of its society. The Australian government states explicitly on its website:

> Australia accepts and respects the right of all Australians to express and share their individual cultural heritage within an overriding commitment to Australia's democratic foundations and to English as the national language.

www.dfat.gov.au/facts/culturally_diverse.html

New Zealand's population has a predominant British ethnicity, although immigration policy has focused more on the micro-states of the South Pacific and, most recently, on migration flows of professionally qualified South Africans and East Asians. A prerequisite for selection for immigration is still proficiency in English.

The business culture in Australia and New Zealand remains very much Anglo-Saxon in nature. However, the work environment tends to be more collaborative than in the UK or

US, which means decision-making can be rather slow and drawn-out. The typical hierarchies are in place in most organizations, but since there is a general distrust of authority, particularly of people who tend to 'flaunt' it, a modest, egalitarian approach is preferred when colleagues are dealing with each other. They can, however, be more direct and critical than their British counterparts, although may not take so kindly towards outsiders joining in the criticism. Humour is an indispensable ingredient of communication, with a preference for teasing others, particularly those who they consider to be 'tall poppies', the term used to denote arrogant people who 'show off' by talking frequently of their own accomplishments.

Latin Americans

The final cluster in the western hemisphere of Figure 3.1 is the Latin American cluster. As happened with the Anglos emigrating to America and Australasia, the immigrants from Spain and Portugal, and to a smaller extent from France, took their cultures to Central and Southern America, and implanted them in foreign soil. The common linguistic, cultural and religious heritage is still strong and is seen in the many activities shared between the 'mother country' Spain and its former colonies, ranging from intensive trade to football tournaments. Similar cultural ties are also to be found between Portugal and Brazil, which was a Portuguese colony before being given independence in the nineteenth century. Portuguese is the official language, and economic, social and cultural ties with the European ex-ruler are still strong.

The term 'Latin' is believed to have been devised by the French in the nineteenth century to reflect the difference between Anglo-Saxon North America and Spanish/Portuguese South America. The term allowed for France, also a Latin country, to claim a role in the development of a continent where a number of countries were demanding independence from their Spanish masters.

This other America, the first rich America, is a deeply divided continent that has not been able to emulate its northern neighbours. Although recent attempts to create some sort of unity at trading level have apparently been successful, conflicts between the many countries of the continent are still prevalent. Furthermore, conflicts within some of these countries, often arising from clashes of interest between the indigenous and 'Hispanic' parts of society, have prevented countries developing economically and socially in the way they would prefer.

Despite the differences between the countries of Central and South America, cultural values are shared. Strong belief in the Catholic religion is a facet of South American society that reflects the importance of the family as well as the distinct male and female roles in society. These features were clearly evident in the Iberian peninsula until recently, but have been watered down through increasing industrialization, the end of authoritarian, centralistic regimes and increasing exposure to other European cultures. In South America, however, such values still predominate. Central governments are strong and societies are generally highly stratified. The gulf between rich and poor is considerable and difficult to bridge. Those in the lower social classes are poorly educated and lack the skills which countries still in the throes of industrialization badly need.

The *patron* exerts considerable power in all aspects of daily life, whether it be in politics, the church, agriculture or business generally. With his high status he can command unquestioning loyalty from those beneath him. Authoritarian behaviour is expected and respect shown.

In those countries, however, where the middle class has grown in line with successful industrialization, such authoritarian behaviour is becoming less prevalent. Harris and Moran (1996) give Mexico as an example of a country undergoing profound social change. Its middle classes are asserting themselves more and more, and this in turn causes tensions between them and the underprivileged as well as revolutionary elements within the country. Just as with other Latin Americans, however, their warm, person-oriented engagement with others is a feature of doing business. Although the country still retains its orientation towards the family, social mobility has increased, and there is now a rapidly expanding middle-class which is asserting its power through hard work.

Exhibit 3.4 — FT

South American unity still a distant dream

By Richard Lapper

For a culturally homogenous region, South America has found it remarkably difficult to forge a united political and economic identity. On the surface, the creation of a South American Community of Nations does, as its proponents claim, seem to represent something of a 'historic moment'.

The problem is that the agreement that was to be signed symbolically on Wednesday in Cuzco, Peru – capital of the old Inca empire – is so loose, so long-term and so tangential to most intra-regional trade that it could be overtaken by broader negotiations with the US. At its core, Wednesday's deal is a merger, over 15 years, of South America's two existing free trade agreements: Mercosur, the customs union comprised of Brazil, Argentina, Uruguay and Paraguay, and the Andean Community, made up of Venezuela, Colombia, Peru, Bolivia and Ecuador. Chile, Surinam and Guyana were also expected to sign the deal, which will eventually free tariffs on currently extremely limited intra-regional trade.

The deal also provides for radical improvements in transport, energy connections and other infrastructure designed to allow traditionally Atlantic-orientated countries such as Brazil and Argentina to conduct business more easily with their Pacific-facing neighbours. For now, the union will not have a separate institutional presence, but it could allow South America to take a common stance in international forums. Brazil, by far the biggest Latin American country, would expect its smaller neighbours to adapt to its positions.

Rubens Barbosa, an independent consultant and former Brazilian diplomat, says a unified South America as distinct from a unified Latin America has long been a goal of Brazilian policy and its achievement would

demonstrate real 'political will' in favour of regional integration. 'This is a major decision in terms of political will,' says Mr Barbosa. In recent years the US has increasingly dealt with individual countries, agreeing a bilateral deal with Chile, and negotiating two others: one with seven Central American and Caribbean countries, and another with Colombia, Peru, and Ecuador.

Nelson Cunningham, a Washington based Latin American specialist, says the US has adopted a hub-and-spoke strategy as 'a way of picking off trading partners and generating momentum towards an FTAA'. In this context Wednesday's agreement can be seen as 'a shrewd counter-move to the American negotiating position. We are watching a fascinating game of global chess'.

Many Brazilian executives complain that the deal is politically driven and that they have not been properly consulted. 'We have had very little participation and the results are weak and vague,' says Lúcia Maduro, an economist with the National Industrial Confederation in São Paulo. It is not clear, either, that Brazil will win international support. Argentina has refused to support Brazil's bid for a permanent seat on the United Nations Security Council and is locked in trade disputes with Brazil within Mercosur. And it is surely significant that neither Argentina's President Néstor Kirchner nor his counterparts from Uruguay and Paraguay even attended the summit.

Source: *Financial Times*, 9 December 2004: 8.

Question

Why do you think it is difficult to make economic agreements between South American countries that appear to be culturally homogeneous?

House et al (2004) characterize Latin America as a collectivist culture, which places great value on pride, loyalty and interdependence in families, but less value on institutional collectivism, i.e. collective distribution of resources and collective action.

This chapter has examined some of the characteristics that bring together a number of countries into five clusters, each of which can be labelled as Western. It has also shown that countries which may share certain similarities do not necessarily enjoy a harmonious co-existence. This issue is reflected in the following activity concerning problems at Airbus, an aircraft construction consortium of European countries.

ACTIVITY 3.1

Problems at Airbus

You will be asked to address a number of questions relating to the problems experienced by a company which has its roots in several European countries: Airbus SAS.

Once you are familiar with the history of the company, as outlined in the first article, read the extracts which follow. These are taken from articles written by interested observers concerning the problems at Airbus. The final extract is taken from a brochure published by Airbus itself.

Airbus was formally established in 1970 as a European consortium whose goal was to gain a share of the aircraft construction market dominated till then by the US. It began as a consortium of French and German companies, to be joined later by Spanish and British companies. When outlining the history of the company, the Airbus website (http://events.airbus.com/about/history.asp) talked of 'overcoming national divides, sharing development costs, collaborating in the interests of a greater market share, and even agreeing a common set of measurements and a common language' and, by doing so, changing the face of the business, and bringing the benefits of real competition to airlines, passengers and crews.

The company has produced a series of successful aircraft, including the world's first twin-engine wide-body jet. According to the company's document ('The Airbus Way', p. 15):

> . . . the [Airbus] fleet has evolved progressively in response to market demand. This includes the . . . double-deck A380, the most technologically advanced plane in the world today.

> Source: www.airbus.com/store/mm_repository/pdf/att00007006/media_object_file_The_Airbus_Way_The_corporate_brochure.pdf

The development of such highly sophisticated aircraft required a reorganization of the company to improve co-ordination, reduce the costs of production and the time between conception of planes and their introduction into service. The French, German, British and Spanish partners, who had operated independently, merged their plane-making assets in 2001 to form Airbus SAS.

Nevertheless, there were considerable problems in bringing the A380 to the market. A two-year delay and a consequent loss in profits of €2 billion forced the company to make drastic cuts in the size of its workforce, to close plants and to outsource many more aircraft parts.

The extract below is taken from an article in the *Financial Times* published on 2 March 2007 and entitled 'Airbus and the damage done by economic patriotism'. The article was written by Xavier Vives, a professor of economics and finance at IESE Business School, Barcelona, Spain.

> France's president Jacques Chirac and Angela Merkel, the German chancellor, made clear that the restructuring of Airbus must maintain 'absolute equilibrium' in employment and technology. The pain of 10,000 planned job cuts has been shared this week between France, Germany, the UK and Spain.

→

Indeed, traditionally the workforce at the aircraft manufacturer is geographically distributed in proportion to national ownership stakes. It is hard to make sense of this from the point of view of productive efficiency. It is an instance of economic nationalism, whereby governments distort private transactions among economic actors by discriminating against foreigners in the name of the national interest.

Economic motives include the preservation of employment or the attraction of economic activity to a certain area. Strategic motives include national security or attempts to capture rents abroad in monopolistic markets. In many circumstances the patriotic approach proves ineffective because it conflicts with economic efficiency, but its endurance derives from protection of the interests of local lobbies. Politicians benefit from the revolving door between political office and the boardroom or by catering to a clientele with a view towards re-election. . . .

The damage caused by economic nationalism includes inefficiency and poor corporate governance. When EADS, parent company of Airbus, was created, it was headed by two chief executives, German and French. In spite of the fact that tensions flourished, the twin-headed structure was maintained even after the crisis caused by problems in the development of the A380 began. As a result, Airbus's reputation has been dented and it has fallen behind Boeing. In other cases, cost-cutting measures are delayed as state aid comes to the rescue of the champion, or competition is distorted because government-supported companies have privileged access to infrastructure and procurement contracts. The market for corporate control suffers as takeover threats from potentially more efficient foreign companies are removed. Finally, national efforts end up being self-defeating as other countries react in kind, neutralising the initial attempt to gain an advantage.

Source: *Financial Times*, 2 March 2007: 17.

One of the causes of the delay in the production of the A380 was the design of the complex wiring system for the aircraft. This extract from a web log by Sam Davis on Electronic Design's Power Management website, gives an insight into co-ordination problems:

Engineering design of a superjumbo jet aircraft is anything but easy; the Airbus A380 aircraft designers can attest to that. You wouldn't expect a wiring problem to delay delivery of an airplane, but that is what has happened. Planes scheduled for delivery in 2006 may be up to two years late – some airlines have already cancelled their orders.

To understand why wiring is critical, you have to know that there are almost 1,200 functions to control the plane, which takes 98,000 wires and 40,000 connectors. The digital design system has 500,000 models, and all those must be kept in sync by mismatched computer-design systems in different countries.

Further complicating aircraft design – nose sections are built in France, fuselages in Germany, wings in Great Britain and tails in Spain, Airbus' A380 aircraft sections will be transported on a special ship from sites in Broughton (UK), Hamburg (Germany), Puerto Real (Spain) and St. Nazaire (France) for final assembly in Toulouse (France).

As reported in the January 2007 IEEE Spectrum article 'Manufacturing mayday,' by Alexander Hellemans, designing the aircraft was much more difficult than anticipated. Engineers in Germany and Spain used the older V4 version of the CAD program to design the wiring whereas engineers in France and England used the newer V5 version. Although the software developer said the two versions were compatible, data was lost when transferring files from one system to the other. Another complication: the French were familiar with the software whereas the Germans did not have as much experience with it.

Because of the wiring design software compatibility issues, problems arose when incorporating wiring changes in the fuselage sections in Germany. 'What happened in Germany certainly was not just a technical problem in the narrow sense,' author Hellemans notes. 'It was an execution failure.' Nick Cunningham, an analyst at the Panmure Gordon brokerage firm in London said it was connected with 'their lack of integration in engineering'.

Source: Davis (2007).

Ian Stokes is project management professor on the aerospace MBA programme at the ESC university business school in Toulouse, France (home of the Airbus company). He has written what he calls a subjective account of the Airbus A380 project. Here is an extract from his account which looks at the cultural issues involved in the Airbus problems:

Time and time again engineering managers and computer-aided design directors say the most difficult part of implementing new software is down to so-called cultural issues. This justifies a high level of support and service from the software supplier as well as a special training investment from the client. In fact, this has been long appreciated by Dassault product managers. Unfortunately, between 2000 and 2004 human resource and training managers were far too busy responding to new legislation – such as those concerning working hours and the recent French directive on the rights of individuals to choose their own training – than to have time to waste on the abstract issues of cultural differences.

These decisions to standardise have come late in the day. Why was there previously no impulse from senior management to insist upon shared design tools? Why were suppliers not involved in a collaborative effort to anticipate problems and to develop some kind of cross-functional translator programme between different versions of the software? Why was no effective and co-operative intercultural exchange of expertise introduced?

Top managers have been distracted by jostling for position in the consortium and lobbying for influence. Critical functions, such as human resources, were diverted by convoluted aspects of legislation and the requirement to produce an equitable distribution of roles and rules. Inevitably, political goals get in the way of project goals, but this did not have to be quite so aggravated, if only the critical success factors of aircraft design had been recognised in time.

Indeed, intercultural teambuilding sessions were set up to kindle a warm feeling of mutual understanding, but they failed to address adequately the fundamentals of co-operating and exchanging know-how on specific tasks related to the job. Instead of being valued for spreading 'connaissances', 'savoir-faire', 'kenntnis' and 'know-how', an increased familiarity with respective intercultural traits left only a feeling of guilt and confusion, fudge and haze.

An Autumn 2006 report highlights an internal intercultural survey at EADS, which portrays the different perceptions that each culture at Airbus has for the others. The French are perceived as being very attached to their networks, respectful of hierarchy, paternalist and showing a preference for a centralised executive. At the same time, they are less formal in their communication and decision-making. The Germans are characterised as being extremely precise and organized, with a respect for hierarchy and formality. At the same time, they prefer collective decision-making and focus on short-term efficiency. The British are seen as being totally focused on financial priorities and are goal-oriented. Their communication comes across as being rather indirect, informal, imprecise, unclear and too subtle to be easily understood. On the other hand they are pragmatic, down-to-earth and prefer straight-forward and practical solutions. The Spanish, who are considered to be strongly patriotic and proud, are appreciated for being considerate, relaxed, flexible, open, creative and co-operative, good team workers, but suffering from an inferiority complex and a tendency to be vague and unreliable.

The remarkable thing about these perceptions is that they are highly stereotyped. However, the scores were not nearly as accentuated as they were a few years ago. In fact, most EADS managers prefer to draw attention to the areas of common ground and the similarities, rather than the differences, and point to a common ambition to transcend national barriers.

Intentions may be good, but in a crisis, each culture tends to look for the obvious solution. The French want a strong man at the top, who is contested by Germans seeking a greater degree of consensus, whilst the British lament about the absence of an economic solution.

The cultural reasons that cause people to react in a particular way are so deep-rooted that they are reflexive and probably impossible to change. Nevertheless, given that Airbus is Europe's premier flagship programme, it seems a pity not to invest in a better understanding of one's own skills in relation to the strengths of colleagues.

Source: Ian Stokes (2006) 'Two billion euros of hurt', www.management-projet.org/projet1/spip.php?article, 28 December.

Here, finally, is another extract from 'The Airbus Way'.

Global knowledge, local understanding

With its head office in Toulouse, France, Airbus operates out of over 160 international locations, including 16 main development and manufacturing sites in France, Germany, the UK, Spain and three wholly owned subsidiaries in China, Japan and North America. Specialist facilities around the world include engineering centres in Beijing, Wichita and Mobile (from 2006); a joint venture engineering centre in Moscow; fast response spares centres in Hamburg, Frankfurt, Washington, Beijing and Singapore; state-of-the-art training centres in Toulouse, Hamburg, Miami and Beijing; and 130 field service offices at key customer locations.

This means that Airbus benefits from a unique workforce that encompasses more than 80 nationalities and speaks over 20 different languages. Such cultural diversity could be seen as a challenge. To Airbus, it represents an invaluable competitive advantage and the lifeblood of the company. Indeed, the Airbus organization is designed to realise the full potential of the enormous mix of experience, expertise and creativity available among its employees, customers, suppliers and industrial partners.

A good example of such multicultural team working are the Airbus centres of excellence, a network of multifunctional teams, which include all the skills (such as engineering, manufacturing and procurement) that are necessary to deliver complete aircraft sections and which are co-located across Airbus' main development and production sites in Europe and North America. This transnational approach enhances flexibility and promotes continuous improvement throughout the Airbus family in every aspect of design and production. It also streamlines production by delegating responsibility and clearing channels of communication.

. . .

Growing together

Airbus knows that it is people who design, build, sell and support aircraft. At the heart of Airbus lies a core of human talent, vision and hard work which keeps the company at the forefront of the industry. In 35 years, what began as a remarkable joining of forces in Europe has grown into a global network. Today, over 55,000 people of more than 80 different nationalities work for Airbus.

Such cultural diversity is the key to Airbus' success. People who join Airbus know they will be part of a truly international organization, where national roots are valued but where many different cultures mix, sharing experience and know-how and developing expertise together in a stimulating environment.

But diversity at Airbus is about more than nationality. Increasing numbers of women are being employed in what are seen as traditionally male roles such as engineering. The company ensures at least 20 per cent of graduate recruits are women.

Source: www.airbus.com/store/mm_repository/pdf/att00007006/media_object_file_The_Airbus_Way_The_corporate_brochure.pdf

Questions

1. How would you define the concept of 'economic patriotism'? What role do you think it may have played in the problems besetting Airbus?

2. To what extent do you consider the wiring problems with the A380 were a reflection of the way the Airbus company was organized, despite the merger of the national components in 2001?

3. Why do you think that intercultural team-building sessions and the reportedly improved perceptions which the different cultures within Airbus have of each other has not necessarily helped Airbus in its problems round the production of the A380?

4. What is your reaction to Airbus' statement in its brochure 'The Airbus Way' that the cultural diversity of the company is 'the key to Airbus' success'?

5. What elements in these texts about the Airbus consortium are reflected the description of the culture clusters in this chapter?

Conclusion

This wide-ranging chapter has considered the five clusters of Western cultures as given in the metaconfiguration devised by the GLOBE project. It has given examples of the cultural features that countries within each cluster share. The European clusters are aligned within European institutions, but there is an ambivalence as to how individual the countries within the clusters should remain or to what extent they should strive for some kind of unity.

The Anglo cluster of cultures, despite individual differences, share a business culture that is proving to be very influential within the other cultures featured in this chapter. The Latin cluster displays strong common values, but industrialization, particularly within Latin America, is gnawing away at these values and causing profound social change.

Points for reflection

1. Considerable prominence has been given in this concept to the Anglo cluster and its approach to business. **What do you consider to be the reasons for giving the Anglo business culture so much attention?**

2. The metaconfiguration used in this chapter shows three clusters within continental Europe. **To what extent do you consider these clusters to be valid? Can you devise other ways of distinguishing (business) cultures in Europe?**

Further reading

Tayeb, M. (2003) *International Management*, Harlow: Pearson Education. The book focuses on the international manager's world, examines cultural differences and their effect on the functioning of organizations. The main theme of the book is 'going international'.

References

Boisot, M.H. (1993) 'Spain: the revolution from outside: Spanish management and the challenges of modernization' in Hickson, D.J. (ed) *Management in Western Europe: Society, culture and organization in twelve nations*, Berlin: Walter de Gruyter: 205-228.

Cooke, A. (1973) *Alistair Cooke's America*, London: British Broadcasting Corporation.

Davis, S. (2007) 'Wiring design faulted for Airbus A380 production delays,' 10 January, http://power.elecdesign.com, article 14634.

d'Iribarne, P., Henry, A., Segal, J.P., Chevrier, S. and Globokar, T. (1998) *Cultures et mondialisation*, Paris: Editions du Seuil.

Harris, P.R. and Moran, R.T. (1996) *Managing Cultural Differences*, Houston: Gulf.

Hickson, D.J. and Pugh, D.S. (2001) *Management Worldwide*, London: Penguin.

Hillmert, S. (2002) 'Labour market integration and institutions: an Anglo-German comparison', *Work, Employment & Society*, 16: 675-701.

Hoecklin, L. (1995) *Managing Cultural Differences: Strategies for comparative advantage*, Wokingham: Addison-Wesley.

Hofstede, G. (1993) 'Intercultural conflict and synergy in Europe' in Hickson, D.J. (ed) *Management in Western Europe: Society, culture and organization in twelve nations*, Berlin: Walter de Gruyter: 1-8.

House, R.J., Hanges, P.J., Javidan, M., Dorfman, P.W. and Gupta, V. (eds) (2004) *Leadership, Culture and Organizations: The GLOBE study of 62 societies*, Thousand Oaks CA: Sage.

Lendering, J. (2003) 'The battle in the Teutoburg Forest (7)', http://www.livius.org/te-tg/teutoburg/teutoburg07.htm

Morin, E. (1987) *Penser l'Europe*, Paris: Gallimard.

Ronen, S. and Shenkar, O. (1985) 'Clustering countries on attitudinal dimensions: a review and synthesis', *Academy of Management Review*, 10 (3): 435-454.

Schneider, S.C. and Barsoux, J-L (2003) *Managing Across Cultures*, 2nd edn, Hemel Hempstead, UK: Prentice Hall.

Vidal, F. (1992) *Le management à l'italienne*, Paris: InterEditions.

Chapter 4

Business cultures in the East

Chapter 3 discussed the GLOBE metaconfiguration and Figure 4.1 is the representation of the degree of overall distance among ten cultural clusters. These clusters are based on the cultural dimensions that the GLOBE project developed from their research. The positioning of these clusters in Figure 4.1 reflects not only the similarities and dissimilarities between the clusters on the basis of the cultural dimensions, but also other factors, including those to do with history, geography and religion.

The proposed five Eastern clusters will be dealt with in this chapter and some elements relating to business culture will be described. These elements are apparent in one or more of the countries within each cluster.

Learning outcomes

After reading this chapter you should:

- Be able to distinguish essential differences and similarities in a number of clusters within the Eastern half of the metaconfiguration given in Figure 4.1.
- Have some insight into the cultural factors that have an influence on business.

Concept 4.1 Eastern culture clusters

This concept will cover aspects of each of the five Eastern cultures in the GLOBE's meta-configuration. This will be done in a similar way to that used in Chapter 3: a cultural feature of one or more countries from each cluster will be discussed and its reflection in work-related values and business practice will be described.

Eastern Europe

A big influence on East European cultures has been the Russian Empire and the Soviet hegemony. The post-revolution regimes in particular had a profound effect on Eastern European countries. Before the Iron Curtain eventually fell, countries under Soviet sway were characterized by highly autocratic, centralized organizations with many bureaucratic levels, reflecting the presence of a dual hierarchy (politics and business worked hand-in-hand) and an

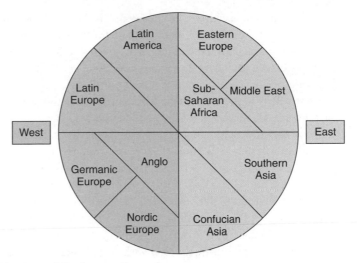

Figure 4.1 Clusters of Eastern cultures
Source: House et al (2004): 201.

obsession with state planning. The legacy of the communist system of administration is what the societies of East and Central Europe have had to contend with since the early 1990s, when Western political and economic practices were introduced. The transformation of highly bureaucratic and centralized economies has taken much longer than anticipated. The withdrawal of centralized control has increased feelings of uncertainty and helplessness. Individuals and companies can no longer rely on the 'system' to help them out; instead they must battle their own way through, develop self-confidence and learn how to deal with a more open, less merciful environment. This transition has, however, caused considerable unrest, and there is still a longing for how things used to be among those unwilling to adapt to the new environment. As Schneider and Barsoux (1997: 101) report:

> Despite the prevailing wisdom that organisations need to be less hierarchical and more flexible, some [eastern European] managers argue that faced with competitive threats and conditions of economic decline or instability, greater centralization and stronger controls are needed.

The opportunity to take on roles and responsibilities similar to those of their Western neighbours is still seen as a threat, especially by those who grew up and worked under the old regimes.

With the political collapse of the Soviet Union, fifteen republics emerged, of which Russia is the largest. This 'new' country, which spans Europe and Asia, has also been struggling since 1991 to replace the social, political and economic features of the communist era with a more democratic political system and a market-oriented economy. Close association with the EU is seen as an important way of developing the Russian economy, but membership is a step too far for many Russians who fear their independence being swallowed up in a greater Europe. Moreover, many question whether Russia is really a European nation, an issue that has been debated for hundreds of years. Is, in geographic terms, the border of Europe the Urals mountain range? Can that part of Russia to the west of the Urals, and where most of the population is centred, be considered as 'European Russia'? Mikhail Gorbachev, who as president of the USSR set many of the reforms in motion that led to the dismantling of the country, pleaded for the building of a 'common European house'. Although the EU and Russia have been exploring the idea of developing a common European economic space, competing political and economic aims and interests appear to have gained the upper hand. Even if Russia's presence on the European business stage is becoming increasingly dominant, there are many who question whether Russians have the same regard for essential values (such as democracy, human rights and freedom) as countries in and close to the EU. Russia and Europe, they argue, are unlikely ever to share such cultural values.

There does appear to be one feature of society in Russia that has survived the recent transition and which continues to play an important role in Russian life. This is a form of social networking called *blat*, which enabled individuals to deal with the scarcity of goods and services of a centrally planned economy. Although the word *blat* was originally associated with small crime, it came to be more associated with caring and sharing, with helping and being helped through a network of personal relationships. These relationships were built up over time, and mutual trust, common understandings and (implicit) rules of behaviour were established that allow favours of many kinds to be reciprocated.

With the increased uncertainties of post-Soviet reforms, *blat* has continued to flourish, essentially to reduce the uncertain nature of a society where services at social, educational, financial and legal levels are weak, scarce, or non-existent. Michailova and Worm (2003: 517), argue that its nature has changed:

> [*Blat*] is becoming increasingly materialised, dominated by pragmatism and market-governed. The transformation of its nature from being based on moral and ethical considerations to having an explicit financial expression is a phenomenon in itself. *Blat* is becoming a negative word again with criminal undertones.

Michailova and Worm (2003) advise business people intent on doing business in Russia to beware of *blat*, that if mutual favours need to be made they should be done on a small scale and between individuals. They point out that the perception there of bribery and corruption is a different one: people are more tolerant of wayward practices, and employees and managers consider it an important element of conducting business.

These considerations help to explain why Eastern Europe has been placed in the Eastern hemisphere of the metaconfiguration rather than being included in one of the European clusters. It is clear that the aftermath of the Second World War involved Europe being divided into two. Eastern Europe became closed off, thrown back on itself and dependent on Soviet communism. Western Europe, on the other hand went under the very strong influence of the US, its enterprising mind, its taste for risk and championing of individual rights. See Exhibit 4.1.

Asia

Although each country in Asia deserves attention, it is nevertheless possible to discern similarities that distinguish these countries from the clusters dealt with so far. The influence of Confucianism and Buddhism in particular has been felt in all the countries in this area

Exhibit 4.1 | FT

A tale of two Russian factories

It takes less 10 minutes to drive from Avtovaz, maker of Lada cars, to its joint venture with General Motors. But to make the journey feels like crossing the border between the Soviet Union and the west 20 years ago.

On one side are grey and crumbling concrete factories, military-style security and unsmiling workers. An office block towers over the plant, with a top-floor restaurant reserved for managers.

On the other is a modern-looking factory, with low-key security, welcoming workers in blue overalls and a canteen where managers and workers eat at the same tables.

Workers in both places are Russian and live in the same city. But one factory is stuck in the Soviet era while the other is part of the modern world.

Inside, the differences do not lie in technology: Avtovaz has a new assembly line, equipped with the latest German and Italian machinery, to produce its slick-looking Kalina model. But as one foreign executive puts it: 'What these guys do not understand is that it is not about a car, it is about people. Spending $5bn or even $10bn in the same environment will not make a good carmaker.'

The real distinctions between Avtovaz and its joint venture lie in management approaches and relations between managers and workers. 'Here everything is different: the work culture, the discipline, the attitude,' says Evgeny Berezin, assembly manager at GM-Avtovaz. 'You can build the same factory as the one here, but it is all in the mind,' he adds.

He says all workers at GM-Avtovaz are encouraged to show initiative and make suggestions, which can be quickly taken on board. Any suggestion at Avtovaz usually gets lost in bureaucracy.

'Avtovaz makes the same model for 10 years – almost unchanged. The car we make here today is different from the one we made a couple of years ago. I like working here because I can see the result of my work. People here have real responsibility.'

Vadim Klassen, who has worked in both plants, says: 'If we learn from [foreign carmakers] we will catch up quickly. If we go down our own path, we never will. But you have to want to learn and know how to learn.'

Source: *Financial Times*, 7 July 2006: 9.

Questions

1. Could you explain what the foreign executive means by saying: 'What these guys do not understand is that it is not about a car, it is about people.'
2. Comment on the last paragraph of the case. Do you agree with Vadim Klassen?

of the world, resulting in cultural values that they share in one form or another. This is one of the reasons for House et al (2004) to divide this region of the globe into the South Asia cluster, where the Buddhist religion predominates, and the Confucian Asia cluster.

One similarity above all is to do with the way relationships are managed. Unlike the West, business is as much to do with the relationship between the parties concerned as the actual transaction. This entails paying considerable attention to building trust and establishing respect while displaying the utmost courtesy, particularly towards those in senior positions. Harmony between the participants of any meeting is required, so everything must be done in a courteous, deferential manner to ensure that nobody is offended or loses face. If harmony is maintained, confidence and trust will build and this in turn will form the basis of consensus and eventual agreement on a deal. Patience is of the essence: time is needed to establish a relationship, to decide whether a deal can be made and, if it can, to actually make the deal.

All these elements cause Westerners considerable frustration when trying to do business in Asia. They often have to try and make deals under time pressure, so go for the hard sell, assuming that vigorous handshakes and tales of past successes will immediately put them in a good light. Egocentric, brash behaviour does not encourage the establishment of a harmonious relationship, let alone any attempt by the Westerner to impose a deadline on any deal.

Nevertheless, deals are made, relationships between Asia and the West do develop, and more and more joint ventures are formed. Asians are always interested in a good deal. According to Lewis (1996: 293):

> Asian correctness and courtesy . . . [and] apparent compliance and reasonable, humble discussion style are all pragmatic strategies to secure, whenever possible, irreversible advantage.

The basis has to be right: a good relationship has to be established to allow gentle haggling to begin.

We will examine the question of relationship-building a little more closely with regard to China, Japan and (South) Korea.

Confucian Asia

The Chinese and guanxi

Relationships in China are the key to business success. Building up a strong network of such relationships, referred to as *guanxi*, is the preoccupation of Chinese businessmen. Trust and confidence are vital elements of such relationships, so that transactions made between people in close relationship do not need to be made in contractual form. In fact, *guanxi* goes much further than an elaborate network of relationships. Those in the network both grant favours and expect eventually to receive favours in return. As Westerners have discovered, it can be difficult setting up relationships without using others who are themselves owed favours. When *guanxi* with someone has been achieved, then the business of penetrating the Chinese market is made easier.

Such a network is indispensable as a source of information and expertise, as a way of developing new relationships, finding business partners and eventually new deals. Its origins are disputed, although it does reflect many of the features of traditional village life in China. It appears to have developed on a large scale as a way of dealing with the state bureaucracy, and to have flourished during the recent opening up of China and consequent economic development.

Those Western companies in business in China are aware of the continual need to develop and maintain these special relationships and will pay them explicit attention in the organization of their activities. A member of staff or whole department will be concerned with *guanxi* or public relations administration. This entails maintaining good relations not just with customers and suppliers, but also with local authorities, financial institutions and tax offices (Burns, 1998).

Related to this is the notion of *mianzi* meaning 'face'. The need to maintain your own dignity and that of others has already been mentioned as a general characteristic of relationships in Asia. In China this is taken a step further. Here, it is to do with your personal and public reputation, to be maintained at all cost and to be used to influence other people in their decision-making. Direct criticism or confrontation of anyone related to business activities is not only an invitation for some kind of damaging retribution, but also results in damage to the *mianzi* of the person who has made the criticism and thereby harmed the other.

The parallels between *guanxi* and the Russian *blat* (as described earlier in this chapter) are immediately apparent, although there are differences. As Michailova and Worm (2003) indicate, *guanxi* is a much older tradition and the reflection of Confucianism's notions that individuals, as social beings, each have their place in a hierarchy of relationships. As such, helping friends within a network is a moral and social obligation: not doing so entails loss of face and prestige. *Blat*, although it also entails making commitments, is more to do with emotions and self-serving pleasure. It is more analytical in nature, confined to smaller networks and more often pursued on a one-to-one basis.

The Japanese and wa

The concept of *wa*, the spirit of harmony, is a principle of Japanese thought, one applied to all relationships – even to the relationship with nature. This spirit is reflected in the considerable degree of collaborative behaviour and consensus-building within an organization. This behaviour is fundamental to decision-making and involves proposals being discussed informally on the work-floor before being pushed up through the organization's hierarchy where each level of management gives its input and suggestions. The managers are to be seen more as facilitators in making decisions rather than the actual decision-makers. Building a consensus within the organization may take time through the need to go into detailed discussion and to give everyone the feeling that they are participating in the decision-making process. Eventually the proposals reach the top and are acted on.

This idea of *wa* is also reflected in the relationship between the organization and its employees. In return for an employee's loyalty and commitment to an organization, the employer will provide job security. In some larger industrial companies this mutual commitment can be for life. This interdependent relationship follows on from other, similar, relationships which the working Japanese have experienced in their lives – with family, school and university. All of them require mutual commitment and loyalty. Some observers see a greater loyalty behind these relationships, that of loyalty to the country. The individual employee identifies with his/her colleagues who, as a group identify with the company, which in turn identifies with the economic needs of Japan.

The whole process of consensus-building may seem long and drawn out to Western eyes. It must, however, be taken into account when doing business in Japan, along with the Japanese disdain of individualism and self-assertion. Moreover, when the implementation phase of a deal is reached, everything happens quickly and enthusiastically.

The South Koreans and the chaebol

Throughout most of its history, Korea has been invaded, influenced and fought over by its larger neighbours, including China and Japan. The Second World War, and Japan's eventual defeat, meant the end of Korea's last occupation but also the division of the country into the communist, USSR-backed North Korea and the US-backed South Korea. North Korea remains outside the global business environment, so South Korea will be the focus here.

One invader that changed Korean norms and values was China. Its Choson Dynasty ruled the country for more than five hundred years and made Confucianism the state religion. Its focus on family life and the need to protect family members and to enhance family fortunes has in turn influenced the way South Korea has developed its economy.

The meteoric rise of the South Korean economy since the 1960s is in no small part due to the role of the extended family in the development of a network of conglomerate businesses. These conglomerates, or *chaebols*, are each active in a large number of business sectors. They are owned by families and run by family members. Each *chaebol*, of which there are around sixty, is a combination of companies held together by cross-ownership and cross-subsidies. As with any family in this part of the world, the leader is autocratic and at the head of a very strict hierarchy. At the same time, relations between members of the clan are strongly communitarian. See Exhibit 4.2.

Exhibit 4.2 — FT

S Korea tries to clip wings of the chaebol

Many believe the conglomerates should be reined in but the government plans only to ease regulations that govern them and their tangled shareholding structures.

By Anna Field

In the 1960s and 1970s, South Korea's *chaebol* propelled the country's explosive growth, helping to transform it from one of the world's poorest countries into an Asian tiger. Now, South Korea is the world's 10th largest economy yet the family-run conglomerates have become what some see as untameable beasts in need of reining in.

'The *chaebol* have become too powerful,' argues Kwon Oh-seung, the chairman of the Korean Fair Trade Commission and the anti-trust regulator leading the charge to stop what he sees as the conglomerates' distortion of the Korean economy.

But rather than pursue a crackdown on the *chaebol*, South Korea's government is pushing a plan to ease the regulations that govern the conglomerates and the often tangled shareholding structures via which their controlling shareholders control vast industrial empires, often with formal shareholdings of 5 per cent or less. The National Assembly is due this month to consider a change that would see the number of companies subject to cross-shareholding restrictions fall from 343 units of 24 *chaebol* to just 24 companies belonging to seven groups.

Under the current regulations, *chaebol* affiliates with assets of more than Won 2,000bn ($2.14bn, €1.65bn, £1.09bn) belonging to groups with assets of more than Won 6,000bn are prohibited from holding more than 25 per cent of shares in an affiliated company.

Under the proposed revision, only *chaebol* with assets of more than Won 10,000bn will be affected. Furthermore, the cross-shareholding limit will be relaxed to allow companies to hold up to 40 per cent in affiliates.

The finance ministry says the move is intended to encourage corporate investment, which is forecast to slow sharply because of economic uncertainties caused by the strong Won and December's presidential election.

The view is backed by industry groups. According to the Federation of Korean Industries, the country's 30 largest business groups expect to invest Won 52,000bn this year, only 0.6 per cent more than in 2006.

The finance ministry argues that any efforts to tame the *chaebol* would potentially hobble an already slowing economy. Indeed, within South Korea there is a fear that the country's GDP would not grow without the *chaebol*.

But Mr Kwon, whose efforts to push through stricter cross-shareholding limits have been stymied by the government, argues the new rules will simply help distort the Korean economy further. Mr Kwon says the current limits can already see affiliates control 40–45 per cent of a *chaebol* company while owners technically hold just 5 per cent.

'The affiliates of large business groups can survive even if they are not competitive,' he says. 'I wanted to make the market function properly so that all those who make quality goods can survive in the market.'

Many analysts say it is time for Korea to wean itself off its dependence on both the *chaebol* and on manufacturing, for it to start developing the service sector, and to allow small and medium-sized enterprises – which employ 80 per cent of the working population – to grow.

The huge size of the *chaebol* is being called into question, especially as Samsung and Hyundai Motor prepare to install third-generation chairmen, a process aided by complex webs of cross-shareholdings.

Mr Kwon argues that in Korea 'power is concentrated in too few hands', singling out Samsung, Hyundai Motor, Hyundai Group, LG, SK and Doosan as the main offenders.

Samsung, the biggest *chaebol*, now has more than 60 affiliated companies – ranging from hotels and a securities trader to shipbuilding and petrochemicals – and accounts for almost a quarter of the Korean stock market's capitalisation and more than 20 per cent of total exports.

'When I compare Korea with other countries, like the US, the UK, Germany, I see that large business groups here have the power to hamper the functioning of markets so I am very concerned,' Mr Kwon says.

The *chaebol* have vehemently resisted attempts to curb their power. Lee Seung-chol of the FKI *chaebol* club argues that the restrictions on large business that the FTC wants to pursue are simply 'wrong'.

'Even though big companies dominate the domestic market they don't dominate international markets. In a global, open economy, market share does not equate to market power,' he says.

But analysts see logic in Mr Kwon's calls for stricter monitoring. 'The resources that the *chaebol* can deploy are massive compared with their potential competitors,' says Hank Morris, a business consultant in Seoul. 'So it makes sense for the government to play referee and be on the look-out for dirty tricks.'

Source: *Financial Times*, 5 February 2007: 2.

Question

Why do you think the South Korean government has not done more to reduce the power of the *chaebol*?

The teachings and works of Confucius and, later on, Buddha have had an enormous historic influence on Asian cultures. However, GLOBE considers it important to put these cultures into two distinct clusters because the countries of Southern Asia share other influences: this cluster 'shares Brahmanism and Buddhist, Islamic and Christian influences' (House et al., 2004: 188).

Southern Asia

According to an article entitled 'Karma capitalism' in US magazine *BusinessWeek* (30 October 2006), a trend in the business world is the development of a certain infatuation with Indian philosophy, This is due in no small part to the influence of a number of the world's leading business gurus who are of Indian descent, such as C.K. Prahalad, Ram Charan and Vijay Govindrajan. Their work contains common themes, including the basic notion that executives should be motivated by more than money alone. To quote Prahalad from the *BusinessWeek* article (page 84): 'It's the idea that corporations can simultaneously create value and social justice.' Companies should not be shareholder-driven, but stakeholder-focused, showing concern for society and the environment as well as those directly involved in their activities. A capitalism needs to be developed which, according to Prahalad, 'puts the individual at the centre of the universe'.

Apart from India, Thailand also has a business culture that embraces the principles of the Buddhist religion. These two countries are characterized below.

The Indians and family

India's culture, while displaying many of the features shared in Asia, places particular emphasis on the family. Every company employee works for the family to maintain and enhance its fortunes. Loyalty to the (extended) family takes priority over loyalty to the company, although here, too, a strong loyalty may develop towards the professional group involved. Loyalty to both family and group can become entwined: success in your profession will give your family added status. This goes, of course particularly for those who are engaged in a family business.

It is in the family business environment that the hard-working nature of Indians is particularly evident. Material success is important, not so much for the individual, but more for the sake of maintaining the family's honour and ensuring a sound future for the family's offspring. To be successful involves not just working long hours but also being creative, coming up with new ideas and trying them out with panache. There may be failures but this is less to do with personal competence, more to do with fate. The Hindu religion, shared by three-quarters of the population, has engrained a deep sense of fatalism into its followers, and as Richard D. Lewis notes (1996), this removes any stigma attached to failure.

Just as Indians accept the hierarchy of gods in their religion, so they accept the strict social hierarchy in their society and the hierarchies in the business environment. They show considerable respect towards their seniors in all aspects of their lives, but also expect these to fulfil the obligations that power bestows. The father is obeyed, but is expected to do everything to promote the family's well-being; the manager may behave in an authoritarian way, but is expected in turn to show care and consideration towards his employees.

Unlike other cultures in Asia, however, the Indians do not accept their lot without showing their feelings. They are renowned for their readiness to express their frustration if their efforts in life are not successful, or the joy experienced when their hopes or ambitions come true. The emotive dialogue in the many films from India's Bollywood film industry are testament to this extensive verbosity. This is a feature of Indian behaviour that foreign business representatives have encountered when pushing their products or services in India, particularly when their audience has the impression that these people are being patronizing. Equivalent products in India may not be as well produced or delivered, but it is not the role of foreigners to tell them this.

On the other hand, what India has in common with the other Asian cultures is the phenomenon of family businesses. Whether you are in India, in Malaysia or in Indonesia, you will find the same preponderance of family firms, and this holds true in all the economic sectors. However, this does not mean that these companies are not without their problems, especially when they break with tradition (Exhibit 4.3).

Exhibit 4.3

A new generation of family firm

By Louise Lucas

All happy families are the same, to paraphrase Leo Tolstoy. But even unhappy ones are not bad for business.

A 'family index' produced by Credit Suisse shows that companies in which the founding family has a stake of 10 per cent or more are good for shareholders' wealth. According to analysts at the Swiss bank, European stocks with a significant family influence have outperformed their respective sectors by an average 8 per cent a year over the past decade. The US experience is similar. Small

wonder that several US companies, including the retailer Gap, are going back to their family roots, five decades or so after the model was nudged aside in favour of public ownership.

Asia, of course, never gave up on family businesses. Mainland entities aside, family-owned companies dominate Hong Kong's Hang Seng Index. South Korea's corporate dynasties are flourishing, even after those pesky scandals. The Lee family has tightened its grip on the

Samsung group by elevating the son of chairman Lee Kun-hee. And Chung Mong-koo 'retains full operational control and decision-making authority for long-term strategic issues affecting Hyundai Motor,' the carmaker says – in spite of being handed a three-year prison sentence for embezzlement.

Dynasties proliferate across south-east Asia: the Malaysian Kuoks, whose interests span hotels and media; Indonesia's Salims in noodles; and the same country's Bakries in mining and telecoms. Taiwan has the Wangs, of Formosa Plastics fame, and the Koos, its oldest business dynasty, now in a spot of bother over the antics of heir apparent Jeffrey Koo junior. Even Singapore, whose corporate landscape is partly in government hands, has family empires.

Does that mean Asian investors have more chance of outperforming benchmarks? Sadly, Credit Suisse has not developed an Asian version of its index.

However, consistent out-performance does not apply to all the region's best-known family companies. Korea's Samsung Electronics underperformed its benchmark in two of the past four years, while Hutchison lagged behind every year. In Singapore, state-controlled DBS outperformed its family-owned banking peers. Other Asian dynasties move in lockstep with their peers – a reflection of the fact that many are rooted in cyclical industries such as property development.

But there are plenty of stars in the family-controlled universe. Henry Yeung Wai-Cheung, an associate professor at the National University of Singapore who has researched Asian family businesses, sees grounds for optimism. Corporate governance and transparency – once conspicuous by their absence – have improved, he says, along with greater globalisation of operations.

Younger generations are moving family businesses into different areas. 'This new phenomenon is leading to a new kind of family firm, more driven by emerging operations, especially in technology,' he says. 'That's a good development – extracting more from the existing franchise.'

And what of the unhappy families? The spat in India between Reliance's Ambani brothers, who engaged in a power struggle when their father died, briefly sent Reliance shares tumbling. But it did shareholders a favour in the long run – the subsequent division of the company unlocked value and pushed both brothers into expansion mode.

Stanley Ho, the Macao casino kingpin, disowned his sister over a row about dividend payments and shareholdings in his gambling empire. But his dynasty continues to produce fabulous returns for shareholders. His son Lawrence's casino joint venture with the son of Australian media magnate Kerry Packer recently listed on Nasdaq and shareholders saw gains of up to 32 per cent on day one.

Perhaps the most startling family rift was last year's bid by Li Ka-shing, the Hong Kong billionaire, to help bankroll an acquisition of his son's telecoms business. Mr Li's proposal, ultimately rejected by shareholders, probably owed more to repairing political relations than sparing his son's blushes. Richard Li's plans to sell PCCW's telecom assets to private equity firms were scuppered by Beijing. But it set back the cause of family businesses. A pity, since it was Mr Li who wrote the epitaph for keeping wealth in the family, in a speech last September entitled 'My third son' – which is how he refers to his charitable foundation.

Mr Li said: 'In Asia, our traditional values encourage and even demand that wealth and means pass through lineage as an imperative duty. I urge and hope to persuade you, especially all of us in Asia, that if we are in a position to do so, that we transcend this traditional belief.'

Source: *Financial Times*, 10 March 2007: 12.

Questions

1. **How can an unhappy family be good for business?**
2. **How does an Indian family business differ from the other family types in Asia?**

Thailand and karma

Unlike Cambodia, Laos and Vietnam, Thailand was not colonized by a European country. One reason was its role as a buffer state between the French and British colonies. Thailand, originally called Siam and then changed to Thailand in 1949 (Thai meaning freedom and also the name of the main ethnic group) has a long tradition of commerce, particularly with Western countries. At the beginning of the twentieth century it developed a new social class composed of merchants and functionaries.

Buddhism plays a dominant role in the values of Thai society. This religion is practised by more than 90 per cent of the population and for its lay followers it is pragmatic in nature, prescribing more than it proscribes. Although *nirvana*, with its sublime ideals, is the ultimate goal, many Buddhists are content to improve their lives by pursuing ethical principles and by asserting personal and social responsibilities ensure peace and serenity. By doing so, they hope to accumulate sufficient positive *karma* (action and result) and so ensure their rebirth in another, happy, state of existence.

This notion of *karma*, defined succinctly by Scarborough as 'the cumulative net effect of merit and demerit over the span of an individual's lives that determines his intermediate and ultimate fates' (1998: 82), contributes to the development of a particular kind of paternalism evident in Thailand. The person in a position of leadership is considered to have attained that status thanks to the accumulation of good rather than bad *karma*. Leadership requires exercising personal responsibility towards the community, being its leader and servant.

In an interview with Chamlong Srimuang, former Bangkok governor, at the East Asia economic summit in Kuala Lumpur (*Bangkok Post*, 9 October 2002: 11) the question of leadership comes to the fore. Chamlong Srimuang considers that leadership – whether in politics or business – requires:

> self-sacrifice or selflessness in one way or another. Such leadership or power over the people lasts longer than the leader's life. Jesus Christ, Mohammed and Buddha, to name a few, are clear examples of such long-lasting spiritual leadership.

In his view, people are not trained/formed to become leaders, but good leaders, which means being able to see clearly the benefit of being hard-working, economical, honest, self-sacrificial and grateful. Trying to be the best is not the key to success. If personal gain is the only goal, this is useless or even dangerous. Being the best is about 'being true to oneself, one's conscience'.

The newspaper article in Exhibit 4.4 describes the development strategy in Thailand based on Buddhist principles, an approach approved by the United Nation's main development agency.

Exhibit 4.4

United Nations endorsed Thai Buddhist economic model

By Kalinga Seneviratne

SUFFICIENCY ECONOMY: In the last two decades, Buddhism's appeal has grown in the West, drawing people seeking a calm not found in the fast-paced world of Internet-driven commerce and communications.

Bangkok, Thailand – While Bhavana (Buddhist meditation), has become a form of modern psychotherapy and influenced Western lifestyles, is there anything in the religion's 2,500-year-old teachings that could influence modern economics?

According to Thailand's much revered King and lately members of the [new military installed] government and a growing number of economists and grassroots development activists, the answer is, yes, there is. They call it 'Sufficiency Economics', a term coined by King Bhumibol Adulyadej in the midst of Thailand's economic meltdown in 1997. It embraces the three pillars of Buddhism – *dana* (giving), *sila* (morality) and *bhavana* (meditation) – and is based on the Buddhist principle of the 'Middle Path', that is avoidance of extremes (of greed).

The Thais have recently got a strong endorsement of this Buddhist development strategy from the United Nation's main development agency. In a report released in

January, the United Nations Development Programme (UNDP) hailed Thailand's new 'Middle Path' development model as a key to fighting poverty, coping with economic risk and promoting corporate social responsibility. . . .

For communities, Sufficiency Economics principles are fundamental to empowerment and building resilience, such as setting up savings groups, revolving credit lines, and local safety nets. For private business it means, 'taking corporate responsibility to the next level' by using this approach as a guide to management and planning.

'This approach encourages them to focus on sustainable profit, to adhere to an ethical approach to business, to pay special attention to their employees, to respect nature, to have careful risk management, and to grow where possible from internal resources,' the report explains. And for the third pillar, the government, the Sufficiency Economy is central to alleviating poverty, promoting good governance, and guiding macroeconomic policies to immunise against shocks. The UNDP report gives many examples of how the Sufficiency Economy model has been implemented in many parts of Thailand, encouraged by models set up under royal patronage across the country.

One such example is of Chumphon Cabana resort, which shows that the benefits of the sufficiency approach are not just confined to the agriculture sector. In the crisis of 1997, this resort on the east coast of the peninsula suffered financial difficulties like so many other businesses. In a desperate attempt to stay afloat, the owner took inspiration from the sufficiency approach.

As a start, she began to plant rice, vegetables, flowers and fruit trees on land within the resort project. To improve the sandy land without the cost of chemicals, she experimented with making organic fertilizer from hotel waste and other materials.

She planted a local variety of rice and installed a rice mill. The husk was used in making the fertilizer and for animal feed. As the resort's land was not enough to supply all its needs, she got the co-operation of surrounding villages to supply the deficit, and also helped train them in making fertilizer and other practices of organic farming. The employees of the resort were especially encouraged to participate.

Next she invented a just-in-time system of supply by posting the following day's requirements of various articles on the local school's notice board. Local production expanded beyond food to include various cleaning materials made from local materials.

As production increased, these articles were also supplied to other resorts in the area. The resort benefited from low production costs and reliable supplies. Surrounding farmers had a secure market and good prices because there were no middlemen.

Soon the resort gained a reputation with the result that other resort owners, farmers, NGOs, and government officials came to learn – which gave the employees a sense of pride. As the owner concluded, 'I think this is a kind of development which makes everybody happy.'

In a 1998 statement on the essence of the Sufficiency Economics model, King Bhumibol said: 'Sufficiency is moderation. If one is moderate in one's desires, one will have less craving. If one has less craving, one will take less advantage of others. If all nations hold to this concept, without being extreme or insatiable in one's desires, the world will be a happier place.'

Source: *Lanka Daily News*, 20 March 2007 www.dailynews.lk/2007/03/20/fea03.asp

Questions

1. In what way does the Chumphon Cabana resort illustrate the Sufficiency Economy model?
2. Which characteristics of this model relate to Buddhism?

This section has highlighted some features of the two culture clusters in Asia and has mentioned a few of the countries in these clusters. Nevertheless, it is hoped that clear differences between these cultures have become apparent, as well as the contrast with the Western cultures dealt with in Chapter 3.

Sub-Sahara Africa

The countries in all of Africa had their frontiers defined by European colonists who divided the continent between themselves at the start of the nineteenth century (Figure 4.2). Ethnic groupings, or tribes, found themselves divided by political boundaries drawn on a map. National identities are difficult to pinpoint, with various tribes inhabiting one arbitrarily

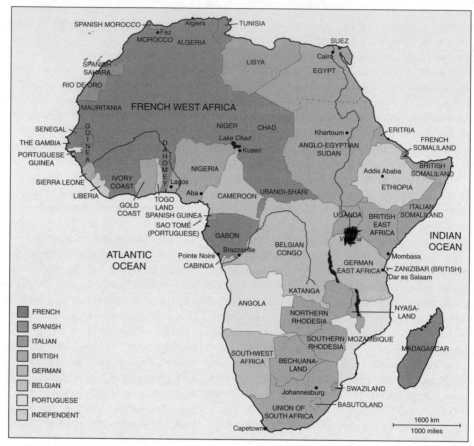

Figure 4.2 Colonial Africa
Source: www.fsmitha.com/h2/map02af.htm

defined country. Africa's inhabitants are diverse in every way – languages, religions, dwellings and economic activities. They live in a wide range of societies, some archaic, others advanced.

The majority of its peoples live outside towns and cities in primitive cultures where archaic, animist religions determine the social order. This organization is based on the patriarchal family following a strict hierarchy in which the patriarch has absolute authority over the whole community of the lineage or clan. This authority is generally handed down through the lineage of the patriarch.

With increasing economic activity and improved local transportation, people migrated to towns from the country to get work and to support their families back in the countryside. Education, imported Christian religions and Islam have often supplanted animist religions in developing urban areas. Despite this increased mobility there is still identification with tribes, although this is weakening over time.

Europeans to some extent developed the lands they colonized, but since moving to independence the dictatorships that arose in individual countries have nullified most of the economic advantages created by development. Only recently has the continent started to make the transition to democratically elected governments and privatized businesses (Exhibit 4.5).

Exhibit 4.5

Why Africa?

To establish a type of nationwide government, [European] colonial administrators effectively set about inventing African traditions for Africa, that would make the process more acceptable to the indigenous population. The most far-reaching inventions of tradition in colonial Africa occurred when the administrators believed they were respecting age-old African custom, whereas a commentator notes: 'What were called customary law, customary land-rights, customary political structure and so on were in fact all invented by colonial codification.' By creating an image of Africa steeped in unchanging tradition the colonizers condemned the continent to live in a reconstructed moment of its past. A vast continental theme park – Africa-land – that hindered development for decades. But perhaps the most pernicious of the traditions which the colonial period bequeathed to Africa was the notion of Tribalism. Just as every European belonged to a nation, every African must belong to a tribe, a cultural unit with a common language, a single social system and established customary law. In Zambia the chief of a little known group once remarked: 'My people were not Soli until 1937 when the Bwana D.C. told us we were. The concept of the Zulu as a discrete ethnic group did not emerge until 1870.'

These were the dangerous sands upon which the colonialists imposed a new political geography. However, once in motion, the process was enthusiastically reinforced by the Africans themselves. Tribes became the object of passionate African imagination. Some chroniclers have endowed their tribes with a retrospective primordial essence. Rather like Yeats did with the similarly disenfranchised Irish.

The British ruled through these local hierarchies, a process which unconsciously promoted the most malleable, collaborative or corrupt local chiefs and where none existed, as we've seen, they simply created one, enabling ambitious individuals and groups to achieve positions of status, dominance and wealth that might otherwise have been unattainable.

To counter this tribalism some African leaders proclaimed the single party state to be the only means to control the excessive, ethnically based competition for the global goods of modernity – education, health and the eradication of poverty. Competitive democracy they said would only lead to penury. Yet one-party rule unrestrained by the moral check of shared community had the same result. It proved to be a mask for oppression, ethnocracy and kleptocracy. Of the 107 African leaders overthrown between 1960 and 2003 two-thirds were murdered, jailed or slung into exile. Up until 1979, 59 African leaders were toppled or assassinated. Only three retired peacefully and not one was voted out of office. No incumbent African leader ever lost an election until 1982.

. . . [Imposing] cultural beliefs on other people, whether by economic muscle or cruise missile, so that they can be more like us is a farce, particularly when the obvious external purpose is regional control of resources and political influence.

Source: Bob Geldof, 'Why Africa? Bob Geldof Speaks at St Paul's Cathedral', www.data.org, 21 April 2004.

An example of a country that has recently been undergoing rapid business development is Nigeria. Here a Western-style 'professional' order has been imposed on relations between co-workers in companies. The workers have responded positively to the hierarchical organization, which runs parallel to the hierarchy within their family. Despite their flexible, easy-going attitude to time they are also responding to the need for regularity and punctuality in work routine.

Shepherd Shonhiwa, a Zimbabwean expatriate and fellow of the Institute of Directors in Southern Africa recently pleaded for Europe to re-assess its view of Africa's business. In a contribution to the *Financial Times* series 'Mastering Management', he noted that African culture had distinctive feelings of communalism rather than separatism. He went on to describe what he considered to be fundamental African personality traits:

● In the main, African culture is non-discriminatory and does not promote prejudice. This explains the readiness with which Africans embrace reconciliation in politics and business.

- Africans have a mentality of inherent trust and belief in the fairness of human beings.
- They have high standards of basic morality, based on historical precedent. These are bolstered by the close kinship observed through totem or clan names and the extended family system.
- A hierarchical political ideology, but based on an inclusive system of consultation. Labour relations and people management practices will optimise this trait.
- A perpetual optimism is an integral part of the African, mainly due to strongly held religious beliefs.

Mutabazi (2001:100) underlines these characteristics when stating that 'the cultural unity of African societies exceeds their diversity'. These societies share a collection of values and beliefs as a result of which every village or town, local administration or company displays the same social phenomena and behaviour. This shared cultural basis of values and rules will have been passed down through many generations within the tribes and passed on through networks of families and friends to communities living in other 'countries'.

Cultural models imported from the West did not succeed in replacing this common African cultural base, one which, according to Mutabazi (2001) is characterized by its relationship to time and (organized) work, as well as its relationship with other people (family, hierarchy, colleagues, subordinates, outsiders). These relations are the same in regions which may be geographically very distant from each other, or very different to each other in terms of climate, religion or language. Mutabazi gives the Ivory Coast and Ruanda as examples of very different countries where, at business level, there are similar attitudes as to how decisions should be made, how managers should give orders. There are also similarities in the way employees behave towards the company. This can be witnessed, for example, in their low rate of attendance, their frequent absenteeism and their lack of initiative.

Furthermore, the great majority of local companies reject the idea of interpersonal competition among employees, as encountered in the North American model. They therefore, for example, do not allocate bonuses to individuals for extra performance or productivity. Certain bureaucratic procedures dating from the French colonial period, such as contracts and other written directives, are also rejected by the Africans. They place greater value on verbal commitments.

South Africa, the Rainbow Nation

The rainbow, South Africa's recently adopted symbol, reflects the country's huge cultural diversity. Apart from the indigenous black peoples there are the white Europeans, Indians, Chinese and other immigrants from various countries in Asia.

Since the dismantling of the policy of apartheid, which not only allowed the white minority to maintain its domination of the country through control of its economic and social system but also institutionalized racial discrimination, South Africa has confidently promoted its multicultural society. The diverse ethnic, cultural and religious groups are now seen as indispensable in the social and economic development of the country. See Exhibit 4.6.

It is therefore difficult to talk of a particular approach to management in this multi-ethnic country. On the one hand, the importance of the tribal/family connections may be of great importance, particularly when it comes to companies in neighbouring countries dealing with South Africans. On the other hand, business relationships may be developed in the office through intensive face-to-face contact.

Exhibit 4.6

Where are the workers?

The following incident took place in a company based in South Africa and which had a Dutch management team. Those employed in the production department were black.

The general manager was pleased with the performance of the production workers, and as is usual in his own country, the Netherlands, he awarded them a bonus at the end of the year equivalent to two weeks' wages.

The Christmas holidays came and went and the New Year started. However, none of the production workers turned up for work, even though the factory was open. Eventually, on 15 January they re-appeared.

The general manager was perplexed. What had gone wrong?

Question

Why was the factory empty for the first two weeks of January?

The true incident described above shows that people at a certain social level in South Africa do not work to earn money but to live. So they survived throughout the first two weeks of January on the two-week extra salary they received in December.

These two approaches reflect the increasingly urban/rural contrast in South African society. Large numbers of blacks are moving into urban areas and falling under the many influences of the others living there, including the large inflow of migrants from neighbouring countries. The prevalent management style is a professional, top-down one, but with an emphasis on conciliation rather than confrontation, thus reflecting the need to maintain social harmony in this multicultural environment.

In the rural areas the more traditional values still apply, with the head of the family determining the manner in which business takes place and the way it is carried out.

The Middle East

The Middle East, stretching from Iraq through the Arabian peninsula and along the north coast of Africa, has for centuries been the crossroads where West and East have met. Here, the Arabs have successfully traded between the two, buying and selling the goods from other countries, as well as their own.

Language and culture are unifying factors, with the Islam religion providing an overarching body of belief and a strong sense of identity and community. Islam spread in the seventh century and along with it the Arab language, which had once been a tribal language in the Arab peninsula. The present Arab states were formed following the break-up of the Ottoman Empire during the first World War.

The family remains at the basis of Arab social structure. As already witnessed in Asia, this means the broader notion of family, a kin group or clan involving several households and cousins on the father's side. The welfare of the family is of primary concern. Family ties bring security but also commitments. These can override the interests of close members in favour of nephews or cousins if the interests of the clan as a whole are better served.

The family is run in a disciplined way by an authoritarian father. The head of the family clan is usually the oldest, competent member of the grouping and runs the clan in an equally authoritarian way. A large proportion of Arab businesses are family-owned and discipline is maintained by a leader having strong central control and a strict hierarchy.

The considerable awareness which Arabs have of their social and economic environment is a noticeable feature of their business culture. They are highly sensitive to the people they are dealing with and may turn down a lucrative business deal because they dislike the people they are dealing with, particularly if these people do not enhance their personal reputation. This is of utmost importance, since damage to one member of the family damages the whole family. It is often contended that when a family concern has to deal with the government it is more often than not a question of two family businesses coming to terms with each other. For, in the government, it is members of the ruler's family who are most likely to hold all the main government posts; outsiders, however talented, are put in less important positions.

The phrase 'Inshalah', often translated as 'God willing' or 'if Allah so wishes', is one often used in everyday conversation and reflects deep-rooted beliefs in pre-destination and fatalism. Its use also emphasizes the extreme sensitivity shown to the context of any discussion. Its exact meaning depends on the subject in hand, the particular purpose of the discussion, and the relationships between the individuals involved. On some occasions it can mean 'yes', on others 'no'; sometimes it can mean 'I'll arrange it', other times 'Don't discuss this further'. Communication can therefore be a hazardous affair for not only outsiders but also for any translators involved, particularly because they must also take account of the intonation and body language used.

Keeping face is often referred to in relation to Arab society and is related to this question of reputation. Admiration and respect are sought after as much as, if not more than, financial success. And this prestige is not for the individual concerned, but for the family to whom the individual belongs. The face or image conveyed to others, especially in public, is therefore given considerable attention, even when this involves dealing with relative strangers. The Arabs are renowned for their generosity and hospitality, but these 'duties' may also be a prelude to seeking some kind of commitment or request.

These comments on family and face highlight a paradox which Hickson and Pugh (2001: 221) refer to when discussing the Arab model of management:

> **Arabs are disposed to handle authority centrally with high power distance, yet at the same time they aspire to an 'open door' for all comers, high or low, and to consultation in the manner of the sheikhs.**

The door is now wide open in many parts of the Middle East, and aspects of Western culture have made their way into many Arab countries. More and more Middle Easterners are also participating in management education programmes in the West and applying the knowledge and skills to their native business environment. This process, however, is being controlled not only by those implementing changes but also by the guardians of Arab society who wish to prevent the norms and values of society as enshrined in civil and religious law from being abused. In short, we can say that Arabic companies are facing a dilemma that brings the globalization of the economy into conflict with affection for cultural values of the past.

However, a middle class is becoming apparent that is trying to reconcile the process of economic modernization with the development of new values, such as tolerance, individualism and concern for the future.

The example of the changes happening in the Gulf emirate of Qatar, as shown in the following text, reflects this process.

Exhibit 4.7

A different breed of foot soldier

By William Wallis

A strange kind of revolution is taking place in the tiny, energy-rich Gulf emirate of Qatar. Until relatively recently a fiercely conservative peninsular state living in the long shadow of Saudi Arabia, Qatar is asserting itself with global ambitions. Women are flocking to universities. Skyscrapers are sprouting from the desert and foreigners and investors are pouring in in search of business. At a time when the Arab street is seen to be stirring in pursuit of change, the transformations under way in Qatar have been engineered not so much by its population as by Sheikh Hamad bin Khalifa al-Thani, the absolute ruler.

In Doha, the foot soldiers of change are a different breed from those crowding other Arab capitals. They are more likely to be from public relations firms and management consultancies, hired from abroad to help promote and develop the emir's 'vision'. Slogans such as 'modernisation without westernisation', or 'modern but Muslim' emerge from PowerPoint presentations rather than street pamphlets or radical preachers. 'His highness,' explains one enthusiastic subject from Qatar's academic community, 'is way ahead of his society. He is trying to position us to benefit from the changes in the world. What's good for the world is also good for Qatar. We are not some kind of freak nation.'

By the standards of the conservative autocracies of the Gulf, Qatar, is, however, becoming distinct in more ways than one even if it shares many of the same challenges. The emir says he wants to build a nation rich in human as well as natural resources, strategically positioned for its service industries, as well as its energy wealth. To achieve this, he is not just changing the skyline in Doha. He is also attempting to remould the mindset of its inhabitants. In the first 24 years of independence from Britain, when other oil rich Gulf societies were assembling the trappings of modernity, Qatar remained a comparative backwater.

From the smallest financial sector in the immediate vicinity, Qatar wants to develop the region's preferred banking centre and has tailored regulations for the purpose. It wants more tourists, more skyscrapers, more international sporting and cultural events and more skills and know-how. Behind these ambitions, say government officials, is a desire on the part of the emir to shake off the apathy that characterised times past.

He and his influential wife, Sheikha Moza, are going out of their way to empower women and instil entrepreneurialism in a population accustomed to being looked after in style by the state, they say. There is also, says Mohamed al-Thani, the economy and commerce minister, a will to invest at home money that might previously have gone abroad. Expense is of little concern. But the tiny size of the local population is, together with a desire not to be seen to compromise the deeply held Islamic beliefs of Qatar's strict Wahabbi culture.

Although there are a growing number of exceptions, most Qatari women do not work and 60 per cent of the population is under the age of 21. 'Qatar is looking to do things that require global experience right from the guy operating the crane, to the engineer, to the financier trying to pull together investors,' says an expatriate government adviser who himself fits the category. In the process, some Qataris complain that the roads are clogging up with traffic, rents have risen by 100 per cent in the past year and the composition and size of the population is changing by the day. About 10,000 labourers have been brought in from south-east Asia for one project alone.

The government wants a booming tourism industry but without the trashier trappings. It is liberalising the economy and wants a world class financial sector. But there is little scrutiny of business and data on public debt, foreign reserves or local population size are not disclosed. Most paradoxical of all, the government wants to develop its non-energy economy without jeopardising the culture and proportion of the local population. Its approach in this respect is far more cautious than nearby Dubai's, where you can now buy a beer with your fish and chips on the beach.

But the larger the non-Qatari population becomes, the harder it may be to stem the flow of unwanted aspects of foreign influence. With so many projects at stake, this appears to be a price the emir believes worth paying. As a non-elected leader with almost limitless funds at his disposal he has the luxury of thinking big and planning long term.

Source: *Financial Times*, 18 May 2005, FT Report – Qatar: 1.

Question

What are the contradictions which Qatar has to deal with?

Concepts 3 and 4 have outlined some similarities – and differences – between countries in each cluster of both hemispheres of the GLOBE metaconfiguration. When doing so they have each highlighted business culture features of countries within each cluster to illustrate fundamental traits they share with others in the cluster as well as to highlight differences with countries from other clusters.

It now seems appropriate to go deeper into the value systems inherent to every culture in a business context, and to bring forward some of the dilemmas these contradictory values can generate. This is the aim of the next chapter, Chapter 5.

ACTIVITY 4.1

In the case study below, a Dutch business consultant gives his account of a problem that he was called in to resolve. The problem involved a South Korean company and a Dutch advertising agency. Before reading the text and answering the questions, read both Chapters 3 and 4.

This activity also prepares the ground for Chapter 5, which examines cultural dilemmas.

My negotiating dilemma

One of my clients was a South Korean company established in the Netherlands. The sales targets they had been given by the headquarters in Seoul were very high. To help them reach these targets they hired an advertising agency. The agency went to work and came up with a total media campaign which the South Korean company accepted and allowed to be set in motion. One ingredient of the campaign was a simple but innovative slogan that quickly caught on.

The advertising agency continued the campaign, which appeared to maintain its success. The initial euphoria within the company had, however, evaporated. Its managers thought the agency's bills were too high, not only because the agency had been working with them for two years, but also because they were suspicious about the actual hours that the agency was spending on producing the advertising. They knew it was difficult to check on the time needed to come up with brilliant ideas, but still they felt that the Dutch were taking advantage of the situation. As I discovered later, a comment which was frequently heard at the top of the company was: 'You have to be careful with those Dutch.'

The Korean company started to withhold payments. The director of the Dutch agency saw this as a typical tactic of the Koreans to get lower prices. He shared the view held by some businesses that Koreans easily breach contracts, a perception that usually comes about because people are generally unaware of how Koreans interpret the word 'trust'. Having tried to explain this to him, it was not really a surprise to hear from the Koreans that they intended to break their contract with the agency. I told them it could damage their name in the market if they did so, and reminded them that all the slogans used to promote their products remained the (intellectual) property of the advertising agency.

Well, the agency threatened to take the Korean company to court to recover the money it was owed. They did so, despite being eager to continue with the contract. Losing it would mean disaster for a company that had only started up a few months before getting the Korean contract.

A meeting took place between the two sides without my presence. During it the Koreans made it clear that they were not going to pay. The young manager representing the agency told the Koreans that they would not be allowed to use the slogans any more if the contract was terminated.

The Korean management called me in and asked me to help.

I had a dilemma. It was in my clients' interest to continue the contract. Breaking it would mean putting an end to the whole advertisement campaign that they needed so much (since they were new in the market). The Dutch had good arguments for the amounts they had charged and were really afraid of losing the contract. If the advertising agency started legal proceedings, the Koreans would have no chance of winning the case.

Source: Adapted from Browaeys and Trompenaars (2000): case 10.

Questions

1. What exactly is the dilemma referred to in the last paragraph?

2. How would you describe the contrast between the South Koreans and the Dutch when they are doing business?

3. How do you think the dilemma could be resolved?

ACTIVITY 4.2

Read the following case study about the problems of exporting flowers to Russia and then answer the questions.

To Russia with love

Jan de Rover sat back in his chair, his feet resting on the piles of paperwork on his desk. He watched a jet flying low over the greenhouses as it came in to land at Amsterdam airport. He was thinking about his next trip to Moscow, where he was trying to sell flowers, which his company grew under glass. 'I'm not looking forward to going,' he told his financial director Rob, who was also watching the plane. 'It's frightening over there, you know?' Sitting up, he leaned over his desk and said: 'You won't believe what the Russian mafia gets up to. Their tentacles are everywhere. And you never know where you are with them, they're so unpredictable. Do you know there was a shooting incident last week – about flowers, would you believe it!'

Jan's company is all about flowers – acres of greenhouses, a dozen trucks to transport the flowers to the flower auction just round the corner, two hundred employees, including seasonal workers, and the office building where everything is managed. He exports 120 million flowers to all parts of the world, including Eastern and Southern Europe, North and South America. Forty dozen flowers are sent to Russia each week. The time factor plays an important role here since flowers will not survive any long transport delay.

The prices of flowers sent to Russia are automatically set 30 percent higher. The difference in price is given to the mafia, otherwise the flowers would never arrive at their destination on time. For Jan this is the only way to overcome the problems caused by the poor infrastructure. Bribes are the only way, for example, to make sure that the flowers get loaded on to local transport before they start wilting. Even then, however, as Jan explains to his financial director, you never know beforehand whether they're going to accept the bribe.

Rob is not happy with these 'facilitation payments' either. Nor is he happy about the fact that the eventual payments for the flowers take ages to reach Holland. In some cases it has taken over a year before the money has been transferred – and then without any excuse or apology. If this happened in his own country, the company would stop any further deliveries. 'If you ask me,' said Rob to his boss, 'I reckon the Russians and the mafia are in it together.' Jan nodded his head in reluctant agreement.

Questions

1. Jan believes that paying bribes is the only way to overcome the problems caused by the poor infrastructure in Russia. Is this really the only way of tackling these problems?

2. How do you explain Rob's comment that 'the Russians and the mafia are in it together'?

Conclusion

Chapter 4 has highlighted some key features of the (business) culture of countries within each of the five Eastern culture clusters in the metaconfiguration devised by the GLOBE project. It has highlighted the importance of relationships and networks, expressed in the form of *blat* in Russia, *guanxi* in China and the *chaebol* in South Korea and has shown generally how Confucianism and Buddhism influence economic activity.

This chapter has also described the important role of the (extended) family in India, Africa and the Middle East, but also how family or tribal values are having to contend with Western ways of doing business.

Points for reflection

1. The GLOBE study put Eastern Europe into a cluster that belongs to the eastern part of the world.

   After reading Chapters 3 and 4, do you think that the cluster really belongs to the hemisphere containing Asia, Africa and the Middle East, or does it really belong to the western hemisphere? Give arguments which support both standpoints.

2. The chapters have underlined the importance of Confucianism and Buddhism in Asian societies. The differences between the two religions have caused GLOBE to create two clusters, one containing China, for example, the other containing India.

   To what extent do you believe that religion still plays an important role in the business cultures of these countries?

3. Sub-Sahara Africa could be characterized as a region of contrasts: on the one hand there is modernity and western influence, and on the other hand tradition and local cultural values.

   How do you account for these contrasts? Could the Middle East be characterized in the same way. If so, why?

Further reading

Harris, P.R. and Moran, R.T. (1996) *Managing Cultural Differences*, 4th edn, Houston, Texas: Gulf. This book documents critical sensitivities that the business person must exhibit in various part of the world. It focuses on building dynamic change into cultural systems and creating synergistic relations in the midst of cultural differences.

References

Braudel, F. (1987) *Grammaire des civilisations*, Paris: Arthaud-Flammarion.

Browaeys, M.-J. and Trompenaars (eds) (2000) *Cases Studies on Cultural Dilemmas*, Breukelen, Netherlands, Nyenrode University Press.

Burns, R. (1998) *Doing Business in Asia: A cultural perspective*, Australia: Addison Wesley Longman.

Harris, P.R. and Moran, R.T. (1996) *Managing Cultural Differences*, 4th edn, Houston: Gulf.

Hickson, D.J. and Pugh, D.S. (2001) *Management Worldwide,* 2nd edn, London: Penguin.

House, R.J., Hanges, P.J., Javidan, M., Dorfman, P.W. and Gupta, V. (eds) (2004) *Leadership, Culture and Organizations: The GLOBE study of 62 societies,* Thousand Oaks, CA: Sage.

Lewis, R.D. (1996) *When Cultures Collide,* London: Nicholas Brealey.

Michailova, S. and Worm, V. (2003) 'Personal networking in Russia and China: *blat* and guanxi', *European Management Journal,* 21, 4: 509–519.

Mutabazi, E. (2001) 'Multiculturalisme et gouvernement des sociétés africaines', in Dahan-Seltze, G. and Pierre, P. (eds), *Mondialisation: les cultures en questions,* Sociologies Pratiques, Paris: APSE: 95–118.

Scarborough, J. (1998) *The Origins of Cultural Differences and Their Impact on Management,* London: Quorum.

Schneider, S.C. and Barsoux, J.L. (1997) *Managing Across Cultures,* Harlow: FT Prentice Hall.

Chapter 5

Cultural dimensions and dilemmas

Figure I.2 in the introduction to Part One mentioned the names of two social scientists, Kluckholn and Strodtbeck. Their book, *Variations in Value Orientations* (1961), has served as a primary source of reference for many researchers into culture and management, including Schein, Adler, Hall, Hofstede and Trompenaars. These researchers developed cultural value orientations when investigating the phenomenon of culture and developed cross-cultural management models for a business context.

Some insight was given in Chapter 2 into the relationship between national cultural values and management. Trompenaars also developed dimensions to measure cultural differences and gain further understanding about cultural diversity in business. What is particularly original about his work is that he presents opposing cultural values in the form of dilemmas.

Concept 5.1 gives an overview of Trompenaars' dimensions and the ensuing dilemmas which a manager may encounter in an intercultural environment. It also highlights some of the differences between Trompenaars' and Hofstede's dimensions.

Concept 5.2 explains the method Trompenaars and Hampden-Turner developed for reconciling the dilemmas outlined in Concept 5.1.

Learning outcomes

After reading the chapter you should:

● Understand the concept of value orientations.

● Have gained insight into Trompenaars' seven dimensions.

● Have explored some cultural dilemmas in business.

● Have learned how cultural differences can be reconciled.

Concept 5.1 Value orientations and dimensions

The concepts of cultural theory have inspired researchers, particularly those relating culture to management, to examine the effect of the norms and values of a society on the individual.

Parsons, an American sociologist who attempted to integrate all the social sciences into a science of human action, argued in his ground-breaking work, *The Structure of Social Action* (1937), that the action of the individual is totally integrated into a social system.

Individuals passively follow the rules of conduct of the specific society in which they are living. The norms of the society are institutionalized and internalized by the individuals in it through a process of socialization. These norms steer their actions and subordinate individuals to the social order, reducing the uncertainty they experience when interacting. Without this social mechanism, interaction would be much less predictable, the motives and reactions of those involved much less certain.

The value-orientation concept

Kluckholn and Strodtbeck (1961: 4) define value orientations as being complex principles that are the result of interaction between three elements: the cognitive, the affective and the directive. This final element is of particular interest since it orders and conducts human thoughts and actions 'as these relate to the solution of "common human" problems'.

They put forward a classification of the universal components of value orientations, including some intra-cultural variations. To enable this classification to be made, Kluckholn and Strodtbeck formulate three assumptions:

1. 'There are a limited number of common human problems for which all peoples at all times must find some solution' (page 10). This forms the essentially universal nature of value orientations.

2. There are many ways of solving problems.

3. Societies have different preferences when it comes to choosing solutions.

These assumptions allow them to determine five problems common to all human groupings. On the basis of these problems they established the variations in five orientations, which have been integrated into the concept in Chapter 6 dealing with cultural values in management.

To enable a clearer understanding of these value orientations, Kluckholn and Strodtbeck (1961: 11–20) illustrate their definitions with examples, many of which relate to the culture prevailing in the US.

1. *Human nature orientation* (goodness or badness of human nature): 'Some in the United States today incline to the view that human nature is a mixture of Good and Evil. These would say that although control and effort are certainly needed, lapses can be understood and need not always be severely condemned' (page 12).

2. *Man–nature orientation* (harmony-with-nature and mastery-over-nature): 'In the conceptualization of the man–nature relationship is that of harmony; there is no real separation of man, nature and supra-nature . . . The mastery-over-nature position is the first-order (that is, the dominant orientation) of most Americans. Natural forces of all kinds are to be overcome and put to the use of human beings' (page 13).

3. *Time orientation* (past, present and future): 'Americans place an emphasis upon the future – a future which is anticipated to be bigger and better . . . The ways of the past are not considered good just because they are past, and truly dominant . . . Americans are seldom content with the present. This view results in a high evaluation of change, providing the change does not threaten the existing value order – the American way of life' (page 15).

4. *Activity orientation* (being, being-in-becoming and doing): 'The doing orientation is so characteristically the dominant one in American society . . . "Getting things done" and "Let's do something about it" are stock American phrases' (page 17).

5. *Relational orientation* (Man's relation to other men): 'The Lineal, the Collateral and the Individualistic "relational" alternatives are analytical concepts for the purpose of making fine distinctions both within and between systems rather than generalizing concepts for the specification of the gross differences between systems' (page 17).

The US, with its many ethnic groups, serves as an ideal example to illustrate the degrees of variation in value orientations. These variations result from the presence of subgroups in every society whose behaviour is more or less patterned according to the value orientations of the dominant group. These subgroup variations contribute to the creation of what Kluckhohn and Strodtbeck (1961: 28) call a 'web of variation' in a society.

Trompenaars follows the same line of reasoning as Kluckhohn and Strodtbeck by proposing dimensions based, in particular, on the orientation of societies with regard to their relations with other people, with time and with nature. However, he goes beyond the framework of anthropology and sociology to show how these dimensions also affect the process of managing across cultures.

Trompenaars' seven dimensions

The standpoint of Fons Trompenaars is that each culture has its own specific solutions for universal problems. In his surveys he presented his respondents with a number of dilemmas and asked them to choose one of a number of solutions. In the first edition of his book, *Riding the Waves of Culture* (1993), Trompenaars attempts to show the effects of culture on management by describing different cultural orientations based on academic and field research carried out in several countries. He rejects the notion that there is one 'best way' of doing business and advocates a better understanding of the cultural dilemmas faced by international companies. Furthermore, if there is a large number of products and services on world markets, attention should be given to 'what they mean to the people in each culture' (1993: 3). Trompenaars examines culture within three main categories: relations with other people, attitudes to time and attitudes to the environment. Some of the dimensions produced reflect those of the authors mentioned above – Parsons, Kluckhohn and Strodtbeck – and these are relevant to business.

Five of the seven dimensions of culture as presented by Trompenaars in *Riding the Waves of Culture* are outlined in Table 5.1 (page 83). This first set of dimensions is based on the five relational orientations borrowed from Parsons which describe 'the ways in which human beings deal with each other' (1993: 8).

Let us have a look at an example, which could be analysed with the dimensions: 'relations to other people'.

Case study 5.1

Statements of commitment

My task was to implement a customer profitability system at a Swedish company located in Amsterdam. The system required a team of people from different parts of the company to aggregate and analyze information related to customer activities. Under my direction, this team of workers had created all the necessary processes and analyses for the customer profitability model. The new system had already succeeded in helping the company's account managers to derive more profits from their existing customers.

Pleased with the results of my team's customer profitability system, the Swedish head of the branch asked me to ensure that the system remained in place even after I had returned to the US. With this in mind, I wrote a formal document that stated the individual commitments of everyone on the team in terms of the profitability system over the next year. My intention was to have each member of the team individually sign up to these commitments. My Swedish branch head believed that the idea to have all the team members agree to their commitments on paper was an excellent one because he believed that the project might otherwise fall apart after I had left Amsterdam.

Upon presenting my commitment document to one Dutch manager with whom I had worked closely, I was surprised by his unease when signing the document. He said that having individuals sign a document in this manner was very 'un-Dutch'. However, if I failed to gain some kind of formal commitment to the project, I felt sure that my Swedish manager would be dissatisfied.

Source: adapted from Browaeys and Trompenaars (2000): case 7.

Table 5.1 Relations to the other people

1. *Universalism versus particularism*: • societal versus personal obligation	*Universalism*: absolute rules apply, irrespective of circumstances and situations *Particularism*: circumstances and relationships are more important considerations than absolutes Example in business: the role of the contract
2. *Individualism versus collectivism (communitarianism)*: • personal versus group goals	*Individualism*: personal welfare and fulfilment *Collectivism*: social concern and altruism Example in business: goals of negotiating and decision-making
3. *Neutral versus affective relationships*: • emotional orientation in relationships	This dimension concerns the contexts and ways that cultures choose to express emotions. Should emotion be exhibited in business relations?
4. *Specific versus diffuse relationships*: • contact versus contract • rapport versus report	*Specific*: company employees are hired in contractually to be part of a system which performs efficiently *Diffuse*: company employees are members of a group working together. Their relations with each other and the organization determine how the company functions
5. *Achievement versus ascription (doing/being)*: • legitimating power and status	In achievement-oriented cultures, business people are evaluated by how well they perform an allocated function. In ascriptive cultures, status is attributed, for example, to older people, those who are of good family or highly qualified

Source: Trompenaars (1993: 8–11) and his other publications.

How can this situation be analysed using Trompenaars' dimensions as given above? Here is how the author of the case saw the problem.

The core of the problem that I was facing was that the Dutch are more communitarianism-oriented than the Swedes. For this reason, the idea of signing individual commitments seemed very 'un-Dutch' to them because they feel more comfortable with group commitments. Still, I knew that my Swedish manager would believe, as I do, that some statement of commitment needed to be signed. This desire for documentation stems from the

Swedish preference for solidifying business relationships through rules and contracts. Additionally, the Swedish prefer job tasks and commitments to be specific. This is shown by Trompenaars' high particularist rating for the Swedish relative to the Dutch. My challenge was to find a means of formal commitment to our project with which my Swedish manager and my Dutch colleagues would be satisfied.

Trompenaars added two dimensions of particular interest to management and business. The dimensions he delineated are to do with attitudes concerning relations with others, time (past, present and future) and the environment (Table 5.2).

Table 5.2 Relations to time and the environment

6. *Sequential versus synchronic time* (monochronic/polychronic)	*Sequential*: Time is tangible and divisible. Only do one activity at time.
	Synchronic: Time is flexible and intangible. Appointments are approximate and subject to 'giving time' to significant others.
7. *Inner versus outer directed* • Internal or external control to the environment	*Internal control*: one's personal conviction is the starting point for every action and this may result in conflict with others and resistance to nature.
	External control: Sensitive to the environment and seeks harmony. Often flexible attitude, willing to compromise.

Source: see Table 5.1.

Although it is important to know the dimensions based on value differences in societies to compare cultures, it is nevertheless necessary for management to define what these dimensions mean in concrete terms, the differing attitudes that result. A useful way of demonstrating these differences is by examining the ways in which dilemmas are approached. Details of these dimensions and the related dilemmas are presented below.

A framework for the new millennium manager

These seven dimensions were essentially the result of Trompenaars' research based on the question 'Where are you coming from?' Are the value-systems of a person predominantly universalistic or particularistic; is that person an individualist or communitarian person? Does the status of that person derive from what (s)he does do or who (s)he is? This approach:

> helps to identify and model the source of not only national cultural differences, but related issues of corporate culture as well as dealing with a diverse work force. This has served to help managers structure their real world experiences. The Trompenaars' database of 50,000 managers worldwide continues to be a rich source of social constructs for identifying and explaining and predicting culture clash.
>
> Trompenaars and Woolliams, 2000: 22

Trompenaars and Woolliams (2000: 25–27) developed a framework for the 'millennium manager' by combining these seven dimensions with a range of dilemmas identified by Charles Hampden-Turner. By using a factor analysis, they reduced the variety of behaviours to seven core competencies that categorize a range of dilemmas. These competencies are defined on the basis of seven dimensions on which the values of diverse cultures vary. The same framework can be used to consider many business dilemmas (Table 5.3). These concepts are abstract but all exhibit bifurcation. Effective behaviours can be defined for each dimension.

Table 5.3 A framework for the 'millennium manager'

1. Universalism-particularism

A high-performing manager recognizes, respects and reconciles allegiance to rule-bound activity or unique circumstances.

In practice, dilemmas are typically between:

- Legal contracts and loose interpretations;
- Emphasis on globalism or localism;
- Human rights or special relationships;
- Low-cost strategies or premium strategy; and
- Extending rules or discovering exceptions.

Thus effective management lies not in the values of rule-making or exception-finding, but between these. How else can the rules be improved except by noting each exception and revising the rules accordingly? In complementarity, how else can exceptional abilities be developed than by noting the highest defined standards and exceeding them?

To their annoyance, managers promulgate a rule only to discover an exception. A scientist would believe he had failed. A boss would feel defied. A moralist would be against the sinfulness of it all. A 'millennium manager' would learn **from** it!

2. Individualism-communitarianism (collectivism)

A high-performing manager recognizes, respects and reconciles the individual employee development, enrichment and fulfilment or the extent the corporation and customers should be the beneficiaries of personal efforts.

In practice, dilemmas are typically between:

- Profit or market share strategy;
- Rights or duties;
- Egoism or altruism;
- Responsibility for self or others; and
- Originating ideas or refining useful products.

3. Neutral or affectivity

A high-performing manager recognizes, respects and reconciles the legitimacy of showing or controlling emotions.

Dilemmas can arise from:

- Being detached or enthusiastic;
- Long pauses or frequent interruptions; and
- Being professional or engaged.

4. Specific-diffuse

A high-performing manager recognizes, respects and reconciles the tendency to analyse and break down the field of experience or to synthesize, augment and construct the experience.

Dilemmas can arise from:

- The bottom line or general good will;
- Data and codification or concepts and models;
- Being results-oriented or process-oriented; and
- Facts or relationships.

5. Achieved or ascribed status

A high-performing manager recognizes, respects and reconciles why status is conferred on people.

Dilemmas can arise from:

- Pay for performance or vindication for worth;
- Status following success or status preceding success;
- Head-hunting or developing in-house; and
- Learning at school or learning through life.

→

Table 5.3 (*continued*)

6. Sequential or synchronic time
A high-performing manager recognizes, respects and reconciles different meaning and priority given to time passing in sequence or coming around and around.
Dilemmas can arise from:
• Highly rational, standardized production or just-in-time production;   • Keeping to schedule or being easily distracted; and   • Winning the race or shortening the course.
7. Inner or outer directed
A high-performing manager recognizes, respects and reconciles whether the locus of control is inside or outside the people involved. For the latter, it is the environment to which people must adapt.
Dilemmas can arise from being:
• Driven by conscience or responsive to outside influence;   • Strategically-oriented or fusion-oriented; and   • Dauntless entrepreneur or public benefactor.

Source: adapted from Trompenaars and Woolliams (2000): 25-27.

Case study 5.2 is a typical example of the cultural dilemma of achievement versus ascription.

Case study 5.2

In search of status

An English friend of mine had finished her studies in the most famous 'Grande Ecole' of commerce in France. She did both her undergraduate and her MBA studies there and then she was hired by a well-known consulting firm in London.

She worked there for four years and reached the level of senior consultant by the age of thirty-three. She was then given an assignment with an oil company based in Saudi Arabia. Until then, she had had no problems in communicating with the client's team-members and had always produced successful results, but she had enormous difficulties with this particular client.

She worked as hard as she could to figure out the structure of the company, its problems and possible solutions. Despite her efforts, however, she could feel that her opinions were not being taken seriously, and that senior managers of the client usually tried to avoid discussing issues with her. Moreover, she had difficulty in getting vital information from employees lower down in the hierarchy, so she was unable to come up with the analyses she wanted.

Although she felt she could really help the company with her knowledge and experience, she found it was difficult to persuade the client to put her ideas into practice. In fact, the better and more innovative her ideas were, the more difficult it was to get them over to the managers in Saudi Arabia.

Source: adapted from Browaeys and Trompenaars (2000): case 5.

Question

Do you agree with the statement given below? Why (not)? Use the example above to explain your standpoint.

At first sight it may appear that two extreme opposing values are contradictory, that they are a contradiction, but they are not. For example, universalism (adherence to well-developed and tested rules) and particularism (adapting rules to the particular situation) are not separate, but different. Situations are more or less similar to the rule, or more or less dissimilar and hence exceptional. Thus we cannot define rules without also knowing what the exceptions are.

Trompenaars' dimensions versus Hofstede's dimensions

Fons Trompenaars, a compatriot of Hofstede's, has on several occasions acknowledged his indebtedness to Hofstede. The seven dimensions he has developed may, at first glance, even look as if they are 'more of the same'. However, as this concept has shown, the nature of these dimensions is different and reflects irreconcilable differences in approach between these two Dutch stalwarts. This is very clear from the response which Trompenaars and co-author Charles Hampden-Turner (1997) gave to the review made by Hofstede (1996) of Trompenaar's model of national culture differences.

Having carried out an empirical analysis of Trompenaars' own data, Hofstede (1996) comes to the conclusion that the questionnaire used by Trompenaars is essentially measuring Hofstede's own individualism dimension by using dimensions that are interrelated. Hofstede questions Trompenaars' research method, claiming among other things that the latter had started his research using preconceived notions taken from mid-twentieth century US litera-ture and had not changed these concepts using the database Trompenaars compiled. Hofstede had concluded his review by implying that Trompenaars was less interested in scholarship, more in commerce: 'He tunes his messages to what he thinks the customer likes to hear.'

In their measured response to Hofstede's review, Hampden-Turner and Trompenaars (1997) concede that Hofstede has taught them a lot and that they basically respect the re-sults of his research. They staunchly defend their approach by giving a detailed account of the statistical methods used and which, they say, Hofstede should consider more carefully. They insist that he does not have the right when assessing their results to view his 'indepen-dent variables' as sovereign and to claim that other cultural concepts are derived from them. As for the question of 'preconceived notions' and implied lack of rigour, Hampden-Turner and Trompenaars strongly defend the US research literature, rejecting the idea that the many researchers whose work they drew on did no empirical research. If anything, it is continental Europe that is more concerned with 'an excess of rationalism and grand theo-ries'. They then turn to the questions Hofstede himself uses in his questionnaires: these are, they argue, borrowed from (or disguised versions of) questions used in various psycholog-ical profile tests used during the 1950s and 1960s in the US, a time when personality research was extremely popular.

As for the dimensions themselves, they consider Hofstede's pursuit of the least number of dimensions to account for observed differences to be 'one dimensional thinking' (1997: 158). Hampden-Turner and Trompenaars see cultures as 'dancing' from one preferred end of a dimension to another when encountering various dilemmas. In that sense, cultures are more like circles with 'preferred arcs joined together' rather than being Hofstede's linear forms where cultures are positioned high or low or in the middle. Faced with dilemmas, they argue, cultures attempt to integrate and reconcile values to come up with a satisfactory response. Their dimensions, they believe, are essentially 'heuristic devices' or speculative formulations that serve as a guide when investigations are being made into 'family resem-blances' between cultures when they are faced with dilemmas.

Rather than being 'the perfect model', which Hofstede is still seeking, Hampden-Turner and Trompenaars see theirs as a 'model-to-learn-with'. They can learn from their respondents – and vice-versa. Hofstede's search for perfection has, they maintain, slowed his learning and hindered renewal. Hampden-Turner and Trompenaars say they have moved on, as can be seen in Trompenaars recent publications, including *'Riding the Whirlwind: Connecting people and organizations in a culture of innovation'* (2007).

Reconciling dilemmas

The dilemmas outlined in each of the seven dimensions devised by Trompenaars and Hampden-Turner, and outlined earlier in this concept, require some kind of resolution. Trompenaars has explored and conceived a methodology which aims to reconcile what appear to be opposing values within each of the dimensions. This will be explained in the next concept of this chapter.

Concept 5.2 Reconciling cultural dilemmas

In his article, 'The practice of reconciliation', Fons Trompenaars (2000: 29–33) gives more consideration to the question of cultural dilemmas in the business context. He proposes a model that can be used to reconcile what appear to be values that conflict with each other:

When businesses cross cultures there are many potential situations in which the reconciliation of differences may be both desirable and necessary. The success of the business being conducted may depend on it. Reconciliation is part of building transcultural competence. There are three essential components of transcultural competence: awareness, respect and reconciling cultural differences.

Especially important are the processes of reconciliation. Without the confidence that reconciliation is possible, awareness can bring pain and frustration can emerge from respect. However, awareness and respect are necessary foundations for reconciling cultural differences. If people lack sufficient awareness of the differences that may exist between cultures, they may easily damage a relationship without intending to do so.

Cultural awareness is understanding states of mind, your own and the person being encountered. You can never be fully informed, since the permutations of options are countless. The seven-dimensional model of culture provides with frames of reference for analyzing ways in which people attribute meaning to the world.

Respect is most effectively developed once people recognize that most cultural differences are in themselves, but they have not recognized most of them. One could say that Westeners think the Japanese are mystics, at times even unreliable. It is difficult to know what they feel or think, they always say 'yes', even in cases where they might feel or think negatively about it. Yet, consider the case where a child has given a nervous and halting performance in her first solo in a school concert. She must go on again after the interval. Might her father not say 'Wonderful, darling' to give her confidence, although he did not actually believe her performance was good?

To sum up, both awareness and respect are necessary steps toward developing transcultural competence. But even their combined powers may not always suffice. People often ask questions such as: 'Why should only we respect and adapt to the other culture? Why don't they respect and adapt to ours?' Another, perhaps more interesting problem is that of mutual empathy (Bennett, 1979). What happens when one person attempts to shift to another culture's perspective when at the same time the other person is trying to do the same thing?

Motorola University recently prepared carefully for a presentation in China. After considerable thought, it was entitled: 'Relationships do not retire.' The gist of the presentation was that Motorola had come to China to stay and help the economy to create wealth.

Relationships with Chinese suppliers, sub-contractors and employees would constitute a permanent commitment to building Chinese economic infrastructure and earning hard currency through exports.

The Chinese audiences listened politely to the presentation, but were quiet when invited to ask questions. Finally, one manager put up his hand and said: 'Can you tell us about pay for performance?'

What was happening here is very common. Even as the Americans moved towards the Chinese perspective, the Chinese started to move towards theirs, and the two sides passed each other invisibly, like ships in the night. Remember that the Chinese who turn out for a presentation by a Western company, may already be pro-Western and see Western views as potentially liberating. This dynamic is especially strong when a country is small and poor. When a drug salesman from a US company meets with a health minister from Costa Rica, the former's salary may be ten times the latter's. The temptation to 'sell out' one's own culture is overwhelmingly strong and, of course, such encounters only harden prejudices. 'See, they all want to be like us.'

However, foreign cultures have integrity, which only some of its members will abandon. People who abandon their culture often become weakened and corrupt. Companies need foreigners to be themselves if partnership is to work. It is this very difference that makes the relationship valuable. Which is why people need to reconcile differences, to be themselves, but at the same time see and understand how the other's perspectives can help their own.

Once one is aware of one's own mental models and cultural predispositions, and once one can respect and understand that those of another culture are legitimately different, then it becomes possible to reconcile differences. Why do this? Because business people aim to create wealth and value, not just for themselves, but for those who live in different cultural worlds. People need to share the value of buying, selling, of joint venturing, of working in partnership.

How does reconciliation work?

In essence, the process of reconciliation leads to a dynamic equilibrium between seemingly opposed values, which make up a dilemma. In fact, reconciliation results in the integration of values through synergy. There are many ways of achieving synergy. The first one is *processing,* the activity in which a dilemma is made into two processes. So if the dilemma is central versus decentral it has to be turned into centralizing versus decentralizing. It is easier to reconcile verbs than nouns.

The second approach is called *contextualising.* Here, one has to decide what is text and what is context. For example, compare the names of two luxury hotels located in Amsterdam:

Le Meridien Apollo Hotel	AMSTEL HOTEL InterContinental

The Apollo Hotel is a member of the Le Meridien hotel group and uses the group's name as its main logo. The Amstel Hotel uses its name in capital letters, and shows its membership of the InterContinental hotels group after its name. Text and context change.

A third option is *sequencing.* You can first centralize and later decentralize. Every process of reconciliation is also a sequence. Finally, the process of *synergizing* is a way to reconcile. Synergizing is best explained by adding the word 'through' between the two opposite orientations. It is the answer to the question: 'How can we increase the quality of our central offerings through better learning from our decentralized operations?'

Reconciliation is preferred over other methods for dealing with cultural differences such as conflict, in which both parties may not benefit. Even compromise has its problems, because in a compromise both parties may still not get what they expected. Reconciliation permits both parties to maintain what is important to them, yet recognize the needs of the other.

Source: adapted from Trompenaars, 2000: 29-33.

The reconciliation approach opens the door to a third dimension, unblocks in some way the duality of the dilemma. In an intercultural business context, recourse to reconciliation may well avoid a situation ending in an impasse.

Getting to know the cultural framework of reference of one's interlocutors seems to be the best way of adapting to their culture(s) and their way of working. Chapter 6 offers an instrument to assist in this exploration.

ACTIVITY 5.1

Individual and group bonus plans: a case for reconciliation

The dilemma below explores the issue of reconciling a cultural dilemma in a business environment (adapted from Trompenaars, 2000: 31–32).

Jeff Mate was the human resources director of an Australian company in household appliances. In the last couple of years, Matehold had internationalized its operations. First, some activities had been transferred to the Mid-West of the USA and some research and development work was being done in the UK because of its excellent education system. Sales were promising, especially in the Pacific Rim markets. A subsidiary had been set up in Japan to develop operations there.

During an international human resources meeting, Jeff raised the question of the need for greater consistency among his colleagues. In the past, the Japanese had worked in Japan and the Americans had worked in the US. Now, however, multicultural teams were slowly being formed, with US, British, Japanese and Australian employees working together. The US HR manager and Jeff proposed an individual incentive system worldwide that would increase the staff's productivity. Mr Kataki from Japan saw big difficulties in implementing the individualized bonus system in the light of the predominantly team-oriented value system of the Japanese. This led to a heated discussion involving all the HR directors present.

In the evening, Jeff was asked to make a decision that would be respected by all.

Question

What would you do if you were in Jeff's position? Choose one of the options given below. Check your answer with your instructor.

1. I would implement the individual incentive programme. After all, everyone responds to individualized monetary rewards. The programme would be based on the success of the Australian employees who produced more effort since they had been recognized for their individual work. And it would improve consistency between the international operations.

2. a) I would recognize that the individual incentive programme alone would not be effective, given the communitarian orientation of some Asian staff.

   b) I would allow the company employees in Asia to choose a group-oriented incentive system in Asia and those working in the more individualistic parts of the world to choose a system based on individual incentives.

3. I would discuss the idea further with the HR staff, asking them to tell me what aspects of the incentive programme they thought would be worthwhile. I would then implement a worldwide programme in which one of the major individual incentives is based on how people support the group.

4. I would introduce a consistent plan worldwide that rewards the group, but which makes the team responsible for looking after individuals either who do not optimally support the group's production goals or who support individual inventiveness.

ACTIVITY 5.2

Read the following case and answer the questions that follow.

Expatriate's first job in Switzerland

Marcus, an American whose parents had been born in India, arrived in Zurich with his Swiss wife. They were both excited about starting a new chapter in their life together. After spending four years in San Diego, they were keen for a change, although Marcus had mixed feelings about job prospects for himself in Switzerland. Four months into their new environment they were elated when Marcus found a challenging new position at Kraft Jacobs Suchard, managing its international assignments programme.

Though this was now a US company (Jacobs Suchard having been acquired three years before) and quite a few expatriates of varying backgrounds worked in the Zurich regional head office where Marcus was posted, there were nevertheless some strong Swiss work attitudes that pervaded the work environment, much to the confusion and chagrin of Marcus.

One area of confusion and some conflict had to do with teamwork and the boundaries of job descriptions. A newcomer to a function or a department, as Marcus was, will have a rather steep learning curve for the first few months on the job. From this perspective, Marcus presumed that his new Swiss colleague Heidi would help with the vast amount of learning that he faced, particularly as there was no formal training for this posting. This was a natural assumption given that this is what he had experienced in various jobs in the US.

However, this was not to be the case in Zurich. Although Heidi did lend some assistance to Marcus (by telling him, for instance, when she normally had lunch), she made it plain that she considered giving any sort of training to Marcus to be beyond her job description. And she stuck to this position adamantly. This left Marcus in a quandary. How could he gain the knowledge he needed to be effective in this new job?

Another point of contention was overtime. Since the Zurich regional head office was in frequent contact with the head office in New York, Zurich staff had to stay later because of the time difference (Zurich is seven hours ahead of New York). During Marcus' interviews for the position, it was made clear that overtime would be required because of this time difference. Marcus did not feel this was unusual for someone in a salaried position, particularly since he had had similar experience dealing with different time zones when working in the US. Heidi, however, did not feel the same way. Her work responsibilities, she felt, ended at 5pm, prompt. Naturally, this left Marcus having to deal most evenings with the less uptight (relatively speaking of course) New Yorkers.

But was this fair? And how could Marcus achieve a more equitable work balance while at the same time build a working relationship with Heidi, whose knowledge he needed to become proficient in his job?

Source: Browaeys and Trompenaars (2000): case 9.

Questions

1. After reading the case, refer to Concept 5.1 and try to identify in which of the seven dimensions you can categorize the dilemma in question.

2. Prepare your answer to the question: 'How could Marcus achieve a more equitable work balance while at the same time build a working relationship with Heidi, whose knowledge he needed to become proficient in his job?'

3. EITHER

   a) Share your opinion with your peers and instructor

   OR

   b) Compare your answer with the author's analysis given below.

Author's analysis

This cultural dilemma is primarily to do with relationships between people. There is, however, a further dilemma that has to do with relationship to time – the overtime issue. From Trompenaars' seven dimensions, universalism versus particularism can provide an explanation. The universalist would typically apply rules and procedures more stringently, whereas a particularist would be more flexible in adapting to a situation.

In this case, it is clear that Heidi was taking a universalist approach towards her job description (and its boundaries), as well as to the question of overtime. Heidi found it difficult, if not impossible, to go beyond her job description boundary to provide Marcus with the training he required. Hers was a very strict interpretation of her job description, and she found it difficult to show flexibility in this situation.

Heidi also displayed a universalist approach with regard to working overtime. Again, she had a very strict interpretation of when her work time ended – promptly at 5pm. Marcus, accustomed to a particularist work environment, was confused and taken aback by this show of inflexibility. Heidi placed more importance on the rules, as exemplified by her job description and her interpretation of her work schedule, than on relationships. Marcus, on the other hand, presupposed that building relationships would have been given priority. And one might say he placed an exaggerated importance on this with it being his first job overseas and he was working in an unfamiliar environment in an unfamiliar job function.

A compromise between the two dilemmas is considered by Trompenaars as being worse than choosing one as opposed to the other. The universalist culture stays within the rules. The particularist culture builds relationships to gain knowledge and share work equally. The following would seem to be a more suitable option towards reconciliation between the two cultures: Marcus and Heidi need to find which knowledge to share and which job responsibilities to split up between them.

In particular, this means sharing the knowledge Heidi needs in exchange for the knowledge Marcus needs and dividing up job responsibilities in such a way that Heidi can finish work at 5pm.

Conclusion

This chapter has outlined the cultural dimensions devised by Trompenaars. These allow cultures to be classified according to certain values, as expressed in the way they confront dilemmas. These dimensions reflect the value-orientation concept proposed by Kluckholn and Strodtbeck since they take into account the relations with others, with nature and with the environment. These dimensions serve not only to distinguish national cultures, but also to show how the values they reflect can affect relations in business and management.

The cross-cultural manager has to face dilemmas. Dilemmas are universal, but the way they are resolved is determined culturally. Chapter 5 gives examples to demonstrate this point as well as the means to resolve them through the principle of reconciliation. The approach to dilemmas by means of reconciliation remains an interesting approach, especially since it takes into account the dynamics of cultures, i.e. the interaction between the interlocutors. Rather than the dimensions themselves, it is the concept of reconciliation that distinguishes the work of Trompenaars and Hampden-Turner from that of Hofstede.

Points for reflection

1. Many researchers in the area of cross-cultural management refer to authors whose disciplines are in the field of social sciences. These researchers appear to rely more on cultural theory than theories of management.

   Is this your opinion as well? Explain your response.

2. Trompenaars and Hampden-Turner consider their dimensions to be essentially 'heuristic devices' or speculative formulations that serve as a guide for investigations into 'family resemblances' between cultures when faced with dilemmas. Their perception of dimensions contrasts with what they term the linear nature of Hofstede's dimensions.

   In what other ways do the two sets of dimensions differ? To what extent do they resemble each other?

3. For cultural dilemmas in business, Trompenaars proposes the reconciliation method as a way of dealing with opposing values. If the definition of 'dilemma' is taken as 'a situation that requires a choice between options that are or seem equally unfavourable or mutually exclusive' (www.thefreedictionary.com/dilemma), **can the reconciliation method be used to resolve all dilemmas? Or do you consider that this approach can only be applied to cultural dilemmas?**

Further reading

Trompenaars, F. and Hampden-Turner, C. (1997) *Riding the Waves of Culture,* **2nd edn, London: Nicholas Brealey.** This book was first published in 1993. Additions to the second edition are significantly influenced by Charles Hampden-Turner's way of thinking. The authors added three new chapters: one on methodology for reconciling cultural dilemmas and two where they discuss diversity within, rather than between, countries.

Trompenaars Hampden-Turner, Culture for Business, www.7d-culture.nl. Website of the company run by Trompenaars and Hampden-Turner. The company provides consulting, training, coaching and (un) learning services to help leaders and professionals manage and solve their business and culture dilemmas.

Trompenaars, F. and Woolliams, P. (2003) *Business Across Cultures,* **Chichester, England: Capstone.** The aim of this book is to provide executives with a cross-cultural perspective on how companies meet the diverse needs of customers, investors and employees.

References

Bennett, M.-J. (1979) 'Overcoming the golden rule: sympathy and empathy' in Nimmo, D. (ed) *Communication Yearbook 3*, Austin, TX: International Communication Association.

Browaeys, M.-J. and Trompenaars, F. (eds) (2000) *Cases Studies on Cultural Dilemmas*, Breukelen, Netherlands: Nyenrode University Press.

Hampden-Turner, C. and Trompenaars, F. (1997) 'Response to Geert Hofstede', *International Journal of Intercultural Relations*, 21 (1): 149–159.

Hofstede, G. (1996) 'Riding the waves of commerce: a test of Trompenaars', *International Journal of Intercultural Relations*, 20 (2): 189–198.

Kluckholn, F. and Strodtbeck, F.L. (1961) *Variations in Value Orientations*, Connecticut: Greenwood.

Parsons, T. (1937) *The Structure of Social Action*, New York, NY: McGraw Hill.

Parsons, T. (1951) *The Social System*, New York, NY: Free Press. Quoted in Trompenaars, F. (1993) *Riding the Waves of Culture*, London: Economist Books: 8.

Trompenaars, F. (1997) *Riding the Waves of Culture*, 2nd edn, London: Nicholas Brealey.

Trompenaars, F. (2000) 'The practice of reconciliation', in Browaeys, M.-J. and Trompenaars, F. (eds), *Case Studies on Cultural Dilemmas*, Breukelen, Netherlands: Nyenrode University Press: 29–33.

Trompenaars, F. and Woolliams P. (2000) 'Competency framework for the millennium manager' in Browaeys, M.-J. and Trompenaars, F. (eds), *Case Studies on Cultural Dilemmas*, Breukelen, Netherlands: Nyenrode University Press: 21–28.

Trompenaars, F. (2007) *Riding the Whirlwind: Connecting people and organizations in a culture of innovation*, Oxford: The Infinite Ideas Co. Ltd.

Chapter 6

Culture and styles of management

In this chapter cultural values are presented that have been extracted from the dimensions examined in earlier chapters. These values are each characterized in bipolar terms and their influence on everyday business activities discussed.

The cultural values are presented as a model of culture that the reader will be asked to apply in one of Part One's final activities. Therefore, by the end of this chapter you will be expected to be able to establish your own cultural profile as a (future) manager, as well as to sketch the profiles of managers from other cultures.

Learning outcomes

After reading this chapter you should:

● Gain a clearer appreciation of the effect cultural values have on the way managers work.

● Understand how a number of management practices are shaped according to the cultural preferences of the managers concerned.

Concept 6.1 Management tasks and cultural values

There are many managerial activities performed across all societies on which cultural values have a considerable effect. The activities chosen below will be discussed in the light of cultural values.

Management tasks

The following management tasks and Table 6.1 to 6.8 are based on material in the participant workbook of *Doing Business Internationally* (1992):

1. **Planning**. This has to do with how the goals and objectives of a company or department are established, as well as determining what actions are needed to achieve them.

2. **Organizing**. This is a big responsibility of managers. They need to decide how the work involved is to be divided up and how it is to be co-ordinated. The use of the resources involved also requires careful organization to ensure effectiveness and efficiency.

3. **Staffing**. The task of allocating employees to particular positions within a company, as well as that of hiring suitable employees for particular responsibilities is demanding. It includes the concern they show for enabling people to fulfil their potential within the company.

4. **Directing**. This has to do with leading the organization and its employees towards its goals. How do managers relate to the employees, how they do they communicate with them, how do they supervise them?

5. **Controlling**. Monitoring the performance of a company or department is a task for which different cultures may use different systems and approaches. This goes also for the ways used to prevent problems or to resolve them. The differences reflect the relations between managers and employees as well as the way performance is perceived.

The way the above tasks and responsibilities are performed will be examined in the light of cultural values.

The effect of cultural values on management

A number of cultural values have emerged in previous chapters when cultural dimensions were being presented and discussed. Since the terminology used often varied, we have used the value concepts presented so far to compile our own list of cultural value orientations, which we judge as having a considerable influence on the way managers perform their activities. This list has been supplemented by other value orientations based on the works of other scholars, Hall in particular, whose ideas on time, space and communication have proved to be especially relevant to management activities.

Figure 6.1 presents the value orientations and characterizes the related values in bipolar terms to clarify the differences. It is intended to be used as a framework of reference when readers are attempting to understand some of the differences they may encounter when

Figure 6.1 A model of culture
Source: adapted from *Doing Business Internationally*, Participant Workbook: 2.3.

doing business internationally and when managing across cultures. This framework will also be used in the Final activity A1.1 of Part One, an activity aimed at developing cross-cultural effectiveness in an international context.

The eight cultural value orientations featured in the model will now be examined in turn.

1. Time focus (monochronic/polychronic)

Time is related to the rhythm of nature. Different cultures have different perceptions of time according to their environment, history, traditions and general practices. Time, therefore, is one of the fundamentals on which all cultures rest and around which all activities revolve.

Hall and Hall (1990) analyse differences in time systems among cultures. These authors distinguish two prominent time systems of particular relevance to management: mono-chronic and polychronic. In cultures where a monochronic perception of time prevails, time is experienced and used in a linear way. People tend to do one activity at a time and dislike having to moving away from a schedule. They are more focused on information than people, and their relations with others may suffer because they do not fit into the schedule of things to be done. In cultures where polychronic time is preferred, people tend to focus on several tasks and are less dependent on detailed information when performing these tasks. Schedules, if kept, are much more approximate and may be changed at any time. What is more important is involvement with other people – they take priority over schedules.

The differences in time focus as characterized in Table 6.1 can be seen in the role given to formal meetings. These may be used more to determine action points and deadlines or

Table 6.1 Characteristics of two attitudes to time

	Monochronic cultures	Polychronic cultures
1. Planning	The focus of activity is more on the task itself and making schedules	The focus of activity is more on relationship in planning
2. Organizing	The approach used is structured, linear and task-focused	The approach is a less structured one, more holistic in nature and people-focused
3. Staffing	Concerns are focused on the shorter term, meeting immediate needs and requirements	The focus is on the longer term, with concern for building relationships over time
4. Directing	The emphasis is on making and following plans, managing the inflow and distribution of detailed information	The emphasis is on being flexible, reacting according to (changed) circumstances, giving priority to people over plans, relying more on the sharing of implicit knowledge and information
5. Controlling	Tendency to use control systems that depend on detailed information and involve strict deadlines	Tendency to use more flexible control systems involving people as well as information

more as an opportunity to reflect on the company generally and to sound each other out on the way things are going or should be going. Actual decisions may come later through further (informal) consultation.

Cultures can also be categorized according to another aspect of time, namely a culture's orientation towards the past, present, and future.

2. Time orientation (past, present and future)

Cultures focused on the past value the upholding of tradition. Changes and plans are made according to whether or not they are in line with the history of the company and the way it usually does things. Those cultures concerned with the present are out for quick results and short-term gain. Those with a view towards the future are more likely to give up short-term gains when there is the prospect of more substantial long-term benefits. Any changes or plans are therefore assessed in the light of expected future benefit.

Hall and Hall (1990) emphasize the importance of knowing which parts of the time frame are given prominence in which areas of the world. They see that countries in the Far East, as well as India and Iran, have cultures oriented towards the past. On the American continent, however, they consider the culture of the urban US to be more oriented towards the present and short-term future, while the cultures of Latin America, are both past and present-oriented.

These differences in values (Table 6.2) can be perceived in many activities, particularly when it comes to negotiations. Those who are 'past-oriented' may be more intent on compensating for previous losses or regaining past successes rather than aiming for a

Table 6.2 Time orientation and management skills

	Past orientation	Future orientation
1. Planning	The emphasis is on continuing traditions and building in long-term time frames if the plan is for a change process	The emphasis is on longer-term plans and long-term results
2. Organizing	Organizational decisions are made within the context of the customs of the society. Past goals and precedents guide the process of organizing	Work and resources are divided and co-ordinated to meet longer-range goals and projections for the future
3. Staffing	Management are slower in adapting the criteria by which they select and train employees	Management select and train employees to meet long-term business goals
4. Directing	Tendency to develop vision and mission statements that emphasize the continuation of the company's values and reputation	Tendency to develop vision and statements which focus on achieving long-term benefits
5. Controlling	Tendency to develop performance objectives in keeping with customary goals	Tendency to develop performance objectives in the context of long-term goals

Exhibit 6.1

Plan your time

Without planning, you'll never have the time for anything. Yes, initially, you may have to spend even more time to make time – but that is a sensible, positive investment. You have to take control of the time at your disposal and decide how you want to spend it. Time is a resource to be husbanded in the same way as you would treat raw materials or finished goods or stock in the business. Time also costs money. So if you have only a finite amount of time, and that time is expensive, it is crucial to plan out how it's going to be spent to most effect. This means clarifying the main purpose of your job.

Ask yourself: what am I here for? Those whose answers identify or match the purpose of the organization for which they work can award themselves several gold stars. Yes. Your purpose is to assist the organization in achieving its objectives, regardless of whether your job function is that of data processing manager, senior welfare officer, sales director or typing pool supervisor. Being organized will help you to achieve those objectives. Having a plan is the first step on the way to that achievement.

Source: Video Arts (1984) *So You Think You Can Manage?* London: Methuen: 20.

resolution that all those involved find acceptable. Plans for the future will tend to be based on past experiences rather than expectations whereby employees are entrusted with responsibility for what happens in the future. See Exhibit 6.1.

3. Power (hierarchy and equality)

The power value orientation is to do with the extent to which the less powerful members of a society expect and accept that power is distributed unequally. As Mead indicates (1994: 66) it is in this area that a culture shows the extent to which it 'tolerates and fosters pecking orders, and how actively members try to reduce them'.

In some cultures, inequality is a given and no attempt is made to make any compensations on a socio-economic level for intellectual or physical inequalities. In other cultures, inequality is regarded as undesirable, necessitating some form of correction through legal, political and economic means.

At work, the level of power and authority are strictly marked out by cultures oriented to hierarchy. There, the employees do their work according to the directives of their boss. In their eyes, the role of the manager is to allocate tasks and to take decisions.

During negotiations, title, status and formal position have less influence in cultures oriented towards equality. There, the hierarchy exists essentially to facilitate the relations between the people in an organization. Managers see their role as more participative than directive. They are more likely to consult employees before taking decisions (Table 6.3).

In companies oriented towards equality there will be more informal structures based on expertise or focused on certain projects. However, hierarchy may still be there below the surface. When risks have to be taken or when there is a budgetary crisis, those with formal

Table 6.3 Effects of hierarchy

	Hierarchy	Equality
1. Planning	More autocratic or paternalistic planning is displayed, in which managers make decisions without consulting employees	Employees may implement the plan in the way they believe is the most appropriate. More participative planning is displayed
2. Organizing	The organizational structure is tightly controlled. Authority and responsibility are centralized	The organizational structure encourages individual autonomy. Authority is decentralized to the lowest possible level
3. Staffing	Subordinates expect bosses to take the initiative to train, develop and promote them	Work relationships should not be strictly prescribed in terms of appropriate/inappropriate behaviours and roles
4. Directing	Leaders are expected to behave in ways that reinforce their importance. Employees like being closely supervised and feel comfortable with a directive supervisor	Managers exhibit participative or consultative styles. In boss-subordinate communications, employees are not afraid to disagree with their managers
5. Controlling	Employees prefer the personal control of superiors over impersonal control systems	Subordinates tend to like working with their bosses to develop, implement, monitor and alter performance objectives

authority may well re-assert their power. An organization with a formal hierarchy that adopts certain features of equality in the way it is run will always feel the tension between control and empowerment.

4. Competitiveness (Competition)

Management may well encourage competition in an organization, particularly where the environment is that of a 'free market'. It encourages employees to take responsibility for the organization's survival and can be crucial in stimulating innovation and developing markets. When competitiveness is valued, the culture is focused on acquiring wealth, performing well and achieving ambitions. The success of a project is determined only by the profit it makes. In other cultures, however, job satisfaction has less to do with making money and more to do with working in a pleasant environment. Here, competition is not so highly valued and not considered to be the main purpose of business. Instead, co-operation is preferred, with the stress on the quality of life, relationships and consensus (Table 6.4).

A company operating in a competitive, dynamic market, but which is keen to maintain or develop co-operation among its staff, will experience a tension between opposing values similar to that felt during other management activities mentioned earlier. Nevertheless, the company will wish to promote creativity among its employees through competition while, at the same time, encouraging co-operation between its employees to ensure effective running of the organization.

Table 6.4 Co-operation and competition

	Competitive	Co-operative
1. Planning	The emphasis is on speed and task performance when implementing plans	Emphasis is on maintaining relationships in plan implementation
2. Organizing	Individual achievement is allowed and encouraged in organizing the work. Managers have more of a leadership role	Group integration is permitted, together with maintenance of a positive working environment and convenient schedules. Managers have more of a facilitating role
3. Staffing	Employees are selected on their ability to act independently	Employees are selected for their ability to work well in groups
4. Directing	The leader's role is to track and reward achievement. The stress involved in the work is generally higher	The leader's role is to facilitate mutually beneficial relationships
5. Controlling	Systems that are predominantly performance-based are preferred	Task performance is recognized as a standard for success; however, other standards are also considered important, including team effectiveness

5. Activity (action: doing or being)

Kluckhohn and Strodtbeck (1961) place 'activity' in their value orientation system because they consider this to be one of the universal human problems. They see every method of human expression as resulting in some form of activity (not in the active or passive sense) which, in turn, shows a preference towards a 'being' or 'doing' orientation (Table 6.5).

Table 6.5 Two approaches to 'activity'

	Doing cultures	Being cultures
1. Planning	Tends to be done by developing measurable, time-framed action steps	Tends to be done with a strong focus on the vision or ideal a company wishes to attain
2. Organizing	Involves developing action-oriented documentation for project management in which task responsibilities are clearly spelled out	Based more on the assumption that implementation is not so much dependent on action steps as on common vision and personal trust
3. Staffing	Account is not necessarily taken of a person's worth beyond his or her ability to carry out organizational tasks	Career development is usually based not only on performance but also on other standards, such as personal or social criteria
4. Directing	Managers are considered to be effective if they have the necessary expertise and competence	Managers are considered to be effective if their personal philosophy, values and style are seen as compatible
5. Controlling	The focus is not only on the tasks to be done, but also on the ways in which they are done. Management of performance is carried out systematically	The focus is less on efficiency and more on effectiveness and adaptability. Management of performance measurement tends to be less systematic

If the orientation is towards being, then this is 'a spontaneous expression of what is conceived to be 'given' in the human personality'. The doing orientation, on the other hand, prefers 'a kind activity which results in accomplishments that are measurable by standards conceived to be external to the acting individual'.

The stress in doing cultures is placed on action and achieving personal goals. Prime motivators are recognition of achievement and promotion. In being cultures, the stress is placed on working for the moment and living the experience rather than achievement itself. The prime motivator is the promise of future rewards while maintaining social harmony.

The contrast between these two types of culture can come clearly to the fore when decisions are being taken during meetings. In a being culture, the status of the 'boss' is unquestioned: it is he who makes the decision. In a doing culture, everybody attending the meeting has a role to play, and these roles can change according to the type of decision, the expertise and experience available. The 'boss' may take the final decision on the basis of the information and analysis emerging during the meeting, or may even delegate the decision to those he considers more competent.

6. Space (private or public)

One aspect of space orientation relates to what is to be regarded as private and public space (Table 6.6). In some cultures, a house, car, refrigerator is not open to public view, in others some or all of these are. Another aspect relates to the invisible boundary around every person, a 'comfort zone'. If this zone is crossed, people feel uneasy or even under threat. In some cultures, this zone is much narrower than in others. The proximity of people in conversation, for example, may be much closer in one culture than in another.

This concept of space can be seen in terms of personality, as Hoecklin (1995: 44) notes when reviewing Trompenaars' dimension of 'specific versus diffuse relationships':

Table 6.6 The influence of personal space

	Private	Public
1. Planning	Tendency to use more individualistic or systematic forms of planning	Public space cultures tend to use more group-oriented or authoritative forms of planning
2. Organizing	The approaches used tend to centre on tasks	The approaches used tend to be more centred on relationships
3. Staffing	The information about how staff are to be employed is more explicit	The information about how staff are to be employed is more implicit
4. Directing	Managers and employees do not share the same office	The location or size of the place where an employee works does not necessarily reflect that person's rank in the company
5. Controlling	Since managers are separated spatially from their employees, they need to use more explicit measures of performance	Managers can use more informal checks on performance

Every individual has various levels to their personality, from a more public level to the inner, more private level. However, there can be cultural differences in the relative size of people's public and private 'spaces' and also in the degree to which they feel comfortable sharing those parts of their personality with other people.

In cultures that are more specific in nature, there are large public spaces or spheres where personal matters are openly discussed, where family worries and individual failings are revealed for all to comment on. Private spheres, however, are very small and not easily penetrated (Exhibit 6.2).

Exhibit 6.2

Private business

A European manager may find himself getting invited by his Chinese business partner to the latter's home, his private space. By doing so, the Chinese is hoping to get to know his partner well with a view to establishing a close relationship. This can prove to be an important basis for (more) business deals.

In more diffuse cultures, public spaces are smaller and more formal, access to which is not easy for strangers. However, once a member of a diffuse culture accepts someone, then that person will be given access to a larger private sphere.

7. Communication (high-context or low-context)

When investigating communication between different cultures, Hall introduced the concept of context and described the role it plays in the communication process (Table 6.7). Context relates to the framework, background and surrounding circumstances in which communication or an event takes place. He distinguishes between high context and low context messages:

> A high context (HC) communication or message is one in which most of the information is already in the person, while very little is in the coded, explicit, transmitted part of the message. A low context communication (LC) is just the opposite; i.e., the mass of the information is vested in the explicit code.
>
> Hall and Hall, 1990: 6

When applying this concept to cultures, he sees the US as a low-context country, because the messages conveyed generally, and in business in particular, are usually clear and explicit. Japan, however, is a high context country, where the most important part of any information is 'hidden' in the text; the situation in which the communication takes place carries most of the information.

Although Hall does not rank countries in terms of their degree of LC or HC, Figure 6.2 reflects the qualitative insights of Hall himself as well as of other scholars in cross-cultural communication as to where certain countries lie on the context dimension.

At one end of the dimension are a number of countries in Asia, at the other a number of Northern European countries, as well as the US. To illustrate the contrast between the two ends of this spectrum. Hall and Hall (1990) describe a typical scene in a US office and

Table 6.7 Communication and context

	Low-context	High-context
1. Planning	Low-context cultures develop plans that are explicit, detailed, quantifiable and information-based	High-context cultures develop plans that are more implicit and less detailed in terms of instructions
2. Organizing	Task-responsibility guidelines are explicit: they are detailed and understood through verbal or written instruction	Job descriptions and responsibilities are implicit and understood according to the context
3. Staffing	Detailed contracts of employment and explicit performance appraisals	The criteria and methods for recruitment, selection, pay and firing are not explicit, nor is the appraisal process
4. Directing	Managers get work done through others by outlining specific goals and ways to achieve them. Communication is explicit and conflict is depersonalized	In high-context cultures, managers get work done through others by giving attention to relationships and group processes. Conflicts must be resolved before work can progress
5. Controlling	Control is more task-driven in accordance with monitoring and control procedures used to ensure performance objectives	Control is more process-driven. Information regarding the various aspects of control is embedded in the cultural context

compare it with one in a French or Japanese office. When an American company director is in his office, he has to work through a stream of pre-arranged appointments, with visitors usually entering the office one at a time. The information needed to do the job comes from a small group of people seen through the day as well as from memos and reports he reads. The flow of information is controlled by supervisors and assistants. Hall then describes the

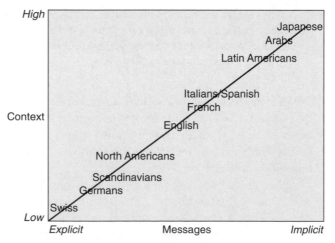

Figure 6.2 Messages and context (adapted from Hall)
Source: Usunier (1993): 103.

equivalent office day in a high-context country such as France or Japan. People are constantly entering and leaving the office, both giving and requesting information:

> . . . the entire form and function of the organization is centred on gathering, processing and disseminating information. Everyone stays informed about every aspect of the business and knows who is best informed on what subjects.
>
> Hall and Hall, 1990: 9

This high/low context orientation will be dealt with further in Part Three.

8. Structure (individualism or collectivism)

The term 'structure' refers to a social structure or, in business terms, an organizational structure, which allows management to distinguish uncertain situations, ambiguity, stress and risk (Table 6.8). This particular value orientation concerns the relation between the individual and the group.

According to Kluckhohn and Strodtbeck (1961), individualism shows the extent to which cultures elevate the role of the individual over the role of the group. When individualism is valued, the 'I' predominates over the 'We'. Individual goals, initiative and achievement are most important and people are encouraged to be independent and self-reliant. There is less need to conform to a group and less distinction made between in-groups and out-groups. Individuals frequently acquire and change their friends and do not hesitate to establish preferred relationships among family relatives.

Table 6.8 Structure and activities

	Individualism	Collectivism
1. Planning	It is expected that those involved in planning will take the initiative to present their views	Plans are developed within the shared values used for measuring and justifying activities in the organization
2. Organizing	Organizational structures emphasize the individual in tasks assignments and resources allocation	Organizational structures emphasize the group; the team is assigned tasks and resources
3. Staffing	Organizations are not expected to look after their employees' career development	Promotion is based primarily on seniority. Managers are evaluated according to how well they conform to organizational or group norms
4. Directing	Leaders expect employees to meet or exceed their responsibilities and defend their own interests. Management entails managing individuals	Leaders expect loyalty in exchange for protection. Group or top-down decisions are the norm, with the leader in quiet control
5. Controlling	Control tends to be exerted by individual standards of excellence. Fear of losing self-respect discourages deviance from standards	Deviation from standards and expectations is discouraged through group-oriented pressure

Exhibit 6.3

Christopher Earley, a US management researcher, gave 48 management trainees from southern China and a matched group of 48 management trainees from the US an 'in-tray task' consisting of 40 items requiring between two and five minutes each (Earley, 1989). The task involved such activities as writing memos evaluating plans and rating job candidates' application forms. Half of the participants from each country were given an individual goal of 20 items; the other half were given a group goal of 200 items to be completed in one hour by 10 people. In addition, half of the participants from either country, both from the group and from the individual goal subsets, were asked to mark each item with their name; the other half turned them in anonymously. The Chinese, collectivist, participants performed best when operating with a group goal and anonymously. They performed worst when operating individually and with their name marked on their work. The individualist US participants performed best when operating individually and with their work attributed to them personally, and performed very poorly when operating as a group and anonymously.

Source: Hoecklin, 1995: 37

Collectivism shows the extent to which the interests of the group prevail over individual interests. Each person in a collectivist society is encouraged to conform, to do what is best for the group and to avoid expressing opinions or beliefs that go against it. Reluctance to co-operate within the group or eagerness to stand out is frowned upon. Clearer distinctions are made between in-groups and out-groups. Relationships are more constant both within and outside the family.

This concept has led to a number of cultural value orientations and presented extreme differences between the values within each orientation. Sometimes, of course, the differences between (some) cultural values may not be as extreme as the differences presented here, so that some sort of accommodation can be made between the representatives of the cultures in question. On the other hand, the contrasts may be such that co-operation is extremely difficult.

Concept 6.2 Other views on values

The previous concept outlined the cultural values and the way they are reflected in management. Values are what people essentially share in a particular culture, what helps them co-exist. Hofstede emphasizes their durability, as does Trompenaars. The latter's dilemma approach, however, acknowledges that in dealing with foreign cultures it may be necessary to talk of reconciliation whereby the parties involved recognize each other's needs while maintaining their own values. As seen in Chapter 5, this process may, according to Trompenaars, entail the development of a third dimension in which the values of the parties concerned are integrated through close synergy. This is a much more productive way of addressing the either/or nature of a cultural dilemma than trying to resolve it through making weak compromises.

This idea of integrating values is much less clear-cut in nature than that of trying to find a trade-off of values during cultural collisions. The complex and unpredictable nature of this integration process, however, seems to reflect much more faithfully the nature of present-day international business and the increasing interdependence between countries and business sectors across the globe.

This interdependence between cultures has led some cross-cultural scholars to question the stability of cultures generally and cultural values in particular. Søderberg and Holden (2002), for example, refer to a recent dynamic approach to the way culture is conceptualized in terms of relations between people rather than in terms of stable sets of values. The cultural identity of people is determined by the context:

> This relational approach to culture and to cultural complexity and the idea of cultural complexity suggest that every individual embodies a unique combination of personal, cultural and social experiences, and thus that ultimately any communication and negotiation is intercultural.
>
> Søderberg and Holden, 2002: 112

The consequence of this standpoint is that making a standard cultural profile is impossible because it ultimately reflects only constructs based on 'the practitioners' and the researchers' own cultural thought patterns and the concepts and categories they are socialized to.

Increasing consideration is therefore being given to the notion of culture as a sharing of 'patterns of meaning and interpretation' (Søderberg and Holden, 2002: 112) resulting from interaction with others. Rather than there being stable cultural communities, there are groups sharing such patterns who, when interacting with others whose patterns they can identify with, may take them on board, be it in adapted form, and/or negotiate a shared meaning and interpretation.

Managers who are involved in globalization may relate to this concept much more readily than to the fixed dimensions of culture as described in Part One. They will see their role as more to do with ensuring that the interaction within multicultural teams is effective and reaping synergetic rewards. Rather than being a matter of dealing with cultures in isolation, their work is 'the management of multiple cultures' (Søderberg and Holden, 2002: 110), thereby ensuring that 'knowledge, values and experience are transferred into multicultural domains of implementation' (page 113).

Earley (2006) is another scholar who sees the concept of culture related to the context, to interaction with others. He is adamant about wanting to avoid what he calls the 'cultural quagmire' of the cultural dimension construct whereby cultural values are an aggregate of individual perceptions and therefore contradict the construct itself (page 924). 'Culture', Earley claims, 'is not a value or set of values; culture is the meaning which we attach to aspects of the world around us' (page 925). Values as culture remains what Earley calls the 'obsession' of cross-cultural research. They should, he maintains, be more focused on meaning as culture. Values are only one element allowing meaning to be attached to the environment. Rather than developing even more value-based classifications on a grand scale, he proposes (more) research based on the concept of culture as a psychological construct whereby an individual is subject to a number of influences. Earley shows how this ties in with a definition of culture made by Rohner (1984: 119–120):

> The totality of equivalent and complementary learned meanings maintained by a human population, or by identifiable segments of the population, and transmitted from one generation to the next.

What is needed, Earley says, is the development of theories and framework that 'link culture to action', which can be used to understand 'the linkage among cultures, perceptions, actions, organizations, structures, etc.' (Earley, 2006: 928). At the heart of this lies the individual, not societies and their 'average tendencies' (the term used by Hofstede to describe the nature of cultural dimension scores).

After reviewing work done to establish the linkage described above, Earley (2006) points to the work done by several authors, including Earley himself, on the 'cultural intelligence' construct. This approach to studying cultural differences examines the extent to which individuals are able to adapt to cultural settings. The focus moves from the context of interaction (such as shared values and meanings) to the behaviour of the individual and the (meta-) cognitive processing involved. Earley admits this approach needs considerable development, but believes it offers a promising way to examine how individual actions are affected by culture.

A number of Earley's ideas are reflected in Chapter 18 where consideration is given to the notion of intercultural communicative competence.

One final activity in Part One provides you the opportunity to reflect on your own cultural values as well as those of others. This reflection will, it is hoped, allow you to develop a clear definition of your own style of working.

ACTIVITY 6.1

Read the case study below, based on the experiences of Larry Zeenny in the Lebanon. It concerns a football agent's attempt to make a deal for his client. When you have read it, answer the questions that follow.

An own goal

The taxi arrived at the impressive mansion in Faqra and I made my way through the blistering sun towards the entrance. I was met by two servants and directed to Mr Haider's room. He had faxed me a contract, the terms of which were ridiculously low, and I was determined to get a better deal for my client.

A peek at my watch revealed it was 11.30. I'd arrived just in time, despite the flight delays at Frankfurt and the queues at Beirut airport. In front of Haider's door I cleared my throat, tightened my tie, gathered all my courage and entered the room. 'Mr Haider, I am delighted to meet you', I said, rather too exuberantly. 'Ahlan Wilhelm, welcome my friend,' said Haider. 'The president will be here in a moment. Please make yourself at home while you're waiting.'

A servant led me to a large room where there were two men and, in the far corner, a beautiful oriental woman. I sat down in a chair and waited for Mr Haider. An elaborate clock chimed twelve, but there was still no sign of him. By now the other three were thoroughly enjoying their lunch, which I had refused out of politeness. To keep my nerves steady I had only accepted a glass of arak. By 12.15 my patience had started to desert me. I was going to be too late for my next meeting. How could I trust Mr Haider if he had already broken his promise beforehand?

Eventually, at 12.30, Mr Haider entered the room. He looked extremely relaxed in his traditional dress and I jumped up to greet him. Before approaching me he first kissed both men and had a brief conversation with the woman. I had prepared myself well for this moment. I gave him a firm handshake and seated myself.

'Ahlan Larry, welcome to Lebanon,' he said. Looking at the table, he added: 'I hope you enjoyed your delicious lunch with my beloved sons, Alain and Elie, and of course with my habibi, Charlotte.'

'Mr Haider,' I replied, 'Thank you for your warm reception, but I ate on the plane. My client is extremely pleased about your interest and he is looking forward to playing for such an illustrious club as Al Ansar. Shall we come to terms as quickly as possible so we can finalize this matter in the best interest of both parties?'

'Shouf Wilhelm,' he retorted. 'Please call me Hashem. But why the rush? We have the time for business until the sun walks out on us! When will your client arrive?'

I told him that my client, a goalkeeper who had played for German, Italian and British teams, as well as for his home country, Denmark, would be unable to attend the negotiations. 'The thing is' (I hesitated: how could I call him by his first name and show my total respect?) 'It's usual for a player to leave such dealings to his agent.'

Mr Haider seemed disgruntled, but agreed to talk. He called his two sons over while his wife quietly headed for the door. As she passed by I respectfully looked her in the eye and wished her a pleasant day.

The bargaining process began and, quite disconcertingly, Mr Haider's sons joined in. Was he hoping to get the upper hand through force of numbers? Could I trust his sons to honour the confidentiality aspect of the negotiation? I was concerned details would leak out to the predators from the international press. After an hour we had reached an impasse, but I couldn't really understand why. Mr Haider refused to provide me with a bank guarantee with respect to my client's salary and signing-on fee. In fact, Mr Haider persistently refused to go into financial matters. These could be discussed the next day, he insisted, since they would not be a problem as far as he was concerned.

But for me they were the problem. And that was why we had reached a stalemate.

Questions

1. What is the significance of the title of this case?

2. How would you define the problem from your perspective?

3. What do you think has caused the so-called stalemate? Refer to the cultural values outlined in this chapter which have had an impact on the way the agent handled his encounter with Mr Haider. Mention, in particular, issues relating to:
   - time focus;
   - competitiveness;
   - activity;
   - space;
   - communication; and
   - structure

4. How do you think Wilhelm can rescue the deal?

5. How can Wilhelm best prepare for any future negotiations in the Middle East on behalf of his football clients?

Conclusion

This chapter has shown the link between theory and practice. Definitions based on research in the field of culture and management have enabled a model of culture to be developed. This model has been applied to the world of international business and the daily tasks of a manager examined in terms of cultural values. The assumption underlying this study is that an individual's framework of cultural preferences influences the way in which their tasks are executed. The case given in this chapter's activity gives an example of this.

Such cultural models, however, may well be too constrictive in nature, particularly when applied to management. By giving the viewpoints of several writers who question the validity of such models, this chapter has given its readers food for thought concerning the application of cultural values to management behaviour, particularly since they do not take account of what may happen when (different) cultures interact.

Points for reflection

1. The concept gives a range of eight cultural values that could affect five management skill areas.

   Can you suggest other cultural value ranges that could be applied? Are there other management skill areas to which these values could apply?

2. There are those who think that when doing business internationally it is necessary to follow certain professional codes of behaviour, such as keeping to deadlines, meeting delivery dates and obeying terms of contract. There are others, however, who consider that business culture rather than business convention has a greater influence on the way people work internationally or otherwise. Managers operating internationally therefore need to take cultural differences into account.

   Which standpoint do you support? Explain why and give examples on the basis of your experience or analysis.

3. You have seen how culture can affect management.

   Apart from being aware of this, what else do you think is needed to perform successfully in a cross-cultural context?

4. Earley argues that culture has less to do with determining values and more to do with meanings. When doing so, he refers to Rohner's definition of culture: 'The totality of equivalent and complementary learned meanings maintained by a human population, or by identifiable segments of the population, and transmitted from one generation to the next.'

   Compare this definition of culture with that made by Hofstede (Chapter 1): 'The collective programming of the mind which distinguishes the members of one human group from another'.

   In which ways do you consider these definitions to be complementary and/or oppositional in nature?

Further reading

Earley, P.C. and Mosakowski, E. (2004) 'Cultural intelligence', *Harvard Business Review,* vol 82 (October): 139-146. This article describes what the authors claim to be the three sources of cultural intelligence. After giving six cultural intelligence profiles to enable readers to assess which one describes them, the authors suggest ways cultural intelligence can be cultivated.

Hall, E.T. and Hall, M.R. (1990) *Understanding Cultural Differences,* **Maine: Intercultural.** Although this book was written primarily for business people, it is oriented towards interpersonal relations with foreigners so it is useful for many other people whose lives involve contact with foreign nationals, either in their personal or professional lives.

Hoecklin, L. (1995) *Managing Cultural Differences: Strategies for comparative advantage,* **Wokingham: Addison-Wesley.** The book explores the effect of culture on each business area and provides a framework for considering cultural factors. The research findings help to clarify what can go on in international management.

References

Doing Business Internationally: The cross-cultural challenges (1992) Participant Workbook, Princeton, NJ: Princeton Training Press.

Earley, C.P. (1980) 'Social Loafing and Collectivism: A comparison of the United States and the People's Republic of China', *Administrative Science Quarterly,* 34: 565–581.

Earley, P.C. (2006) 'Leading cultural research in the future: a matter of paradigms and taste', *Journal of International Business Studies,* 37: 922–931.

Hall, E.T. and Hall, M.R. (1990) *Understanding Cultural Differences,* Yarmouth, ME: Intercultural.

Hoecklin, L. (1995) *Managing Cultural Differences: Strategies for comparative advantage*, Wokingham: Addison-Wesley.

Hofstede, G. (1991) *Cultures and Organizations: Software of the mind,* London: McGraw-Hill.

Kluckholn, F. and Strodtbeck, F.L. (1961) *Variations in Value Orientations*, Westport, CT: Greenwood.

Mead, R. (1994) *International Management: Cross-cultural dimensions,* Cambridge, MA; Oxford: Blackwell Business.

Rohner, R.P. (1984) 'Toward a conception of culture from cross-cultural psychology', *Journal of Cross-Cultural Psychology,* 15 (2): 111–138.

Søderberg, A.-M. and Holden, N. (2002) 'Rethinking cross cultural management in a globalising business world', *International Journal of Cross Cultural Management,* 2 (1): 103–121.

Video Arts (1984) *So you think you can manage?* London: Methuen.

Developing cross-cultural effectiveness

The concepts presented in Part One have allowed a framework of reflection and knowledge to be developed about national cultures and businesses cultures. Part One has also shown how close the relations are between culture and management.

Such insights are essential for working and succeeding in an environment different to one's own. However, it is not enough to learn the different styles of doing business inherent to certain culture(s). International managers also need to develop personal capabilities, particularly cultural analysis skills which will enable them to operate effectively in a variety of cultural contexts.

Learning outcomes

After completing this activity, you will be able to:

- Analyse the effect of cultural variables in business and management practices.
- Adapt business skills to work across different cultures.

INTRODUCTION

There are three steps in developing cross-cultural effectiveness (*Doing Business Internationally*, 1992: 2.32):

- **Step one:** *Self-awareness: gaining insight into your own culture.* It is necessary to analyse yourself, to discover your own style with respect to the eight cultural variables in Figure 6.1.
- **Step two:** *Cross-cultural understanding: understanding the culture of others.* Acquiring knowledge and understanding of the national culture and the business culture of the society or country in question is a requirement, as is insight into its preferences in terms of the cultural variables given in Figure 6.1.
- **Step three:** *Adapting your professional skills to the culture and working style of the society or country in question.* Account needs to be taken of both the preferences within each cultural variable and the effect of these variables on working styles. Furthermore, strategies need to be established to enable a manager to succeed in the country in question.

ASSIGNMENT

The assignment involves:

- Making a cultural profile of yourself (step one as described above) and a profile of another culture (as described in step two). To facilitate this task, your instructor can download a Microsoft Excel file entitled 'Cultural Profile' from the website dedicated to this book.
- Making a comparison of the differences between your own culture and another culture.

- Making an analysis of the main differences in cultural values and the way they change management roles.
- Determining the management strategies needed to make a success of your job in the country chosen.

Step one: self-awareness

The first step is to identify your own cultural values by making your own cultural profile:

1. Refer back to Figure 6.1. The figure summarizes a model that can be used to establish a cultural profile.
2. Re-read, if necessary, the definitions of the cultural parameters in Chapter 6.
3. Make your own cultural profile by giving a score for the eight cultural parameters given in the Excel document entitled 'Cultural Profile'. Create your own profile in the spread sheet. A version of the (uncompleted) Excel sheet is given in Table A1.1.1. You are required to enter a score against each parameter that reflects your own value on a range of 1 to 5.

Table A1.1.1 Make your own profile

Parameter	Value = 1	Value = 5	Your score (from 1 to 5)
Time focus	monochronic	polychronic	
Time orientation	past	future	
Space	private	public	
Power	equality	hierarchy	
Structure	individualism	collectivism	
Competition	co-operative	competitive	
Communication	low context	high-context	
Action	being	doing	

These values can be plotted on a profile diagram (Figure A1.1.1).

Figure A1.1.1 Step-one profile

Step two: cross-cultural understanding

The second step is to analyse the preferences of the culture in which you are going to do business. How do you perceive the culture of this country?

1. Choose another country where you know some of its inhabitants. Collect relevant documentation on this country.

2. Make up the cultural profile of the country you have chosen in a similar way as your own by giving a score for the eight cultural parameters in the cultural profile document (Excel sheet). See the examples of cultural profiles in Table A1.1.2 and Figure A1.1.2.

Table A1.1.2 Your cultural profile score and that of chosen country

Parameter	Value = 1	Value = 5	Your score	Other score
Time focus	monochronic	polychronic	1	5
Time orientation	past	future	3	3
Space	private	public	1	4
Power	equality	hierarchy	2	5
Structure	individualism	collectivism	1	4
Competition	co-operative	competitive	5	1
Communication	low-context	high-context	1	5
Action	being	doing	4	2

Figure A1.1.2 Step-two profile: own and chosen country

3. Compare your own cultural profile with the profile of the culture that you are going to work with:

   ● What are the differences and the similarities in which parameters?

   ● What, in your view, are the critical issues when representatives of the two cultures profiled work together?

Step three: adapt your professional skills

Cultural preferences (Figure 6.1) affect the way you perceive and perform the professional and management skills required.

1. Re-read the concept 'Management tasks and cultural values' in Chapter 6.
2. Make an analysis of the impact of the main differences in cultural values between you and the country chosen on five management tasks: planning, organizing, staffing, directing and controlling (Table A1.1.3).
3. Then, think about how you can adapt to operate in the business environment of the chosen country taking into account individual, national and management cultural differences.

Before answering points 2 and 3, read the example below. This text explains differences between the Netherlands and Japan in terms of cultural values regarding management tasks and the strategies needed for the launching of a new product.

Table A1.1.3 Cultural differences summary

Management tasks	1. Differences in cultural values regarding management tasks 2. Management strategies
Planning: Defining goals and objectives	1. 2.
Organizing: Defining tasks and relationship structures	1. 2.
Staffing: Acquiring appropriate human resources	1. 2.
Directing (leading): Leading the employees towards the goals of the organization	1. 2.
Controlling: Monitoring performance and giving feedback on achievements	1. 2.

Planning

1. Differences in cultural values regarding management tasks
Japanese customer relationships are based on trust and long-term perspectives. When the introduction of a product in this market is being planned, it is necessary to exercise patience: time is needed to build relationships and this has to be taken into account when sales targets and market share objectives are being established. The marketing plan needs to emphasize long-term relationship building. The planning should be schedule-driven, but not with too many detailed instructions. On the other hand, the goals and objectives set should be very detailed and quantifiable, and accepted as a shared objective by all involved.

2. Management strategies
As manager, one should have concrete ideas on what the plan has to be. Top-down planning is expected. Plans should be challenging to motivate sales people. If the Dutch approach was used, and employees were

allowed the room to discuss and participate in the planning, the Japanese would set very conservative goals to avoid risk. The initiative clearly has to come from the manager.

Organizing

1. Differences in cultural values regarding management tasks

Once staff have been hired, they need to be organized: tasks need to be allocated, geographical areas assigned and a reporting structure put in place. Japanese people are used to a relatively strong hierarchical structure. Since informal and casual management communication is characteristic of the Dutch, the expected flexibility in an organization will therefore be lacking. Procedures and protocols will need to be followed if goals are to be achieved in the long run.

In contrast to the focused, step-by-step approach to planning, where adherence to time schedules is very important, the task does not need to be specified in such great detail. Relationships rather than detailed plans are more important for selling the product. Tasks will nevertheless need to be clearly assigned to a specific person or a team. If there is any ambiguity, people will react defensively.

2. Management strategies

The assignment of specific customers to specific, reliable salespeople could be of crucial importance. Each salesperson or sales-team needs to be the right 'fit' for the customers concerned, so that the best possible relationships can be built.

Staffing

1. Differences in cultural values regarding management tasks

Bearing in mind the above-mentioned emphasis on building long-term relationships, people should be hired who have the social skills required. For a product launch in Japan to be successful, local sales and marketing people who are reliable and trustworthy need to be recruited.

2. Management strategies

To motivate employees, a manager should show that he takes care of their interests. To ensure their cooperation, he needs to apply a system of seniority that employees will accept. Salaries can be lower than in the Netherlands (owing to differences in Japanese living standards), but achievements should be rewarded with bonuses. Training is to be initiated by the manager although the score on competitiveness would suggest differently.

Directing (Leading)

1. Differences in cultural values regarding management tasks

Japanese sales employees are used to strong directive control and detailed instructions on how to proceed. Absence of this directive attitude or a sudden casual form of management can confuse employees, cause uncertainty and lead to undesirable behaviour.

Marketing people familiar with the local market can avoid cultural mistakes in communication about the product. However, since the Japanese are not used to participative management, they should be instructed carefully as to the expectations of the Dutch management. If an idea is put forward, it may well be accepted because the Japanese are reluctant to show their disagreement and cause possible conflict. As a result, the wrong ideas can end up being taken on board.

2. Management strategies

Group coherence is very important in the Japanese culture and therefore the best results probably will be achieved if this value is applied. This can be done, for example, by making the group responsible for meeting sales targets.

Again, time based management is expected and therefore the Dutch manager should adapt his directives accordingly.

Controlling

1. Differences in cultural values regarding management tasks
Conflicts must be resolved before work can progress. That means that, whenever a deviation to the plan has been observed, the feedback given should be carefully communicated, preferably in an indirect way. Japanese people are used to security in their job through lifetime employment. Any corrective measures should therefore be carefully considered.

2. Management strategies
Strategies should involve building good relationships with employees.

Reference

Doing Business Internationally: The cross-cultural challenges (1992) Participant Workbook, Princeton: Princeton Training Press.

This final activity is based on a case study that takes a practical and relevant approach to the investigation of cultural relations. It could be used as a framework for readers who intend to study the relations between employees from different cultural backgrounds who are working in one company.

Learning outcomes

After reading this case and answering the questions you will:

- Gain insight into how cultural sensitivity can be assessed through careful, sensitive questioning.
- Understand how essentially qualitative data can be interpreted in a reflective manner by a team of interviewers from different cultures who have themselves undergone considerable international exposure.

The research paper below was presented by the authors at a Sietar Europa Symposium entitled 'Europe on the Move: Fusion or Fission?' The paper investigates how representatives of three European cultures cope with each other's cultural differences when they are working together.

Galderma – a case study

An empirical study of cross-cultural relations between French, German and British managers in an international company

By M.-J. Browaeys, R.L. Price, and C.R. Seifert

1. INTRODUCTION

In the light of continuing European integration – economic and otherwise – the aim of the investigation was to gain insight into how three dominant members of the present-day European Union – the German, French and British – cope with each other's cultural differences when working together. The starting-point was one company in which the three cultures mentioned were working together, and had been doing so since the company came into being in 1981. It was hoped that the results of the investigations, outlined below, would lead to a framework that could be used when examining other companies operating internationally.

2. GALDERMA INTERNATIONAL

Galderma International is the first co-operative venture between L'Oréal and Nestlé. Started in 1981, it is an international company selling skin preparations and products to dermatologists on the world market. The company's initial range of products consisted of those produced by Alcon, Nestlé's US subsidiary, and those developed by L'Oréal. As well as having research and development centres in France, the US and Japan, Galderma produces products at its plants in France and Canada. Galderma's parent company is in Switzerland, with corporate services in Paris. Galderma employs 2,300 people in thirty-three fully owned subsidiaries worldwide. Among its European subsidiaries are those in France, Germany and the UK.

   The management of the holding company is staffed by several nationalities, as is the laboratory. The interviews carried out by the researchers (who each represented one of the three cultures under investigation) took place at the Paris headquarters, at the R&D laboratory near Nice in southern France and at the German subsidiary. In Paris, the chief executive (président-directeur général) of the company was interviewed, as well as all members of the board of management. In Nice, all those people in managerial positions were interviewed, with one exception; in Germany, the director and product portfolio manager. In total, thirteen managers were interviewed.

3. INTERVIEW METHOD

The interviews revolved around open-ended questions about how the managers in question interacted with managers from other nations within their specific working environment. In particular, they were asked to give their perceptions of the two other cultures involved in the research and to give their own perceptions of their own cultures in the eyes of the other cultures.

The interviewees were not asked a standard list of questions, although a number of basic questions were composed beforehand to serve as a framework for each interview. The interviews were carried out in the interviewee's native tongue in such a way that the experiences of the subjects were drawn upon to a maximum, with minimum influence from the interviewers as to the nature of the answers given.

The responses were then considered, reflected upon and analysed by the interviewers, each of whom represented one of the three cultures in question. During this stage of the research, the interaction of the differing perceptions relating to the researchers' cultural backgrounds acted as a control on the subjectivity of the final analysis.

4. THE MANAGERS IN QUESTION

4.1. Their background

All the managers interviewed had undergone a university education in science and/or management studies, part or all of which had been taken abroad. They had all worked outside their home country before coming to work at Galderma. The majority of them had worked in two foreign countries, one of which was the US, one in Europe. All had English as their native or second tongue.

4.2. Their perception of other cultures

During the interviews the various nationalities present in the managers' working environment came up for discussion. The comments that the interviewees made are given below, arranged in terms of the particular cultural aspects touched upon.

a) The French view of the British

All the French managers interviewed in the company commented on how the British communicate. The comments ranged from 'their soft expression' through 'they don't always say what they mean' to 'you have to decode what they say'. These comments applied to situations where the code of communication was English or French. Some remarks focused specifically on the communicative behaviour of the British when operating in English. One particular comment reflects the tenor of others given: 'They tend to bring considerable nuance to their expression, which frequently begs the question: "What are you trying to say exactly?"'

This behaviour led one of the French interviewees to say that it was sometimes necessary to treat the British in a gingerly fashion, to use kid gloves, to be less direct in communication with them than they would wish. If criticism had to be given or disagreement expressed, the interviewee felt obliged to be very careful in finding a form that would not cause the British to feel too offended.

Another interviewee concluded that there was a general lack of understanding between the two nations. Deep in the collective unconsciousness of the French, he said, there was an incomprehension of the British that has to do with the feeling that they still remain the traditional enemy of the French, despite 'ententes cordiales', 'rapprochement' and other diplomatic manoeuvres.

Most interviewees commented on the need for the British to make their presence felt, to be regarded as important within the company. 'They enjoy a position of power and enjoy reminding others of the power they possess,' was one typical comment. One interviewee talked of their wish to 'recreate the world', i.e. the tendency to fantasize about how the department/company/country/world would be like if they had total control. This was something they tended to do in the company of other Anglo-Saxons when drinking in a local bar after finishing work. Several interviewees described the behaviour of the British in the company as *fanfaron*, which implies that they display a certain boastfulness when talking of their role in the company.

As for their general effectiveness in the company's operations, the general impression drawn from the interviews was not positive. Several informants made the point that, although they may be effective in helping to determine policies, they lack effectiveness when carrying them out. One person talked of how her English colleague preferred to delegate implementation of a policy if it was likely to meet resistance among members of the department. Another talked of a lack of courage in seeing matters through. He talked of a lack of *rigueur* – the British being 'wishy-washy', either because they did not know what they really wanted, or because they were afraid to commit themselves to an action or decision that might later rebound on them. Another interviewee went further by saying that the British were known to have gone back on decisions they made or supported earlier. This view was contested by another informant who maintained that if the Brits made a 'gentleman's agreement', they always stuck to it.

Comments made by three interviewees on the British attitude to work shed further light on the question of the general effectiveness of the British in the company. One said bluntly: 'They don't work'; another said they were not *travailleur*; another: 'They stop work at 4pm' (the French tendency being to work until 6–7pm). All three were positive about the essential friendliness of their British colleagues, but essentially wished they would talk less and work more.

Another aspect concerning working with colleagues is highlighted by two comments on the difficulty the British have in dealing with female colleagues. The Brits, they maintained, were not used to dealing with women who occupied a similar position to themselves in the hierarchy, and have even greater problems with women who are above them.

One interviewee summed up his experiences with the British by saying that they were not international, but rather members of an exotic island race that just went its own way – on the left-hand side of the road!

b) The British view of the French

A common thread in all the comments given by the British interlocutors was the bureaucratic administration of the French. The headquarters of Galderma as well as the laboratory are situated in France, and both are subject to French law. The criticisms relate to the bureaucratic nature of public employees in civil administration and the health sector in particular.

For one informant, the battle with French bureaucracy is the focus of his activities with the company, although he is rarely in face-to-face contact with the bureaucrats themselves. Instead, he devises strategies to outsmart his adversaries, and uses French nationals to carry them out. A number of informants referred to their experiences with bureaucracy elsewhere in the world and conceded that the problems they had undergone or were undergoing in France caused no particular irritations.

In relation to the above, one informant talked of the 'bloody-mindedness' of the French, another of their individualistic nature. The former explained that this had to do with excelling within a very rigid hierarchical system, the latter explained that working together with others was not a particular strength of the French. He attributed this to the fact that, unlike the British, the French do not have sport as part of their school curriculum. 'Sport encourages team-play,' he added, 'and this is something which the British are good at doing.'

The same two informants talked about dealing with the French at meetings. Although both considered themselves proficient in the French language, there were times, they admitted, when it was more convenient for them to go into English if they wished to communicate effectively. This often put the French at a considerable disadvantage: the subtlety of the English language was something only native speakers of English could use, and something the French colleagues could neither use nor appreciate. The result was, they admitted, occasional miscommunication and misunderstanding.

A further informant, who said he made a point of speaking in French at all times, found that the French could display strong emotions at such meetings: one moment they were 'up in the air', the next they were calm. This 'roller-coaster' of emotions was something he found difficult to deal with: 'When I explode – which isn't very often – I tend to stay up in the air for the rest of the meeting. When this happens the French sometimes find it difficult to deal with me.'

Another interviewee would not be drawn into defining what was typically French in the behaviour of his colleagues. 'There are no French,' he maintained. He acknowledged, however, that to become partially integrated into French society it was essential to have some knowledge of French culture. He meant essentially French literature and referred specifically to Voltaire, Racine and La Fontaine.

Just as the French see the British as being imperious in nature, so the British see the French as being nationalistic. One manager added that they were protectionist about their presence in this international company – a recent round of staff cuts involving French employees had provoked considerable local publicity, although a further round involving non-French employees had caused hardly any reactions. Another manager added that the French encourage the non-French to take an active interest in their culture and language – 'they need to justify their culture'.

c) How the British think the French see them – and vice versa

Not all respondents were able to deal with this area, preferring instead to talk in terms of personalities. One manager, however, did make remarks concerning the French view of the British. The French, he said, tend to think of the British as being rather pragmatic in their ideas – they prefer the concrete to the 'airy-fairy'. This point was pursued by another informant who said that the French found it difficult to talk in English with the British about 'concepts'. They considered French a much more suitable language for discussing more abstract matters than English. A third manager thought his French colleagues found him rather phlegmatic. While they expressed their opinions/feelings in no uncertain terms, he tended to hold himself back.

As for the French, one informant talked of the British reaction in the UK to his critical comments about the role of Britain in the EU. 'They were scandalized by my open criticism,' he said, adding that he felt the British thought he was being much too outspoken. Moving on, he talked of certain prejudices the British have towards the French – 'a certain envy' was how he put it, particularly of the lifestyle they lead.

d) The French view of the Germans

Two contrasting views appeared to predominate in the company, one based on the stereotype image of the Germans, the other on the presence of one German manager who was seen as the very opposite.

The stereotype image is reflected in comments such as 'their authoritarian character', 'their pride in themselves', 'their rigidity', 'their imperious nature', 'their monolithic presence'. Despite these remarks, there was a general feeling, expressed and implied, that working with the Germans was not too unpleasant an experience. This is based on comments such as 'they may be somewhat rule-bound, but at least they are easier to understand (than the British)', 'You can count on them, even if they are rather direct'. 'My contacts with the Germans may not have been very warm, but at least they get things done.'

Several respondents raised the matter of lack of warmth in day-to-day contact. One manager commented on the tone of voice used by the Germans as being sometimes unpleasant She referred in particular to requests which a German manager makes in French on the phone. These tended to sound more like orders, particularly with the more direct modal forms being used. The same respondent said this would be bearable were it not for the lack of 'chit-chat' preceding the request. The expectation on the French side is therefore that the channel of communication be carefully prepared. If not, the imperative nature of the request is all the stronger.

One particular feature of the Germans that received some attention in the interviews was their very careful approach to business, careful both in the sense of being very precise and accurate, as well as in the sense of being conservative, reluctant to take risks. One interviewee gave a concrete example of this behaviour in relation to the sales forecasts of the German subsidiary for one particular product. He said the subsidiary had been told to sell this product, although the Germans had doubts about its potential success as a result of their own marketing research. Their reservations were clearly expressed in the low sales forecast for this product they sent to headquarters. 'When actual sales turned out to be ten times the number forecast,' he added, 'the Germans were delighted and proud to have achieved such wonderful sales figures!'

The interviewee in question called such conservative forecasting 'sandbagging', thus implying that the Germans were prepared for the worst by presenting such modest sales forecasts. This sort of behaviour naturally put the Germans in a good light, he said somewhat scornfully, when the estimated and actual sales were compared at headquarters. The downside, however, was the fact that the German subsidiary ran out of stock after a while, and could not meet demand.

This essential prudence, as it was called, contrasted strongly with what the same informant called the French preference for 'bold strokes'. Several other managers talked admiringly about the German *Gründlichkeit*, but at the same time remarked upon the disadvantages this brings: 'stick-in-the-mud attitudes', a 'reluctance to take our (French) creativity seriously', the need to 'argue till the cows come home before you can convince them'.

One manager said that this view of the Germans predominated and that the Germans were aware of this. As a result 'they work twice as hard to prove that this (authoritarian, inflexible) image is not a true one'.

As said earlier, one German member of the management team was considered to be different. He was regarded by several French interviewees as 'soft', 'a product of the late 1960s', the period of student revolts, thus an anti-authoritarian figure, a 'Green' who was ecologically aware.

e) The German view of the French

The comments recorded in this area were limited and further interviews need to be made. Nevertheless, the following observations are worth noting.

'The French,' one interviewee remarked, 'are more concerned with ideas than with detail. They are not particularly thorough, have a certain disdain for detail – and this can be somewhat vexing for someone who is concerned with getting things right.' Related to this was the following comment: 'The French are very good at defining goals, but are not particularly concerned as to how the goal should be reached.'

Favourable comments were expressed by three interviewees about the French lifestyle, although the fact that life is family-oriented makes it difficult to integrate. The less disciplined ways of the French were also commented on – the lack of punctuality was appealing to one, more of an irritation to another. One German commented on the influential role of the French Grandes Ecoles and the preponderance of their graduates in top management not so much on the basis of merit, more as a result of their simply being graduates of these schools.

f) The British view of the Germans

The views expressed by the French on the contrasting German images were frequently reflected in the observations made by the British managers. One manager, when talking about his German colleague said: 'X is the exception to the rule' – and went on to give the stereotype image of the Germans as portrayed by John Cleese, the British comedy actor who has portrayed the Germans as goose-stepping, authoritarian, Hitleresque figures. Other descriptions of the typical German were: 'the regimented, inflexible type', 'the worker who goes by the book – if it's not in there, he doesn't know what to do'.

In line with the French observations made earlier, two managers talked of the immense effort made by the Germans to integrate. One said that despite all these efforts, X is still perceived as being Germanic in character; the other said that Y was pursuing with some success an 'affiliatory style of management'.

One gut reaction made to the question concerning Germans and their colleagues in general was: 'The French do not like the Germans.'

g) The German view of the British

One interviewee expressed exasperation with the British. They were seen as great fun to be with – their social lifestyle and sense of humour being very enjoyable. They were masters of communication in their own tongue, and it was fascinating to see how they used their language to such great effect. On the other hand, on the basis of experiences with the British subsidiary, it was not always possible to rely on them. The managers there, he remarked, were extremely co-operative and 'promised you heaven', but the realization of these promises depended on others who lacked the same commitment. Promises were therefore not always kept. Moreover, their skill in English was frequently used to conceal their real thoughts, so it was occasionally necessary to read between the lines to get at what they were really thinking. A very difficult task.

5. PERCEPTIONS OF THE MANAGERS: SOME CONCLUSIONS

5.1. The cultures remain

The responses to the questions and reflections upon them lead to a conclusion that, whatever insights they have displayed concerning themselves and their international colleagues, the interviewees remain essentially French, German and British.

This is an obvious conclusion, perhaps, but one that counters the comments of a number of those interviewed. One proclaimed: 'I'm a European'; another (French) interviewee stated: 'There are no French'; a third remarked: 'There are no differences between cultures, it's only a question of personality.' Such comments are not necessarily a denial of the culture in question, but more, we believe, a wish to show that the interviewee is able to exist, even flourish, in another culture and is not being dragged down by the ballast of his/her own culture.

Nevertheless the 'Frenchness', 'Germanness' and 'Britishness' remain, even though the interviewees had been exposed to other cultures, were living in other cultures and taking on board many of that culture's ways. Many informants may be unable to say explicitly what it is to be French, German or British, i.e. to describe features of their cultural identity. These features are, however, implicit in the way they describe the other culture with which they are working.

5.2. Cultural sensitivity

Although the previous section presented the comments in such a way as to highlight some of the common threads woven through the individual comments on the cultures in question, it does not make clear to what extent the degree of cultural sensitivity varies from one respondent to another. This was therefore another stage to the analysis.

This stage involved returning to the raw material of the interviews, reflecting on it carefully as individual interviewers and as a group of interviewers and assessing as carefully as possible the cultural sensitivity of each person interviewed. The questions which, it was decided, the interviewers should ask themselves were the following:

- to what extent is the interviewee aware of the cultural background of the colleagues with whom (s)he is dealing?
- to what extent is the interviewee aware of his/her own cultural background?

6. A CATEGORIZATION OF THE INTERVIEWEES AT GALDERMA

6.1. Graphical representation of interview results

As stated earlier, the 'raw material' of the interviews, i.e. the responses given to the questions, were reflected upon by the three Interviewers. On the basis of their individual reflections, each interviewer allotted a score ranging from 1 (low) to 5 (high) to the persons interviewed. The score consisted of two numbers: the first represented the degree of perception which, it was felt, each interviewee had acquired concerning his/her own culture; the second number reflected the degree of perception which the interviewee was judged to have reached vis à vis other cultures. Once the interviewers had deliberated with each other over the individual scores they had allotted, a median score was awarded to each interviewee and plotted (Figure A1.2.1).

6.2. Initial observations on the graph

The graph shows that the majority of the interviewees have, in our judgement, a rather high score when it comes to their perception of other cultures. When it comes to their own culture, however, the degree of perception is generally lower.

The top left of the graph, where a high degree of perception of one's own culture and a low degree of perception of other cultures is marked, is scarcely occupied.

The scores allotted to the majority of their managers at Galderma tend to be clustered around the centre of the figure.

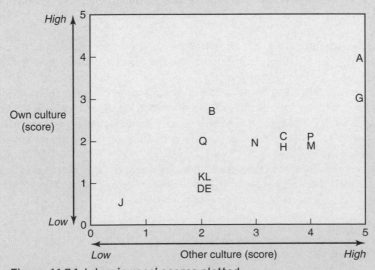

Figure A1.2.1 Interviewees' scores plotted

Figure A1.2.2 **Shared characteristics of interviewees**

6.3. Categorization of the scores

The field on which the scores are plotted can be divided up into quadrants (Figure A1.2.2).

The interviewees to be found in each quadrant can be said to share certain characteristics with regard to their cultural awareness.

Those in quadrant **1**, such as interviewee J, show great interest in the question topics, but become aware of the intercultural phenomenon only as the interview progresses. In quadrant **3**, interviewees such as M are able to analyse their own culture, but do so in an implicit manner by indicating ways in which another culture differs from their own. They talk at length about other cultures and display a high degree of perception, frequently using detailed examples drawn from their own experiences to support their analysis. They also attempt now and again to give explanations for the cultural attitudes which they have described.

In quadrant **4**, the two interviewees plotted – A and G – are both able to make a critical analysis of companies which are representative of their own culture. They explain how necessary it is to adapt one's manner of communication to that of the host country.

Just like the interviewees in quadrant **3**, they are able to talk at length about other cultures, citing many examples. They go further, however, by characterizing the cultures in terms of their professional activities and by explaining why they prefer to work with one culture rather than another.

Quadrant **2** has not yet been referred to since only one interviewee has been plotted there, B. This subject is, however, clearly set apart from the others. He deals with his own culture in terms of opinions and observations, but does not make any attempt to analyse it. He does show a certain interest in his culture, but his remarks are based more on intuition rather than reflection. He knows the other cultures which he presents in terms of clichés and *idées reçues*. He is very descriptive and categorical in his judgement.

After further reflection concerning the responses of these interviewees, according to the quadrants in which they have been plotted, it is possible to come to a concise definition of each of these four categories. This can serve as a framework for further study of managers working in international companies.

7. THE FOUR CATEGORIES

7.1. Definitions and comments

The four categories defined below correspond to the four quadrants on the graph in Figure A1.2.2.

Category 1

People who have given little or no reflection to their own culture and therefore have minimal knowledge or aware-ness of it. The question of cultural differences has not occurred to them.

This category accounts for those who display a minimal degree of cross-cultural awareness. Such people have never con-sidered what it is to be a member of a culture, are unable to describe what being French, German or British is all about. The fact that their culture may be different from others is not something they have ever had to deal with.

We encountered few representatives of this category during our interviews. This is not surprising bearing in mind that we were dealing with a collection of managers who had all had experience of living and working abroad. We would, how-ever, expect to find many more representatives of this category in national companies with international ambitions.

Category 2

People who have some knowledge of their own culture, but who have little or no awareness of the other culture(s) in question. They tend to be judgemental when there are cross-cultural differences.

A person belonging to this category is usually able to make general comments about his/her own culture and can refer to what (s)he considers to be typical features of the behaviour displayed. As for the other culture(s), the person in question is aware that (s)he is dealing with someone from a different cultural background, is familiar with some of the features of that background. When it comes to working with representatives of the culture(s) in question, the person is not aware of the influence that his/her cultural background has on their working together. Instead, the person tends to make judge-mental remarks and opinionated comments on the other culture(s) without showing understanding of them.

Although only one respondent is clearly placed in this category, we would expect to come across many more represen-tatives of this category in other companies.

Category 3

People who are trying to adapt fully to the other culture, but do not reflect on their own culture while doing so.

The people in question here have clearly gained insight into the cultural background of the people with whom they are working. Their comments are perceptive and non-judgemental. They have adapted to their working environment. How-ever, they have not gained insight into their own cultural background, have not perceived how the other cultures perceive them. Interaction with other cultures is perceived by their standpoint only, no account is taken of the other culture's perception of themselves and the reasons for this.

Category 4

These people adapt consciously to the other culture(s) while reflecting critically on the culture(s). They can func-tion effectively in the other culture(s) while reflecting critically on their own.

A person in this category has reflected on both his/her own culture and the culture(s) encountered. A degree of aware-ness has been reached which enables questions to be asked such as:

'Why is X reacting that way?'
'Why is X causing me to react in this way?'

On the one hand the person is attempting to account for what (s)he may consider to be abnormal behaviour in terms of the other's cultural background. This implies relating such behaviour to what may be 'normal' for the culture in question. On the other hand (s)he is also attempting to consider why (s)he considers this behaviour abnormal anyway. This there-fore implies that the person is trying to elicit what (s)he considers to be 'normal' behaviour, i.e. behaviour which corresponds to his/her cultural norm.

This does not imply that such questions can be answered, but the fact that they are asked shows that the person is busy reflecting on his/her situation, on the interaction with those around. This very attitude puts that person in a position where (s)he is taking stock, coming to terms with the culture(s) in question and adapting where possible. If this is not possible, the person can ask 'Why cannot I adapt?' This critical reflection and further experience with(in) the culture in question may lead to an enhanced understanding of the person's own culture and the other culture. In short, one can talk of the person moving along a spiral of experiential learning, referring constantly to the person's own culture and that of the other(s).

7.2. Some reservations

The problem with such a categorization is, of course, its seductive simplicity. People are forever attempting to characterize facets of human behaviour, and this could be seen as another vain attempt. Moreover, these categories of cultural awareness cannot adequately deal with the process each individual undergoes when dealing with other cultures. The interviewers themselves recognize the complex nature of this process, one which involves posing questions about one's own culture as well as about the other(s), coming up with hypothetical answers to these questions, trying them out, finding other answers if the original answers do not appear to be valid, trying these out and so on. Gaining awareness, then, is an erratic to-and-fro between one's perception of one's own culture and the other culture, during which differences are determined, reflected upon and in some way accounted for.

Nevertheless, the categorization does give some indicators of what the interviewers believe to be the degree of sensitivity attained by the subjects questioned. Moreover, this categorization can be used as a somewhat primitive instrument with which to examine the degree of cross-cultural awareness of individual managers as well as the composition of a management team when other companies active in international business are being investigated.

Questions

1. Read sections 1–4 of the paper in which the researchers give their findings.

   a) Draw any general conclusions you have about the interviewees. Have they, for example, become less 'French', 'British' or 'German' and more 'European'?

   b) The conclusions drawn by the researchers are given in section 5. Compare your conclusions with theirs.

2. Now read sections 6 and 7.1. of the paper. Here the researchers have categorized their findings from the interviews carried out.

   a) Give your opinion of the validity and usefulness of the categorization in this case.

   b) What is your opinion of cultural categorizations generally? Refer to the concepts in Chapter 2 and Chapter 5.

   c) Compare your response with that of the researchers as given in section 7.2 of this paper.

3. The authors refer to the fact that they did not ask a standard list of questions, but used a basic list of questions composed beforehand as a framework for the interviews.

   a) Compose a list of the framework questions you think were used.

   b) Compare these with the ones actually used by the researchers (provided on the instructor's website).

   c) Try using these questions as a basis for a short interview with a colleague. Listen carefully to the responses given and try to use as many follow-up questions as you can to clarify or broaden the responses given.

   d) Discuss the results of the interview and the questioning strategy used. What do you, as both interviewee and interviewer, think worked well and how could the interview have been more effective?

4. This paper presents a small-scale research project, the results of which are essentially qualitative in nature.

   a) What, in your opinion, are the advantages and disadvantages of this approach in cross-cultural management research?

   b) What role, if any, does it have to play alongside the quantitative-oriented research described in Part One?

Part Two

CULTURE AND ORGANIZATIONS

Introduction to Part Two

By examining the effect of culture on organizations, this part aims to develop the cross-cultural competence you need for working in international business. This cross-cultural competence involves being aware of:

- the impact of culture in the international business environment, particularly the issue of cultural diversity.
- the influence of culture on companies operating in the global market-place, particularly on the way they are led.

A small case study for starters

An appropriate way of starting the examination of managerial competence within a context of cultural diversity is to consider the case of Mr Takahashi and the perfume.

Mr Takahashi and the perfume

Lekan, a large wholesaler specializing in interior furnishings, needed to boost its sales. Its domestic market was stagnant and its export sales, although increasing gradually, were not delivering the anticipated volume. The company desperately needed to make a large deal, preferably in the expanding Asian market.

After intensive efforts by its marketing department, Lekan was eventually contacted by a Japanese company, Ligato, which was interested in purchasing floor coverings. The two companies met on several occasions in Tokyo and a large deal was finally made. A dinner was arranged to celebrate the successful conclusion of business.

Mr Roberts, the senior sales manager who had headed the Lekan team of negotiators, had brought along gifts for Mr Takahashi, his Japanese counterpart. With heartfelt expressions of gratitude, Mr Roberts handed over a bottle of 25-year-old malt whisky and then Chanel perfume which, he said, was intended for Mrs Takahashi.

Mr Takahashi did his best to conceal his anger and disappointment. He left the celebrations, however, without signing the contract.

Why did Mr Takahashi react the way he did?

It was not the malt whisky that upset Mr Takahashi, but the present for his wife. In Japan it is not done to buy perfume for a woman because it implies that she has an unpleasant odour. Mr Roberts' present had been unintentionally insulting. Had he known how the Japanese perceived such a gift, then the deal could have been signed and sealed. Before we ask ourselves how best to prepare for this kind of situation we need to look more closely at the context of cultural diversity and cultural competence.

The context in which a manager operates

It has been known for some time that the process of globalization is a reality for business. The same is true of cultural diversity. People from different cultures interact with each other more and more frequently, not only on an international level, but also nationally and at local level.

Bearing this continuing globalization in mind, Bartlett and Ghoshal (1989) came up with a model for the organization of the future: the *transnational organization*. As Concept 12.1 will describe in detail, this model has both the managers at company headquarters but also those in charge of the subsidiaries abroad being responsible for the co-ordination of units within the whole organization. The transnational company, which combines the abilities of the multinational, global and international firm, now represents the territory of the modern manager.

Managers in such an organization perceive the cultural diversity present as an opportunity, as long as they are able to handle it. This means that they need to learn about the methods and tools that will help them to optimize their managerial skills. In this way they can eventually adopt the most appropriate attitude in a specific cross-cultural context. This acquired complex of skills is referred to as 'transcultural' competence.

Acquiring transcultural competence

To define a competence of this nature in detail, consider Figure II.1 based on the concept developed by Le Boterf (1994).

This model shows *Knowledge* on one side and *Know-how* on the other. People develop competence via a combination of knowledge and know-how, which when combined through the channels of communication and interaction help to form the desired level of

Figure II.1 What is competence?

competence. To sum up, competence involves a full range of resources related to knowledge, skills and cognitive abilities. The ability to integrate these resources represents the key to competence. For Le Boterf, competence is at the heart of the complexity surrounding the ordinary and cannot only be defined as the capacity to solve a problem. In the context of management, Le Boterf sees this competence in the following terms:

> . . . the good manager is not the one who exhibits the same behaviour in all circumstances, but the one who knows how to modify management strategy according to the situations encountered.

Le Boterf, 1994: 24

To return to Mr Roberts and the perfume, he will make sure that he is not confronted with the same situation again. He will investigate why Mr Takahashi did not sign the contract and learn more about Japanese business culture generally. Integrating this with his managerial know-how, he will then modify his behaviour according to the situations, especially since knowledge itself entails learning from experience.

Learning about cultures

An effective way of learning from experience is by studying examples. Just as in medicine and in human sciences, the objective of case studies is, in the first place, the development of the capacity to reason and not the achievement of a precise solution. Bearing this in mind, the primary function of the case study method is to learn how to deal with complex and non-structured problems. After an analysis of the situation, the effect can then be imagined of different actions in line with one's own experience in comparable situations.

The case study approach is directed at the development of cognitive abilities of an individual such as structuring knowledge, reasoning and problem-solving, as well as the learning process itself. The most important factor, however, is 'memory' because it provides individuals with the ability to store information. All situations heard, read or studied, put together in the form of case studies, will find a place within a database. This database will form the knowledge of an individual. Know-how is all about calling on the right knowledge at the right moment to identify a problem.

This implies that the competence of a transnational manager will involve possession not only of the knowledge or experience in the field of cross-cultural relations, but also the development of a 'memory of cases'. A manager will draw on this memory to adopt the appropriate attitude in a given situation. This will eventually permit individuals to act at the right moment without thinking.

A special form of case study is the 'critical incident', such as the one given at the start of this introduction. Here, there is no need for a comprehensive case analysis. Instead, the reader is confronted with a specific situation, in a context with its own particular dynamics whereby the interaction between the people concerned is unique.

As Bosche (1993) remarked, we learn much more about culturally different people in the dynamics of their interaction than by learning about their cultural backgrounds; it is this interaction which is the motor of learning. Critical incidents are therefore particularly suitable for learning about cultures and, just as in Part One, will continue to be present in the activities of this part of the book.

We will now outline the various components of Part Two.

Chapter and concept overview

Chapter 7 Culture and corporate structures

This chapter examines the places that national culture and the business environment occupy in the notion of corporate culture.

- **Concept 7.1 Organizational structures.** This concept shows how models of organizational structure evolve in line with the changes in context and with the influence of cultural differences.
- **Concept 7.2 Corporate cultures.** The focus of this concept is corporate culture and its constituents. Two forms of classification are described, one using time and risk, the other using the degree of formalization and centralization.

Chapter 8 Culture and leadership

This chapter looks at the evolution of thought with regard to leadership, cultural elements involved in defining the role of leaders as well as attributes of leadership within and between cultures.

- **Concept 8.1 Different conceptions of leadership.** Having outlined the developments in Western ideas on leadership this concept looks at present-day thinking on the subject, particularly the influence of Eastern ideas.
- **Concept 8.2 Leadership in the international context.** This concept considers cultural variables which may be contingent on leadership effectiveness. It then considers the question as to whether there are attributes reflecting good leadership which are to be found in all cultures.

Chapter 9 Culture and strategy

This chapter addresses the role culture plays in determining strategy, especially strategic alliances in the global marketplace.

- **Concept 9.1 Cultural view of strategy.** The relationship between culture and strategy is explored, as is the way national culture influences a company's strategy.
- **Concept 9.2 Strategy alliances and business cultures.** This concept examines the question of culture in merger strategies and the difficulties for all kinds of co-operation on the cultural front.

Chapter 10 Cultural change in organizations

Fundamental organizational change involves changing the culture of the organization concerned. This chapter examines the role of culture in this process.

- **Concept 10.1 Organizational change as a cultural process.** Once the process of organizational change and the mechanisms involved have been presented, the concept considers the cultural insights needed for change to succeed.
- **Concept 10.2 Organizational change in a global environment.** This concept examines how external factors influence the culture of an organization and presents an assessment instrument for diagnosing discrepancies between its culture and its business environment.

Chapter 11 Culture and marketing

This concept investigates the influence of culture on marketing and advertising in an international environment.

- **Concept 11.1 Marketing in the cross-cultural environment.** Once the present-day approach to marketing, involving the whole company, has been addressed, the question of intercultural marketing is discussed, one that involves adapting products and marketing strategies to the international consumer.
- **Concept 11.2 Advertising across cultures.** The question of brands is addressed, their relation to national images, and how their meaning is managed across cultures.

Chapter 12 Cultural diversity in organizations

This chapter considers the general question of cultural diversity in organizations and the nature of the transnational organization.

- **Concept 12.1 Cultural competence in transnational organizations.** The concept examines ways in which managers can deal with cultural diversity as well as turn it to their advantage.

Final activities

Part Two contains two final activities:

1. **Making cultural profiles of brands.** The first of the final activities requires you to create cultural profiles of brands of your choice. Before doing so, you will read a study in which the authors develop their own cultural profiles of a range of brands. The model they use is based on the cultural model used in Part One.
2. **A case study** about a joint venture between two chemical manufacturers in South-Africa presents strategic and cultural issues round a joint venture.

What you will gain

After working through Part Two you will gain more insight into:

- The influence of culture on all aspects of the organization: its structure, its leadership, strategy and marketing.
- The skills necessary for dealing competently with cultural diversity when operating in international business.

References

Bartlett, C.A. and Ghosal, S. (1989) *Managing across Borders: The transnational solution*, Boston, MA: Hutchinson.

Bosche, M. (1993) 'La problématique interculturelle' in Bosche, M. (ed) *Le management interculturel*, Paris: Editions Nathan: 31-48.

Le Boterf, G. (1994) *De la compétence*, Paris: Les Editions d'Organisation.

Chapter 7

Culture and corporate structures

This chapter describes the relation to be found between the structure and the culture of an organization. This relation is a very close one because structure is not independent of culture but an element of the organization's culture. To gain a better understanding of this relation, structure and culture have been separated into two concepts.

Concept 7.1 focuses on the forms of organizational structure and how these have evolved. This is because models change or adapt in line with new forms of organization that emerge over time according to the context and influence of cultural differences.

Concept 7.2 refers to the classifications of corporate culture proposed by experts in the area of organizational culture. Such classifications are useful, although different forms should be put forward to reflect the different facets of an organization's culture. It is this range of ideas that gives particular interest to this concept.

Learning outcomes

After reading this chapter you will gain an understanding of:

- The relation between the structure and the culture of an organization.
- Forms of organizational structure.
- The levels and values of corporate cultures.

Concept 7.1 Organizational structures

The term 'organizational structure' describes the way an institution is organized to carry out its objectives and pursue its projects. It allows relations within the organization to be formalized by describing the tasks, jobs and positions of its personnel, as well as the limits and responsibilities of the work units. It also indicates the kind of hierarchy within the organization, the levels of authority and power as well as the formal lines of communication between the employees. In short, organizational structure forms the basis of the organization's culture. That is why the structure of an organization is used to analyse its culture.

Several factors influence the structure of an organization. Size is one: if a company is small, it can be flexible and engage the whole staff in a range of activities. The business environment is another factor: the structure of a large-scale organization, for example, will need to be more decentralized if it sells its products in many markets, whether they be regional or international. Another important factor is the influence internal and external factors can have on the organizational structure. Fatehi (1996) makes a distinction between internal requirements (the choice of technology, the type of activity being undertaken, the particular strategy pursued) and external factors in the external environment that influence an organization's fate. The way internal and external forces are combined gives each enterprise a different structure, one that allows it to realize its particular goals.

Fatehi (1996), however, does not see any fundamental differences between multinational organizations and domestic ones, apart from the fact that multinationals need to take account of factors such as the physical distance between headquarters and the subsidiaries, their mutual relations and the legislation of the countries where the subsidiaries operate. The fact that multinationals operate across national borders means that the need for co-ordination and integration will be greater than in domestic organizations.

Forms of organizational structure

Generally speaking, two main types of organizational structures can be distinguished: a traditional hierarchical structure and a structure with several lines of reporting. In the former, the staff is divided up according to function, product, service or location; in the latter, the structure takes the form of a project team or assumes a matrix structure. For several years now, another form of structure has been making its appearance, one that has assumed increasing importance – the network structure. This form facilitates partnerships between organizations.

According to Fatehi (1996:104): 'Functions, products and geographic areas remain the three basic models of organizational structure.' Bearing in mind these domains, he puts forward a detailed classification of five organizational structures which he defines as follows:

1. *Geographic structure.* In this structure, employees are grouped according to region (or country/continent if they are multinationals). At the head of each division there is a senior-level executive who shares responsibility for the area with the human resources manager. Headquarters maintains control of 'strategic planning' as well as control of the operations of each company. A number of regional divisions may retain the possibility of producing and selling according to local needs.

2. *Functional structure.* Here, responsibilities are arranged according to functional areas: at the head of each function – marketing, finance, research and development, etc. – is a senior manager who reports directly to the company's chief executive. Where a company has several product lines, the 'functional managers' do not always have the same objectives. These differences of opinion may be passed to headquarters, where executives could spend more time resolving such conflicts than they do making strategic decisions.

3. *Product structure.* The organizations using this model organize their staff according to product lines, which are in turn grouped according to product divisions. All the functions relating to the product being sold and the market being served are controlled by the divisions. This structure allows a product to be launched simply through the creation of a new division. Although the rest of the company may be less destabilized as a result, such autonomous units can pose problems relating to control and co-ordination.

4. *Mixed structure.* This structure is often preferred by organizations who wish to extend their international business activities. They are looking for a form that allows different structures to be combined. Multinationals may wish, for example, to combine:

- area knowledge with product and functional skills; or
- the functional divisions with product divisions; or
- the geographic areas with product lines; or
- the functional skills with the geographic divisions.

5. *Matrix structure.* A matrix organization does not follow the traditional hierarchy since it does not respect the principle that each employee has just one superior. Moreover, the management of this type of organization acknowledges a lateral authority. The two 'lines' – functional and project – share responsibility. In general, this system facilitates the co-ordination and integration of projects, but it also has the disadvantage of relying on more managers (thus increasing costs) and of possibly increasing internal competition. This may, in turn, create conflict among people in the organization (Case study 7.1).

Case study 7.1

Accountability: where does the buck stop?

A classic bureaucracy usually has a number of relatively independent business units reporting to head office. Head office prescribes the strategy for each of these components and checks that the strategy is being carried out. A certain decentralization may be allowed, whereby the units fill in elements of the overall strategy and are responsible for monitoring the process but, essentially, the buck stops at HQ.

Philips, the Dutch electronics multinational, with a vast range of products and a growing number of markets worldwide, was one of the first companies to adopt a matrix structure. Hindle (2006) points out that the company superimposed geographical 'silos' on the company structure that cut across the traditional functional units. This meant that: 'The boss of the washing-machine division in Italy, say, would report to the head of Philips in Italy as well as to the washing-machine supremo in the Netherlands.' The basic problem Philips encountered with this sort of organization was to do with accountability. Was the country boss (in the case of washing-machines the one in Italy) responsible for the profit-and-loss account, or was it the head of that product division in the Netherlands?

The tug-of-war between country bosses and product heads eventually resulted in Philips re-organizing itself again in the late 1980s. Businesses were grouped together into units (built around products such as consumer goods, lighting and medical products). These units were based at Philips' headquarters and local operations ('national offices') were to report to the director of the unit in question.

Hindle (2006) points out that this structure has been modified slightly as a response to criticism that too much attention was being given to technology and the development of new products and not enough to the company's customers. Changes include the creation of the position of chief marketing officer. Moreover, collaboration between units is being encouraged and incentives have been put in place to get employees to move between geographical regions or product areas. This need to cross organizational boundaries has also been reflected in the running of workshops for top managers across the company to discuss issues which are of concern to the whole company.

Current thinking on other organizational structures

The organizational structures described above are still common. However, the phenomenon of globalization has brought about the appearance of new organizational forms or adaptations of existing forms to keep pace with economic reality.

Network structure

This form of organizational structure has gained considerable favour, thanks mainly to developments in technology and a network's apparent ability to deal more effectively with global competition. Rather than being a pyramid hierarchical structure, a network has company units with a horizontal system of communication. This implies that responsibility and decision-making is dispersed to local subsidiaries and alliances (Deresky, 2003).

Network structures also have to do with managing the cross-cultural transfer of knowledge. Holden (2002) considers networking as an activity of cross-cultural exchanges of knowledge. This activity has the shape of a negotiation involving interlocutors being chosen and, at the same time, access being given to the resources of organizations that are culturally or geographically different.

The practice of networking facilitates organizational learning and is the essential characteristic of a 'learning organization' (see Concept 8.1 for a definition). Networking uses 'socio-interactive communication' to support the strategy and the mission of the organization. This network is indispensable for companies needing to learn about the rapidly changing business environment in which they are involved.

Transnational structure

Bartlett and Ghoshal (1989: 59) were among the first to propose a new structure that corresponded more effectively to the strategy of internationalization among companies: the transnational structure. They argue that international enterprises must adopt a multifaceted strategy to respond to the complex environment within which they operate. In other words, they must opt at the same time for international, multinational and global strategies to become what the authors call a 'transnational company'. In such a company 'innovations are regarded as an outcome of a larger process of organizational *learning* that encompasses every member of the company'.

Such a company has the following characteristics:

- It is dispersed, interdependent and specialized.
- National units make differentiated contributions to integrated worldwide operations.
- Knowledge is developed jointly and shared worldwide.

A decade after the emergence of the transnational organization, the authors asked themselves about the future of this model: How must the transnational model evolve to respond to the needs of the future? (Bartlett, Ghoshal and Birkinshaw, 2004: 756). This question addressed predictions that the end of large worldwide companies was in sight, to be replaced by either more flexible small companies, or by 'virtual corporations' thanks to the evolution of technology. While maintaining the concept of the 'transnational company', the authors suggested that 'large companies' should no longer be described in terms of a formal structure divided into business, geographic and functional units, but in terms of processes. This description reflects more accurately a style of business management that involves the entrepreneurial process, the integration process and the renewal process. The influence of culture is to be found not only in the choice of structure but also in the sum of processes occurring within the organization. This implies that the managers have to adapt their attitudes and skills to their new roles.

Cultural assumptions and organizational structure

In this sphere of internationalization, relations between people from various cultural backgrounds are increasing and companies have to manage these differences. What effect do these differences have? Do the employees who make up the cultural diversity in the company have an influence on the organizational structure? Furthermore, how do cultural assumptions affect organizational structure? To what extent is cultural diversity reflected in international organizations?

To address these questions, Hoecklin (1995) refers to work done by Adler (1983, 1986). This shows the impact of cultural diversity on international organizations and the stages they need to go through before they can call themselves global. They propose a model representing four kinds of organization and their cultural assumptions:

1. *Multidomestic* structure. The organization is presented as a set of sub-units in several countries. They are autonomous and have no interaction with each other. Cultural diversity has no effect on the organization as a whole.

2. *International* structure. The homogeneity of the organization is considered to be normal. The culture of the organization – including the national culture of the top management – is considered to be universal, one that is to be applied at domestic firm level. So cultural diversity is regarded as a source of conflict: it leads to inefficiency and is therefore undesirable.

3. *Multinational.* In this structure, on the other hand, diversity is inherent to the organization because of its geographical spread. The structure recognizes that diversity can cause problems resulting from cultural differences, but at the same time recognizes that diversity can benefit the organization as a whole.

4. The final type of structure, the *Transnational* structure – as described by Bartlett and Ghoshal (1989) – gives enterprises their 'global' status. This differs from the others through the fact that it generates its own evolution without having to rely on forces outside the enterprise. Heterogeneity, and all the problems it may bring, is indispensable. The diversity present allows mutually beneficial relations to be created.

This classification takes account of the importance of cultural diversity when it is tied to a certain type of organizational structure. However, it is necessary to go more deeply into the meaning of cultural diversity to be able to assess its effect on organizations (Chapter 12).

It must be said that the types of organizational structure given above are based principally on the Western model, which does not necessarily reflect the practice and tradition elsewhere. Nevertheless, it is hoped that new structures will emerge – transnational as well as network structures – that allow organizations to respond more effectively to a complex global environment.

Concept 7.2 Corporate cultures

Concept 7.2 discussed models proposed by various writers that allow national culture to be given shape. It also examined the place national culture occupies in the notion of corporate culture. The conclusion drawn was that, over time, a corporate culture may be based on the 'original' organizational culture, or the national/regional culture – or a combination of both. Concept 7.2 will focus on the 'corporate' element of culture and present models to take account of two key criteria: the business environment and the national cultural setting.

According to Deal and Kennedy (2000: 13), 'The business environment is the single greatest influence in shaping a corporate culture.' In other words, the type of industry in question, as well as the type of product and the markets involved, play an important role.

The national cultural setting also has an influence on how companies manage their business. The cultural assumptions with regard to the relations between employees and their organization, the hierarchical system in place, the company's mission and aims, all these elements have an influence on the preference for a particular organizational culture.

Corporate culture and management

Most domains of management use the concept of culture. For strategy, culture is a diagnostic element and also acts as a framework of reference for instigating strategy. It is also a framework of reference in human resource management for the implementation of change and the involvement of the people in the process. Marketing has to do with the commercial culture of the firm and even finance shows the relation between cultural values and accounting systems. However, according to Thévenet (1999), it is still not clear whether the implicit values inherent in every management system are the same as those of the corporate culture.

If management is defined as an activity based on three aspects – action, the management of people, and the achievement of objectives – to what extent does culture affect management?

First, culture is of interest to management if it offers the possibility of increasing efficiency at various levels. If culture is taken into account, then the potential for analysis is greater and this allows the manager to explain how an organization works before deciding whether it needs to be changed.

Second, culture helps to understand the organization as an entity, as a collection of individuals who have together created a heritage of references based on the experience of the group. This serves as a framework of reference for situations in the future.

Finally, the company has a raison d'être: it is there to achieve certain objectives, to reach certain targets. It is management's task to achieve these by looking for behaviours that allow the best performance. Culture is also a source of behaviour and therefore a source of performance.

Levels of corporate culture

To define 'corporate culture', Schein (1999) starts with his general definition of culture and its three layers. He calls the first level 'artefacts', i.e. everything visible in an organization: the structure, the way the offices are arranged, the office doors (are they open or closed?), the frequency of meetings, the way people dress. However, what is easily visible or observable does not always explain why things are as they are. Answers to questions such as 'why do they do what they do' allow people to gain only a certain understanding about the 'artefacts' and behaviour patterns. It is the second level, 'espoused values', that reveals the strategies, objectives and philosophies of the organization.

Still, according to Schein, it could be that two organizations share certain values such as integrity, teamwork, customer orientation and product quality, without having the same visible behaviour. This shows there is a deeper level of thought and perception driving the overt behaviour. This is the third level, 'shared tacit assumptions'. The history of the company, all the values, beliefs and assumptions of its founder(s) and 'key leaders', as well as certain individuals or small teams who have made the company successful, all these elements form the culture of an organization. If the organization continues to perform well, then these beliefs and values are shared with newcomers and, through a joint learning process, they become tacit assumptions about the nature of the world and how to succeed in it.

In conclusion, Schein (1999) insists that cultural assumptions consist not only of the internal workings of a company, but also above all how an organization sees itself in relation to its environment. This forms the culture content of the organization, which must:

- Survive in the external environment (mission, strategy, structure, processes . . .);
- Integrate human aspects (common language, relationships . . .); and
- Take account of the national culture in which it is operating.

Corporate values

Other writers stress the importance of values. Deal and Kennedy, for example, (2000: 21) consider that values – which they define as being 'the basic concepts and beliefs of an organization' – form the basis of corporate culture: 'Values provide a sense of common direction for all employees and guidelines for their day-to-day behaviour.' They add that 'rational' managers show little concern for the system of values of an organization; they are more interested in its structure, policies and procedures, strategies or budgets. This lack of concern undermines both the leadership of the organization as well as commitment. The everyday business environment, however, requires that choices be made and values are an indispensable guide for making such choices.

According to the same authors, three characteristics emphasize values and distinguish companies from each other:

1. The organizations have an explicit philosophy as to why they are conducting business.
2. The management places great importance on communicating the values that shape the company in terms of the economic choices and the business environment of the company.
3. These values are shared at all levels of the organization, from the shop floor to the board room.

Identifying corporate cultures

Deal and Kennedy (2000: 15–16) are among the first to examine in detail the phenomenon of corporate culture. Their book is intended primarily to serve as a primer on cultural management for business leaders. Using concrete examples taken from companies that, according to them, know how to manage their culture, they examine the role of the leader as a 'mediator of behaviour' and the positive effects of building culture. The main belief is that a company is not only a place where things are produced, but also an institution whose principal resources are people. And it is these people who manage themselves by using 'the subtle cues of a culture'. A strong culture – which they see 'as a system of informal rules that spells out how people are to behave most of the time' – allows the behaviour of people to be guided and to 'feel better about what they do, so they are more likely to work harder'.

As stated in the introduction to this concept, the business environment in which a company operates has a considerable influence on the culture of the company. That is why Deal and Kennedy (2000) present a classification of the types of cultures on the basis of a study they made of various firms and their business environment. Using two factors – how much risk is involved in the firm's activities, and how much time is needed before a company and its employees know how successful their decisions or strategies have been – they distinguish four categories of culture. These categories provide a useful framework for classifying organizational cultures.

- *The tough-guy, macho culture.* This culture takes a lot of risks and quickly finds out whether its actions have been successful. A police force or a hospital can be seen as representatives of this type of culture. The construction or cosmetics industries, or even management consulting and the whole entertainment industry, are other examples, particularly since they have to deal with a lot of internal competition. This type of culture puts great emphasis on youth and speed. Decisions must be made quickly, even if there is a risk that they may not be the right ones.

- *Work hard/play hard culture.* This is a 'fun' and action culture with a tendency to pursue low-risk activities that give quick feedback. This culture is to be found in the sales department of a company or in a factory. The feedback is gained rapidly and everyone knows whether or not the work has been carried out according to the rules. There is a strict control system preventing big risks. This culture attaches particular importance to consumers and their needs. In contrast to the 'tough-guy' culture, which is 'find a mountain and climb it', the 'the work hard/play hard' culture rests on 'find a need and fill it'.

- *Bet-your-company culture.* This form favours high risk, but in an environment where feedback is slow. A lot of time passes – maybe months and years – before the employees see the benefit of the decisions taken by the company. This type of organization may invest millions in a project that will take years before it is completed – or not. The risk of the company going bankrupt is considerable. That is why relations within the company are such that discussions are encouraged to make sure that the right decision is taken.

- *The process culture.* There is little feedback within this sort of culture, and the activities are low-risk. This is typical of banks, insurance companies and financial departments, as well as in highly regulated industries such as pharmaceutical companies. As in the work/play culture, the financial interests are low but, unlike that culture, the employees receive no feedback. This lack of feedback forces employees not to worry about what they are doing but how they are doing it.

Stereotyping corporate culture

The classification model just described, whereby organizational culture is divided into four groups, has been taken up by other writers. Other criteria, however, have been used for the classification. Trompenaars and Woolliams (2003: 101) dedicate a whole chapter of their book *Business Across Cultures* to corporate culture. They describe it as the 'driver' of the organization: '"Management of culture" is now about creating a corporate culture in which people will work together to achieve the organization's goals, reconciling dilemmas that originate from issues of corporate culture.'

Just as in a society, an organization is composed of individuals with different personalities who form and share a culture. Trompenaars and Woolliams (2003: 107–111) put forward a model based on 'organizational relationships' – those between employees, between employees and their superiors and the relations within the group as a whole. By using a model that combines two dimensions – task or person (high versus low formalization), hierarchical or egalitarian (high versus low centralization), they come up with four culture stereotypes:

- *The Incubator* is like a team without a leader. Its main characteristics are that it is person-oriented and focused on self-realization, commitment to oneself and professional recognition.

- *The Guided Missile* has a low degree of centralization and a high degree of formalization. It is task-oriented with a management by objectives approach and a focus on the power of knowledge/expertise, commitment to tasks and pay for performance.

- *The Family* culture is characterized by a high degree of centralization and a low degree of formalization. It is power-oriented, with a stress on personal relationships (affinity/trust) and an entrepreneurial character.

- *The Eiffel Tower* has a high degree of formalization together with a high degree of centralization. It is role-oriented, with power attached to the position or role. The formality is reflected in the importance given to job descriptions and evaluations, rules and procedures, order and predictability.

To conclude this concept, Delavallée's conclusion (2002) appears correct, in that globalization of trade, identical management and production techniques have narrowed the differences between companies. What remains different is the culture of each company. That culture exists in its own right and, being the result of the company's history, belongs to it alone. Unlike a production method, a corporate culture cannot be copied. That culture is a way a company can differentiate itself from its global competitors. Therefore, if the company has adapted to the demands of its environment, culture remains the most effective way of maintaining a lasting competitive advantage.

This chapter has presented two ways of categorizing companies according to their structure or culture. It would be worthwhile investigating a possible correlation between the two to see if certain types of organization are more suited than others to developing specific corporate values inherent to a particular type of culture.

ACTIVITY 7.1

Read the case study below about a joint venture between a Saudi-Arabian and a German company, then answer the questions.

Bad blood

Our group, the Venture Group – a mother company in India, with as branch head, Mr Soota – received an offer to invest $2 million in a joint venture between Brigitte Zankyl GmbH in Munich and DXB-Al Fayed Corporation in Saudi Arabia. The proposed project was to build a plant in a small town near Riyadh to make blood transfusion tubes to sell in the Middle-East. The German company had the technical expertise; the knowledge, capital and funding required was to be provided by our company. At this point, Venture was in the process of negotiating the contract.

DXB-Al Fayed was a partner in the business because it had managed to negotiate and win a favourable contract with the government for the purchase of the plastic tubes. The Saudi Arabian company was in a very comfortable position: it had no financial stake in the project and was a 35 per cent partner in the business by virtue of its good contacts with the Saudi government and its in-depth knowledge of the local market.

A few senior managers from our company were asked to go to Riyadh to explore the viability of the investment. Two weeks later, after our managers had returned, the company was more convinced than ever that this was going to be a wonderful project. We only had to wait for another three weeks since the German negotiating party was going to negotiate and conclude the contract after having received the necessary approval from us.

A large delegation of nine people, including lawyers from Germany, prepared themselves for the negotiations. On the first evening after negotiations had started, we heard by phone from the German side that things were looking good.

The next day, however, we received a call from the Saudi party. They informed us that they were not willing to sign any contract with the German party and, if possible, we should try instead to team up with them. Mr Habib commented on the phone: 'I am sure that we can work with you, but Mr Zankyl and Mr Kirchdorfer are people we do not trust! We get the feeling that they are trying to fleece us. They are trying to pretend they are doing us a big favour; they think they are lords, but Allah is there watching us all. There is no place for being crooked. We have tried to work with Westerners before and they always try to be difficult. The only solution I can see is that we contract with you: you run the project. We don't care if you outsource the technology and expertise from Brigitte Zankyl, but our only condition is that they do not become a partner in our business!'

Mr Soota was becoming concerned and, to try and diffuse the situation, asked Mr Habib to calm down. 'Mr Habib,' he said, 'I apologize on behalf of my business partners in case there has been any misunderstanding. I am sure we can resolve the matter. Would you like me to fly down there early tomorrow morning so that we can resume discussions using a clean slate?'

Mr Habib appreciated Mr Soota's remarks, adding: 'I wish the German side could understand us as much as we understand each other. They do not care about what we think! All that matters to them is dollars, dollars and more dollars. Our esteemed minister Mr Sherrif gave us his word and promised us that, Insha-Allah, the government would sign the purchase contract next month, but the German lawyers told us that they would only like to see contracts in black and white and said that our word was not enough. Do they want to imply that, I, Sheikh Habib, am a liar? If they don't trust us, then I have to be honest and admit that we do not even trust them since business should be for mutual benefit and not dictated. I am sorry, but please do not expect me to respect somebody who thinks that we are dishonest and unprofessional in our approach. Mr Kirchdorfer said that our small family concern needs to gear up and act more professionally to manage the new project! But we know how to run our business – we don't need the Germans for that!'

Source: adapted from Browaeys and Trompenaars (2000): case 4.

Questions

1. Why do you think Mr Habib did not want to do business with Brigitte Zankyl GmbH?

2. In his analysis, the author of the case proposes four reasons for explaining what happened. What do you think is the most likely reason?

   a) The two contracting parties had perhaps agreed on the first level of organizational integration but had unfortunately ignored the inter-personal and cultural integration aspect of organizational synthesis, which very much provides the necessary foundation for the success of any strategic alliance. Had both parties made a conscious and deliberate effort to understand one another as individuals with an appreciation for one another's cultural bearing, perhaps the matters would not have got out of hand.

   b) The Germans and the Arabs are at opposite extremes on the monochronic–polychronic scale, therefore communication did not take place in a normal manner. Furthermore, the exigencies of the Muslim religion often complicate the interchange of ideas even more. Yet Arabs are used to dealing with foreigners and readily forgive them for not behaving like Arabs as long as they do not feel personally challenged and insulted.

   c) In the negotiations, when the German experts in finance, marketing and law met their Arabic counterparts, the Germans' approach was perhaps to try and clarify facts and determine who held the decision power. To the Germans, the Arabs appeared to be evasive and secretive, not revealing anything. For the Arabs it was not just the 'facts' that the Germans seemed to be prying into, but also the mutual understandings between the leaders and themselves.

   d) Having a 'specific' culture, the German managers perhaps found it particularly easy to insult their opposite 'diffuse' Arab partners. This is because they do not understand the principle of losing face, which is what happens when something is done that people perceive as being private. It can be inferred from the scenario that Mr Habib would have perhaps felt very insulted in front of his colleagues if the German contracting party had demanded proof of his claims about the government order.

3. What would have been the most appropriate attitude for the Germans to adopt? Explain your choice.

   a) One serious pitfall for 'universalist' cultures (Germans) in doing business with the more 'particularist' ones (Saudi Arabians) is that the importance of the relationship is often ignored. The Germans saw the contract as definite, whereas the Arabs perhaps regarded it as only a rough guide or approximation. For the Arabs, relationships have a flexibility and durability that contracts often lack. Particularists get suspicious when hurried. It is important to create a sound rational and trustworthy basis that equates the quality of the product with the quality of the personal relationship.

   b) As close working relations develop among the alliance participants, psychological contracts, based on trust and shared goals, replace the formal alliance agreement. Firms that are adept at managing strategic alliances use a flexible approach, letting their alliances evolve as conditions change over time. They not only invest adequate resources and management attention to these relationships, but also integrate the organizations so that the appropriate points of contact and communication are managed.

   c) The only solution for good communication for the 'linear-active' Germans should have been to make some concessions towards extroversion. Many find this difficult, even painful, but the rewards for doing so can be considerable. If people keep their distance, just like the Germans did in Riyadh, the Arabs will think that their physical presence is considered distasteful, or that these people are cold individuals. Arabs speak volubly and earnestly to someone they like, so the contracting party should have also attempted to do the same. When talking business with Arabs, one must always do so against an intensely personal background.

4. What would you do next if you were in Mr Soota's position? Explain why.

Conclusion

According to this chapter, to analyse the culture of an organization, it is necessary to take into account its structure. There are many organizational structures, ranging from geographic and matrix structures through to network and transnational structures. The last two seem to be the most suitable for the globalization of business. The choice of structure depends on the strategy and the mission of the organization, as well as its cultural diversity. While cultural diversity has little impact on national organizations, it can affect structure at all levels in international organizations.

However, an organization is not only characterized by its structure, but also by its specific corporate culture. Deal and Kennedy show that the culture of a company is strongly influenced by its history, by the people who compose it, and also by its attitude towards the business environment. Therefore, the corporate culture of a company - even if it is classified somehow - has unique characteristics that differentiate it from others.

Points for reflection

1. An organization's structure and culture are often seen as one and the same. Its structure is often given more serious consideration than its culture. If the size of the company increases or decreases, or if the business environment evolves, any consequent change - internal or external - often involves a change to the organization's structure. Its culture, on the other hand, is often ignored or seems to be the last resort for dealing with the company's problems.

   What do the structure and the culture have in common?

2. Even if their classification systems differ, the scholars who introduced the concept of corporate culture, such as Deal and Kennedy, and Schein, describe the basis of corporate culture using the same criteria as those used for the concept of culture. As indicated in Part One, each culture can be seen as having three layers: the 'behavioural' or 'explicit' level; a second layer containing the 'norms and values'; and a third containing its assumptions and beliefs.

   Because the systems of norms (rules of behaviour), values (what is good or bad) and beliefs appear to vary from company to company, can you therefore say what could be the function of organizational culture?

3. The culture of the organization concerned determines the success - or otherwise - of a matrix system. If conflicts are resolved through establishing clearer boarders of responsibility and authority, the result may well be a system as bureaucratic as the one it replaced. In other words, a structure created to cope with the rapidly changing demands of the multinational environment may eventually show itself to be incapable of achieving that very goal.

   To what extent can it deal with the degree of uncertainty inherent in the system, as well as the way authority and responsibility is shared?

Further reading

Deal, T.E. and Kennedy, A.A. (2000) *Corporate Cultures: The rites and rituals of corporate life*, **Cambridge, MA: Perseus.** Despite the changes of business in the past two decades, this book, written in 1982, remains relevant. In their new introduction, the authors argue that the basics – the artefacts of organizational life and the shared values – are as strong as they were in organizations twenty years ago. Their work remains, as they say, 'still deeply committed to the embryonic ideas, launched a while ago and still viable today'.

Bartlett, C.A., Ghoshal, S. and Birkinshaw, J. (2004) *Transnational Management*, **4th edn, New York, NY: McGraw-Hill.** This edition reviews the overall content of the 1989 edition. The authors discuss transnational management and focus on cross-border companies and management. It provides a fulfilling and realistic approach to the management of today's multinationals.

References

Adler, N.J. (1983, 1986 and 1991) *International Dimensions of Organizational Behaviour*, Boston, MA: Kent.

Adler, N.J. (1983) 'Organizational development in a multicultural environment', *Journal of Applied Behavioural Science,* 19(3): 249–365.

Bartlett, C.A., Ghoshal, S. and Birkinshaw, J. (2004) *Transnational Management*, 4th edn, New York, NY: McGraw-Hill.

Bartlett, C.A. and Ghoshal, S. (1989) *Managing Across Borders; The transnational solution,* Boston, MA: Hutchinson.

Browaeys, M.-J. and Trompenaars, F. (eds) (2000) *Cases Studies on Cultural Dilemmas,* Breukelen, Netherlands: Nyenrode University Press.

Deal, T.E. and Kennedy, A.A. (2000) *Corporate Cultures: The rites and rituals of corporate life,* 2nd edn, Cambridge MA: Perseus.

Delavallée, E. (2002) *La culture d'entreprise pour manager autrement,* Paris: Editions d'Organisation.

Deresky, H. (2003) *International Management: Managing across borders and cultures,* 4th edn, Upper Saddle River, NJ: Prentice Hall.

Fatehi, K. (1996) *International Management: A cross-cultural approach*, Upper Saddle River, NJ: Prentice Hall.

Hindle, T. (2006) 'The Matrix Master', *Economist,* 21 January: 3–5.

Hoecklin, L. (1995) *Managing Cultural Differences: Strategies for competitive advantage*, Wokingham: Addison-Wesley.

Holden, N.J. (2002) *Cross-Cultural Management,* Harlow: Pearson Education.

Schein, E.H. (1999) *The Corporate Culture Survival Guide,* San Francisco, CA: Jossey-Bass.

Thévenet, M. (1999) *La culture d'entreprise*, Paris: PUF Que sais-je?

Trompenaars, F. and Woolliams, P. (2003) *Business Across Cultures*, Chichester: Capstone.

Chapter 8

Culture and leadership

The previous chapter examined types of company structure and the range of corporate cultures to be found within them. By gaining insight into a company's culture, managers can see more effectively how a company works and how it can improve its performance. It is this role of management in the cultural context that Chapter 8 will examine in detail. This involves looking briefly at (Western) theories of leadership and the recent influence of Eastern ideas on them, before considering the notion that there are assumptions about leadership across all cultures.

Learning outcomes

After reading this chapter, you will gain an understanding of:

● Evolving ideas with regard to leadership, particularly those Western ideas influenced by Asian concepts of leadership.

● The notion that there are attributes of leadership shared across all cultures, even though these are perceived differently in different cultures.

Concept 8.1 Different conceptions of leadership

Before examining the role of leader, it is necessary to look at the concept of leader. A number of theories about leadership have been devised over the years, most of which emanate from the US and Europe. They contain many definitions of the term in the business context, but most assume that leadership has to do with an individual intentionally exerting influence on others to structure the relationships in an organization. Where definitions differ is with regard to how the influence is exerted and the outcome of the attempt to influence.

Related to this is the question of the difference between a manager and a leader. One can be a leader without being a manager and vice versa. The manager is often seen as the embodiment of stability within an organization, whereas the leader is more oriented to ensuring the success of the organization. The roles can be seen as contradictory, but at the same time complementary. Kotter (1990) compares the two (Table 8.1).

Table 8.1 Comparing management and leadership

	Management	Leadership
Creating an agenda	Planning and budgeting: establishing detailed steps and timetables for achieving goals, then allocating the resources necessary to make that happen	Establishing direction: developing a vision of the future, often the distant future, and strategies for producing the changes needed to achieve that vision
Developing a human network for achieving the agenda	Organizing and staffing: establishing a structure for accomplishing plans and staffing that structure with individuals; delegating responsibility and authority for carrying out the plan; providing policies and procedures to help guide people; and creating methods or systems to monitor implementation	Aligning people: communicating the direction by words and deeds to all those whose co-operation may be needed so as to influence the creation of teams and coalitions that understand the vision and strategies, and accept their validity
Execution	Controlling and problem-solving: monitoring results v plan in some detail, identifying deviations, and then planning and organizing to solve these problems	Motivating and inspiring: energizing people to overcome political, bureaucratic and resource barriers to change by satisfying basic, but often unfulfilled, human needs
Outcomes	Produces a degree of predictability and order, and has the potential of consistently producing results expected by various stakeholders (e.g. for customers, always being on time; for stockholders, being on budget)	Produces change, often to a dramatic degree, and has the potential of producing extremely useful change (e.g. new products that customers want, new approaches to labour relations that help make a firm more competitive)

Source: Kotter (1990): 6

The first leader

The prototype leader in a business context is the entrepreneur who founds a company. That person will have a strong influence from the start. He/she will determine the mission of the company and the environmental context in which it operates. Schein (2004) describes the founding process and the mechanisms which the leader may use to implant and maintain the corporate culture:

- What the leader considers important and pays attention to, what must be measured and controlled. This has considerable influence on people in the working environment.
- The way a leader reacts to difficult situations and crises. This shows others within the company how they should react in similar situations.
- The priorities a leader sets when allocating resources.
- The examples set by a leader. These teach and reinforce desired values and behaviours.
- The criteria a leader uses to allocate rewards and status as well as to reinforce desired behaviours.
- The criteria used for recruitment, selection, promotion and dismissal.

However, as many entrepreneurs have discovered, once they stand back from the company they started, the company culture takes on a life of its own. The leader's pioneering work may have resulted in the establishment of routines in all aspects of the company's operations. Such routines/habits may, however, be difficult to break if there is felt to be need for change in response to a dynamic environment. The increasing size of a successful company and the consequent decentralization of its operations may water down the power and influence exerted by those who have replaced the leader. This management team may not recognize the need for change when the company undergoes some sort of decline and may instead cling to power, preferring to keep things going as they have always done and blaming the environment for the change in its fortunes. Then it is up to the leader to re-assert his position and to instigate changes to revitalize the company. Or hand over the reins to a successor or new leader from the management team.

In recent history, it is the industrial revolution that spawned the founder/leader as well as the study of organizations. The next section will give a brief account of the development of organization theory with emphasis on the role of the leader/manager.

The theories evolving around the leader

Research on organizations and the decision-makers focused originally on the organization of work systems. The production process, including the increasing specialization and division of labour emerging from the industrial revolution, was the focus of attention. What was the best way for a leader to get the job done in the most efficient way possible? This led to the development of **principles of scientific leadership** towards the end of the nineteenth century, whereby the questions of planning, organizing, leading and controlling a group of employees were approached in a scientific way. Standard methods for doing a job were developed – the worker was not required to think, only the leader. Chapter 6 touched on these issues when examining cultural elements relating to the tasks of the manager.

Bureaucratic organizations were the eventual product of this approach to managing production processes, particularly as a response to much larger companies. In such bureaucracies the leader heads a carefully designed hierarchy of authority, where responsibilities are clearly defined. Functions within the organization become specialized, information- and control-centralized. The totally rational approach of this model is emphasized by the uniform application of standard rules and procedures. All employees play a role in this bureaucratic world that is totally separate from the one they play in their private lives. Examples of bureaucracies include not only government departments, the police and military, but also large companies.

Alongside these process-focused theories emerged ideas about the ideal leader. The first clearly definable trend was the **trait approach**, which took many ideas from historians, psychologists and sociologists. The theory was developed that some people have traits – and skills – which will make them seek out and reach positions of leadership and be effective in them, whatever the situation, whoever the 'followers'. Great leaders throughout history were examined and the features they had in common. Stogdill (1974), for example, reviewed studies of leader attributes and made a list of characteristics of a successful leader from different countries. These included:

- high intelligence;
- considerable verbal fluency;

- overall knowledge;
- considerable initiative involving energy, ambition and persistence;
- height: tallness implies authority!

The question of **human relations** within organizations only began to achieve prominence as a result of research carried out in the late 1920s and early 1930s by Elton Mayo. His book *The Social Problems of an Industrial Civilization* (2007), originally published in 1933, describes experiments carried out at the Hawthorne Works of the Western Electric Company in Chicago, USA. Mayo showed how attitudes and feelings influence the productivity of the workers. Job satisfaction was created more through teamwork and co-operation with management rather than financial incentives or improved working conditions.

Attempts were made to marry the scientific and human approaches by focusing on the role of the decision-makers. If they are to operate successfully, they need to find a compromise between rational, goal-oriented behaviour and non-rational behaviour among an organization's employees.

Task orientation versus relationship orientation

With the shift to the human factor came a shift in emphasis with regard to the recipe for leadership success. The style of leadership behaviour became the base for analysis, particularly as to how leaders interacted with groups under various conditions.While a leader needs to remain task-oriented to ensure effective performance of the organization, he has to be a relationship-oriented leader to ensure greater satisfaction among subordinates. The successful leader, it was maintained, managed to balance both task and relationship concerns. Maintaining this balance was necessary to ensure the effectiveness of the group.

The **X and Y theory** of McGregor (1960) gave a startling contrast between the task-oriented view and human-oriented view. The message accompanying this theory was that managers should take a more positive approach toward employees, delegate authority, making jobs more challenging, providing rewards for superior performance, and treating workers with respect.

Theory X is based on a pessimistic approach and assumes that people have an inherent dislike of work and will do a lot to avoid it. They generally lack ambition, avoid responsibility and seek security in the workplace, lack imagination, creativity and initiative. The theory X manager is results-driven, demands and does not ask, has little interest in human issues, and shows little concern for the morale of the workforce. The X manager does not listen to suggestions for improvement, sees criticism as threatening, holds responsibility but is the first to hold subordinates accountable for failures.

Theory Y is based on an optimistic approach and suggests that people actually like working under suitable conditions; they are self-starters, willing to accept responsibility, are creative and imaginative. The Y manager believes people, under the right conditions, want to learn to accept and to seek responsibility. The Y manager wants employees to participate in decision-making and problem-solving – people's creativity can be used to solve problems and further the organization's success.

One drawback to this approach was that it gave little consideration to the influence of different situations in which a leader may operate and how these affect the effectiveness of the leader. Theories were developed to try and establish the factors determining an appropriate match between leadership style and demands of the situation. The implication of this approach is that there is no universal answer as to what makes an effective leader. If there is one answer that can be given, it is 'it depends . . .'

Therefore, in the search of leadership effectiveness, the focus of the research being done in North America shifted from the person to the context in which leadership takes place. Fred Fiedler (1967) established a new perspective on the study of leadership, and many studies since have adopted a similar approach.

The contingency theory considers how performance of the workers in an organization is the result of the interaction of two factors: leadership style and situational favourableness. Leadership effectiveness is the result of interaction between the style of the leader and the characteristics of the environment in which the leader works. This environment is characterized by three factors:

- Leader–member relationship: the degree of confidence, trust, and respect.
- Task-structure: the extent to which it is necessary to spell out the goals, procedure and guidelines to the workers.
- Position power: the extent to which the leader or the group holds the power. The leader's power may be boosted by the expertise shown and the authority to reward or punish.

Fiedler (1967) presents two extreme situations, describing all the contingent factors:

- A highly favourable situation in which everyone gets along well, the task performed is clear and the leader enjoys considerable power. In this situation, all that is needed is someone to take charge and show direction.
- A highly unfavourable situation in which the leader has a battle of wills with the workforce and the task is not clearly structured. The leader needs to be strong to counterbalance the power of the workforce and to show direction in an ambiguous environment.

In the latter situation, suggests Fiedler, actions can be taken to improve the situation:

- Change relations with the workforce (spend more time with group, change the composition of the workforce, and offer additional rewards).
- Change the nature of the task (make the task less or more structured, create unusual tasks, ask for the workforce's help in restructuring the task).
- Change the position of power (raise the leader's authority by making full use of all powers available, allowing information to be spread by the leader only; reduce the leader's power by inviting the workforce to participate in decision-makings, delegating powers and authority).

Fiedler's theory is implicitly related to leadership in North America: no mention is made of cultural impediments to improving the leader's situation (see Concept 8.2). The context within which the contingency theory was developed was that of (North American) companies running bureaucratic systems whereby the core functions of planning, organizing and controlling workforces could be exercised efficiently to ensure maximum economies of scale and increased output.

This way of functioning had indeed appeared to be working well: the growth and profitability of the US economy had soared during the 1950s, 1960s and most of the 1970s. By that time, however, the increasing presence of Japanese products in the US domestic market was beginning to take its toll. The car and electronics sectors in particular were being hit hard by innovative, well-made and well-priced products from Japan. The attention of researchers in management inevitably turned increasingly to the Japanese way of doing business and their approach to management.

The Z theory

Reference has been made in Chapter 4 to the Japanese concept of 'Wa'. This is the notion of harmony, reflected in the considerable degree of collaborative behaviour and consensus-building within an organization. This is in turn reflected in the **Z theory**, developed and introduced by William G. Ouchi (1981). He describes the basic elements of the Japanese management approach and explains what US business people can learn from their Japanese counterparts.

Theory Z is a kind of extension of McGregor's X and Y theory in that it combines elements of theory Y with features of modern Japanese management. Ouchi's theory assumes that employees are disciplined, have a strong moral obligation to work hard and want to establish close, co-operative working relations with their colleagues as well as those for whom they are working. They can be trusted to work hard as long as management can be trusted to give them maximum support and to show concern for their well-being. This entails the organization giving consideration to the workers' families and traditions since these are as important as work itself.

Management's job is to ensure that employees increase their knowledge of the company through training and job rotation. Rather than becoming specialists, the employees develop a range of skills that can be applied in many parts of the company's operations. Through gaining considerable familiarity with the company's operations while being trained to develop their skills and decision-making competence, the workers are expected to develop a loyalty to the company and to devote themselves to it for their working-life. If they are eventually promoted to a high managerial position, they will be very knowledgeable about the company and the way it operates and will in turn be in a position to apply management Z theories to new employees.

This theory moves on from theories X and Y in that it focuses less on management and motivation from the manager's viewpoint, and more on the attitudes and responsibilities of subordinates. It reflects the fundamental concept found in Japan, and one which managers have as their starting-point, that all employees share a collective responsibility for the fate of their company. To that end, individuals are encouraged to develop their potential within the company. Rather than being tied to one position, they are expected, with training, to function in different positions.

This approach was very different to that taken in North America, where the principles of scientific management still tended to predominate, even though they had been softened to some extent by a greater emphasis on human relations. Nevertheless, the Z theory has had an enormous effect on management in the US. Its many advocates point out that 'type Z' companies are among the most successful and fast-growing types of businesses in the US.

The new leadership

A transformational rather than a transactional leader

The perception of leadership has changed in line with the development of ideas concerning organizations and management described above. Leadership theories nowadays place less emphasis on planning, allocating responsibilities and controlling, and give more emphasis to motivating and inspiring subordinates, creating change and empowering others. The new leader creates, communicates and embodies a vision that can influence changes in the attitudes and assumptions of subordinates, builds their commitment to the organization and inspires trust, confidence and loyalty. This is the new **transformational leader**.

Barnard Bass (1985) makes a distinction between the transformational leader, as described above, and the traditional leader, whom he describes as a **transactional leader**, someone who has more of a 'business-like' relation with subordinates. The starting-point for the latter is essentially that of exchange between leader and subordinates: 'I'll look after your interests if you look after mine (and the company's)'. In other words, transactional leaders appeal to the self-interest of all parties.

In his later work on leadership (written with Avolio, 2002) Bass makes it clear that there is need in business for both types of leadership. The most effective leaders, he and Avolio discovered, were both transformational and transactional in their leadership style. Exhibit 8.1 considers the notion of 'charisma' in leaders.

At present, a lot of energy, particularly in the US, is being invested in the concept of leadership. The certainties of the recent past as to the role of the leader have given way to much thought and examination of the elusive nature of leadership. More inclusive models of leadership have come to the fore, including one called 'quiet management' which

---

Exhibit 8.1

A gift from the gods?

Max Weber, a German sociologist, used the term 'charisma' when describing the qualities some leaders have that enable them to motivate others to achieve outstanding performance. This term – a Greek word meaning 'a gift from the gods' – is used frequently when describing transformational leaders. Robert House (1977) tried to define the charismatic leader by referring to:

- personality, which has a profound effect on their followers;
- the need for power, which motivates them to be a leader;
- their strong feeling of self-efficacy: they feel they are essentially capable; and

- their conviction in the moral rightness of their beliefs.

One crucial element is their ability to inspire those around them to create a dedicated, loyal workforce by articulating a clear, compelling vision.

Republican politician George Bush (senior), when campaigning for the US presidency, was asked why he focused on the short-term objectives and not on the longer term. Bush's reaction was:

'Oh, the vision thing.'

advocates a quieter, less dramatic leadership at all levels of an organization. To quote Mintzberg (1999: 30):

> Quiet management is about thoughtfulness rooted in experience. Words like wisdom, trust, dedication and judgement apply. Leadership works because it is legitimate, meaning that it is an integral part of the organisation and so has the respect of everyone there. Tomorrow is appreciated because yesterday is honoured. That makes today a pleasure. Indeed, the best managing of all may well be silent. That way people can say, 'We did it ourselves.' Because we did.

Although such an idea may have been crafted in the US, it does demonstrate how the very nature of leadership has undergone considerable cultural influence from leadership in eastern cultures, particularly those of China and Japan. Lao Tzu, the sixth-century Chinese philosopher who was an older contemporary of Confucius and proponent of Taoism, believed that human life, like everything in the universe, is constantly influenced by outside forces. He believed that simplicity offered the key to truth and freedom and told his followers to try to understand the laws of nature through careful observation. In this way they could develop their intuition and increase their personal power; and to use that power to lead life with love, and without force. His works have considerable resonance in today's uncertain world and some of his quotations parallel the ideas of many contemporary thinkers with regard to leadership. The quote from Lao Tzu below contains similar ideas to those put forward by Mintzberg with regard to the idea of collective leadership:

> A leader is best when people barely know he exists, not so good when people obey and acclaim him, worse when they despise him. But of a good leader who talks little when his work is done, his aim fulfilled, they will say: we did it ourselves.
>
> (http://uoleadership.uoregon.edu/resources/quotes)

The role of the leader in a 'learning organization'

The type Z theory heralded the concept of the learning organization, which itself was a response to the increasing uncertainty and complexity of global business. Peter Senge, one of the architects of the concept, saw that learning, or rather the rate of learning, could offer organizations an immense, sustainable advantage in a world where competition is becoming increasingly stronger. In his seminal work, *The Fifth Discipline*, Senge (1990: 3) defines learning organizations as:

> . . . organisations where people continually expand their capacity to create the results they truly desire, where new and expansive patterns of thinking are nurtured, where collective aspiration is set free, and where people are continually learning to see the whole together.

Organizations are not, in his opinion, structured to allow people to reflect on what they are doing or to become engaged in their work. People need tools and guiding ideas to cope with and give real meaning to the situations they face. Senge (1990) advocates the mastery of disciplines that enable people to gain a broader view of the organization's operations, to see themselves not as powerless figures in the corporate landscape but as participants who shape that very landscape. Rather than just coping with the present they are also helping to create the future. Rather than being traditional heroes who charismatically rescue their organization from a crisis, leaders of learning organizations have a more important, if less flamboyant, role to play. They are essentially responsible for learning in the organization:

they design the learning processes, create, foster and manage a shared vision, and help people to understand what brings about change. Such leaders have to counter the 'mental models' that hold back members of an organization from participating fully in its operation by bringing about a fundamental shift of mind among the members of the organization. This entails 'discover[ing] how to tap people's commitment and capacity to learn at *all* levels in an organization' (1990: 4).

This concept has offered a framework of reference on leadership by outlining the development in thought with regard to leadership. It has shown how many of the theories developed came from North America and Western Europe, but also how recent ideas have been heavily influenced by the approach taken by Japanese management. The next concept will take some of these ideas on leadership, consider some of the cultural implications and go in search of attributes of leadership that can be applied across cultures. Meanwhile, Case study 8.1 gives further thoughts on the nature of leadership.

Case study 8.1

Define your leader

The session 'Define your leader', 29 January 2001, at the annual meeting of the World Economic Forum started with the experiences of two people with 'outstanding stories', in the words of moderator John R. O'Neil, president of the Center for Leadership Renewal in the US. Lorraine Monroe, director of the School Leadership Academy in the US, admitted she 'loved the power of leading'. She outlined a list of characteristics of great leaders that she had largely gained from her experience as a head teacher in failing schools. In her view, successful leaders:

- can identify and articulate a dream, and inspire a team to carry it out;
- are creatively crazy;
- can identify people who can replace you;
- can fire people, though this takes guts;
- have done the job themselves, so carry credibility with the team;
- are able to balance home and work – particularly difficult for women;
- can emanate a vision, and realize when this is no longer the case, and are prepared to quit before people notice.

Warren Bennis, professor of business administration and founding chairman of the Leadership Institute at Marshall School of Business of the University of Southern California, focused on what he called 'finding your voice'. This is a combination of self-awareness and character, the ability to differentiate 'what you want to be from what you want to do'. Great leaders all know their real selves and have sometimes taken extraordinary steps to discover this, like Gandhi who spent a year listening to Indian villagers to understand his destiny.

O'Neil quoted a definition of leadership used in the Basque country:

- show up on time;
- all of you show up on time;
- tell the truth and work hard;
- work hard but don't let the outcome be attached to your ego.

→

Asked about the role of charisma in a leader, Bennis said that the leader was 'a social architect whose role it is to create the ecology of learning'. Many great leaders, including Martin Luther King, whom he had known, were accidental leaders. King had a symbiotic relationship with his followers – it was he who followed them to jail, at first. In Monroe's view, the leader has to 'galvanize' activity.

Challenged by a participant to distinguish between a leader and a manager, Monroe said that managers 'don't give joy'. In her view, the ideas person is the leader. 'You can hire managers, but it is hard to hire a dreamer.' O'Neil stated that most leaders evolve with time and are sufficiently self-critical to 'know that what was great last year needs to be scrutinized the next'. A comment from the floor suggested that leaders need to lead from the front to handle crises, but could be just as effective as 'servant leaders', leading from behind at other times. Monroe said a true leader is sensitive about knowing when to drop back.

On the question of whether some people are natural leaders and others followers, Bennis said that some leaders had an enormous desire to lead, others learned the skill over time, and yet others decided to drop leadership. O'Neil said that a common problem was when good leaders 'lose their creative connection' and didn't realize it. At the same time, they lost their powers of empathy: 'They think they are listening, but in fact they no longer are.' Some leaders fail because they suffer from hubris, often fed by subordinates. Other leaders become alienated and then very bored.

Acknowledging that it is difficult to explain leadership, Bennis said that leaders tended to have a stronger moral voice 'which touches the human heart'.

Source: www.weforum.org/site/knowledgenavigator.nsf/Content/_S3330?open

Question

From your reading of the text, which elements do you think support the thesis that 'Leaders are born not made'? Which other elements from the text do you believe support the idea that people can be trained to become leaders?

Concept 8.2 Leadership in an international context

This concept will first consider the extent to which aspects of culture can influence 'Western' ideas of leadership before examining the question of whether there are attributes of leadership that can be found in all cultures.

Cultural contingency factors

As mentioned earlier, Fred Fiedler (1967) has had a considerable influence on leadership theory. The idea that leadership effectiveness is the result of interaction between the style of the leader and the characteristics of the environment is seductive.

However, if culture is taken explicitly into account, leaders may not be able to exercise all the variables that Fiedler describes because of cultural constraints. Instead of being in a position to influence the workforce and the dominant culture, they may be forced to alter their own leadership behaviour to conform to the cultural realities they face. Managers working in an international environment may need to take account of cultural differences and adapt their style of leadership accordingly.

Two areas where cultural attitudes and values can obviously have a big effect on styles of leadership have already been touched upon in Part One: the wielding of power and the handling of uncertainty.

In those societies where **power** is more evenly distributed among the members, the difference between the more powerful members and the least powerful members is small. In those societies where there is a wide variation in power distribution, the difference between the most powerful and least powerful is large. Here, large differences in power are legitimate and acceptable. Should an attempt be made to reduce the distance between the leader and the workforce by increasing accessibility between the two and attempting to engender a friendly interaction, the subordinates concerned may well feel uncomfortable with these changes and may indeed attribute some sinister motive to the actions. In such an environment, subordinates' expectations have a considerable influence on whether certain leadership behaviours are feasible. In cultures where there is a large power distance, an ideal leader may well be expected to display great authority, but to do so to the benefit of those being led. A benevolent autocrat or paternalist is not expected to ingratiate himself gratuitously with his subjects. Age, experience and accumulated wisdom will account for more than the actual ability to do the job.

The second factor is to do with the way cultures handle **uncertainty**. This ties in with the question of task structure as a contingency factor raised by Fiedler (1967). Cultures with strong uncertainty avoidance are unwilling to take risks and to assume heavy responsibilities. In the workplace they prefer to work by the book, to rely on rules, regulations and instructions. They avoid ambiguities in their tasks and prefer to be told how to carry out their tasks. In Fiedler's terms, therefore, the leader may well need to show direction and make sure that tasks are unambiguous and well structured.

What Fiedler does not address in his contingency theory is the nature of the leader who is making decisions as to how best to lead. Is his own cultural profile not a contingency factor which has to be taken account of? If he is himself risk-averse by nature, can he be expected to lead a company to success in a competitive environment, particularly if the employees in that company are similarly risk-averse?

Inevitably, discussion turns to an individual leader in a particular company in a particular cultural context. By doing so, the focus is less on the general tendencies displayed by a certain culture, its companies and its representatives and more on particular examples. Evans et al (2002) rightly warn their readers of applying a cultural perspective that only takes account of 'central tendencies'. The variance within a culture can, they maintain, be as great as the variation of means across cultures. Although the authors acknowledge that the cultural perspective offers considerable insights into attitudes towards power and uncertainty, they recognize that culture may be used as an excuse for not trying to make changes to ensure a company's success. Indeed, increased sensitivity to cultural differences may discourage attempts to get people to adapt to practices (if not values) used in other cultures. Moreover, cultural factors do not stand alone when a company's fortunes are being considered. Others factors – including economic ones – need to be considered when determining how best to lead a company. Consider the Case study 8.2.

Case study 8.2

Turnaround

The experiences of Carlos Ghosn are worth dwelling on in this context. Born in Brazil, of Lebanese parents, Ghosn helped create and led a strategic alliance between a French and a Japanese car manufacturer. Ghosn managed to persuade the Japanese side of the alliance not only to accept radical changes to the way the company operated but also to implement these efficiently. Ghosn was parachuted in by Renault to join a company with debt of $20 billion. Within one year of his arrival, Nissan's net loss of $6.1 billion had become a net profit of $2.7 billion. This transformation in the company's fortune was brought about by an outsider who managed to cut costs and transform business practices.

What was the secret of Ghosn's success? Many articles, case studies and books have tried to reveal the answer, but from Nguyen-Huy's lucid account (2004) alone, it is clear that Ghosn listened carefully to the company's woes at all levels, became aware of how distressed all employees were about Nissan's poor performance, and of how their pride in the company had been undermined. The need to restore Nissan's 'face' was clearly an important factor in persuading the company's employees that what became known as the 'Nissan revival plan' was the only feasible solution. Good intentions, however, need to be put into practice, and Ghosn's concern with implementation helped assure the plan's success.

This happened in a country where everything is done to avoid uncertainty and where careful, drawn-out consensus-building within the company and its other stakeholders is normally a prerequisite of any change in business procedures and direction, and where seniority is the basis of a person's authority within a company.

Universal attributes and cultural variables

The question of the **universality of leader behaviours** is one of a number of issues dealt with in the Global Leadership and Organizational Behaviour Effectiveness research programme. As was described in Part One, GLOBE is a long-term programme designed to conceptualize, operationalize, test and validate a cross-level integrated theory of the relationship between culture and societal, organizational and leadership effectiveness. One of its elements has been to try to discover whether there are attributes across all cultures involved in the project that are considered to contribute to outstanding leadership.

The findings of the project confirm the general hypothesis that operational and managerial practices are usually a reflection of the cultural orientation of the society where they are being carried out. As for leadership attributes, the project findings have managed to pinpoint two aspects of leadership that are reported to be highly effective in all the societies studied. These are:

● Team-oriented leading, where the emphasis is on building effective teams and implementing a goal common to team members.

● The 'communication of vision, values and confidence in followers' (House et al, 2004: 7)

However, variations between societies have been found with regard to other dimensions. The perceived effectiveness of participative leadership – the extent to which leaders involve others in making and implementing decisions – was highest among Anglo cultures,

Northern European cultures and Germanic Europe. Another factor, autonomous leadership, was subject to even greater variation in the findings. This newly defined dimension refers to independent and individual leadership, which involves a high degree of social distance from subordinates. It was perceived as contributing slightly to organizational effectiveness in East European countries (except for Hungary) and Germanic Europe (except for the Netherlands). On the other hand, in Anglo countries, Latin America (apart from Argentina) and the Middle East (apart from Egypt), it was perceived as ineffective.

The findings with regard to another newly defined dimension, self-protective leadership, showed a similar degree of variation. This leadership focuses on maintaining the leader's safety and security and involves elitism as well as a tendency to create conflict with others. Leaders who practise self-protective behaviour were regarded as being slightly effective in Albania, Taiwan, Egypt, Iran and Kuwait. In all other countries, however, they were considered to be ineffective, particularly in France and countries in Northern Europe.

It should be noted here that the detailed findings of the research showed that there were specific attributes of leadership which were universally regarded as ineffective, most of which relate to the 'self-protective' dimension (see the second column of Table 8.2). The first column lists attributes to be found universally that reflect good leadership. The third column shows cultural variations with regard to acceptance or rejection of certain attributes.

Although the GLOBE project has made use of sophisticated multiple measurement methods to validate its hypotheses, one question that arises when examining the lists of attributes in Figure 8.2 concerns their manifestation in different cultures. House et al (2004: 727)

Table 8.2 Attributes of leadership

Universal attributes that reflect good leadership	Universal attributes that impede good leadership	Cultural variations of acceptance/rejection of attributes
<ul><li>integrity (trustworthiness, honesty, fairness)</li><li>charisma (encouraging, positive, motivational, confidence-building behaviour showing dynamism and foresight)</li><li>team-oriented leadership (effective in building teams, communicating and co-ordinating)</li><li>decisiveness</li><li>intelligence</li><li>orientation towards excellence</li></ul>	<ul><li>Irritable</li><li>egocentric</li><li>loner</li><li>non-explicit</li><li>asocial</li><li>dictatorial</li><li>ruthless</li><li>unco-operative</li></ul>	<ul><li>independent, autonomous, individualistic</li><li>subdued, self-effacing, self-sacrificial</li><li>domineering, ruler</li><li>status-conscious, class conscious, elitist</li><li>enthusiastic, compassionate, sensitive, sincere</li><li>orderly, formal, logical, procedural, habitual</li><li>intuitive</li><li>risk-taking, cautious, able to anticipate</li><li>wilful, ambitious</li><li>evasive, indirect, cunning</li></ul>

Source: Tables 21.2, 21.3 and 21.4 in House et al (2004).

give an example with regard to the attribute 'integrity' – which is universally considered to be desirable:

> ... does it mean the same thing to a Chinese as it does to an American. How do people in different cultures conceptualise, perceive and exhibit behaviour that reflects integrity?

The next phase of the GLOBE project intends to address such daunting questions, to identify the behavioural manifestations of the leadership attributes that it has investigated.

The **universality of transformational leadership** is given particular attention by de Hartog et al (1999). They note many hypotheses developed with regard to leadership across cultures using Hofstede's dimensions. These include:

- Collective cultures will find it easier to be persuaded by transformational leaders.
- High-uncertainty avoidance cultures will flock to charismatic leaders, but will shy away from leaders who display innovative behaviour.
- More masculine cultures will appreciate strong directive leaders, whereas more feminine cultures will prefer leaders who are more considerate and consultative.
- High power distance cultures will appreciate a dominant display of authority, whereas low power distance cultures will prefer leaders who show themselves to be just like those they are leading.

The authors then refer to studies on transformational leadership that show how different countries have different components of transformational leadership. Studies done in the Netherlands, Scandinavia and Australia, for example, suggest that being participative is an important part of being a transformational leader. Such societies are seen as strongly egalitarian, with low power distance, and transformational leaders are expected to allow a measure of participation in decision-making. The 'tall poppy syndrome', referred to in Part One, whereby Australians tend to pour scorn on those who stand out because of their achievements, highlights the negative attitudes in that society towards charismatic leaders. Such leaders must do their jobs well, keep their feet on the ground, show humility and not take themselves too seriously.

Den Hartog et al refer in particular to Bass (1997) who proposes that transformational leadership may be universal, but this does not exclude the possibility that the way transformational attributes are expressed may differ between cultures. The concept of charisma, for example, may well be shared among all cultures, but what each culture perceives as charismatic behaviour may differ.

A further issue with regard to universal attributes of leadership is that of **gender**: are some universal attributes more prevalent among male or female leaders?

One starting-point is to try and determine whether there actually are gender differences in leadership. The literature on leadership and gender is mainly US-oriented and frequently examines the influence gender has on aspects of leadership. Feminine leadership styles are generalized as being concerned for the welfare of others, democratic and charismatic. These features are related to the stereotype view of women as being warm, sensitive, considerate and expressive. Masculine leadership styles are generalized as being less interpersonal-oriented and more focused on the task. The stereotypical traits related include decisiveness, aggression, independence and objectivity.

One theory frequently put forward in the literature to account for these differences is based on the division of labour in the home: qualities required for domestic activities, of which women take the major share, are to do with rearing children and maintaining family cohesion. Men, the theory maintains, perform more tasks outside the home and require qualities that enable them to survive and even thrive in a competitive environment.

If feminine leadership styles are different to male-oriented ones, the matter of their effectiveness brings up the question of contingency. So many factors within an organization need to be considered when determining which style of leadership is appropriate. Task-oriented behaviour (as evident in transactional leadership) may be more appropriate at times, and relation-oriented behaviour (as evident in transformational leadership) more appropriate at others. In the same way that male leaders may need to pay more attention to interpersonal skills alongside their 'natural' authoritative, decisive behaviour, female leaders may see themselves compelled at times to perform in a task-oriented way while still practising their 'natural' intuitive, empathic skills.

Gender can be regarded as just one of many social differences that play an important role in the development of leadership styles. Developing an appropriate, effective style of leadership may be hampered by *gender stereotypes* clouding the perception subordinates have of what makes a successful leader. Overcoming these stereotypes, while focusing on the characteristics appropriate to the position, remains key for any candidate for leadership, whether male or female.

Do these considerations concerning gender and leadership apply across cultures? Although international research in this area is thin on the ground, one survey carried out across a number of countries – both in the East and West – still has a certain resonance. In Judy Rosener's survey (1990), members of the International Women's Forum, together with matched male counterparts, were asked to describe, among other things, their leadership performance as well as the ways they used to influence those with whom they worked. Male respondents generally saw their job performance as a series of transactions with subordinates whereby rewards were given for satisfactory performance, and punishments given for inadequate performance. They saw the power they used as coming from their formal, hierarchical position within the company. Female respondents, on the other hand, saw their leadership role as getting subordinates to see the bigger picture, to move beyond self-interest and consider the interest of the group as a whole. Female leaders considered their power to come less from their position in the organization and more from their own character – their charisma, their interpersonal skills and their ability to work hard. Rosener summarizes the differences between male and female leaders in terms of the transactional and transformational behaviour referred to earlier.

This survey, as well as other limited research carried out in the area where leadership, gender and culture interact, suggests that differences between genders in one culture are also found in other cultures. Male and female leaders, it appears, display differing behavioural tendencies whatever their country of origin. Although leadership style may be based on gender, differences in the leadership style employed are based more on culture than on gender.

This concept has briefly described cultural variables that apply to conceptions of leadership. It has also shown that there are consistent elements of leadership recognized across cultures but whose form may vary between cultures. Moreover, this concept has indicated that some modern concepts of leadership generated in the West appear to have their antecedents in the East. Different cultures, it seems, can generate similar perceptions of leadership, even if the contexts within which leadership is affected are very different.

ACTIVITY 8.1

Le patron, der Chef and the boss

By Alison Maitland

Have you heard the one about the three captains of industry? The Brit insists he is happy to have his decisions challenged. The German stresses the importance of humility. And the Frenchman enjoys wielding power without having to consult first.

Far from being a joke, these are the revealing findings of a new survey of 200 chief executives, chairmen and directors in the UK, Germany and France. It is often assumed that rules about leadership apply regardless of culture or nationality. But the survey suggests this is an over-simplification. It highlights big differences in national attitudes to responsibility, status and decision-making that global companies would do well to understand.

The research, co-ordinated by MORI for DDI, an international human resources consultancy, labels French captains of industry as 'autocrats', Germans as 'democrats' and British as 'meritocrats'.

In support of these catchy generalisations, it finds that fewer than three in 10 French bosses are happy to be challenged about the decisions they make, compared with half of Germans and more than nine out of 10 business leaders in the UK. The French prize the autonomy they gain from the job. Nearly two-thirds count 'the freedom to make decisions with minimum interference' as one of the three best things about being a leader.

'I enjoy the decision-making without having to confer with others,' says one Gallic captain of industry. Only 46 per cent of bosses in Germany and 39 per cent in the UK regard this as being important.

The ability to hand-pick their team is another perk of the job for the French, but one that is less highly rated in Germany and Britain.

For business leaders in the UK and Germany, the best thing about the job is developing talent in the company. Seventy per cent of British bosses and nearly 50 per cent of Germans – but only 14 per cent of French ones – rate this among the top three benefits of leadership.

Although few of the 200 captains of industry choose 'being in a position of power' as one of the three best things about the job, the French are three times more likely than the British, and eight times more likely than the Germans, to regard this as important, the survey finds.

'In Germany, you accept the responsibility of authority but you don't talk about it, whereas typically in France, if you belong to the upper echelons of management, or if you own a company, it's a badge of success that you wear in every aspect of your life,' says Steve Newhall, managing director of DDI Europe.

Public recognition is more important in France, reflecting the kudos attached to a senior position in business, he says. Just over 30 per cent of French chief executives and directors rate this as one of the three best things about being a leader, compared with 16 per cent in Germany and just two per cent in the UK.

Is it possible that these differences simply reflect greater honesty from the French about enjoying the exercise of power, while the British and Germans consider this would be politically incorrect? Mr Newhall admits it is hard to be sure, but he says the anonymity of the interviews makes it likely these are genuine differences.

'The intention was to get as honest an answer as possible and to probe behind the PR,' he says. 'The French are more likely to respond in that way because it's something that's acceptable within their cultural norms. We know about the *grandes écoles* system where the elite are prized. In the UK, "the establishment" is used more as a derogatory than a positive term.'

He says he is not suggesting that one leadership style is better than another. But executives of international companies need to be like chameleons, able to adapt to the corporate and national culture in which they are working, while not abandoning their individualism.

'The danger for any leader is only being able to operate within one of these styles. If you take an autocratic style into a culture that expects a more democratic or meritocratic style, the chances are that you will trip up.'

German leaders stand out in the survey for their social conscience and their concern about the responsibility that goes with power. Nearly half say that one of their top three concerns is having to make tough decisions that affect people's futures – compared with only 28 per cent of leaders in the UK and 20 per cent in France.

'Sometimes the amount of influence I have frightens me,' says one German boss. 'I have to be very cautious and thoroughly weigh up the pros and cons of any decision.' Another comment: 'You have to remain humble: personal vanity and over-estimating your ability will lead to the downfall of the enterprise.'

Given such modest responses, it is perhaps paradoxical that deference is strongest in Germany, with nearly 60 per cent of business leaders saying their decisions are likely to go unchallenged. Four in 10 German bosses cite fear of failure as a top concern, compared with just over two in 10 in Britain. Mr Newhall believes this reflects the lingering stigma of failure in Germany, which contrasts with the Anglo-American preference to see failure as an opportunity to learn and move on.

Leaders in the UK appear the most upbeat, perhaps because of the more stable economic environment, the research finds. What keeps them awake at night are external pressures, such as new legislation and corporate governance issues.

For French leaders, warring egos in the management team are a big concern. While this may simply reflect Gallic style, the DDI report suggests that French chief executives' fondness for independent decision-making may lead to friction.

Despite the many differences, some worries and beliefs are shared across all three countries. Lack of personal time is a common concern. The importance of the team is widely appreciated.

'Again and again, in private one-to-one interviews, whether face-to-face or on the phone, captains of industry stated their focus to be on responsibility rather than power, and on their team's success rather than their own,' says Mr Newhall.

This emphasis on collaboration is epitomised by a German boss who says: 'I see myself as a service provider in a company run as a democracy, where everyone pulls together to achieve the strategies we have worked out together.' A French respondent concurs: 'We are working in an ever more complex environment, and working efficiently within a team is the best way.'

A final common theme is that the risks increase the higher you get, and that nothing can fully prepare you for the challenge of running a company. Enjoy it while it lasts. As a German respondent puts it: 'It is a long hard climb to the top of the mountain. There is a nice view, but it is quite windy.'

Source: *Financial Times*, 9 January 2006: 10.

After reading the article

1. Look again at the text and try to determine what questions were used in the survey.

2. Enter key examples in the table below of behaviour or attitudes that reflect the label given to each type of leader at the beginning of the article

Le patron: the autocrat	*Der chef:* the democrat	*The boss:* the meritocrat

→

3. How reliable in your opinion, are the results of the survey? Refer in particular to the comments made in the text about the 'honesty' of the respondents.

4. If you were asked to classify the business leaders in your country, which of the above labels would you use to describe them? Give examples of behaviours that reflect your labelling.

5. If the title of the article had been 'La patronne, die Chefin and the female boss', how valid do you think the results of the survey would have been? What behavioural or attitudinal differences – if any – would you have expected to see in the survey?

ACTIVITY 8.2

In his article entitled 'Six country comparisons' in *Cross Cultural Management: an International Journal* (vol. 2 no. 4: 15–23), Tony Morden (1995) compared six countries in terms of their national and business cultures, as well as their working practices and management style. Below is a summary of the sections devoted to each country's management style, where reference is made specifically to the X, Y and Z theories mentioned in Concept 8.1. Read the summary, then answer the questions that follow.

Management styles in six countries

The Netherlands

Decision-making within a Dutch company is 'slow, formal and deliberate'. The approach is a rational, analytical one, whereby all those involved, including managers who are senior in rank, work together to achieve the most effective outcome.

The need to build consensus is uppermost. The actual formal meetings where the decisions are taken are usually preceded by informal consultation, referred to by Morden as 'management by walking around' (MBWA). This reflects the emphasis on Theory Y and Z, as does the decentralized and autonomous approach to getting the task done. Rather than being someone who prescribes action, the manager is seen as facilitating and co-ordinating action agreed upon through consensus.

Brazil

A typical organization has a strong hierarchy with control enforced from the top. Theory X is reflected in the way that managers exercise authority and direct subordinates. Here, MBWA is used to check that underlings are doing what they are told to do and at the same time to give fatherly reassurance. With improved education and a developing economy, Theory Y is being applied which entails increased responsibility.

However, decision-making still tends to be centralized and done so on a short-term basis since economic conditions (especially inflation rates and high dependence on global commodity markets) discourage longer term planning.

Germany

German managers see their company as a 'community of individual people working together'. This view is reflected in a participative style of management that reflects the notions in Theory Z. This means that time is needed to make decisions: procedures must be followed scrupulously and comprehensive information gathered.

Although consensus is regarded as important, managers are expected to 'lead by example'. They are expected to be decisive while drawing upon the expertise and experience of the team they are leading. When managers delegate authority, they do so in a clearly defined manner, reflecting their own managerial skills as well as their concern for the development of their subordinates as contributors to the organization's development.

Japan

Maintaining harmony within the company at all levels is reflected in the way that all those who will be involved in implementing a decision are involved in the making of it. A proposal is circulated which is added to and/or amended by those involved. The final version is then passed up to senior management who decide whether or not to implement the proposal.

Management style is 'beyond Theory Z'. Even though hierarchy is important (and essentially based on age and seniority), deference to it is subservient to maintaining harmony and meeting production and quality targets. Everyone working in the company shares a communal responsibility for ensuring that the best decisions are made and goals attained.

Employees work together and each work-group is responsible for maintaining their performance and for meeting the standards required.

South Korea

The chief executive heads a hierarchical and disciplined organization and is usually a strong figure who commands great respect and wields considerable power. Such leaders are often charismatic, deeply involved in the company as well as in civic affairs.

Employees are regarded as a valuable asset in an environment where the chaebol are competing with each other. Training is regarded as an integral part of business activity and required of all large companies.

Managers need to be competitive and risk-oriented and ready to take bold decisions, but only after carefully analysing all the relevant issues and alternatives. Approval from the top is usually required and once gained will allow a carefully organized implementation.

Theory X predominates through the need for authority, discipline and order.

Spain

Strategic decisions and business plans generally tend to be formulated at the top. The boss is regarded more as the benevolent autocrat, bold in his actions while showing concern for the interest and security of his family of employees.

Middle managers are not involved in decision-making, not even when they have to implement what has been decided. Meetings tend to be used more as a tool of management control rather than of communication and consultation. If there is delegation, then this done for a short time-frame and with clear instructions.

The boss will however make informal use of personal contacts within the company, people who can be trusted and who can deliver useful input.

Theory X therefore tends to predominate, despite the personalized and humanistic facets displayed.

Questions

1. Theory X is referred to when the management style of Brazil, South Korea and Spain is being described. Which factors do the management styles of these three countries share that reflect Theory X? Which factors indicate any differentiation between the styles?
2. What do you consider to be the main differences between the Netherlands and Germany in terms of Theory Y and Theory Z?
3. Management style in Japan is considered to be 'beyond Theory Z'. What does this entail exactly?

Conclusion

This chapter has shown how the concept of leadership in the West has evolved. Originally perceived in terms of scientific principles, it has taken on a much more human orientation, reflecting the influence of the way leaders behave in Asia. Although leaders in the West nowadays show greater concern for employees, their attitude and motivation, traditional styles persist in some cultures, as the activities have shown.

There appears to be a consensus across cultures as to what makes an effective leader (including integrity, charisma, decisiveness and being team-oriented). However, the way in which these attributes are expressed in actual behaviour can vary considerably from culture to culture. The same applies in a way to the question of gender and leadership: the differences in leadership style between males and females observed in one country are also seen in other countries, but the ways in which behaviour tends to reflect these differences is based more on culture than gender.

Points for reflection

1. Ouchi put forward the Z theory to explain how Japanese management works and to show the Americans what they could learn from their Japanese counterparts. Many advocates of the theory indicate that type Z companies are among the most successful types of US companies.

   How do you account for their success, bearing in mind that the principles of scientific management still predominate in that country?

2. One element of transformational leadership referred to in this chapter is charisma. Research shows that it is a universal attribute of good leadership. However, certain facets of charisma are valued differently in different countries.

   Look again at Figure 8.2 and try to determine which of these relate (positively or negatively) to the concept of charisma. Once you have done this, try to work out which of these attributes are prevalent in your country when it comes to perception of charismatic leadership.

3. Companies are becoming increasingly aware of the need for relation-oriented skills in their global endeavours. Female managers working for Western companies, for example, could generally be regarded as potentially effective managers in, say, Asia because of their person-oriented leadership skills. The consideration women show others, as well as their ability to empathize, are features which are said to be held in high esteem in that part of the world.

   Why do you think that some multinationals nevertheless tend not to give serious consideration to female candidates for managerial positions in, for example, Asia?

Further reading

House, R.J., Hanges, P.J., Javidan, M., Dorfman, P.W. and Gupta, V. (eds) (2004) *Leadership, Culture and Organizations: The GLOBE study of 62 societies,* **Thousand Oaks, CA: Sage.** One of the aims of this book, as described in Concept 8.2, is to find out how leadership is understood differently across cultures. The GLOBE project is a long-term research programme based on an integrated theory of the relationship between culture and societal, organizational, and leadership effectiveness. Apart from proposing a range of cultural dimensions (dealt with briefly in Part One), the book gives an interesting review of leadership theories.

References

Bass, B.M. (1985) *Leadership and Performance Beyond Expectations,* New York: Free Press.

Bass, B.M. (1997) 'Does the transactional-transformational paradigm transcend organisational and national boundaries?', *American Psychologist,* 52(2): 130-139.

Bass, B.M and Aviolo B.J. (eds) (2002) *Developing Potential Across a Full Range of Leadership: Cases on transactional and transformational leadership,* Mahwah, NJ: Lawrence Erlbaum Associates.

Den Hartog, D.N., House, R., Hanges P.J., Dorfman, P.W. and Ruis-Quintana, S.A. (1999) 'Culture specific and cross-culturally generalizable implicit leadership theories: are attributes of charismatic/ transformational leadership universally endorsed?', *The Leadership Quarterly,* 10(2): 219-57.

Evans, P., Pucik, B. and Barsoux, J.-L. (2002) *The Global Challenge,* New York, NY: McGraw-Hill/Irwin.

Fatehi, K. (1996) *International Management: A cross-cultural approach,* Upper Saddle River, NJ: Prentice Hall.

Fiedler, F.E. (1967) *A Theory of Leadership Effectiveness,* New York, NY: McGraw-Hill.

Hofstede, G. (1980) *Culture's Consequences: International differences in work-related values,* New York, NY: McGraw-Hill.

Hofstede, G. (1991) *Cultures and Organisations: Software of the mind,* New York, NY: McGraw-Hill.

House, R.J. (1977) 'A 1976 theory of charismatic leadership' in J.G. Hunt and L.L. Larson (eds), *Leadership: The Cutting Edge,* Carbondale, IL: Southern Illinois University Press: 189-207.

House, R.J., Hanges, P.J., Javidan, M., Dorfman, P.W. and Gupta, V. (eds) (2004) *Leadership, Culture and Organizations: The GLOBE study of 62 societies,* Thousand Oaks, CA: Sage.

Kotter, J.P. (1990) *Force For Change: How leadership differs from management,* New York, NY: Free Press.

Mayo, E. (2007) *The Social Problems of an Industrial Civilisation,* London: Routledge.

McGregor, D. (1960) *The Human Side of Enterprise,* New York, NY: McGraw-Hill.

Mintzberg, H. (1999) 'Managing quietly', *Leader to Leader,* 12 (Spring): 24-30.

Morden, T (1995) 'Six country comparisons', *Cross Cultural Management: An international journal,* 2(4): 15-23.

Nguyen-Huy, Q. (2004) 'Building emotional capital for strategic renewal: Nissan (1999-2002)', Insead case study (http://knowledge.insead.edu).

Ouchi, W.G. (1981) *Theory Z: How American business can meet the Japanese challenge,* New York, NY: Avon.

Rosener, J.B. (1990) 'Ways women lead', *Harvard Business Review,* 68(2): 119-25.

Senge, P.M. (1990) *The Fifth Discipline: The art and practice of the learning organisation,* New York, NY: Currency Doubleday.

Schein, E.H. (2004) *Organisational Culture and Leadership,* 3rd edn, New York, NY: Wiley.

Stogdill, R.M. (1974) *Handbook of Leadership: A survey of theory and research,* New York, NY: Free Press.

Chapter 9

Culture and strategy

Strategy is not only an element of managing organizations, it is found in all areas of management, from marketing through human resources to communication. This chapter takes the concept of strategy as it is used generally in business and addresses the relationship - if one exists - between strategy and culture. Concept 9.1 addresses this issue, while concept 9.2 attempts to explain the influence of culture - whether corporate or national - in strategic applications such as mergers and acquisitions.

Learning outcomes

After reading this chapter you will gain an understanding of:

- The relationship between strategy and culture.
- The role of national culture in the formation of company strategy.
- The effect of strategy on international mergers and acquisitions.

Concept 9.1 Cultural view of strategy

Since the 1960s, companies have been looking for strategies to use in their competitive environment and so help realize their objectives. The question is: what link, if any, can be made between strategy and culture?

Strategy and corporate culture

Is culture used to formulate strategy, or is it just a component of strategy? According to Schoenberger (1997), the relationship between company culture and strategy is closer than would appear. Strategy can be seen as less to do with making decisions and more to do with knowledge, i.e. what the organization knows or what it thinks it knows. This knowledge also includes the way it interprets the world and its position in it. It is the company's imagination that determines how this world could or should be. This means strategy undergoes the influence of culture since it is through its culture that a company creates an understanding of itself as well as an interpretation of the world. When this world presents new problems or changes, then culture devises a company's strategic response to them.

Looking at the question from this standpoint, strategy is a product of culture. At the same time, however, since the strategic orientation of the company has in the past moulded specific practices, relations and ideas, culture is also a product of strategy. Culture and strategy are therefore inextricably connected. What companies need to resolve, says Schoenberger (1997: 14), '. . . is not so much how to *adapt* the corporate culture to a new strategy as to understand how culture *produces* strategy'.

Schneider and Barsoux (2003) argue that their definition of culture – a solution to the problems of external adaptation and internal integration – could also be used as the definition of strategy. The process is the same: strategic decisions are made to adapt to the environment and these are implanted and integrated within the company by means of human resources. The actual departments where strategic plans are made, the tools, models and jargon used are simply cultural artefacts. The application by management of the strategies chosen have created beliefs and values, and behind these managerial practices are assumptions. But do these assumptions have the same meaning in different cultures?

Cultural models of strategy

Deresky (2003) wrote that most companies use strategic planning to evaluate their future prospects and so decide on strategies to be taken to accomplish their objectives in the long term. Although the strategic planning process is an ideal way for doing so, this does not prevent decisions being influenced by the personal judgement, experience and motivation of the managers who make them. This implies that a change in management can radically change the eventual strategy of the company. This is what Schneider and Barsoux (2003: 122) emphasize when they say:

Assumptions regarding internal integration are relevant to questions such as who is involved and who takes the decision.

Furthermore, when it comes to strategic management, Schneider and Barsoux (2003) divide management from different countries into two types according to their behaviours, values and assumptions (concerning uncertainty, control, power, human activity and time):

● Controlling model: the departments responsible establish strategic plans and present them to top management, or to the board for their consideration. The company's reports are the main source of information about its environment, and these are fairly quantitative and objective in nature.

● Adapting model: responsibility for strategic decisions lies with all levels of the organization. The information obtained is qualitative and subjective in nature because it comes from personal sources, friends and colleagues.

Cultural factors of strategy

Following the same line as the previous authors, Fatehi (1996) adds that formulating strategy is not just a question of collecting information, but also deciding what is to be done with it. Such decisions are in no way 'free of human biases' and in fact the whole process of collecting and examining information is a perceptual one based on culture. If this is so, in what way is the formulation of strategy affected by cultural differences?

Fatehi (1996) suggests that two areas in particular are influenced by culture:

Relationship with the environment

To illustrate cultural differences in this area, Fatehi uses what he refers to as the 'mental framework' of two types of person. The first is 'engineering-oriented' and goes looking for information to support a strategy (change) whereby the environment can be altered to the benefit of the company. This orientation rests on the belief that humans can control their surroundings. The second is 'symbiotic-oriented', believes in close ties with nature and therefore looks for another, non-destructive strategy for dealing with the environment. Fatehi (1996) refers to the fatalist beliefs of Buddhists and the conviction amongst Muslims that events are predetermined. Both recognize the limits humans have when trying to control their environment.

Relationships among people

Fatehi also distinguishes differences in the question of interpersonal relationships within a company. Formulating strategy is just one of the functions of management involving a predictable pattern of relationships. Within a certain hierarchy the reaction of a subordinate to the order of a superior will be in line with expected modes of behaviour. To show differences in attitude among employees towards a company's strategy, he contrasts US and Japanese companies. The former consider possibilities of success as 'environmental opportunities'. They formulate their strategies in such a way that they do not have to demand individual sacrifice of their employees. Japanese companies, on the other hand, may demand a number of strategic choices, of which one or more could involve personal sacrifice from their personnel. The individual employee, however, does not see this demand as a self sacrifice since it is made for the benefit of the company.

Trice and Beyer (1993) also take up the question of the role played by cultural factors in corporate strategy. They too dwell on the differences between US and Japanese companies. Although there is intense competition between the two, the way they compete is shaped by cultural differences. Competition is inherent to US culture: companies in the US compete fiercely for market domination. Neither the laws in place nor the managers and their way of thinking make it easy for companies from different sectors to co-operate with each other, not even outside the US. The Japanese culture, however, is more to do with co-operation and harmonious relations – as was described in Part One. Nevertheless, they can be as competitive as their US counterparts. The difference is that Japanese companies practise competition to achieve collective goals against 'outsiders'. This type of competition preserves internal harmony and benefits the country as a whole.

The effect of national culture on strategy

In what way can national culture affect strategy? Not only on the choice of strategy but also on the way it is realized. So, this is about leadership and the decision-making process. Tayeb (2003) describes how, for example, Swedish managers spend more time taking decisions than their British counterparts. The British, on the other hand, require more interaction and consultation with experts. Schneider and Barsoux (2003) also refer to the cultural elements of decision-making: who makes the decisions, who is involved, where the decisions are taken (in a formal meeting, or elsewhere). Not to forget the matter of time: how quickly are the decisions made? The whole process reflects different cultural assumptions.

Tayeb (2003) mentions another area where national culture impinges on strategy: the product and services sectors. Consumer demand for certain products will differ from country to country, from region to region, and this will influence the different markets. The needs and preferences of the consumers need to be taken into account when analysing the resources and capacities of the organization, particularly when business overseas is concerned.

Finally, the question of national culture comes to the fore when a multinational has to make strategic decisions about the maintenance – or otherwise – of the national culture in its local subsidiaries. As Bartlett et al (2003: 672) indicate, if a corporate strategy is used, managers at headquarters will not necessarily have a clear insight into the business environment and the cultural differences at play in the foreign markets where the multinational operates. They underline the importance of the role of the country manager in the implementation of company strategy. This manager is at the centre of the strategic tension between defending the company's market positions against global competitors on the one hand, and satisfying the demands of the local subsidiary on the other. These demands usually include meeting the requirements set by the host government, responding to the specific needs of local consumers and reinforcing the company's competitive position with local (potential) resources. The country manager assumes the role of 'cultural interpreter' who is expected to be able to give information about the national situation to 'those whose perceptions may be obscured by ethnocentric biases'. In short, it is necessary to understand the national culture of the host country, to respect the local cultural norms and, at the same time, to understand the corporate goals, strategies and values and communicate them effectively to the local employees.

Implications for international managers

Why is it that one company succeeds in the global market and not another? Some analysts claim that success is due to strategy, others say it is on account of structure or technological innovation. Black et al (1999) argue that the key to success is the people involved. It is they who formulate the strategy and implement it, it is they who create and shape the organizational structures and it is they who invent and use the technology.

In this regard, global assignments can be very important strategically for the company. The managers sent from headquarters to the subsidiary abroad can not only concentrate on the specific needs of the local market but can also analyse the tendencies in the global market for the benefit of the whole company. By going on an international assignment, the managers involved can also develop their individual knowledge and competencies, particularly since they need to understand and work with people from another culture. As Black et al (1999: 3–4) write:

> Managers who fail to develop these skills, and organizations that fail to develop these managers, risk being irrelevant in the twenty-first century.

But how is a manager to develop these skills? How is a manager to gain insight into the attitudes of those involved in a cross-cultural situation and modify his management strategy accordingly? This does not mean that the manager has to have a fixed 'new' strategy for whatever circumstances. She/he will realize that the strategy is not to have the same strategy, but to modify it according to the situations encountered – especially since knowledge itself entails learning from experience. This learning is therefore to do with applying skills and knowledge learned in one context to another context. Once a manager has acquired this competence, then she/he is able to make judgements and adapt to different situations.

This cultural understanding is particularly important in mergers and acquisitions, as the following concept shows.

Concept 9.2 Strategic alliances and business cultures

To develop strategies for the global market, companies are turning to alliances. Strategic alliances can create considerable advantages. First, they can help realize increased economies of scale and reduced marketing costs. Furthermore, they can result in access to new markets, know-how and technology. Moreover, if the alliance is a close one, a takeover or merger, risks can be shared and products developed jointly. Through carefully managed co-operation, the results of rapprochement between companies can be seen relatively quickly. Not that everything is necessarily plain sailing: extra problems may well arise – especially those relating to culture.

This is an area of concern to managers only when things are not running smoothly. The focus is often first on the business advantages, including the merging of products and/or services, strategic fit in the market, and the financial savings. The matter of cultural fit is given relatively little attention at the start. Only when problems arise, particularly when they interfere with the business goals established through an alliance, are they given real attention.

Merging cultures

As Delavallée (2002) points out, an alliance between companies – whether through a merger or a takeover – is one area where the most serious cultural problems arise. Only a major organizational change within a company causes a similar amount of anguish and conflict. The success or failure of an alliance is down to the human factor, not the bottom line.

And the human factor is all to do with how people come to terms with each other, how the employees of two companies work together to help realize the goals of the alliance: the cultural dimension, therefore. However, as Delavallée (2002) stresses, this is often ignored or forgotten about. The systems making up the organization of the two companies that are coming together must harmonize, if not become one. The merger process involves making a coherent whole out of the sub-systems of the organization of each partner-to-be. These sub-systems comprise goals, structures, techniques and culture. The merger process, therefore, has three levels: strategic, organizational and human.

On the strategic level, Delavallée (2002) uses the work of Cartwright and Cooper (1993) to explain the strategies used during company mergers. According to them, there is not just one merger strategy but four: assimilation, deculturalization, separation and integration. The type of merger strategy used depends on:

- how strong the influence is of the buyer on the culture of the company being absorbed; and

- the degree to which the company to be absorbed is bound to its own culture.

Compatibility between cultures is rarely taken into account while the merger process is under way. When the two sides are highly incompatible – a discovery often made months later when people actually start working together – the shock can be overwhelming.

If a merger between two national companies can lead to a culture shock when the two teams have to work together, what can be expected when there is a merger between companies from different countries or cultures? Furthermore, what will happen when a manager is sent on an international assignment?

Culture shock

The term 'culture shock' used above refers generally to the unpleasant experience that can be had when coming into contact with other cultures. Marx (1999) has developed a model to describe the notion of culture shock, a model adapted from that of the anthropologist Oberg (1960). According to Marx, international managers experience culture shock psychologically at three levels. She uses what she calls the 'culture shock triangle' to describe these levels (Figure 9.1).

Marx (1999) insists on the fact that the culture shock phase is an integral part of the adaptation phase and, as such, should have no negative connotations. This is a normal reaction of people who confront the strange, the unknown, the foreign, but gives no indication of future success.

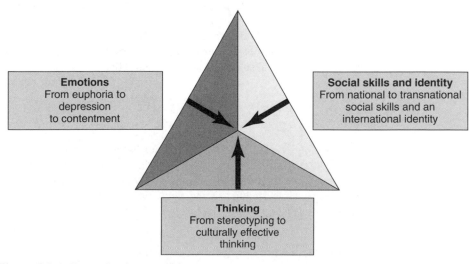

Figure 9.1 Culture shock pyramid

Source: *Breaking through Culture Shock* by Marx, E., Nicholas Brealey Publishers. Copyright 2001.

However, the success – or otherwise – of a merger between companies at international level depends not only on managers who are well prepared for this culture shock and who have the interpersonal skills necessary. Success depends also on the motives and strategies of the companies wishing to co-operate with or take over another firm.

International company strategy

The current company is no longer what it was nor is it what it will be. This applies just as much to national as to international companies. Every day, the media report mergers and acquisitions in every country and every business sector. In 1998, Paul Koster (1998: 37) was predicting that mergers and acquisitions would go on for decades: 'It is not a wave. There are only more or less intense episodes.' Today, the intensity is evident, particularly in Europe, where consolidation in many business sectors is rife. The hostile nature of some takeover battles has received considerable publicity, as has the increasing number of acquisitions made by 'foreign' private investment companies. 'Companies have cash to spare and the prey is cheap. It is a question of swallow or be swallowed' (Hendriks, 2004: 27).

As the examples below show, the forming of these kinds of co-operation, ranging from mergers and takeovers to joint ventures, alliances and partnerships, does not occur without difficulty:

> In the acquisition of KLM by Air France there are also American partnerships to be integrated. However, the American competition authority does not accept that they want to make international agreements in Europe. It is not yet clear to what extent this dispute can further delay the takeover. Neither Air France nor KLM want to comment. 'We do not comment on matters happening on the other side of the Atlantic Ocean,' was the official reaction from Air France in Paris.
>
> *NRC Handelsblad,* 22 March 2004.

> The Swiss pharmaceutical company Novartis mentions in public a potential merger with Aventis. Novartis is only prepared to discuss a merger or takeover with the French–German company Aventis after an official invitation from the board of directors of Aventis. Furthermore, Novartis demands that the French government keeps out of the negotiations, or, at least, remains neutral. Earlier this month, the French government announced its opposition to a takeover of Aventis by Novartis.
>
> *Financieel Dagblad,* 24 March 2004.

The post-merger period often shows companies taking the opposite direction to that planned. The case of the British–Dutch steel company Corus illustrates this:

> Two years ago, two years after the merger between British Steel and Hoogovens, Corus decided that the British part would continue to produce for the British market, even though production in the Netherlands was cheaper. According to CEO Philippe Varin it is too expensive to close the existing plants and to expand in IJmuiden. Instead there will be capital investment in modernization in England.
>
> *Financieel Dagblad,* 29 March 2004.

As we see above, not only is the study of management after cross-border acquisitions of interest, but also during the acquisition phase, as we see above, when the alliance forged on paper is being given shape.

What are then the implications of this globalization for cross-border relations? What impact can this culture phenomenon have on the internationalization of business, on marketing or on human resources?

The merger of two companies presupposes a change of 'culture' in the new organization. If, in addition, the companies are established in two different countries, the complexity of the exchanges, of the interactions between cultures increases and gives rise to other problems than those in a merger between two national companies. What can be observed is an organizational situation being transformed, along with all the accompanying elements of cultural change. A merger is by no means a simple process but a complex evolutionary process due to the inevitable change of culture(s) involved.

Mergers and acquisitions: a strategic or cultural issue?

In this area of mergers and acquisitions, the company becomes integrated into the management's process of globalization and internationalization. Therefore, as Pierre (2001: 141), emphasizes, this requires 'a permanent adaptation of the manager' because 'the environment is in perpetual change and the international executives appear continuously 'under construction' through a never ending professional maturation'.

What are the reasons compelling companies to seek an alliance? According to the protagonists the reason is purely economic, particularly financial, whatever the sector.

'Ahold looks for takeovers after 2006. Company directs focus on Europe,' is a headline from a financial newspaper (*Financieel Dagblad*, 1 June 2004). The article explains: 'the objective of the current takeovers is to reduce the imbalance in income'. Others have acted similarly: 'Scottish Bank makes large takeover in US. Royal Bank of Scotland (RBOS) buys the American bank Carter One for $10.5 billion in cash. This makes RBOS the seventh-largest American bank' (*Financieel Dagblad*, 6 April 2004).

What role does the cultural element play in these forms of cross-border alliance? This element is usually completely ignored when merger plans are being drawn up for a merger, as well as at the start of the alliance. When KLM and Air France had just completed their merger (to create for themselves a stronger position in the market), cultural issues were far from their minds. This was suggested in their reactions to a question concerning Easyjet's latest results:

> **Without saying it aloud, the disappointing results of Easyjet are for both parties the proof that they were right about their plans to merge. Problems for Easyjet? 'We have our own problems to solve', they both said, laughing.**
>
> *Financieel Dagblad* 6 April 2004.

Sorting out financial questions resulting from the merger was clearly the priority for both parties.

It is often the case that cultural factors come to the fore only when mergers and acquisitions do not meet strategic expectations, or necessitate a change of strategy. Even then, cultural factors may not be explicitly referred to:

> **The board of directors of the British-Dutch steel company Corus has to offer, at short notice, positions to Dutch directors. This was stated by the Russian steel baron Alisher Usmavov (a shareholder in Corus, who has a 12% interest in the company).**
>
> *Financieel Dagblad*, 29 March 2004.

Nevertheless, as Thévenet (1999: 10) remarks, the cultural element in companies is to be found everywhere: 'In all our investigations, not one company has ever showed itself to be interested in culture per se, but everybody works on culture to resolve concrete problems: problems of strategy, mergers, mobilization of the staff, reorganization, even communication.' This explicit attention to culture is all the greater when a company is operating across borders.

This does not mean, however, that the cultural problems occurring in mergers are related solely to national cultures. This is confirmed by Trompenaars (2004) when describing the Sony/Philips alliance: the problems that had arisen were less to do with differences in national culture and more to do with the strong market orientation of Sony coming up against the technical orientation of Philips.

However, it remains obvious that those advocating a merger of some kind often underestimate the differences in the local cultures that have been brought together under one roof. Moreover, they tend to ignore the cultural confrontations that take place and which, in many cases, provoke resistance to any changes on both sides. This resistance is often the manifestation of collective fears intrinsic to the merger or takeover. These fears are often justified, because not only does the organizational culture change, but also the company's strategy. That is why any change needs to be managed carefully so the fears can be identified and monitored. The phenomenon of change in relation to culture will be developed in the next chapter.

ACTIVITY 9.1

Shell's reorganization

In 2005, two companies, Royal Dutch Petroleum Company and Shell Transport and Trading Company merged to form one company: Royal Dutch Shell plc.

Read the two articles below. These describe the developments in the organization of Shell. Then answer the questions that follow.

Our strategy in action: Creating the culture and organization to deliver

We have made significant progress in changing our culture and organization to ensure that we can deliver our strategy. The unification of the parent companies under Royal Dutch Shell plc in 2005 has provided us with a clearer, simpler, more efficient and accountable form of governance.

The chief executive now reports to a single board comprising 10 non-executive directors and five executive directors and a key advantage of this single, smaller board is that it provides a very clear and direct line of accountability to shareholders. Royal Dutch Shell now has a single headquarters in The Hague (the Netherlands). The centralisation of a number of activities in the headquarters is helping to reduce duplication and helping us to operate in a more streamlined and efficient way.

The structural changes are also helping to reinforce our work to simplify and standardise many of our business processes. In particular, the integration of the oil products and chemicals businesses into one downstream organization has so far been very successful in creating a more dynamic, responsive and effective organization. We have seen particular benefits at sites which contain both refineries and chemicals manufacturing plants.

By sharing services and integrating their activities we can operate much more efficiently. It also means we have been able to share and adopt best practice more quickly and so improve operational performance.

Source: Royal Dutch Shell 2005 annual report, www.shell.com/annualreports.

Marriage after a century of cohabitation: Shell prepares for the next merger round

On the top floor of London's towering Shell Centre, a cavernous boardroom looms over the Houses of Parliament, filled with high-backed chairs and rows of angled microphones. For decades, British and Dutch directors from two separate companies have held eight 'conferences' a year, alternating between there and the Netherlands, to decide on the business of Royal Dutch/Shell Group. But if shareholders today approve the most radical restructuring in its history, the London room will fall into disuse. Instead, board members will assemble each time in the more intimate surroundings of a gabled building topped by a clock tower in The Hague.

After nearly a century of quirky cohabitation, shareholders of Royal Dutch Petroleum and Shell Transport and Trading will today be asked to approve the formal marriage of the two, which together make up the world's biggest publicly traded oil company after Exxon-Mobil and BP.

The union will put the relationship on a new footing and fundamentally alter the way the company is governed. Shell's eccentric corporate governance structure – long a source of befuddlement to outsiders – will be scrapped in favour of a modern, 'Anglo-Saxon-style' system designed to bring it into line with Exxon and BP, its more successful rivals.

Executives say the shift represents a dramatic transformation of the company's conservative and consensus-driven culture – changes they say are badly needed if it is to compete in a rapidly changing oil industry. But critics ask why it took them so long to accept the need for change and why Shell had to be forced into it by shareholders following a scandal last year in which the group was forced to slash what it had recorded as proved reserves of oil and gas no fewer than five times. That reduced the level of reserves by one-third, led to a boardroom purge and brought $150m in fines imposed by US and British regulators. Investors question whether the merger will do enough to alter the ponderous way in which the group operates.

'We changed a lot of the culture of this company,' insists Jeroen van der Veer, appointed as Shell's first-ever chief executive following the reserves scandal and the decision to streamline the group. A soft-spoken Dutchman with a kindly manner, Mr Van der Veer – still eager to show that he and the other executives have taken a firm grip following one of the worst crises in its history – adds: 'We were very much a "bottom-up" company. Now there is certainly more direction from the top. I try to give very high clarity on where to go.'

He makes it clear that the direction the group is headed will include takeovers. Shell had missed out on the wave of mega-mergers in the late 1990s that saw Exxon merge with Mobil and BP buy Amoco. The failure to participate was prompted largely by a prediction that oil prices would remain low – at about $10 a barrel instead of the $60 seen today. But Shell's dual structure also meant it would have been hard for the group to use its stock as currency to finance takeovers, as its rivals were doing.

With today's high oil price, the cost of any deals is much higher. But Mr Van der Veer says the company must be ready for the next wave of consolidation in the industry. 'If you study – and I do that fairly regularly – the last 100 years of the oil industry, it is one long story of consolidation,' he says. So you [had] better [be] prepared. You must have the tools in your toolkit.'

The necessary tools were absent when the reserves crisis hit. Shell seemed paralysed. It took some measures to improve the way in which it booked reserves and addressed other compliance issues. But investors were unhappy about the speed at which it was moving after Mr Van der Veer and his new team took over in March last year. Advisers intervened on behalf of large institutional investors to try to press their views about the need for a thorough overhaul of the company's structure. Shareholders wanted an end to the company's dual-board system which, they maintained, hamstrung the company with a cumbersome decision-making process and obstructed accountability.

At first, the group resisted the calls. 'They thought the structure was doing well and when the reserves debacle hit, to some extent they were in denial,' says one senior adviser to the company. 'They quickly went away from that into a phase where I quite frankly realised they didn't know what to do.'

Shell had periodically considered altering its structure, most recently during the 1990s. At that time, the company was doing well and there was little support for change. But things had now changed and reformers saw their opportunity.

Two broad options were on the table. The first was to create a single unified board while maintaining separate Dutch and British companies – a so-called 'dual-header' company such as Rio Tinto or BHP Billiton. This choice represented →

a tidying-up of the existing arrangement and had the advantage of being easier to do. But the big-bang approach of a full merger had the virtue of simplicity and would do away with the complex corporate structure that so bothered investors.

Any changes also had the potential to upset the delicate balance of power within the group that had existed for 98 years. Royal Dutch was in the ascendant when they joined forces in 1907. The then troubled Shell side was forced to join up with Royal Dutch on somewhat humiliating terms – a 60/40 split in the Dutch company's favour.

Under the new plan, however, the merged company will be incorporated in Britain and listed on the London Stock Exchange. 'For some people in the Netherlands, seeing by far the largest company in the Netherlands become a plc with its primary listing in London is quite a difficult issue,' says one director.

To offset the perception that it is becoming too British, the company will be headquartered in The Hague and will be a tax resident of the Netherlands. The 60/40 split will also be maintained. A senior adviser to the company says: 'The idea was to try to preserve the Anglo-Dutch heritage in as many ways as possible. There was a tax advantage to having the headquarters in The Hague, which made no sense to give up. To the extent that you needed to pacify political interests in the Netherlands, that clearly served the purpose. Equally, having a UK listing played to the UK gallery.'

Shell executives insist the changes are not cosmetic. Mr Routs, head of downstream operations, says he is already seeing tangible benefits. 'If I compare differences in the team in terms of operating, it is night and day,' he says. 'We are now a more transparent, supportive, action-orientated executive team that makes things happen. There is not a lot of consensus-seeking in the old way of expressing it. We come to conclusions faster. We come to deals faster.'

The reorganization of the company would not have happened without the reserves crisis, many believe. But Shell still does not accept that the reserves crisis was a result of its management structure. That has left investors baffled. If there is no connection between the reserves crisis and the structure, then why change at all? Conversely, if much of what is proposed is 'common sense', as Mr Routs now says, then why was it not done sooner?

Some believe that the directors of Royal Dutch/Shell agreed to the restructuring not because they really believed in it but as a sop to disgruntled investors. As a senior adviser to the company says: 'The reserves debacle had seriously dented shareholder confidence and I suppose [the big-bang approach] was ultimately also a way of demonstrating to shareholders that we can deliver.'

At the height of the scandal last summer over the level of oil reserves it had booked, Jeroen van der Veer, the group's lead executive, held a number of meetings with shareholders in the US, The Hague and the City of London. The discussions centred on investor demand for a structure that would foster accountability and transparency in decision-making.

Investors say it took several meetings for Shell executives to accept that the status quo was not an option. A year on, investors hope the combined structure will help prevent any future scandal. Few are entirely satisfied, though, and remain watchful lest Shell slip back into its secretive previous ways.

Source: *Financial Times*, 28 June 2005.

After reading the text

1. How would you characterize, in cultural terms, the nature of Shell when it was a 'cohabitation' of Royal Dutch Petroleum and Shell Transport and Trading?

2. What changes in the culture of Shell are the 'marriage' of the two companies expected to bring?

3. What were the reasons for the strategic decision to merge the two companies?

4. How did the reserves crisis precipitate the changes?

5. What do you consider to have been the key managerial and cultural factors involved in the merger process?

6. What evidence can you find in the text to suggest the possible emergence of a 'third culture' within the new company?

ACTIVITY 9.2

The text below is an adaptation of an article written by a lawyer who specializes in company reorganization, mergers and acquisitions, when he was working for an international group of tax consultants.

Cultural differences during international takeovers and mergers

Cultural differences have played an important role in many of the cases I have been involved in. Sometimes they have helped to speed up a transaction, sometimes they have delayed a transaction – and even prevented a deal being made.

Some of the differences I have experienced are, in my opinion, to do with language. By language I do not mean the use of different mother tongues but also the use of the professional language prevalent among consultants. In our profession, it is easy to forget that not all our clients and others involved in our cases will understand the language terms we use. This goes not only for our international clients, but also for one group of specialists communicating with a different group of specialists in the same company.

Other differences have to do with customs, different ways of doing things. I have been involved in several cases where such [cultural] differences have played a crucial role. A number of these are outlined below.

A British baker's takeover

A British concern wanted to take over a Dutch family bakers. Although the former used internationally recognised norms when determining the value of the Dutch firm, (these differed considerably from the norms used by the Dutch side), the deal was more or less finalised. All that had to be done was to work out how best to keep on managers of the Dutch bakers for a while once the takeover had taken place. The British buyers, aware of the family's considerable knowledge of and experience in the market, were keen to keep its members in position for a few months.

The takeover was completed, but it soon became clear that the Dutch managers could not come to terms with the regime of the new owners. The strict accounting procedures coupled with the new book-keeping approach gave them a number of headaches, as did the new company's answerability to its shareholders. In the end this all proved too much for the Dutch family and their stay-on was reduced from one year to six months.

A Finnish–Norwegian merger

I represented a Norwegian oil company in its discussions with a Finnish oil company over the integration of their respective plastic divisions. The Finns used the services of an American lawyer; the Norwegians used my firm since, apparently, it was considered large enough and with enough international experience to do a good job. The idea of using a British firm had been considered but eventually rejected: British lawyers were considered to be too expensive, complicated and drawn out in their dealings.

The intended merger itself was on a very large scale: one hundred companies were involved in several countries. Many external parties were also involved, including a British investment bank, which was in charge of the whole project. It relentlessly pushed the project forward knowing that if the merger did not come off it would receive no fee for its efforts.

Once a letter of intent had been agreed upon and 'due diligence' reports completed, the real negotiations began, with co-operation on an equal footing being the main goal. The Norwegian party had noticed during its 'due diligence' investigations that several of the Finnish companies involved had caused environmental pollution. This would involve a costly cleaning-up operation and, along with other issues, would make it difficult for a 50-50 deal to be reached. Nevertheless, after a number of long, drawn-out negotiations in several European cities (to underline the European character of the merger), the contracts were signed in England.

During the process, clear differences in working practice between the American and Dutch lawyers emerged. The Finn's American lawyer made a note in detail and required every point to be covered – preferably twice – in the agreement. This slowed down the whole process, particularly when the American lawyers acted as if they were the spokespersons of the company and even appeared to be making decisions on the company's behalf. The Dutch lawyers behaved as they usually do: they are there to advise the client along with other advisors (accountants, tax consultants etc.). They consider it natural that in the end it is the company's directors who determine policy and take the decisions.

Further differences emerged in behaviour during the negotiations. The lawyers representing the Finnish partners showed a rather aggressive attitude throughout and this contrasted strongly with the quieter, more modest approach of the Norwegians' lawyers. The Norwegians were somewhat intimidated by the American lawyers and had to be reassured that the less contentious approach in no way undermined the justness of their cause.

A French takeover of a Dutch concern

Language turned out to be a barrier when a French group of companies decided to take over a Dutch company. During the research phase prior to the negotiations, the French sent several employees from the Alsace region of France to carry out interviews in the Netherlands. They assumed that the dialect spoken by these colleagues would enable them to communicate with their Dutch counterparts. When this did not turn out to be the case, everyone involved started using English.

English was used during the negotiating phase, but its role in the actual written agreement was hotly disputed. The French preferred to have the takeover contracts written in French, the Dutch in Dutch. In such a situation, a contract written in a neutral language is the best solution, especially since legal terms written in one language can have a very different meaning in another. If both sides can agree on a neutral language, then agreements can be reached on what the legal terms used actually mean.

In this particular takeover, neither side would back down and, for a while, the language question threatened to scupper the whole deal. Eventually, however, after a further round of protracted negotiations, an agreement was reached and the deal went through. The takeover contract was drawn up in French for the French group of companies and in Dutch for the Dutch concern. An English version was made for reference during face-to-face encounters.

Source: adapted from Browaeys (1996): 41-50.

1. The author of the article above mentioned some cultural differences he has encountered in dealing with companies abroad: language (different mother tongues and professional language) and customs (different way of doing things). Note the kinds of cultural differences – language, customs or others (say what they are) dealt with in the three cases:

   a. A British baker's takeover;

   b. A Finnish–Norwegian merger;

   c. A French takeover of a Dutch concern.

2. Describe the differences in attitudes and working practices of the lawyers and the people involved in the process of the three mergers/takeovers.

3. Write a conclusion to this article: make a synthesis of the three cases and answer the question: what have I learnt from this account about the cultural aspects in international mergers and acquisitions?

Conclusion

This chapter has dealt with the close relationship between the organizational culture and the corporate strategy of a company. The organizational culture is actually a part of the strategy in the sense that it influences not only the formulation of a strategy, but also the way it is implemented in the company. Furthermore, as Schneider and Barsoux point out, in the process of strategy development lie the same levels as in culture: artefacts, values and assumptions.

This relation is particularly obvious in mergers and cross-borders acquisitions since both involve not only the companies themselves but also their cultures. However, most companies see mergers actions as being a strategic way to deal with globalization, without taking into account the cultural problems inherent in the emergence of a new culture in the new organization.

Points for reflection

1. Strategy is often linked to change. Globalization compels companies to internationalize, so they must choose a strategy that enables them to remain competitive in the global market. Strategy is also linked to the future. It is a question of choosing strategies appropriate for enabling them to achieve long-term objectives. Having to face an environment often perceived as hostile and unstable, a company needs to redefine its strategy, to give it a new orientation. Are these attitudes towards strategy common to all companies?

   What role can culture play in defining strategy?

2. What is important in the process of creating a global culture is dealing with diversity, opposite poles, and the complementarity of ideas. This means that the creation of a global culture in cross-border organizations has to do with the opposition between ideas.

   The question therefore arises: how can the local cultures of two organizations with their different forms of logic and principles be united while ensuring that their duality is maintained?

Further reading

Deresky, H. (2003) *International Management: Managing across borders and cultures*, **4th edn, Upper Saddle River, NJ: Prentice Hall.** Takes a global perspective in foreign environments while taking into account the variables of culture. Cross-cultural management is evaluated in the context of global changes.

Fatehi, K. (1996) *International Management: A cross-cultural approach*, **Upper Saddle River, NJ: Prentice Hall.** This work uses the concepts of managing from an international perspective while emphasizing the cultural differences and the difficulties of working with people from diverse cultural backgrounds.

References

Bartlett, C.A., Ghoshal, S., and Birkinshaw, J. (2003) *Transnational Management*, 4th edn, New York, NY: McGraw-Hill Education.

Black, J.S., Gregersen, H.B., Mendenhall, M.E., and Stroh, L.K. (1999) *Globalizing People Through International Assignments*, Harlow: Addison-Wesley.

Browaeys, M.-J. (ed.) (1996) *The Challenges of Cross-Cultural Management*, Breukelen, Netherlands: Nyenrode University Press.

Cartwright, S. and Cooper, C.L. (1993) 'The role of culture compatibility in successful organizational marriage', in *Academy of Management Executive*, 7(2); quoted by Delavallée, E. (2002) *La culture d'entreprise pour manager autrement*. Paris: Editions d'Organisation: 55-70.

Delavallée, E. (2002) *La culture d'entreprise pour manager autrement*, Paris: Editions d'Organisation.

Deresky, H. (2003) *International Management: Managing across borders and cultures*, 4th edn, Upper Saddle River, NJ: Prentice Hall.

Fatehi, K. (1996) *International Management: A cross-cultural approach*, Upper Saddle River, NJ: Prentice Hall.

Hendriks, P. (2004) *FEM Business Magazine*, Amsterdam, The Netherlands: Reed Business, 6 March: 27.

Koster, P. (1998) *FEM Business Magazine*, Haarlem, The Netherlands: NVU Media, 19 June: 37.

Marx, E. (1999) *Breaking Through Culture Shock*, London: Nicholas Brealey.

Oberg, K. (1960) 'Culture shock: adjustment to new cultural environments', *Practical Anthropology*, 7: 177-82, quoted by Marx, E. (1999) *Breaking Through Culture Shock*. London: Nicholas Brealey: 5.

Pierre, P. (2001) 'Eléments pour une réflexion critique sur le management interculturel,' *Sociologies Pratiques*, 5: 119-143.

Schoenberger, E.J. (1997) *The Cultural Crisis of the Firm*, Oxford: Blackwell.

Schneider, S.C. and Barsoux, J.-L. (2003) *Managing Across Cultures*, 2nd edn, Harlow: FT Prentice Hall.

Tayeb, M. (2003) *International Management*, Harlow: Prentice Hall.

Thévenet, M. (1999) *La culture d'entreprise*, Paris: PUF Que sais-je?

Trice, H.M. and Beyer, J.M. (1993) *The Culture of Work Organizations*, Upper Saddle River, NJ: Prentice Hall.

Trompenaars, F. (2004) in Verbakel, F., 'HRM moet verzoenen in plaats van uitsluiten', *Gids voor Personeelsmanagement*, 83, 4: 20-22.

Chapter 10

Cultural change in organizations

So far, this book has examined organizational culture in terms of the various models put forward by researchers, the concepts of leadership and the cultural contingencies and variables involved. Furthermore, it has looked at the question of company strategy and corporate culture. All these elements come together when it is a question of a company's culture needing to adapt to ensure its success or even survival. This chapter examines the process of adaptation, its starting point being that any real change in an organization involves changing the underlying culture of the organization.

Learning outcomes

After reading this chapter, you will gain an understanding of:

● Certain mechanisms for changing an organization's culture as well as an instrument for diagnosing the changes required;

● The tensions between national culture and organizational culture in the change process, particularly the emergence of a so-called international corporate culture.

Concept 10.1 Organizational change as a cultural process

Whether an organization thrives, survives – or otherwise – depends on numerous factors, both within the company and outside it. There are, of course, external factors to which a company needs to respond, or circumstances to anticipate in the way it organizes its operations. Rapid technological change, changes in industries and markets, new deregulation policies, increased competition and the development of the global economy can all be seen as potential threats to a company's survival, or potential opportunities.

But success has also to do with internal factors. How can an organization adapt? Is it able to change its behavioural practices, its structures, to deal with external pressures? Admittedly, the culture of a company is dynamic. However, does it need to change its core values to survive or will changing cultural artefacts suffice? It is generally acknowledged that successful change has to do with maintaining both continuity and change, retaining the cultural foundation on which the company rests while changing its strategies and practices. In short, can essential elements of culture be brought in line with responses to the external forces pushing on the company?

The process of change

André Laurent (1989) addresses the difficulties involved in the process of change. The view of workers to organizational change, and the management thereof, is inhibited by their assumptions and conceptions. For a start, they may have fixed ideas as to how an organization should be structured. They may not, for example, consider any options to the hierarchical pyramid, where movements up and down are clearly defined. The idea of unity of command may also be taken for granted. Such concepts, the products of classical (Western) management thought, may not be appropriate when the organization has to take on fresh tasks or technologies, or deal with new people or environments. Moreover, the whole idea of change may be naive, if well-intentioned. People focus too much on the benefits from change without giving consideration to the idea that change is not an organizational shift from A to B, but a transformation from A into B.

These two differing concepts of change, shift versus transformation, reflect the 'doing' orientation of Anglo-Saxon cultures and 'being' of many Eastern cultures, mentioned in Part One. In 'doing' cultures, people and groups are mostly defined in terms of what they do, what they achieve. In 'being' cultures, people and groups are defined more in terms of affiliation, the relationships they have with others in the organization. In 'doing' cultures organizational change is perceived more in linear fashion, a question of putting the past state of affairs behind and pushing on with the new. In 'being' cultures, however, the past state of affairs undergoes gradual transformation so that it eventually becomes a new state of affairs.

Laurent advocates a dual approach to organizational change: both the instrumental and social nature of the organization must be considered. Managing change in the sense of ensuring the continuing running of the organization, re-assigning tasks, maintaining overall stability, may well be necessary in the process, but it is not enough. What is also needed is inspirational guidance, a leader who engages people's minds through vision. In his terms, our minds are the receptacles of culture, and as such give meaning and guidance to our experiences. Minds cannot be managed, but they can be transformed through inspiring leaders who spread visions that advocate new meanings and new lines of thinking.

Such concerns are shared by Deal and Kennedy (2000: 158). Many company managers, they maintain, are concerned about change, but do not pay attention to the cultural issues involved. They may go about dealing with tangible factors, such as changing job descriptions, replacing managers, changing the company structure even, but essentially, 'the business of change is cultural transformation'.

> These actions . . . are not the kind of long-term, all-encompassing behavioural and cultural changes we are talking about. When we speak of organizational or cultural change we mean real changes in the behaviour of people throughout the organization.

In their view, the decision to become, for example, more marketing-oriented or to become cost-effective cannot be taken without subjecting the company to a fundamental cultural change that involves everyone. The change is not just a matter of changing routines but of identifying with role-models who embody a new purpose or goal. Such fundamental change does not occur overnight: it is often a gradual and sometimes painful transformation.

The mechanisms of change

Chapter 8 summarized how Edgar Schein (2004) addressed ways in which a leader can implant and maintain the corporate culture. Such means can be used to change the culture of an organization.

Schein (2004) also lists what he calls 'secondary' means. These are mechanisms for shaping and reinforcing the culture that are only effective if consistent with the primary means:

- The design and structure of the organization.
- The systems and procedures used.
- The 'rites and rituals' used in an organization.
- The design and layout of the organization's physical space.
- Stories of important events and people.
- Formal statements of the organization's philosophy.

When a manager is intent on getting employees to perceive things differently, all the primary mechanisms must be used. Moreover, according to Schein, they must all be consistent with each other.

Chapter 8 also noted how Schein's model refers to the group-learning process when responding to problems externally and internally. External problems are concerned with responding to the environment. Internal problems arise from managing the internal development of the organization. For Schein, culture plays an important role in determining how environmental developments are perceived by members of organizations, and secondly how members of the organization react to the strategies designed to respond to those environmental developments.

In his article 'Organisational culture: what it is and how to change it', Schein (1989) presents what he believes to be the culture issues predominating at each phase of a company's growth. In addition, he discusses the change mechanisms that could be operating during each phase of growth. These phases only apply to private organizations and the kind of change possible depends on the extent to which the organization is ready for change as a result of either an external crisis or internal an internal push for change. Table 10.1 summarises his insights.

Table 10.2 summarizes how Schein (1989) believes the cultural change mechanisms work.

Can organizational culture really be changed?

Table 10.2 triggers an important question: is it possible to bring about fundamental transformations? An analysis by Deal and Kennedy (2000) reflects the belief that the culture of an organization is deep-rooted, particularly if, in Schein's terms, it is in a mid-life or maturity stage. A culture that has developed along with the organization and been passed on from generation to generation will be difficult to change and involves all kinds of relations between individuals and sub-groups.

If the external factors referred to in Chapter 7 are believed to have a strong influence on the organizational culture, the values, beliefs and behaviours that employees bring to the

Table 10.1 Growth states, functions of culture and mechanisms of change

Growth stage	Function of culture/issue
I. Birth and early growth Founder domination, possible family domination	• Culture is a distinctive competence and source of identity • Culture is the 'glue' that holds organization together • Organization strives towards more integration and clarity • Heavy emphasis on socialization as evidence of commitment
Succession phase	• Culture becomes battleground between conservatives and liberals • Potential successors are judged on whether they will preserve or change cultural elements
Change mechanisms 1. Natural evolution 2. Self-guided evolution through organizational therapy 3. Managed evolution through hybrids 4. Managed 'revolution' through outsiders	
II. Organizational mid-life • Expansion of products/markets • Vertical integration • Geographical expansion • Acquisitions, mergers	• Cultural integration declines as sub-cultures are spawned • Loss of goals, values and assumptions creates crisis identity • Opportunity to manage direction of cultural change is provided
Change mechanisms 5. Planned change and organization development 6. Technological seduction 7. Change through scandal, explosion of myths 8. Incrementalism	
III. Organizational maturity • Maturity or decline of markets • Increasing internal stability and/or stagnation • Lack of motivation to change	• Culture becomes a constraint on innovation • Culture preserves the glories of the past, hence is valued as a source of self-esteem, defence
Transformation option	• Culture change is necessary and inevitable, but not all elements of culture can or must change • Essential elements of culture must be identified, preserved • Culture change can be managed or simply allowed to evolve
Destruction option • Bankruptcy and reorganization • Takeover and reorganization • Merger and assimilation	• Culture changes at fundamental levels • Culture changes through massive replacement of people
Change mechanisms 9. Coercive persuasion 10. Turnaround 11. Reorganization, destruction, rebirth	

Source: Schein (1989): 66.

Table 10.2 Mechanisms of cultural change

Natural evolution	The culture will evolve a culture of what works best if the organization is not undergoing too much stress from the environment. This may also involve what Schein calls a 'general evolution' to the next stage of the organization's development through diversification and growing complexity. It may also involve 'specific evolution' where sub-cultures may emerge around the increasing number of sub-units in the organization
Self-guided evolution through organizational therapy	The organization gains insight into own strengths and weaknesses, e.g., by using an outside consultant to 'unfreeze' the organizational culture and so allowing dramatic changes to occur
Managed evolution through hybrids	This approach is useful where the culture needs to change, but the organization may lose its identity as a result. People from inside the company are used in key positions, people who realize there is a need for change but may meet less resistance than outsiders
Planned change and organizational development	Differentiation through growth and increasing complexity may lead to increasing sub-cultures coming into conflict. A consultant initiates a change programme to reduce conflict, one that involves some sort of culture change
Technological seduction	Technological changes may bring about cultural change because they change behaviour patterns and compel the organization to examine the way it carries out business
Change through scandal, explosion and myth	Change may occur through discrepancies between the values that are espoused by the organization and the practices that it actually performs. 'Whistleblowers' may reveal, for example, how ethical standards are being bypassed in certain operations, safety procedures ignored, promotion policies undermined. Such exposures often lead to assumptions being reconsidered and cultural changes being made
Incrementalism	Cultural change is implemented gradually over several years and is hardly noticed. Recruitment and selection policies, for example, may result in all key positions in a company being filled by people who act according to assumptions that are different to those of the old culture
Coercive persuasion	A culture turnaround, usually in a mature culture, where change agents – possibly senior managers – challenge old assumptions, put forward new ones and give key managers psychological safety by rewarding them for embracing the new assumptions
Turnaround	A turnaround individual or team has a clear idea of where the organization must go and how it is to get there. Some or all of the above mechanisms may be used while the present culture is unfrozen and psychological safety offered to reduce resistance
Reorganization and rebirth	An unusual occurrence, whereby the group that bears the old culture is removed and replaced by a new group and a fresh culture

organization, then there is little conviction that an organization can be changed unless the external environment changes in line with the desired changes. If organizational culture is seen as dependent on internal factors, then there is a belief that culture can be directed and changed. Ideas as to how these changes are brought about vary: some concentrate on the role of the leader as instigator of changes or as facilitator, others focus more on how to initiate change at the three levels of corporate culture as defined by Schein (norms, values and beliefs; then behaviours and norms; then symbols and artefacts).

The notion that cultural change is easier to implement in an organization with a 'weak' culture rather than a 'strong' culture is contested by Laurent (1989). Both are in a way doomed to extinction. The organization with a weak culture may eventually crash, even if there is an initial burst of creativity from its disparate body of workers. With employees who each give the organization a different meaning and who each have a different view of what needs to be done, a weak culture is poorly co-ordinated, lacking direction and consistency. The organization with a strong culture may be throttled by rigid norms and behaviour and the resulting dearth of innovation.

Rather than the strong–weak paradigm, Laurent advocates a more conceptual differentiation, which takes account of the extent to which an organization knows itself and the environment in which it operates. The higher the degree of awareness, both internally and externally, the better an organization can interpret its environment and deal with it.

Schein (2004) takes this awareness-raising issue further. He suggests that one way of trying to 'grasp' the corporate culture is for members of the organization to examine their culture together and assess some of the main assumptions. One or more of these may need to be abandoned or re-defined so that those involved can help decide the way the organization needs to evolve. The leader can play a key role here in getting the 'self-guided' evolution under way and managing the process.

A degree of culture change will almost always be necessary, Schein maintains, because what has been learned has become routine. Bringing unconscious values and norms to the surface and then questioning them and redefining then may lead to a considerable anxiety: the subjects involved may feel that their sense of identity or integrity is threatened. Everything must be done to reassure those involved, to show them that changes are possible and that they will not be humiliated in the process.

This brings us back to the role of transformational leaders, discussed in Chapter 2. Their role is to provide that reassurance through communicating a vision of how things should be, of convincing those who feel under threat that there is a brighter, happier future for the organization.

An enquiry into secret accounts held by the European Commission is an example of the sort of crisis that can trigger organizational change.

Exhibit 10.1

Irregular practices at the European Commission

Brussels launches probe into secret accounts

A widespread inquiry into secret bank accounts and fictitious contracts across the European Commission has been launched.

There is fear that the 'vast enterprise of looting' that fraud investigators found at Eurostat, the Commission's statistical arm, may exist elsewhere in the European Union's executive. Although problems were identified at Eurostat by trade unions in 1997, by internal Commission audits in 1999 and 2000 and by Paul van Buitenen, a whistleblower, in 2001, they were not taken seriously until newspaper reports surfaced in May 2003.

Neil Kinnock, EU administration commissioner, has since revealed the 'relatively extensive practice' at Eurostat until 1999 of setting up secret and illegal accounts, into which millions of euros are thought to have disappeared. The secret bank accounts at Eurostat were set up by Commission officials to hold money paid through inflated contracts to sub-contractors.

The commission has responded by initiating three disciplinary proceedings, suspending all directors and ordering an investigation into the work of some thirty heads of unit.

Source: *Financial Times*, 17 July 2003

Extract from the 2003 annual report dealing with protection of the European Community's financial interests and the fight against fraud:

Progress in the implementation of the Reform within the Commission

The modernization of the European public service continued to progress during 2003, in parallel to the work relating to the deepening of the antifraud reform of May 1999. In particular, the financial and administrative reform conceived in the White Paper of March 2000 on the internal reform of the Commission is being completed with the entry into force of the new Financial Regulation on 1 January 2003 which changes in particular the internal control system, and the decision of July 2003 on the Specialised Financial Irregularities Panel. As a result of the political agreement reached on 19 May 2003 in the Council and the opinion of the European Parliament of 19 June 2003, the Commission adopted an amended Proposal for the Staff Regulation. As from its entry into force on 1 May 2004, this Staff reform will have a major impact on the managing practices of departments and will contribute in particular to the prevention of irregularities. . . .

In response to the irregular practices detected at Eurostat, the Commission adopted complementary horizontal reinforcement measures: the September 1999 Code of conduct on the relations between the Commissioners and their services was revised in order to improve the information transmitted to Commissioners and to enable them to assume their political responsibility. To this end, a group of Commissioners including the President ensured that all the relevant information and/or allegations of fraud, irregularity and other reprehensible acts coming in particular from OLAF, IDOC and the Internal Audit Service are the subject of a rigorous follow-up. The group of commissioners is assisted by a high-level interdepartmental group.

Source: Report from the Commission Protection of the European Communities' financial interests and the fight against fraud, Annual report 2003 (http://eur-lex.europa.eu/LexUriServ/LexUriServ.do?uri=CELEX:52004DC0573:EN:NOT).

Questions

1. How would you describe the effect that the whistleblower's actions had on the European Commission?
2. In what way do you think the 'culture' of Eurostat might have been changed as a result of the actions?

Change in an organizational culture does seem possible, but the effort involved may be considerable and time-consuming. Apart from the question of motivation, the key aspect is clearly that those involved need to go through a process whereby they gain clear insight into important cultural assumptions and then work out which of these help or hinder the organization's future. A 'transformational' leader can be critical to such a process.

Concept 10.2   Organizational change in a global environment

So, organizational change in companies operating across a number of cultures is not just instrumental (becoming more cost-effective or market-oriented) but also transformational (giving new ways of thinking). How, therefore, does a multinational deal with change if it not only has to deal with policy changes, but also internal factors that may vary considerably from one part of the company to another? Equally important is how the multinational can handle the external factors that are said to have such an influence on the culture of the organization? (Laurent, 1989)

The tension between organizational and national cultures

The first issue to be addressed is the one briefly described in Part One: the tension between organizational culture and national culture. Nancy Adler (2002) wondered whether organizational values in some way pushed aside or diluted the national culture of the organization's environment. She refers to the seminal research carried out by Laurent in the eighties. The conclusions of this research were that cultural differences among managers working for a multinational company were significantly greater than those cultural differences among managers working for companies in their own (native) country. Although restricted to Western managers, Laurent's investigations showed that 'nationally bounded' collective perceptions of organizations did not appear to be diminished in any way through international business. On the contrary, as Adler indicates, these appear to be reinforced through the international exposure.

The conclusion is that the national companies of multinationals are likely to prefer different ways of bringing about the organizational changes that headquarters wishes to implement. To use the terms adopted in Concept 10.1, the transformation of an organization from A to B may involve following a different path in one part of the multinational than in another, even if the end-result (B) is the same. The means used to reach the desired change will also depend on how the national organization determines what the starting-point should be. In other words, the outset of the transformation to B will depend on how the national organization interprets its own present situation (A).

Does an international corporate culture exist?

Despite the all-important influence of national cultures, there is often an opinion expressed that there is a growing class of transnational business people who share a similar education, work experience and are developing their own global business culture. Moreover, the companies for which they work are, it is argued, themselves developing commonalities in terms of efficient production processes, quality control, workers' rights and environment issues. More and more international norms concerning business are being established through various agencies and these are being followed by an increasing number of globally active companies. So, the argument runs, both the increasing homogeneity among international managers and the increasing convergence of business practices is leading to the establishment of a common management culture among more and more international companies and their national constituents and which has no roots in any particular national culture.

These arguments appear to be supported by investigations done by Rohit Despharde et al (1998). They investigated whether there were any commonalties when comparing the organizational performance of multinationals based in Japan, the US, England, France and Germany. They found that, although the companies operated very differently, the most successful businesses surveyed used a similar organizational strategy. Whatever the country of origin, each successful multinational was most likely to foster competitive, entrepreneurial values. In particular, they found that those companies where innovation was most valued were the most successful.

Their findings may indeed highlight values which account for the success of the companies investigated, but to suggest that these companies have adopted an organizational culture at the expense of national cultures is considered by many in the field to be wishful thinking.

There may indeed be a growing consensus among multinationals as to what is best practice for international business. However, the idea that a shared organizational culture of many multinationals is pushing aside national cultures not only downplays the deep-seated nature of national cultures, but also discourages the transfer of know-how between the culturally different subsidiaries of the company, particularly when it comes to organizational change. Moreover, there is always the risk that multinational constituents become estranged from their national roots and that local relationships of all kinds are put under strain.

In short, a true multinational does not subordinate national cultures, but regards them as a source of learning and increased synergy within the company. To return to the analysis made by Laurent (1999: 93) and summarized at the start of this concept, this increased learning and synergy:

> . . . cannot be the result of a rational management decision. It requires an evolution in ways of thinking – from a parochial and ethnocentric conception of management and organisation to a world view.

Mapping corporate culture change

At this stage it is worthwhile looking at the framework of reference used in the survey carried out by Despharde et al to take the issue of corporate culture change further. Cameron and Quinn (1999) categorize organizational effectiveness perspectives and associated types of organization (Figure 10.1). They emphasize that this categorization should not be seen in any way as comprehensive. It is, however, based on many scholarly analyses of corporate culture and has, they claim, proved its value in many subsequent investigations into corporate culture change.

As can be seen in Table 10.3, two dimensions are used to differentiate effectiveness criteria. one emphasizes either flexibility and discretion or stability and control; another emphasizes either internal orientation (integration and unity) or external orientation (differentiation and rivalry). These two dimensions produce four quadrants, which each represents a set of values that are at the base of judgements about organizations. The quadrants are contradictory or competing on the diagonal. Hence the name of the model, the competing values (CV) framework.

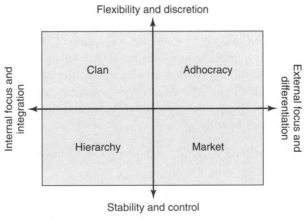

Figure 10.1 The competing values framework
Source: Cameron and Quinn (1999): 32.

Table 10.3 The characteristics of the CV framework quadrants

Hierarchy culture	Values tradition, continuity, rationalization and regulation. It focuses more on internal than external (market) issues, and values stability and control over flexibility and discretion. This is the traditional 'command and control' model of organizations, which can work effectively if the goal is efficiency and the organizational environment is stable and simple
Market culture	Also values stability and control but is more focused on external rather than internal issues. This culture values profit, productivity, competitive advantage and achievement
Clan culture	Focuses on internal issues and flexibility and discretion rather than seeking stability and control. It values team-spirit, participation, consensus and mutual support.
Adhocracy culture	Focuses on external issues and values flexibility. Its values are adaptability and innovation

The characteristics of these quadrants, as described by Cameron and Quinn (1999), are summarized in Table 10.3.

This categorization is not clear-cut: all organizations have aspects of all four cultures. An 'adhocracy', for example, which is intent on creativity and flexibility, still needs to contain some 'hierarchy' values if it is not to run out of control; a 'market' culture may be so focused on making profit that individuals – and their health – may become secondary to the whole operation; a 'clan' culture may allow for so much uncontrolled individualism that the company's tasks become secondary. However, over time, one type of culture tends to predominate. High performance entails, therefore, balancing conflicting and competing demands.

The elements in the model, as well as the language used, can be used to discuss organizational culture and change. As such, the framework serves as a basis for diagnosing the predominant culture of an organization and for assessing whether it is responding appropriately to the challenges and changes in the environment. Equally important, the framework helps in the diagnosis and management of the interrelationships, congruencies and contradictions in the organization. Altogether, the framework helps leaders to improve in a comprehensive way the organization's performance and value creation.

The 'organizational culture assessment instrument' used to carry out the diagnosis is described in detail by Cameron and Quinn (1999). It takes the form of a questionnaire in which respondents complete questions covering six items. The questions are answered first in terms of the organization's current culture, then answered again in terms of what the respondents think should be developed in the culture to respond to future challenges. Once the present and future profiles of the organization have been drawn up, they can be examined from several angles:

- What type of culture is most heavily emphasized (what basic assumptions, styles and values are dominant)?
- What discrepancies are there between the present and future profiles (what needs to be done to close the gap)?
- What is the degree of congruence between the individual responses to the questions (to what degree are the values and assumptions shared)?

An organization's profile can also be measured against an average industry profile (Cameron and Quinn provide a range of these, mostly from the US but also in Europe, South America, Africa, Australasia and Asia). Comparing the two profiles allows insights to be developed concerning the cultural changes needed: is the organization out of line with the requirements of the sector's environment, or is the mismatch itself a source of competitive advantage?

As a final point, it is worth returning to the survey by Despharde et al, which used the competing values framework. Although they came to the conclusion that successful international companies were likely to foster very similar competitive, entrepreneurial values, they also noted differences of emphasis when it came to categorizing these companies according to the CV framework. They found, for example, that the Japanese companies under investigation fostered 'hierarchy' and 'clan' values while at the same time stressing competition and performance, English companies, although fostering values associated with 'adhocracy', also displayed 'clan' values of loyalty and cohesiveness. French companies embraced many values associated with 'hierarchy' cultures, but also embraced the virtues of entrepreneurship and innovation associated with the 'adhocracy' culture. These findings confirm the 'competing' nature of the framework, but also clearly imply that congruity between an organization's cultural values and national cultural values are a measure of a company's success.

ACTIVITY 10.1

The summary of events given below concerning Michelin's joint venture in China is based on the detailed account given in the autumn 2005 issue of *The Link*, the learning interface of China European Business School, Shanghai (www.ceibs.edu/link/index.shtml).

Michelin in China implementing a human resources strategy

In 2001, Michelin, the world's leading tyre manufacturer and based in France, set up a joint venture in Shanghai, China, with Shanghai Tyre and Rubber Company Ltd. The Chinese tyre market was expected to almost treble within three years, so Michelin was happy to invest $200 million in the company.

The new company, in which Michelin had a 70 per cent stake, was mostly made up of employees from the Chinese partner plus a small team of expatriate managers and managers recruited from other international ventures in China. The expatriates were used to lay the foundation for future operations and to support the management team that had originally run the Chinese company. This team was kept in place to facilitate the integration process.

Michelin wished to implement its well-established personal management philosophy in the new company. This was the way to develop the personal and professional effectiveness of the workforce as well as help individuals develop their career in the company. The company badly needed managers who could work in a joint venture environment, so this active approach to human resource development compensated for the dearth of suitable managers available in China.

The management approach Michelin wished to have adopted was based on Michelin's five core values based on respect for: customers, people, shareholders, the environment and facts (www.michelin.com/corporate/front/templates/affich.jsp?codeRubrique=76&lang=EN).

These values were immediately recognizable and not difficult for the Chinese employees to accept. But were they aware of what the implementation of these values through the management approach entailed?

The personnel department in Shanghai, as well as its counterparts in other Michelin production plants, was responsible for creating and maintaining a strong, open and shared company culture, one that was a source of social cohesion and motivation. It encouraged individual employees to advance themselves professionally according to their performance, →

skills and ambitions. Just as on other Michelin sites, the department was set apart from the business units. The personnel managers had no formal position in the hierarchy but worked closely with partners, the managers of the business units. During the employees' progress within the company there was continual evaluation and face-to-face dialogue involving the employee, the unit manager and the career manager from the personnel department.

In her analysis of the personnel situation in the Shanghai plant, the human resources director of Michelin China described the difficulties that the integration of this approach into the joint venture would cause (Qi, 2005). Clearly, this could not be done overnight. The concept of appraisal and the role of career managers did not fit into the concept that the Chinese have of management and the importance given to hierarchical relationships. Other elements of the HR approach that would be difficult for the Chinese to accept included the notion that support functions such as human resources were as important as functional departments and the expectation that employees should speak openly about themselves and the working environment.

The starting point of any integration needed to be for both sides to understand each other's ways of thinking. In this way initial fears and suspicions could be removed and the process of building mutual trust set in motion. The employees who had been recruited from other joint ventures and who had become familiar with Western practices acted as a bridge between the expatriates (who were mostly involved in the technical process) and the line managers (who were Chinese). In addition, considerable resources were dedicated to training courses and study abroad for (potential) managers.

Four years after the creation of the joint venture, the HR director saw some progress, but that integration was by no means complete. Although some employees were unable to adapt to the changing environment and left, the majority appeared to be willing to accept Michelin's approach to human resources. The career management system was 'taking shape' and the process of dialogue between employees, career managers and line managers was under way. At the same time, the expatriates had gained a deeper insight into how the Chinese culture works.

As the writer indicates, one core value of the Michelin culture – respect for people – lies at the core of the integration process. Respect by both sides of both sides. The process was therefore not about establishing the Michelin way, or the Chinese way; it was about establishing the Michelin China way.

Questions

1. Summarize what you believe to be the 'Michelin China way'.

2. Which of the values, as described in the competing values framework, do you recognize in the case with regard to Michelin and its Chinese partner?

Conclusion

Chapter 10 has described the role of culture in organizational change. It has outlined the cultural issues which, according to Schein, are prevalent at the various stages in a company's development, and it has summarized the actions he proposes as mechanisms of change.

One crucial factor in any change process is the extent to which a company is aware of its culture and of the operational environment. Using the competing values framework devised by Cameron and Quinn is one way of assessing whether a company and its employees are responding appropriately to the environment; this framework has been outlined in the chapter.

Chapter 10 has also shown that, even if the culture of a multinational organization needs to be changed, any transformation carried out will need to reflect the national culture while at the same time ensuring that the subsidiaries involved remain integral parts of the whole multinational.

Points for reflection

1. As the text indicates, companies tend not to give explicit attention to cultural issues when planning and implementing organizational change. Laurent advocates a dual approach to address this situation.

   What type of leader is required in this approach and what does that leader need to do? Where does this approach belong in Table 10.2 (Schein's 'mechanisms of change').

2. Concept 7.2 summarized a classification of the types of cultures, made by Deal and Kennedy (2000) on the basis of a study they made of various firms and their business environment.

   What are the similarities between this and the cultures defined in the competing values framework presented in Figure 10.1? What differences do your perceive between the two – and how do you account for these?

Further reading

Schein, E.H. (2004) *Organizational Culture and Leadership,* 3rd edn, San Francisco, CA: Jossey-Bass. This is the third edition of the book published originally in 1985. Schein offers his readers considerable insight into the dynamics of organizations and change. Using the findings of contemporary research, as well as referring to many of the organizations with whom he has worked, Schein examines occupational cultures as well as the ways in which leaders apply the principles of culture to achieve organizational goals. He also addresses the question of cultural change within an organization, specifically the role of the leader in this process. One aspect that Schein considers indispensable – and which he says is almost completely ignored in most leadership books – is the question of organizational growth and the different role which culture plays during each stage of growth.

Cameron, K.S. and Quinn, R.E. (1999) *Diagnosing and Changing Organizational Culture,* Upper Saddle River, NJ: Prentice-Hall. This book provides an instrument for diagnosing organizational culture and a framework for understanding organizational culture. It then describes a step-by-step process for producing an organizational culture profile, identifying the ways in which the culture of the organization should change, and formulating a strategy for accomplishing that change. The book contains an assessment instrument that readers can use to determine their own cultural profile as leaders/managers/employees in an organization.

References

Adler, N.J. (2002) *International Dimension of Organisational Behaviour*, Cincinnati, OH: South-Western.

Cameron, K.S. and Quinn, R.E. (1999) *Diagnosing and Changing Organizational Culture,* Upper Saddle River, NJ: Prentice Hall.

Deal, T.E. and Kennedy, A.A. (2000) *Corporate Cultures: The rites and rituals of corporate life*, Cambridge, MA: Perseus.

Despharde R., Farley, J.U. and Webster Jr., F.E. (1998) 'Factors affecting organisation performance: a five-country comparison', MSI Report no. 98-100.

Evans, P., Doz, Y. and Laurent, A. (eds) (1989) *Human Resource Management in International Firms,* London: Macmillan.

Laurent, A. (1989) 'A cultural view of organizational change' in Evans P., Doz, Y. and Laurent, A. (eds) *Human Resource Management in International Firms*, London: Macmillan.

Qi, L. (2005) 'Learn to agree to differ', *The Link,* autumn 2005, Chinese Europe International Business School on its website: (www.ceibs.edu/link/index.shtml).

Schein, E.H. (1989) 'Organisational culture: what it is and how to change it' in Evans, P., Doz, Y. and Laurent, A. (eds) *Human Resource Management in International Firms*, London: Macmillan: 83–94.

Schein E.H. (2004) *Organizational Culture and Leadership,* 3rd edn, San Francisco, CA: Jossey-Bass.

Chapter 11

Culture and marketing

Marketing is no longer an isolated function of the organization. This means that its activities such as creating markets and satisfying consumers can no longer be realized without the contribution of the whole organization. The focus of this approach is principally on the consumer. Marketing is the integrating part of the organization, linking it to its environment.

Concept 11.1 goes beyond the boundaries of the domestic firm to examine marketing in an international environment, with all the adaptations this requires, especially in marketing research.

Concept 11.2 focuses on communication in an intercultural environment, especially advertising, as well as on management of meanings related to brand names for international markets and to country of origin images.

Learning outcomes

After reading this chapter, you should have an understanding of:

- The cultural differences in marketing practices in the world;
- The nature of cross-cultural research in marketing and its components;
- The role of communication in international marketing.

Concept 11.1 Marketing in a cross-cultural environment

Marketing is an integral part of a company's activities. It tries to balance customer needs with the aims and resources of the organization. Wall and Rees (2001) separate out marketing activities in terms as follows:

1. Market analysis with at least three elements:
   - *environment analysis*, which involves making an inventory of the risks and opportunities in the company's environment;
   - *buyer behaviou*r: the company needs to establish the profile of its (potential) customers and to know how and why they buy;
   - *market research*: this is the way information concerning the company's customers and environment is collected.

2. Marketing strategy. Once a market has been scanned using the above tools, the company has to develop a strategy to give a meaning and direction to its marketing activities. The following strategies are often used:

- *market segmentation*: taking a group of (potential) customers who share certain characteristics (such as age or income range or occupational profile)

- *marketing mix*: comprising, apart from the product itself, price, promotional activities and place.

The various marketing activities are integrated into the organization through planning and management itself. Through planning, market opportunities can be evaluated in relation to the resources of the enterprise with a view to attaining its goals. Management is intent on running the whole process effectively so that the customers' needs and wishes are met.

However, this classification of marketing activities in terms of market, strategy, planning and management, as well as the strategy of the marketing mix, has its critics. Some experts see these approaches as being traditional ones that no longer meet present-day needs.

Traditional view and new ideas and concepts

As Mercado, Welford and Prescott (2001) note, experts are increasingly questioning the effectiveness of the marketing mix approach. They argue that market-driven management should be more than a succession of 'ordered functions'. They see a modern concept of marketing with a stronger customer focus, one that entails not only the notion of anticipating and responding to customer needs, but also that of defining and delivering customer value through a market-oriented business strategy. This means that that the whole marketing function of a company should be integrated into all parts of a company. There should no longer be a separate unit for marketing; the function should be seen as a collective one whereby departments link up to perform various tasks and processes.

This prescription is, according to Mercado et al (2001), closely linked to the development of relationship marketing. Here, too, the focus is less on the marketing mix and more on the development of relationships that firmly link the company to the market. These relationships comprise not just personal and organizational ones, but also the creation of networks that the authors define as 'sets of relationships and interactions performed within specific relationships'. Relationship marketing is essentially about connecting with customers through continual transactions and exchanges whereby the expectations of customers are not only met but also, if possible, exceeded.

Problems with cross-border market research

This fresh approach to marketing is seen as the most appropriate and effective way of dealing with consumers within the expanding and increasingly integrated markets, Europe being a prime example. There remain, however, problems for marketers and market researchers. Mercado, Welford and Prescott (2001: 394–395) define them as follows:

- *Language barriers.* Language poses a real problem when it comes to identifying behaviours common to different nationalities. Translating from one language to another is one problem, but also assessing the differences between countries when it comes to the meaning of the translated words.

- *Sensitivity of questioning.* Europeans show differences in the information they choose to communicate. The Greeks, for example, may not be worried about revealing information on their income, whereas the British are reluctant to do so.

- *Research techniques.* Most of marketing research techniques emanate from the US. They focus on the ability of individuals to express their sentiments and feelings. Some customers, whether in Europe or Asia, are reluctant to talk openly about such matters and prefer instead to be asked questions on more practical issues.

- *Cultural differences.* When surveys are being carried out across cultures about the way people live, behave and think, it is important to take into account the cultural context when analysing responses to questionnaires. If this is not done, the research findings may be misinterpreted and the real meanings undiscovered.

- *Suspicion.* People in certain countries are becoming increasingly suspicious about what happens to information gathered through marketing surveys. They are, therefore, increasingly reluctant to participate in such surveys.

- *Statistical comparisons.* Cross-country comparisons of statistics are difficult to perform since the data are established locally and are based on practices that differ between countries. Demographic information, educational qualifications and social groupings may be different, as well as the relative amounts spent on promotion and advertising.

- *Fragmentation.* Many multinational concerns have decentralized structures whereby operating companies enjoy considerable autonomy. Research done by a local company across different countries and markets may lack a consistent method, be fragmented and inconclusive.

An example of the problems defined above is illustrated in Case study 11.1.

Case study 11.1

What is behind the question?

In his article on linguistic sensitivity in cross-cultural organizational research, Lawrence M. Gales (2003) refers to the differences between France and the US with regard to the centrality of work in one's life.

He refers to research into job satisfaction across cultures. Researchers have used well-tried survey instruments in English, translating them into the languages of the cultures in question. However, as the author points out, a translation of this kind will not necessarily 'capture the nuances of work life and job satisfaction within a given culture' (2003: 135). A question such as 'How satisfied are you with your salary?' translated into French may not adequately reflect the concern that the French give to the quality of life. Job satisfaction will probably have a different meaning to those living in a culture – such as that in France – where work does not play such an important role in self-fulfilment.

International marketing

According to Wall and Rees (2001: 266), international marketing can be simply defined as 'marketing activities that cross national borders'. They do add, however, that these activities occur at three levels in line with the focus of a company's operations:

- Companies whose sales for the most part are made in the domestic market and consider exports to be less important.

- Multinational companies selling throughout the world that consider their country of origin or host country in the same way as the other market environments in which they are involved.

- Those companies – usually multinationals – that want to adopt a global marketing strategy by identifying products or services with certain similarities in certain markets, and pursuing a single, global marketing strategy for them (Coca-Cola being an obvious example). Consumer products as well as industrial products are all potential candidates for global marketing particularly when there is little or no need to adapt them for local consumption (telecommunications and computers are examples).

Companies with a **sales orientation** try to sell the same product in a large number of countries when consumer characteristic are similar and, as Daniels and Radebaugh (2001) point out, there is a 'spillover' between countries when it comes to product information.

Increasingly, however, exporting companies are having to adopt a **societal orientation**. This entails not only knowing how a product is bought, but also how it is disposed of; not only knowing why a product is bought, but also how it could be modified in some way to make it more socially desirable.

A change in orientation may be necessary because of legal, cultural or even economic reasons. Such a change may compel the enterprise to modify its products to meet the needs of local consumers. The real reason for a change in orientation is often a cultural one. A switch from one product to another, a change in colour preferences or choice of materials is difficult to predict. Marketers just cannot determine in advance what the consumer is going to buy – not even when they are surveying their home country. Making such predictions in foreign markets is as difficult, if not more so, when it comes to selling new products, or at least products which are unknown to the consumers there.

The intercultural marketing approach

The question of adapting products and marketing strategies to suit the needs and wishes of the consumer lies at the heart of the intercultural marketing approach. Intercultural marketing is, according to Usunier and Lee (2005), as much to do with localizing as with globalizing. The intercultural marketing approach takes account of criteria related to geography and nationality while, at the same time, using criteria to do with consumer attitudes, preferences and lifestyles related to age, class and ethnicity, as well as occupation.

Intercultural marketing is made easier if the conditions for identification with the products are present in the target market. If consumers are to buy a certain product they need to identify with it in some way. Usunier and Lee (2005: 232) also maintain that consumers:

> buy the meaning that they find in products for the purpose of cultural identification, based on the desire for assimilation in a certain civilization.

The elements involved in the process of cultural identification are, according to the authors, twofold:

- the notion of *identity* (the need to reproduce the national culture such as it is, the desire to feel at home)
- the notion of *exoticism* (the desire to escape from one's culture and to experience other values, other ways of living).

These notions are closely interlinked in a rather ambiguous way in the identification process, so a straightforward description of the approach is difficult to make. That is why it is preferable to make clusters of countries or consumers who share 'meaningful cultural characteristics'.

There are, in their analysis, 'geographical cultural affinity zones' which, to a large extent, resemble national cultural groups; and 'cultural affinity classes', which are formed using different kinds of segmentation. Usunier and Lee (2005: 232) give an example of such a class composed of people between the ages of fifteen and twenty from Japan, Europe and the US:

> They have a tendency to share common values, behaviour and interests, and tend to present common traits as a consumer segment; their lifestyles converge worldwide irrespective of national borders.

Such cultural affinity classes can be an ideal target for standardized products because they have a sense of belonging to a common age, gender or income group across different countries. They may also share a common channel of communication, particularly the web and satellite television.

Cross-cultural consumer behaviour

A certain understanding of cultural differences is indispensable for effective communication with consumers from different backgrounds. However, according to Kaynak and Jallat (2004), the importance of geographic frontiers and politics will gradually diminish because of changes in the economic environment and the evolution of consumer behaviour. Europe offers an example of such changes, as do the young generations of consumers in more and more countries. They increasingly behave in the same way. Even in China there is evidence of the influence of the Confucian system of values retreating among the young to make way for a more individualist attitude in their buying habits.

Although differences in the cultural and economic environment remain, there is increasing uniformity in consumer taste and consumer behaviour. This already appears to affect the marketing strategies of companies operating at an international level.

Usunier and Lee (2005) point out, however, limitations to the way behavioural intentions are determined. Significant differences in consumer behaviour may be determined and the need to adapt a product established. This is not, however, sufficient in itself because the intentions of the consumers need to be established. The behavioural intentions models, which were assumed to be applicable universally, showed different weightings between attitudes and norms.

To what extent, therefore, is it possible to talk of transposing theories to do with consumer behaviour? There are certainly similarities between cultures, but to really understand consumer behaviour, the characteristics of the consumers' culture and their underlying models must be taken into consideration.

Marketing is also a process in which communication plays an important role. Consumers buy not only the product but the meaning which goes with it. This idea will be developed in Concept 11.2.

Concept 11.2 | Advertising across cultures

Branding

Some say that the brand often sells better than the product. Among many products on the market, the buyer recognizes 'his' or 'her' brand before actually buying the product. The seductive power of the name seems therefore to count as much as the way the product is made.

How can we define what a brand is? Well, for a start, it is the brand that identifies a product/service or range of products/services. In a legal sense, provided it is registered, this form of identification becomes a trademark. As such, the brand (eventually) becomes instantly recognizable and can to a certain extent market itself, so reducing promotional costs.

Decisions regarding brands require careful consideration. Daniels and Radebaugh, (2001) list the many choices that may have to be made:

- Have a brand or not;
- Use the manufacturer's brand or a private brand;
- Decide on one brand or use multiple brands;
- Employ one worldwide brand or use local brands.

The final choice is one multinationals need to face. Using one uniform brand internationally makes economic sense, but problems can arise as a result, particularly when it comes to language (Case study 11.2). A name originally chosen for one particular market with a particular language may have a different association in other language areas. The name chosen may also be difficult to pronounce because other languages may not have the sounds attached to the original name, or because the pronunciation of the name may create a

Case study 11.2

Jif and Cif

Unilever developed a liquid cleaning product that was first sold in France under the name Cif. When it proved to be successful, it was introduced in other markets. For the British and Dutch markets it was renamed Jif because, the story goes, the manufacturers were concerned that the name 'cif' might be associated with 'syph', the slang word for the sexually transmitted disease syphilis. The word 'jif' is found in English phrases such as 'See you in a jif' or 'This won't take a jif' – implying that something will happen quickly. In 2001, however, Unilever decided to use just one brand name for the product across Europe – Cif. Although it seems logical to have the same name for the same product for marketing purposes, the change may also reflect the fact that syphilis is no longer a common subject of discussion in the UK.

The name Jif is still used in Australia, New Zealand and Norway. In Canada, it is called Vim, which was the name given to a similar product first manufactured by Lever Brothers in the UK in 1905.

meaning different to the original. Such problems may be all the greater if the brand is promoted using a different alphabet.

As Daniels and Radebaugh (2001) rightly point out, problems with promoting brands internationally are exacerbated by the lack of knowledge of foreign languages among consumers. English, French and Spanish are so predominant that the native speakers of these languages do not learn (or, we may add, are not exposed to) other languages as much as speakers of 'minority' languages such as Dutch, Greek or Finnish.

Brands and national images

As we have seen, the brand name can provoke associations of ideas and emotions in such a way that consumers are not just buying a product but also the image it conveys. In terms of a consumer's purchase criteria, image is an important facet of the product, along with quality, innovation, design, and ease of use as well, of course, as price. In terms of international marketing, how do consumers perceive products from countries other than their own? What is the relationship between the nationality of a product and the image it evokes?

A number of authors, including Usunier and Lee (2005) see this relationship as a very important one, not only in terms of the 'made in' label, but also in terms of other elements that contribute to the consumer's perception of product nationality. These include:

- The image of national products as compared with imported or international products.
- National images of generic products.
- The national image of the manufacturing company.
- The image diffused by the brand name.

Such elements are not necessarily related to one country (e.g. pasta to Italy), but to several countries (e.g. wine), or even to a geographical area (yoghurt to the Balkans).

Usunier and Lee (2005: 289) note the role of stereotypes in associating a product with the national image of a country. There are, they maintain, a small, but important number of consistent stereotypical images:

> . . . the image of the robustness of German products, the image of France as associated with luxury goods, the image of Korean products as being cheap.

Such shared perceptions, however, do change, as Usunier and Lee (2005) conclude from their investigations, and seem to do so rapidly. This is particularly the case for products from Japan and the newly industrialized countries of Asia. This applies also to countries that have cultural and language similarities through their colonial past, but which have very differing perceptions of the meaning of products.

Another factor that can change shared perceptions is the matter of 'country of origin'. As Usunier and Lee (2005) indicate, multinationals sell the same products under the same brand worldwide. These products may, however, differ considerably from one economic zone to another, containing components from the company's country of origin as well as from the areas where they are sold. For example, how 'French' is a Peugeot that has been assembled in the UK or Spain, containing parts from different European countries – including France – as well as from Asia?

Case study 11.3

Skoda transformed

The perception of brand name Skoda has undergone a massive change since the early 1990s. Skoda was originally the name of a Czechoslovakian car manufacturer nationalised by the new communist regime after World War II. The cars it made before the 1989 'Velvet Revolution' were available in western as well as east Europe. Although behind the Iron Curtain they were considered to be superior to cars from other communist countries, they were seen in the West as cheap but poorly made and unreliable. Jokes about the car – along with those made by the Russian equivalent Lada – were heard frequently:

'How do you double the value of a Skoda? Answer: Fill it with petrol.'

'Why does a Skoda have a heated rear windscreen? Answer: To keep your hands warm when you push it.'

Once the German car maker Volkswagen had taken a 30 per cent stake in the company in 1991 (eventually taking total control of the company in 2001), things changed. Through intensive training and extensive investment in the plant, research and product development, the quality of Skoda products improved considerably. The cars were soon earning high praise from the motoring press. However, the accolades the company received were not immediately reflected in sales figures in the West. Nevertheless, through clever marketing campaigns in Europe (and parts of Asia and Latin America), consistently positive reviews from the motoring press and multiplying 'word-of-mouth' recommendations from satisfied buyers, sales started rising rapidly.

In the UK, marketers found it particularly difficult to shake off the old Skoda image. Commercials were made, however, that faced up to this image in an honest but humorous way. In one of these, for example, a Skoda driver returns to his car where a parking attendant is waiting. The attendant says: 'I'm afraid some little vandal has stuck a Skoda badge on the front of your car'. The commercial ends with the picture of the handsome new Skoda (Fabia or Octavia) and, beneath it, the slogan 'It's a Skoda. Honest!'

Market researchers found that this and other similar commercials, in which the 'new' image played with the 'old' image, had a very positive effect on consumer awareness. They helped boost sales during the 18-month promotion period. Moreover, the percentage of British consumers who said they would not consider buying a Skoda fell by more than a third after one year into the campaign.

Source: 'Skoda goes from trash to treasure,' American Marketing Association, 18 February 2002 (www.marketingpower.com/content16161S1.php).

Some multinationals underplay the country of origin and focus on the 'country-of-brand'. So, Daimler-Benz talks in its corporate advertising of the company 'being home in more than 200 countries' (Usunier and Lee, 2005: 292). See Case study 11.3.

Related to this change of focus is the increasing appearance of products that are 'made in the European Union'. What sort of associations are this label expected to evoke among consumers within the EU – and those buying the product outside the EU?

Communication: advertising

To communicate with the customer and the outside world – whether the focus is on the organization in question or on its products – marketing uses advertising as its principal channel.

Advertising is often defined as the channel of communication used not only to inform the public, but also to persuade the consumer to buy a product or service. Some consider advertising as a universal phenomenon, an indispensable part of everyday life; others focus on its power, the power not only to persuade people to buy, but also to create a need. In any case, advertising in its simplest form is information intended to create a link between the producer and consumer. But there is clearly a purpose behind this, namely to sell! Its essential purpose is to publicize a product and so create a demand for it. And when a product has become known, advertising maintains the recognition and reputation it has acquired while maintaining the consumer's wish to buy the product.

In the end, of course, it is all about the consumer. Those busy with international marketing must go beyond questions of language and behavioural differences to try and find out the meanings consumers in different cultures give to products, brands, messages and behaviours. Even 'lifestyle' research and other investigations to determine market segmentation pay increasing attention to the way culture affects consumers' perception of products and services.

When it comes to launching a product in another cultural environment, there are obstacles, even when the country in question seems to have a business culture similar to that where the product is already being sold. Case study 11.4 highlights such obstacles.

Case study 11.4

Product launch in Uruguay

A few months after an Argentinian food manufacturing company had launched a number of product categories in Uruguay, it decided that the next launch would be cake and dessert mixes. The sale of these products would help to build the brand rapidly and would contribute high volumes to the company's operations.

It was entering a market where there was only one competitor, and it had a 90 per cent market share. The company thought the launch would (literally) be a 'piece of cake': the country's culture was similar to its own, so what could go wrong? The products were launched together with a TV commercial where the only change was to give the voice-over a Uruguayan accent.

About three months later, the products were still on the shelves. The distributor was not sending any new orders but calling instead to ask what should be done next.

The company decided to run focus groups to find out what was happening. What it discovered was surprising. Consumers, women aged twenty to forty-five, middle class mothers who were the purchase decision-makers for this type of product, explained that it was a disgrace to buy a pre-packaged cake or dessert. The true identity of a mother or a wife was only proven when she could cook something delicious for her loved ones. These women even prepared gelatine at home out of chicken bones (a very time-consuming and disgusting process). Making cakes from packets was out of the question: only the housewives could give them the right flavour and ingredients – and cakes were easy to make anyway. There was a market for pre-packaged ingredients, but only a small one, for those occasions when the housewives had no time to prepare cakes in the normal way.

The company was not prepared for this feedback and started wondering whether its main competitor was aware of this. It was time to start a campaign to educate the customer.

Source: adapted from Browaeys and Trompenaars (2000): case 6.

Question

What should the company have done to make the launch of its cake mixes a success? Look at a possible analysis of the case study.

The company had no control over this (external) market, but was willing to accept what the market provided them with. The company should have kept its focus on the customer and maintained a flexible attitude towards them. This meant taking advantage of the existing forces and not contradicting them, in a circle that would have worked positively for them – in line with Trompenaars' framework (Chapter 5).

Rather than assume there was a market for the dessert mixes because cultural similarities between the home and export country were considerable, the company should have investigated the actual demand. The fact that there was only one supplier of this type of product should have driven the company to find out why no others had entered the market. If the company had decided there was a market, it should have created advertising which clearly informed the (potential) Uruguayan consumers of the advantages of the product.

Using cultural dimensions to examine a product concept is also what Hoecklin proposes. Taking a cultural approach in marketing and advertising gives added value in the sense that it provides indispensable information to the marketers. From Hoecklin's viewpoint (1995: 106):

> . . . the more the marketers understand about the way a particular culture tends to view status, expressions of emotion, friendship, rules, humour, enjoyment, public life versus private life and so on, the more control they have over creating an ad that will be interpreted in the way in which they want.

The product or service is therefore no longer presented to the public as it is, but presented in a symbolic way to create adhesion. The advertising presents the product in such a way as to attract the consumer and when doing so, focuses its message on the benefit the product brings the consumer, not on its qualities. Advertising and other promotional campaigns adapted to the local market allow the image of the product in question to be directly associated with the product concept in the mind of the consumer. Consider Case study 11.5.

Case study 11.5

Sensodyne toothpaste

To illustrate this 'glocal' strategy, consider the information to be found on a tube of Sensodyne bought in Holland and on a tube bought in France:

- *Same product:* both tubes show identical ingredients (in English) and the same product description ('Sensodyne for sensitive teeth') in their respective languages.
- *Same message:* the Dutch tube gives the following message in Dutch: 'Daily use of Sensodyne protects sensitive teeth and prevents the pain from returning.' The French tube gives the following message in French: 'If used daily, it prevents the sensitivity from returning.'
- *The difference:* on the Dutch tube: 'Brushing twice a day brings a lasting result.' On the French tube: 'After three weeks' use you will be able to notice the improvement in your dental sensitivity and regain the pleasure of savouring everything you like.'

Managing the *meaning* of brands across cultures

Incorporating understanding of a consumer's culture takes into account the emotional element, necessary if a product is to be successfully launched in a new market. As Hoecklin observes (1995), companies operating internationally are managing the meaning of brands across cultures while building the strength of their brand and extending the number of markets in which they are selling and promoting their brand. Their attempts to adapt to the cultural differences in communication and product use have reached a sophisticated level: companies are increasingly intent on making sure that the intended meaning of the brand coincides with the *perceived meaning* of the message.

This approach underlines the importance of the notion of perception. In psychological terms, perception is a complex act whereby the individual is not just observing but also reconstructing his environment. He is not just discovering, but also interpreting it by applying shapes or patterns. If cognitive theories of perception are applied to advertising, they indicate that a product must always involve the receiver to a sufficient degree. If this does not happen, the information given will not retain the consumer's attention, even if the information is considered shocking. Generally speaking, consumers will avoid everything that contradicts their system of thought, or will reduce its importance when interpreting it. From this, one can deduce that differences in cultural systems also determine what is seen and how it is perceived.

According to Hoecklin (1995: 111), for effective communication to take place, 'consumers' *perceived* meaning of a product or service must coincide with the advertiser's *intended* meaning'. From a cultural viewpoint, this means that 'the intended meaning of products brands' must coincide with 'the perceived meanings' of consumers who come from different cultures. The most cost-effective way of ensuring that this happens is to standardize the product or service concept globally, but allow for local adaptation of the message. Figure 11.1 illustrates this approach.

In Figure 11.1, quadrant 1 contains truly global products and services. The product concept is the same everywhere and the advertising is standardized. This approach allows considerable economies of scale and cost savings in the marketing of the product.

Quadrant 2 contains products and services where the brand concept is globalized (as in quadrant 1) but the message – the promotion – is adapted to the local culture. Sales are increased globally by matching the perceived meaning and intended meaning in each particular country/culture.

Figure 11.1 The managing meaning matrix
Source: Hoecklin (1995): 101.

Case study 11.6

Vicks inhaler

British skier Alan Baxter finished in third place at the Winter Olympics in Salt Lake City in 2002. Two days later, when he was still celebrating his victory, he was told by the Olympic authorities that he had tested positive for drugs. He was eventually disqualified and had to return his bronze medal. All this because he used an American inhaler rather than a British one.

While preparing for the big event, Alan bought a Vicks inhaler stick to help him breathe more easily and so improve his sleep. The packaging and the product looked exactly like the one he used regularly in the UK. When he went for the doping control it did not cross his mind to declare his use of the product. Unfortunately for Alan, the US product differed significantly. It contained a substance that is on the proscribed list of the International Olympic Committee: levmetamphetamine.

Despite his appeal that he had no idea that the US stick contained the substance – and that the substance itself would not have improved his performance anyway – the IOC stuck to its decision: the substance was detected and an offence had been committed.

Source: 'The Highlander laid low' by Steven Downes, *Scotland on Sunday*, 10 March 2002 (http://scotlandonsunday.scotsman.com/sport.cfm?id=268802002).

The success of the approach in Q1 is limited: few products and services can be marketed this way. Hence the tendency to go for the 'glocal' approach in Q2, as indicated by the upward arrow from Q1. The arrow from Q3 to Q1 shows the move by producers of local product concepts to create a larger market through standardizing the product concept but using differently coded messages to ensure its success in different countries/cultures.

The approach in quadrant 4 applies to products for which the global message is the same, but which contain different ingredients corresponding to the particular preferences of a country. An example is a soft drink that is promoted using global marketing, but which contains a different amount of sugar in a certain country where local taste differs slightly from the 'mainstream' taste. Case study 11.6 shows the unfortunate consequences when it is assumed that a product with the same name and function is assumed to be the same in one country as in another.

Managing the meaning of brands across cultures is not so much to do with presenting the products themselves, but the value they communicate. The basic values attached to the products are supplemented by values specific to each cultural group.

ACTIVITY 11.1

Read the case and answer the questions that follow.

Coping with variables: a comparison of Indian and European hauliers

Hauliers in India and Europe both face a competitive environment, and buying the best lorry for the job is just half the battle. Both have to contend with a number of variables if they are to generate a healthy profit. And the variables for the Indian haulier are very different from those faced by his European counterpart.

The main difference between these haulage sectors is the room to manoeuvre which these variables afford. In European countries, many variables are fixed: some are set by government regulations and others offer almost no choice. In terms of

Figure 11.2 Differences in hauliers' management tools

infrastructure, for example, when it comes to road conditions and speed limits, there are very few variables to be found. Equally importantly, every competitor can take full advantage of these facilities, so they offer no competitive advantage at all. In India, however, the road network shows many differences: some four-lane highways are available in the urban areas, while single lane potholed dirt roads are the only option for trucks in rural areas.

Figure 11.2 indicates the differences in management tools for the hauliers between both continents. The 'crossed' variables are fixed in the market. These clearly limit a haulier's management decisions regarding investment in one area of variability to extract greater economies from another.

There are, for example, many variables attached to the truck driver in India. A haulier could decide to employ either a trained and experienced truck driver (who knows the ins and outs of the truck and how to use it profitably), or to hire an inexperienced driver (who has only worked as a co-driver and knows little about profitable truck use). Either driver could be put to use in Europe and India, although the European haulier would doubtless incur a loss if he used the inexperienced driver (assuming this driver had been able to get a driver's licence in the first place). If the Indian haulier employs an experienced driver, he can make more profit on account of the driver's reliability and efficient use of fuel. On the other hand, he knows this driver will ask for higher pay. If he uses an inexperienced driver, he can compensate for any loss of efficiency by overloading the driver's truck or by putting him on a very old truck. In that way the haulier can still make a profit.

Both India and Western Europe have government-imposed restrictions on vehicle design and the use of trucks, although European regulations are generally a lot stricter. The few regulations that India does have can be manipulated easily because they are not being strictly enforced. Corruption among police officers is common and both hauliers and drivers frequently use this as a way of escaping regulatory restrictions.

Payload capacity is strictly fixed in Europe. Trucks are free to transport as long as they keep to the limits imposed by law. Truck manufacturers and the trailer and body building industry have come up with lighter vehicles so that heavier payloads are possible, but these new trucks are available to the whole transport industry, so the payload is not a variable. The picture is very different in India. Here, government regulations and manufacturers' maximum payloads do not 'count'. The sky is the limit when it comes to load volumes: any load can be transported, as long as it stays on the truck.

The power – or otherwise – of government legislation has considerable influence on the thinking process of an Indian haulier. Unlike in Europe, a haulier in India cannot claim financial compensation from a business supplier if the contract is discontinued without proper reason. Most transport contracts in India contain a clause allowing the supplier to discontinue the contract if he believes he can get a better deal elsewhere. Therefore, unlike his European counterpart, who is quite sure he has a deal when a contract is signed, the Indian haulier still has to face some uncertainty and insecurity, especially if he is saddled with high monthly financial instalments over and above his normal living costs. The Indian haulier will therefore want his trucks on the road as much as possible to pay off these costs. No wonder, then, that drivers have to work long hours driving overloaded trucks.

Source: adapted from Engelaer, F. and Vloet, D. (2005) 'Analysis of the Indian truck market,' Nyenrode Business University.

1. Consider the following statement about variable 'legislation and legal liability':

Legislation can have a serious impact on market developments and the performance of current business models all over the world. The Indian government has announced its intention to bring legislation on transportation up to European levels. By doing this, it clearly demonstrates its appreciation of European developments in the industry. However, the implementation of such legislation does not necessarily result in a change of mentality or a change in the process. One needs to understand, however, the influence of at least one specific difference between the legislation in India and that in the EU to understand the thinking process of an Indian truck owner.

Using the information given in the case (and/or your experience), give your opinion on the above statement.

2. Consider the comparative analysis in Table 11.1 of marketing communication in the truck market, between Western Europe and India.

Notice the differences between Europe and India concerning:

- communication flow;
- responsibility of the dealers, manufacturers, importers;
- marketing strategy; and
- marketing activities.

Table 11.1 Marketing in Europe and India

Europe	India
The flow of marketing communication starts with and is directed by the manufacturers. They set the marketing boundaries with which an importer has to comply; the importer in turn controls a large part of the marketing flow of a dealer. Manufacturers and importers are mainly responsible for mass communication, while dealers account for most relational marketing activities. They visit their 'accounts' (as they are called) and organize test drives and demonstrations. The marketing strategy of European truck brands focuses on existing customer relations rather than on new prospects.	The communication flow is comparable to Europe, with manufacturers controlling the process. Dealers might be less pro-active than in Europe, but this is certainly no longer the case for all dealerships. The main difference is that, in the Indian truck market, the focus is more on new prospects and first-time users, and less on existing customers than in Europe. Indian sales brochures focus on functionalities, while European brochures focus more on visual aspects.

Conclusion

This chapter presents ideas about international marketing and points out problems for cross-border marketing research. The focus is more on the consumer than on marketing methods, because it is the consumer who first presents the most important cultural differences. Even if there is a certain standardization in consumer behaviour, manufacturers still continue to adapt their products to suit the consumer markets where they are sold.

Another element of international marketing which deserves special attention is communication. To succeed, communication through the various channels of advertising needs to create a balance in the relation between the product itself, the message and the perception that people in a certain country may have about this product.

Points for reflection

1. The cultural differences in the behaviour of the consumer appear to be diminishing, competition is becoming more global than national, the marketing function of an enterprise involves not only the complete organization but also its environment, and multinationals are selling their products under the same brand,

   Is it necessary, as marketeer, to make a choice between global marketing and intercultural marketing?

2. Although advertising has been around for a long time, techniques have certainly evolved and the channels used have multiplied, with websites now playing an important role alongside television and radio, the press and posters. Nowadays consumers – in Western Europe at least – seem to appreciate advertising more than they used to. This is because it reflects the expectations of the consumer: more and more advertising is less to do with pushing the consumer into buying a product or service at any cost and more to do with keeping the consumer up-to-date on new products and services, providing more information and, most importantly, acting as a form of buying guide. The messages given are also clearer, more relevant and believable.

   How do you account for this change? Use the concepts to support your arguments.

   How is advertising perceived in your country? Do you see the same evolution as that described above?

Further reading

Usunier, J.-C. and Lee, J.A. (2005) *Marketing Across Cultures,* 4th edn, Harlow: Pearson Education. The first edition of this book, written by the French professor Jean-Claude Usunier with the title *Commerce entre cultures* was published in 1992 and translated into several languages. The author's cultural approach offers a major contribution to international marketing. The influence of culture on relevant aspects of marketing in an international environment is given a comprehensive analysis in the book. The fourth edition updates the subjects and cross-cultural cases, but more importantly the book deals more thoroughly with the phenomenon of globalization, thanks to the contributions of its Australian co-author Jil Ann Lee.

References

Browaeys, M.-J. and Trompenaars, F. (eds) (2000) *Cases Studies on Cultural Dilemmas,* Breukelen, Netherlands: Nyenrode University Press.

Daniels, J.D. and Radebaugh, L.H. (2001) *International business: Environments and operations,* 9th edn, Upper Saddle River, NJ: Prentice Hall.

Gales, L.M. (2003) 'Linguistic sensitivity in cross-cultural organisational research: positivist/postpositivist and grounded theory approaches,' *Language and Intercultural Communication*, 3, 2: 131-140.

Hoecklin, L. (1995) *Managing Cultural Differences: Strategies for competitive advantage,* Wokingham: Addison-Wesley.

Kaynak, E. and Jallat, F. (2004) 'Marketing in Western Europe: a monolith or a multidimensional market', in Kaynak and Jallat (eds) *Marketing Issues in Western Europe: Changes and developments,* Binghamton, NY: International Business Press: 1-14.

Mercado, S., Welford, R. and Prescott, K. (2001) *European Business,* 4th edn, Harlow: Pearson Education.

Usunier, J.-C. and Lee, J.A. (2005) *Marketing Across Cultures,* 4th edn, Harlow: Pearson Education.

Wall, S. and Rees, B. (2001) *Introduction to International Business*, Harlow: Pearson Education.

Chapter 12

Cultural diversity in organizations

The word 'diversity' is ambiguous, especially when associated with the term 'organization'. An organization can be a domestic one, with many of its employees who have their roots abroad – reflecting the social diversity of the country in question. It can also be an international organization whose cultural diversity is reflected in its foreign subsidiaries. At the same time, diversity can refer to the collection of groups who form the organization: groups differentiated in terms of gender, mother tongue, education, as well as their position or salary.

Concept 12.1 examines how managers can deal with cultural diversity and how they can turn this diversity to their advantage.

Learning outcomes

After reading this chapter, you will be aware of:

● The skills managers need to manage cultural differences in a global environment.

● The features of management culture required in multinational companies.

Concept 12.1 Cultural competence in transnational organizations

Globalization is one of the most discussed topics in business. International business research is directly affected by a globalization process that does not seem to end. Furthermore, researchers of other disciplines are also being urged to reflect on this process, which concerns all institutions of human society.

Compared with political, social and educational institutions, however, businesses appear to be the most suitable candidates for globalization, particularly those in the industrial, financial and service sectors. According to de Woot (2000), companies in these sectors have cleared most obstacles in the globalization process: that of size (with multinationals), that of time (with long-term strategies), that of complexity, and finally that of information and communication. The globalization of companies seems to be linked to the cultural diversity of organizations, which in turn is connected to the internationalization of organizations.

Management culture and multinationals

As many writers on the subject indicate, the globalization of the economy causes organizations a major problem – the management of cultural differences.

Steinmann and Scherer (2000) raise some fundamental issues with regard to the effects of the globalization process on managerial functions. These include the way the executives of a company conceive the interaction between the different cultures present. If, for example, a multinational embraces operating companies in Asia, should it advocate western values (what Steinmann and Scherer call a 'strategy of proclamation') or should it embark on the new process of intercultural learning, based on the application of reasoning (a 'strategy of learning')? This last option seems to them the best way of settling the intercultural conflicts in multinational companies.

What sort of management culture is to be found in multinationals? Théry (2002) distinguishes three types:

- A dominant management culture that is a copy of the multinational's home country (e.g. American management in a US multinational).

- A dominant transnational management culture created by the mother-company's founders using clearly defined specific values, a culture present in all the multinational's operating companies.

- A minimum management culture, leaving considerable room for national cultures in all their diversity.

In all three cases, the multinational must perform two roles at once: an integrating role and an adapting role. It not only has to ensure that the companies forming the group remain integrated and thus able to continue as a multinational; it also has to ensure that it respects the different national groups of clients and employees by making the necessary adaptations.

Transnational organization

That globalization has become a reality and that it is still progressing at high speed is not in doubt. The same holds true for the increase in cultural diversity in domestic and international companies where people from different cultural backgrounds work more and more together. In view of these changes, Bartlett and Ghoshal (1989) propose a model for the organization of the future: the transnational company (see Concept 7.1). The 'transnational' is a management mentality combining the abilities of the multinational, global or international firm: flexibility, efficiency and the transfer of expertise. The managers at the headquarters and in the subsidiaries abroad are responsible for co-ordinating these capacities throughout the different units of the organization. Trompenaars and Hampden-Turner (1997: 188) state 'the transnational corporation is polycentric rather than co-ordinated from the centre'.

Bartlett, Ghoshal and Birkinshaw (2003) go further. They believe that top management must bring added value to the transnational company in the same way as the executives operating at all levels of the organization. This means that the top managers are not just content to create an operational framework in which the responsibilities of the functional and geographic groups are clearly defined. They also have a federating role by integrating the different influences of these groups in the management process. While recognizing that diversity and internal tensions can be the source of new ideas, it seems that the role of top management is rather to create a common vision for the future, a shared set of values to reflect managers' goals.

Cultural diversity and transnational organization

What is diversity? Gómez-Mejìa, Balkin and Cardy (2001) see in the notion of diversity a human characteristic that allows a differentiation to be made between people. On the one hand there are individual characteristics, such as race, age or gender, over which the individual has no or little control. On the other hand there are characteristics an individual can act on during his life, such as work background, geographical situation and education. In everyday business life, managers may well see their employees as individuals. However, they should also be aware of the diversity and the characteristics inherent to each specific group. In fact, diversity among employees may well not only cause misunderstandings but also obstruct team work and productivity. Good management is therefore crucial to prevent this happening.

Consider the case of a transnational organization. How do the managers there perceive cultural diversity? Adler (2002: 157) refers to a survey (Adler and Ghadar, 1990) to show that it can be a source of both problems and advantages.

Problems caused by cultural diversity are to do with communication and integration, particularly when the organization requires its employees to think and act in the same way. The more an organization demands transparency and convergent opinions, the greater the ambiguity, complexity and confusion. Problems with diversity also arise when certain practices and procedures are adopted by the organization across the board. Export managers may use the same marketing campaign across countries without taking account of the different cultures involved.

As for the possible advantages of cultural diversity, Adler (2002) notes that some managers describe multicultural organizations as being more flexible and open to new ideas. Other managers find such organizations to be more aware of consumer needs. Diversity is also considered an advantage when the concern needs to reposition itself, to generate ideas, to develop projects, to open itself up to fresh perspectives.

Within organizations operating in an international environment, partners, collaborators and co-workers will be brought into intercultural situations that need to be turned to their advantage to prevent failure of the strategy of internationalization. This means that knowledge, tools and working methods need to be acquired to help develop the attitude and behaviour desirable in a specific cross-cultural context. Managing diversity in this kind of organization and its environment demands, at all management levels, a competence that one might call 'transcultural'.

Transcultural competence

To develop the capacity to act effectively at international level, companies must opt for intercultural management, in other words management which adapts its way of communicating, negotiating and leading to the cultural context of the country in question. According to Théry (2002) imparting recipes or dos and don'ts is not the answer: such quick fixes are too anecdotal and offer no insight into the situation at hand. Nor is providing instruments for 'cracking' cultural codes the answer on its own. What is needed is to apply a global approach across the board, or a country-by-country approach. Moreover, the managers involved must become aware of their own cultural preferences and, case by case, look for ways of working that are adapted to those of another culture.

Trompenaars and Woolliams (2000) argue that cross-cultural comparisons are helpful to demonstrate the different ways in which dilemmas are approached. In particular, they have observed that some cultures begin from their own orientation and accommodate the opposing dimension in a process of reconciliation. In contrast, some cultures (managers) are quick to abandon their own orientation and to start from the opposing viewpoint before returning to their initial orientation to ensure it is accommodated in the reconciliation process (see Concept 5.1).

The authors found that Americans with a transcultural competence do not put their own cultural stereotype ahead of foreign values. Thus, the authors might argue that good communities and teams generate outstanding individuals. As for the question of women in middle management, Trompenaars and Wolliams note that women tend to have a higher propensity to reconcile than their male counterparts. Women also appear to be more synchronic than men. However, when severely challenged and unable to reconcile a dilemma, women also show a certain readiness to adopt a compromise whereas men – in this case Americans/Anglo Saxons – tend to fall back on their own comfort zone, which may be dogmatic in nature.

In an article, Trompenaars and Woolliams (2000: 20–21) explain their viewpoint on transcultural competence:

> Over the last ten years, many business school researchers, consultancies and organizational psychologist groups have developed a range of competency frameworks that claim to delineate effective behaviours of high performing managers. They often form a reference for job design, person specification, organization structuring and training needs analysis. These models often seek the same end but often differ considerably as they each try to encapsulate the existing and traditional body of knowledge. Often, these are only prescriptive lists, like a series of ingredients for a recipe.
>
> Many of the derived underlying behaviours owe their origin to observations of business practice or research in American/Anglo-Saxon studies. Their often ethnocentric nature can cause managers operating internationally additional problems. These prescriptions for behaviour, we increasingly find, do not transfer to other countries or other types of organization from where they were originally developed and tested. At first sight they seem to prescribe a change of behaviour in new destinations as in 'When in Rome, do as the Romans do'. A different set of competencies or framework seems, therefore, to be required for a different destination culture – and even for working with a diverse workforce or in a transcultural team. As a consequence, it becomes like trying to impress on your first date. Our approach is completely different.

The approach used by Trompenaars and Woolliams (2000: 25) is what they call 'the new framework of transcultural competence'. This framework, described in Chapter 5, entails the ability to bridge the differences between the native and destination culture through developing the propensity to reconcile seemingly opposing values. This principal of reconciliation is what lies at the heart of transcultural competence. The extent to which managers display this competence is, on the basis of feedback received by peers on their business performance, closely correlated to the degree of success these managers achieve in business abroad. The amount of experience working on international assignments and with a diverse workforce is also closely correlated to their degree of success.

Contrary to what would have been expected, internationalization has reinforced the importance of cultural diversity, rather than reducing it. It is therefore a question of a company having a management that can actually manage this diversity in some way. This means having managers who are able to adapt and who can use the intercultural situations present both within and outside the company to the company's advantage. Managers need to acquire tools and working methods to allow them to develop sufficient competence in the cross-cultural context to turn diversity into a competitive advantage.

Intercultural competence is everyone's business. It is not just a requirement for expatriates, but also for managers who work in multicultural teams. The question as to how this competence can be acquired, or at least developed, is partially addressed in the introduction to Part Two. The particular skills relating to the all-important communicative component of intercultural competence are examined in Chapter 18.

ACTIVITY 12.1

Diversity versus localization within a telecommunications company in Latin America

INTRODUCTION

This case study is related to the field of cultural management and focuses on a large international telecommunications company, which has operations in Latin America. It is specifically related to the networks division of this company.

The telecommunications industry has seen huge growth during the last couple of years in this part of the world. One important factor is that the GSM technology has been adapted as the standard in most Latin American countries and the local operators have adapted their mobile networks to this technology. The operations of the company in question consist of providing equipment and services for the local operators so they can build, operate and maintain a GSM mobile network. During the last few years there has been important growth in terms of revenues, personnel and offices. The company is present in most Latin American countries (Figure 12.1).

To manage the growth of the personnel in this region efficiently and effectively, the company is using two approaches. First, existing employees of the company are moved to Latin America and offered positions for a fixed period ('expatriates'). Second, employees are being hired from the country itself ('locals'). With regard to this second approach, the network division of this company is facing a cultural dilemma: should it maintain a diversified organization in the specific country or should it 'localize' the organization?

Diversity can be defined as a mixture of people with different groups of identities, such as gender, age, education, ethnicity, language or marital status. Diversity can also be related to work, such as seniority, management status, income or functional level of an employee. The advantages of diversity might be that it increases creativity, generates different opinions and opens the mindset. This element of diversity plays an important role in the company. In fact, it sees itself as a multicultural company in which diversity is an important asset that enables the company to achieve extraordinary results. On the other hand, 'localization' of personnel is also an important driver as it can, for instance, bring down costs and so make the company more competitive in the market. Another advantage of localization can be that it increases cultural awareness within the company of the country within which it is operating. Locals naturally understand their customs, behaviours and language better than outsiders do.

1. Argentina
2. Bolivia
3. Brasil
4. Chile
5. Colombia
6. Ecuador
7. Guatemala
8. Mexico
9. Panama
10. Peru
11. Venezuela

Figure 12.1 Company's presence in Latin America (2005)

COMPANY VALUES AND DIVERSITY

The corporate culture of the company is embedded in its culture and values. Despite the company's rapid growth, including that of the network division, it has continued to stress a corporate culture more typical of an independent, innovative and creative start-up. The objective has always been to maintain this culture, no matter how large the company might become. The company believes the best way to achieve this goal is through leadership rather than traditional management. This first entails the leaders disseminating the company's four values, defined in the 1990s, to everyone in the organization. These values are: customer satisfaction, respect, achievement and renewal. They are applied worldwide and form the core element of the company culture as well as the basis for operations.

Furthermore, the company has defined goals with respect to diversity, a concept it defines as: 'Any demographic and individual attribute that defines each person as a unique individual. It means all the ways we are different from each other.' First of all, the company wants to encourage innovation which, it believes, can best be achieved by well-managed teams whose members come from diverse cultures. These teams are usually more creative and find better solutions than homogeneous teams. The company also aims to improve its understanding of customers. This can be best achieved through it mirroring a diverse marketplace to meet customer needs and so anticipate future opportunities. Finally, the company wants to maximize the pool of talent available. This entails attracting and retaining the best people within a competitive environment.

QUALITATIVE RESEARCH

To identify the corporate culture embedded in the company's values, qualitative research was conducted among forty middle managers of the company in Latin America. An investigation was also carried out to identify the company's corporate diversity policy and the attitude of the employees in this particular region towards it. Topics were analysed such as 'the (dis)advantages of diversity' versus 'the (dis)advantages of localization' in Latin America and the extent to which the company should 'localize' different functions. The total group was further split into three subgroups to identify any differences in views between certain types of employees. The following subgroups were made (Figure 12.2):

- Latin and Europeans;
- Locals and Expats; and
- Females and Males.

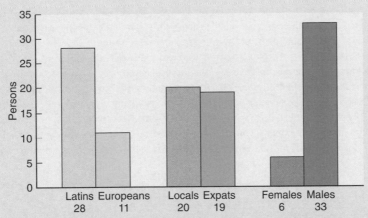

Figure 12.2 Subgroups of respondents to the questionnaire in the Latin American region

RESULTS OF THE RESEARCH

Cultural dimensions of the company in Latin America

From the research comes the identification of the characteristics of the corporate culture and the cultural dimensions of the company in Latin America. Figure 12.3 shows the characteristics of the corporate culture (using Trompenaars' model; each shade represents a different corporate stereotype of culture). The three most dominant characteristics of

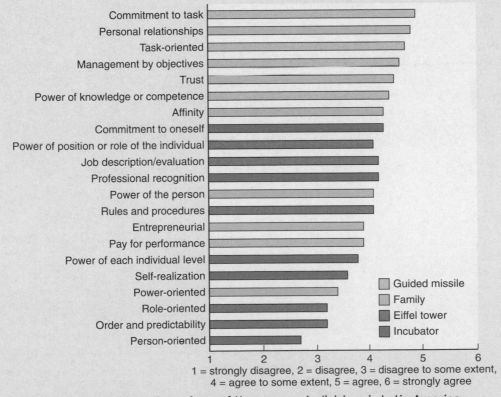

Figure 12.3 Corporate culture of one of the company's divisions in Latin America

the company culture in Latin America are 'commitment to tasks', 'personal relationships' and 'task-oriented'. On the other hand, a characteristic such as 'person-oriented', which basically means that a company exists only to serve its employees, is a characteristic with which the respondents of the company are not identified.

The results were based on the entire group: no distinction was made between different subgroups. It is interesting to look at each subgroup and analyse how people in it identify themselves with, for instance, cultural dimensions. Figure 12.4 shows the trends among the three subgroups in Latin America in terms of cultural dimensions. The 'diffuse' dimension, for example, which is the degree of involvement in personal relationship among colleagues, is a cultural dimension valued much more highly by Europeans and Expats than by Latins and Locals. This might seem to be atypical since Latins naturally value this dimension more highly than Europeans. An explanation for this result might be that all the Europeans are also Expats in Latin America and therefore are much more open to having close personal contact among their colleagues.

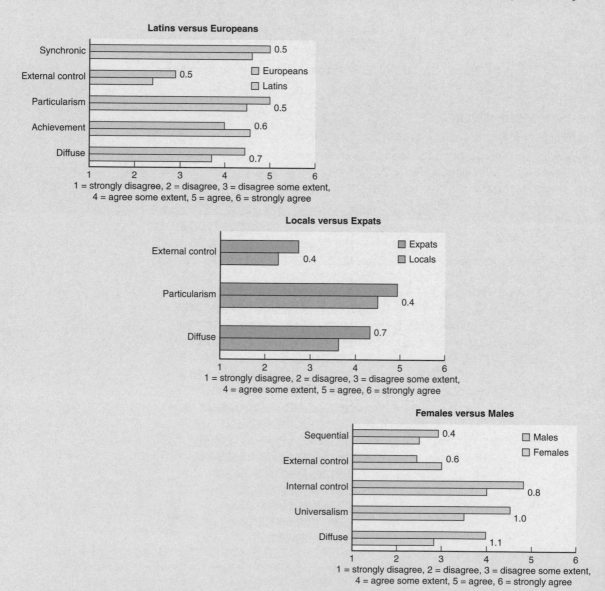

Figure 12.4 Largest differences among the three subgroups regarding cultural dimensions

The results might have looked different for Europeans when based in their own country in Europe. Another example is that the females do not see the company as 'diffuse', which means that the females do not tend to share many personal issues among their colleagues. Their male colleagues, on the other hand, see 'diffuse' as a dominant cultural dimension of the company in Latin America. Males tend to share their personal life and issues much more easily among colleagues.

Advantages and disadvantages of localization versus diversity

The research also consisted of open questions by which those interviewed were asked to identify advantages and disadvantages of localization and diversity. Table 12.1 summarizes the responses.

Table 12.1 Localization versus diversity: advantages and disadvantages

Localization	
Advantages	**Disadvantages**
<ul><li>Cost reduction and cost efficiency</li><li>Knowing the local culture, better insight, understanding of the local reality, local way of thinking</li><li>Customer intimacy and understanding customer needs</li><li>Language</li><li>Locals are able to solve things faster</li><li>Everybody understands each other's position when discrepancies arise</li><li>More realistic approach to solving problems</li></ul>	<ul><li>Lower awareness of company culture or company way of working. Local culture cannot be appropriate for company culture</li><li>Limited experience, lower exchange of experience</li><li>Lack of global connections and global guidance</li><li>Less control</li><li>Certain local habits may not be supportive to business</li><li>Local people tend to create their own rules</li><li>Creation of small political groups</li><li>It creates too narrow a mindset</li></ul>
Diversity	
Advantages	**Disadvantages**
<ul><li>Different opinions, mindsets, points of view</li><li>Stimulates more creativity</li><li>Brings in more experience</li><li>Puts flavour in work environment</li></ul>	<ul><li>Cultural barriers and distance might lead to misunderstandings</li><li>Language (difficult to understand and communicate)</li><li>Higher costs</li><li>More difficult to manage and misbelieve</li><li>Adaptation of foreigners to local culture might be a risk</li><li>Locals are not as well respected as they should be</li></ul>

It is also interesting to see the differences in opinion within each subgroup regarding the (dis)advantages of localization and diversity. A Latin might have a different perception or preference from a European. The same can be said about a Local compared to an Expatriate (who may be either a Latin or a European). Some typical 'quotes' show the different perspectives within each subgroup:

→

Advantages of localization:

Local: 'Knowledge of the local situation can be very important in particular places like Latin America. The cost of these resources is significantly lower.'

'The deep knowledge, contacts, behaviour, networking and cultural aspects bring potentially better positions for dealing with the local culture of the customers and suppliers. Also the roles that do not add value to the overall business are better contracted locally to reduce the cost of the operation.'

Expat: 'Apart from minimizing the disadvantages of diversity, localization in general matches the cost levels our customers can accept. Also, certain jobs, especially in the field and customer support functions, would prefer local personnel for language and cultural reasons. The company will additionally have access to the local ways of doing things, which are most often the most efficient.'

Disadvantages of localization:

Latin: 'The company culture is still based on its European background (transparency, respect, flat organizations, etc.). If key positions are localized without there being a good understanding of the person's background, there is a high risk of basic principles being lost.'

European: 'Less possibility of ensuring that the local organization stays in line with the way the company works.'

Advantages of diversity:

Local: 'People with different experiences in other projects in which our company participated enriched others with a broader knowledge of the mobile business around the globe. Diversity itself motivates tolerance. This means that people of different nationalities, education and language working together is itself a challenge that creates an environment of co-operation and flexibility to work under potentially difficult circumstances.'

Expat: 'Having foreigners keeps the company's way of working alive, and ensures that our company does not become too "localized" in terms of behaviour. A diverse organization also impresses our customers: They have the feeling that they are getting the best of the company's global reach.'

CONCLUSIONS

On the basis of the research findings, conclusions can be made with respect to the cultural dilemma: why should the company have a diversified organization and what are the main reasons for having localization?

The main incentives for having a diversified organization in Latin America can be summarized as follows. First, having cultural differences and multicultural teams in the organization in Latin America can lead to more creativity and better solutions. Furthermore, diversity is necessary for remaining in business. This is because the organization in Latin America has been growing fast during the last two years with a lot of new local employees, so experienced employees (mostly foreigners) must be kept inside the organization for it to remain successful and competitive. With regard to its customers, the company feels that it needs strong international back-up support in Latin America to ensure that its customers get the best possible attention. Finally, diversity keeps the company way of working alive.

As for localizing resources in the region, this is needed to reduce costs to stay competitive in the market. Furthermore, the company should have local knowledge in Latin America to gain a deep understanding of the market and to be close to the customer. Localization also helps to remove possible language barriers and to gain a closer cultural match with local circumstances (customers, suppliers, customs etc.).

Source: adapted from a case written by Roberto Danker (2006), Nyenrode Business University

Questions

1. Look at Chapter 5 for a description of Trompenaar's seven dimensions, and then examine how the author in his case study describes the results for the 'Diffuse' dimension with regard to the three sub-groups (Figure 12.4).

Do the same analysis for the two dimensions 'External control' and 'Particularism', using the information given in Figure 12.4 and Trompenaar's definitions of these dimensions.

2. Read the quotes from the different sub-groups and then decide which (dis)advantages of Localization and Diversity are most referred to.

3. Discuss the conclusions given by the author at the end of the case study.

4. Below is the author's answer with respect to the cultural dilemma: 'Which positions should be localized, and which not?'

Author's analysis

The cultural dilemma comes down basically to the following question: which positions should be localized in Latin America and which not? The results of the survey show that the organization does not have a clear answer to this question. All respondents, whatever subgroup they belonged to, replied that the localization 'policy' was not clear. However, if we look at the issue of localization in terms of different job grades, and the percentages involved, the survey findings show that for positions such as assistants and engineers the localization is around 90 per cent. Furthermore, the survey shows a tendency whereby the higher the position inside the company, the less localized it should be. For higher management positions the localization is at least 75 per cent or more. Considering the 'Latin - European subgroup', the Latins believe there should be higher localization for high management positions (around 75-80 per cent). The Europeans would like to see a lower localization percentage (50-75 per cent). The reason for this might be that Latins believe that higher management also has to deal with political issues in the country, in which case a local person is more suitable. The Europeans believe that the company headquarters needs to keep control of local subsidiaries such as the one in Latin America, and that the localization should therefore be less.

a) Discuss this opinion with your peers.

b) Using the information given in the case and/or your knowledge of the area in question, what other solution, if any, could you put forward?

Conclusion

This chapter has examined how managers in multinationals can best deal with cultural diversity and do so to the company's advantage. One problem was addressed: how can managers embrace the values of the country in which each subsidiary is operating while ensuring that the subsidiary remains an integral part of the multinational? Bartlett and Ghoshal's concept of the transnational organization, with its flexibility, efficiency and transfer of expertise, was put forward as a way of resolving the local/global issues because it allows the integration into the management process of the influences of the diverse culture groups within the organization. The case study in this chapter gave an example of how cultural diversity was addressed within a multinational company.

The chapter finally put forward the notion of transcultural competence as exemplified in the process of reconciliation (referred to earlier in Chapter 5). Using the reconciliation approach can turn cultural diversity into a competitive advantage.

Points for reflection

Certain companies regard the management of cultural diversity as a way of developing new competencies that give them certain advantages. They are, for example, able to recruit and hold on to good employees, to diversify their markets, and to promote creativity and innovation. For most of the time, however, it is just a question of managing differences between genders and ethnic minorities.

What, in your opinion, are the reasons for companies adapting their recruiting, training and communication policies to the cultural diversity of their personnel?

Further reading

Adler, N.J. (2002). *International Dimensions of Organizational Behaviour*, **4th edn, Cincinnati, OH: South-Western Thomson Learning.** This book, devoted to cross-cultural management, examines what Nancy Adler calls 'the international dimensions of people's behaviour in organizations' and which she defines as 'a new field relative to the traditional study of management'. This work is particularly interesting because it deals with studies of human behaviour carried out in essentially North American organizations while, at the same time, adopting an approach to take account of the diversity and complexity involved in the globalization of present-day organizations.

References

Adler, N.J. (2002) *International Dimensions of Organizational Behaviour*, 4th edn, Cincinnati, OH: South-Western Thomson Learning.

Adler, N.J., and Ghadar, F. (1990) 'International strategy from the perspective of people and culture: the North American context,' in A.M. Rugman (ed.) *Research in Global Strategic Management: International business research for the twenty-first century; Canada's new research agenda*, Vol. 1, Greenwich, CT: JAI Press: 179–205.

Bartlett, C.A., Ghoshal, S. and Birkinshaw, J. (2003) *Transnational Management,* 4th edn, New York, NY: McGraw-Hill Education.

Bartlett, C.A. and Ghoshal, S. (1989) *Managing Across Borders,* Boston, MA: Harvard Business School Press.

Gómez-Mejìa, L.R. Balkin, D.B. and Cardy, R.L. (2001) *Managing Human Resources,* 3rd edn, Upper Saddle River, NJ: Prentice Hall.

Steinmann, H. and Scherer, A.G. (2000) 'Considérations philosophiques sur le pluralisme culturel et le management' in Ricciardelli, Urban, Nanopoulos (eds) *Mondialisation des sociétés multiculturelles,* Paris: PUF: 99–130.

Théry, B. (2002) *Manager dans la diversité culturelle,* Paris: Éditions d'Organisation.

Trompenaars, F. and Hampden-Turner, C. (1997) *Ridings the Waves of Culture,* 2nd edn, London: Nicholas Brealey.

Trompenaars, F. and Woolliams, P. (2000) 'A new unified competency framework for the millennium manager,' in Browaeys, M.-J., and Trompenaars, F. (eds), *Case Studies on Cultural Dilemmas,* Breukelen, Netherlands: Nyenrode University Press: 21–28.

Woot, Ph. de (2000) 'Ambiguïtés de la globalisation' in Ricciardelli, Urban, Nanopoulos (eds) *Mondialisation des sociétés multiculturelles*. Paris: PUF: 155–170.

Part Two Final activity A2.1

Making cultural profiles of brands

A strong brand is reflected in the culture of the organization, which is itself a reflection of the people working in it. This relationship is the focus of the study below.

The authors of the original study on which the text below is based, examined and compared a number of different brands of one company. To assess the extent to which the brands differ from each other, they developed a model which is an adaptation of the model used in Part One to determine a cultural profile. The model used in their study maintains the layout and some of the values of the Part One model, supplemented with others conceived by the authors. Using this model, the authors drew up a cultural profile for each of the brands in question in line with the authors' observations and perceptions.

Learning outcomes

After completing this activity you should be able to:

● Indicate cultural differences used in the marketing of brands;

● Determine the cultural profile of your choice of brands using an adapted version of the model used in Part One to determine a person's cultural profile.

Exhibit A2.1.1

Brands and their cultures

This text is based on the Master's thesis written by Erik Sierkstra and Robert Stal (2005, Nyenrode Business Universiteit). The company and brands used in the original thesis have been fictionalized.

Cherlon, with its headquarters in New York, is an international manufacturer of cosmetic products. It has brand teams in each of its operating companies responsible for the sales and marketing in their specific country. Within Cherlon Germany, it is said that the employees radiate the characteristics of the brand they are currently working with. This paper will consider four brands and their respective teams at the operating company's Berlin headquarters. The important features of each brand will be discussed and then contrasted.

METHODOLOGY USED

The cultural profile model used by Browaeys and Price (Part One, Final Activity) will be applied, but in amended form to enable research into brands in general, and the differences between them in particular. The first element added to the model is that of *Control:* the extent to which head office exercises control over the different brands (flexible/rigid). Two other elements *Appearance* and *Behaviour* have been added to the profile model to enable the degree of formality in people's behaviour to be assessed. Two further additions have been made to assess the *Fashion* sense in the brand (trendy/classical) as well as the *Affinity* of the brand with the parent

223

company – the extent to which the brand is associated with Cherlon (weak/strong).

The three values used in the original cultural profile are adhered to: *Time Focus* (monochronic/polychronic), *Power structure* (hierarchy/equality) and *Action* (doing/being). These values are aspects of a brand's culture and can be extracted easily from interviews. They are all artefacts, as it were, of a brand culture and the values of one brand can be easily compared with those of another.

To gain insight into each of the brands, interviews were carried out with employees working for one of these brands. All of these employees had worked for other brands, mainly at Cherlon's head office. The questions asked of each interviewee were focused on how the culture of the brand which the employee was currently busy with differed from other brands he knew or had worked for. Other questions were also asked to determine how the culture of the employee's brand in the country in question differed from the same brand's culture in another country's subsidiary.

THE BRANDS

Four brands were chosen for analysis from Cherlon's products. They each occupy a unique position in the company's portfolio and the images they radiate are different to each other's.

The brands described below were chosen from the:

- Women's professional products division
- Men's professional products division
- Luxury products division
- Consumer products division

To show the difference between these brands, a cultural profile was made of each.

Brand A: Mara from the women's professional products division

Mara stands for passion for fashion. The products are manufactured specifically for use by hairstylists and colourists. This division tries to create a strong band with its clients by ensuring that a brand representative visits its main professional clients at least once every five weeks.

Apart from this intensive contact, the brand also has a foot in the door in the fashion world. As a hairstylist at fashion shows and a sponsor of young talent in the industry, Mara stays in close contact with the market.

Figure A2.1.1 Mara's cultural profile

Mara's cultural profile

The first feature of the brand that emerged from the interviews was its obvious flexibility. The way the product is to be marketed is left entirely to the subsidiary. This is because the division's marketing is based on door-to-door (salon-to-salon) and must therefore be adjusted for each market (Figure A2.1.1).

Mara seems to have a polychronic time focus. This means that the people working with the brand do many things at once and do not always stick to a planned schedule. Furthermore, the culture appears to be both a being and a doing culture. Although the brand truly 'lives' in the team (being), its members also have to come up with their own ideas about how to market and sell the product (doing). The hierarchy of the brand team appears to be quite flat, despite the expectations for German organizations. While the behaviour seemed to be neither formal nor informal, the team-members who were seen walking around were dressed in stylish suits (rather formal). The affinity with the mother company seems to be strong since the people in the brand team look neat, stylish and fashion-aware, reflecting head office culture. Finally, the style seen within the Mara team was very trendy in terms of hairstyle and, even though people were wearing suits, as mentioned earlier, they were trendy suits, giving the impression that the people were representing a trendy brand rather than a classical one.

Brand B: Ragel from the men's professional products division

The men's professional products division was recently acquired by the company. Although it has been integrated into the company, the head office is still in London, where

Figure A2.1.2 Ragel's cultural profile

Ragel is originally from. The image of Ragel reflects the trendy, life-in-the-fast-lane of London's young inhabitants. The brand offers consumers a high-priced luxury hair-care product. This is offered to both men and women, although the focus at present seems to be on men. Ragel is a product for a younger market.

Ragel's cultural profile

From Figure A2.1.2, one can see differences between Ragel's cultural profile and that of Mara. The parent company's control over this brand seems relatively rigid. The brand team involved can decide for themselves where they want to place posters, advertisements and TV commercials. All these, however, have been designed in London where Ragel's head office is found. Since the team is not directly involved in the design process, one would expect its members to be dissatisfied with the inflexibility of their task. The interviews, however, did not reveal any discontent.

The timing seems to be a mix of polychronic and monochronic. Although any planning is strict, some leeway is offered to allow the team to apply their personal touch. The impression emerged that Ragel was more a being brand rather than a doing brand: it appeared to be more a brand that judges a person for what they are rather than how they perform. The brand conveys a certain sense of equality as evidenced in the way the team's work area has been designed (no closed-off rooms, only glass divisions) and in the way the members mix when having lunch together (marketeers with salespeople, administrators with art-designers). Their attire as well as their behaviour appears rather informal: the brand manager as well as the rest of the team walk around the office in jeans rather than suits (internally). In terms of its overall style, Ragel is trendy.

Of all of Cherlon's brands, Ragel seems to have the weakest affinity with its parent-company. It gives the impression of being a brand on its own, separate from the group while still belonging to it.

Brand C: Lussu from the luxury products division

Lussu is the only daughter of a vigilant father, an eternal beauty who seems so fragile that she must be handled with great care. This image is reflected in the culture of the brand. Cherlon's head office is the 'father' of Lussu's beauty and Lussu is the flagship of the Cherlon group, a treasure well guarded by head office. This is why it seems so difficult for anyone to make any changes within this brand until they have proved themselves worthy of doing so.

Lussu's cultural profile

The profile in Figure A2.1.3 clearly differs from those of the other brands. Because of its value, Lussu is a rigidly controlled brand. It has a planning system that works according to strictly regulated launch times and controlled tasks and targets. The brand seems to be a strong 'doing' brand, one that is focused on meeting targets and reaching goals rather than using to the full the personal qualities of its team members. Lussu seems to be one of the most hierarchical brands within the company, where every step seems to be controlled by head office. It appears also to be a very formal brand, both in terms of attire and behaviour. Lussu's affinity with its parent company is very strong: it is a proud image of the company. Finally, Lussu seems more of a classic brand than a trendy

Figure A2.1.3 Lussu's cultural profile

one. Though it is up to date with fashion, as all brands of the company should be, it seems to target mature, 'classy' ladies who are willing to spend money on their looks.

Brand D: Tifla from the consumer products division

Tifla is what one could call the young face of the company, a brand based on high sales and strong image. This brand is used to sell products such as haircare, skincare, make-up and styling products to young people. Brand B is based on high sales and a good image. This seems to be company's representative brand in the consumer products division.

Tifla's cultural profile

Tifla seems to be more tightly controlled than the other brands discussed (Figure A2.1.4). This is a brand based on high volume sales for revenues and, for this reason, control from head office is considerable. The divisional manager at the local subsidiary does, however, have certain discretion over the launch price of a new product and in-store promotions. For this reason, the timing involved can be considered more monochronic than polychronic. This brand seems to have a rather 'soft' hierarchy: attire seems relatively informal, as does the behaviour. This ties in with the brand being the young face of the company, even though it is not the most informal. Tifla's affinity with the company group is very strong and this is visible on the packaging where the name of the parent-company appears in slightly smaller letters below the brand name. Tifla is also trendy: it needs to spot the newest fashion in the market and mass-produce it. Those working for the brand wear trendy clothes, reflecting the brand's image

and showing once again that those working with the brand live up to its image.

Concluding remarks on brands across cultures

There are some large differences in the cultures of the brands described above. One can see, brand by brand, what cultural values are important within these brands and how these differ. One can imagine, therefore, how problematic the transfer by an employee from one brand team to another can be: the employee will be expected to dress differently, communicate with people differently, act differently and make other adjustments to become 'a part of the brand'. This just shows how much the brands 'live' in the company as a whole. Were this not the case, then any transfer from one brand to another would entail simply selling a different product. However, at Cherlon, a person changes along with the change of brand. That is why the differences in cultures described above are so important.

Questions

1. By referring to the figure 'Model of culture' in the closing activity for Part One, make a similar model for 'brand cultures' using the parameters chosen by the authors of this study.
2. Re-read the definitions of the topics in Concept 6.1: Time focus (polychronic/monochronic); Activity (being/doing); and Power (hierarchy/equality). Define briefly the five new values of the model used by the authors in making the profile of the brands.
3. Summarize the differences and similarities between the profiles of the four Cherlon brands.
4. Choose a real company on the internet that works with several brands. If you wish to stay within the area of cosmetic products you can refer to www.cosmeticindustry.com/links/cosmsites.html for links to international companies. You can also refer to other industries such as beer manufacturers (e.g. Interbrew), clothing (e.g. Benetton or Levis), or soft drinks (e.g. Coca-Cola or Pepsi Cola). Look at the information available – text as well as images – and try to make an initial profile of contrasting brands within the company. If possible, talk to people familiar with the brands in question and even with people working for the brands. Then develop a cultural profile for each brand using the model referred to in question 1. If necessary, you may adapt some of the values used in the model.

Figure A2.1.4 Tifla's cultural profile

This activity is based on a case study into how two chemical companies in South Africa addressed the strategic and cultural issues involved in a joint venture. The author was involved in setting up the joint venture and ends his case with a critical assessment of the measures implemented to ensure the venture's success on the cultural front.

Learning outcomes

After reading this case and answering the questions you will:

- gain insight into the issues involved when two companies that are culturally different, despite being in the same country, set up a stand-alone joint venture.
- be aware of the issues of power involved in such a venture and the difficulties in resolving them.
- understand how active measures can promote the creation of a new organizational culture within such a joint venture.

Creating chemistry – a case study

This case is adapted from one written by Fain Ferguson in Browaeys, M.-J. (ed) (1996) *The Challenge of Cross-Cultural Management*, Nyenrode University Press

Why a joint venture?

A couple of years ago, two large chemical manufacturers in South Africa – AECI Limited and Sasol Limited – agreed to combine certain operations and to form a separate entity as a joint venture. The new venture formed was called Polifin. As the company now stands, AECI and Sasol own 80 per cent of the shares with the remaining 20 per cent being traded on the stock exchange or held in employee share benefit schemes. Although the company is now run as a separate entity, it is still effectively controlled by AECI and Sasol boards of directors/shareholders.

The objective of the project was to combine complementary manufacturing plants from the two separate companies to benefit from the effects of internal transfer pricing and the synergies that would be created. It was felt that greater economies of scale, better production scheduling, more efficient customer service and the creation of a monopolistic niche could be achieved by the joint venture. The reason for creating such a joint venture, and not just a sales agreement, was to create a company that was separate from the other two companies and one that could grow and develop products and processes that would not be achieved with just a sales agreement. Furthermore, the size of the combined forces would give credibility to the operation in the market place.

Bringing about the joint venture

From inception, a separate management team was created to run this project. The team included managers and staff from both founding organizations as well as new staff. It was expected to co-ordinate, create and manage the changeover of functions and staff to the new company. Decisions had to be made to match reporting methods, to resolve personnel issues (such as staff grading, pension benefits, medical aid and staff pre-requisites) and to determine the type of control given to divisions. The project was made more complicated than the start of a brand new operation by the fact that these functions already existed and now had to be modified or changed to fit with the new strategies and directions taken.

A new plant was built to increase the capacity of the organization and a completely new head office was created, with sales, some division heads and corporate administration being included. This move, again, provided management with a number of decisions as to where to locate, the type of offices and the size required and allocation to be given to the various divisions.

The two companies involved (AECI and Sasol) had very different reporting requirements as well as information needs. Information had to be supplied at different times to each during the month and the information-gathering process often had to be duplicated to supply exactly the information requested. The fact that these two companies had different year ends also complicated life within Polifin. Fortunately, the product flow was in a linear fashion with most divisions only being reliant on one other division. As a consequence of this, there were not a lot of serious cultural issues that the divisions had to address.

Culture issues

As already mentioned, a large percentage of the staff came from AECI and Sasol. The companies were run differently, with AECI being used to much more informal management and decentralization of power to the divisions. Sasol on the other hand was a fairly hierarchical company with protocols that were written and unwritten law within the organization (for example office sizes went specifically on the level of seniority in the organization with formal titles being used and staff having to go through the 'right' bureaucratic channels to get issues addressed). The cultural issues will be addressed at various levels.

National culture

Two of the sub cultures within South Africa are English and Afrikaans. The English culture is based on open and informal communications, and frequently challenging nature of authority. The Afrikaans culture on the other hand is characterized by distinct respect for elders and discipline (especially within a school environment) and the need to obey this discipline and not to question authority at all stages.

Professional culture

As is typical of the chemical industry, senior management mainly had backgrounds in chemical engineering and thus found it easy to understand one another in this respect. Other functions such as accounting were staffed by people with similar backgrounds. Consequently, the issue of professional culture did not appear to have much effect on the joint venture.

Organizational culture

The existence of two sub cultures led to a problem in defining the best corporate culture for the venture. The culture of the AECI staff was informal with a number of business issues being discussed over a 'beer' in the evening and an informal, open-door, first-name basis. On the other hand, the Sasol staff were characterized by a head of the division controlling all the information flows in and out as well as being the representative with senior management. The culture was hierarchical and formal with much empire building behind the scenes.

The analysis above reveals the problem faced at Polifin. Two distinct operating styles needed to be satisfied and supported, or even modified to create a new culture.

Power issues

The need to win the confidence of senior managers as well as the need to assert power over other divisions led to power issues. A couple of examples are required to illustrate this:

- The corporate accounting division had the task of co-ordinating and reporting financial information monthly, quarterly and annually. Because of the stringent requirements of the controlling shareholders and the fact that the head was second in charge of the joint venture, and responsible for the day-to-day running of the organization, the division was given a lot of power to force compliance with their reporting requirements. The problem was that the divisions that came from the AECI group were used to their own standards and deadlines and refused to co-operate. The result was that at the end of each month, a couple of telephone calls were required to ensure compliance.
- Senior staff from Sasol wanted their own parking bays and would really create a stir if anyone else was found using them. The need to affirm their seniority was strong.

- Ex-Sasol division heads would only pass on information about their figures on 'a need to know' basis. They protected their information base, apparently hoping to be able to use informational advantages as leverage during the year. It reflected the culture of hierarchy and forcing of reliance so that they were noticed.

A **frontstage** to the organization can be identified, showing it to be fairly dynamic without too many formal procedures in place, one which is undergoing a few teething problems in its rush to meet consumer demand.

There is also a very different situation **backstage**, where the culture was definitely one of power struggles. The environment had an adversarial feeling in which ex-Sasol employees faced ex-AECI employees, both sides supported by 'their' divisions. Clearly the full benefits of synergy were not being obtained.

Bringing the cultures together

Measures had to be taken to bridge the two regimes and to define a new culture to go with the new stand-alone business.

Bridging culture

Occasions were created whereby employees had the opportunity to interact. A number of annual events (such as the annual managers' conference) were arranged to bring the two regimes together and to create a new sense of belonging. Management tours of plants were arranged to meet the staff and to let staff know who the managers were. Sporting events and social activities helped create interaction among staff and to create healthy competition among divisions.

Other instruments were used:

- In-house magazines were introduced to create a feeling of internal culture as well as to get to know the 'people' within the organization.
- Computer systems throughout the organization were eventually harmonized.
- A new logo was created and a distinctive image of the company portrayed to the public, giving the employees something to work towards and feel part of.
- Once the stock was listed, shares were awarded to staff throughout the company.
- New policies and procedure manuals were written to define the expectations of the new company.

Neutralizing power imbalance

The method used to stop the creation of power empires was to instigate job rotation. Managers who previously operated in a hierarchical manner were suddenly thrown into situations that required a different approach. This would, it was hoped, lead to a change in management approach and would help to modify the structural inefficiencies. Furthermore, this rotation could lead to a good bridging of the backstage cultures: new managers could develop a deeper understanding of the underlying issues.

Power was also removed from division managers. Divisions had previously been allowed to handle their own cash and run separate bank accounts. This was now done centrally to simplify the cash position of the organization.

Managers had also to complete newly-formatted reports. They now had to comply with the new information requirements and learn how to present their information in a different way.

The results of the measures

The outcome of the project was the eventual creation of a new identity and culture that could definitely be identified from the outside (frontstage culture). However, there was still a way to go to achieve a new internal culture (backstage culture). The divisions insisted on maintaining their own way of collating information and often supplied information to, for example, the corporate accounting division in different formats and with varying degrees of detail. The efficiency of the organization still needed improvement because lack of total compliance increased the time spent making inquiries at the divisions.

In economic terms, the project appeared to be successful: the results exceeded expectations and surprised the controlling shareholders. The synergies achieved created a monopoly within the South African market that was able to undercut internationally competitive prices. The market became a price taker and this resulted in impressive profits and cash flows. The funding of new projects could be made from cash rather than from borrowings.

The combination of the various divisions created benefits, with raw material inputs being more efficiently used to create the finished goods at a cheaper price and better quality. There were fewer stock failures through increased understanding of the flow of products. Managers who previously worked on a seller/purchaser basis now had closer contact to each other and understood each other's needs better.

Boundary-spanning performance

An important lesson to be learnt from this exercise was that a better awareness of the cultural differences (and how culture affected the various operations) could have led to fewer conflicts. Cultural issues could have been addressed in advance instead of being left to simmer until conflict brought them to the surface. Perhaps better planning at the start-up phase would have negated the culture differences. This could have involved reviewing the structure of divisions, defining a new, company-wide standard that allowed employees to start at similar levels, and organizing cross-cultural workshops to create awareness. Furthermore, the development of policies, procedures and practices could have been defined at the start instead of being developed in an ad hoc manner.

The focus of not just the functional aspects but the interpersonal aspects could have been addressed a lot better than they were. Up-front discussion and negotiations with staff members could have assuaged a lot of their worries.

Finally, there is a saying that 'time heals all wounds' – and this seems to be relevant here. As time goes by, people will create their own culture within an organization and will slowly drop/adapt their old cultures. Eventually, staff will retire and be replaced with new staff who will become socialized in the new culture.

Questions

1. What were the reasons compelling the two companies to set up a joint venture?

2. What do you consider to have been the main cultural issues at the outset?

3. How were these issues addressed at the start? What was done later to deal with the cultural problems?

4. The author suggests how the cultural conflicts could have been addressed from the start of the venture. Give your opinion of his suggestions and suggest any other actions that could have been taken both at the start and during the development of the joint project.

Part Three

CULTURE AND COMMUNICATION

Introduction to Part Three

The relationship between culture and communication is an intriguing one. Although the process of communication can be seen as a way of transmitting the beliefs, attitudes, behaviours that identify a certain culture, this very process can also be regarded as an agent in shaping this identity. Although people, when communicating, draw on the meanings of the culture to which they belong, this very culture owes its existence to the exchange of information between its members.

Communication between cultures is culturally determined to a considerable extent. The cultural factor has come to be considered as the prime cause of difficulties in the interaction between individuals and groups who perceive themselves as belonging to different cultures. This explains to some extent the considerable amount of literature devoted to intercultural communication generally and to communication in international business in particular. Rather than attempting to summarize all the theories and empirical studies in the many studies in this area, Part Three focuses on ideas considered to be of particular interest.

At this point, however, it is worth considering two key terms used in studies on communication and culture. One has been used in the previous paragraph – **intercultural communication**. Another term, **cross-cultural communication**, is also frequently used in the same context. Gudykunst (2004) clearly explains the differences between what may appear to be terms with similar meanings. Intercultural communication is to do with communication between people from different national cultures and comprises all aspects relating to the study of culture and communication. Cross-cultural communication has to do with the comparison of the various ways people communicate across cultures. Cross-cultural communication is therefore a 'sub-domain', which means that understanding intercultural communication is a prerequisite to understanding cross-cultural communication.

Part Three will not stick rigidly to the distinction between intercultural and cross-cultural communication; the intention is to deal with those subjects relevant to communication both in and between cultures without necessarily classifying them.

Before examining these subjects, however, it is appropriate to first consider the process in graphic form when two representatives of different cultures are communicating. Figure III.1 displays the communication process between the two, including the frame of reference each communicator uses, as well as key filters through which messages sent and received must pass.

Frame of reference

When communicating, each sender/receiver is unconsciously referring to a framework consisting of:

- Their knowledge of the subject under discussion.
- Their experience in professional or individual terms.

Figure III.1 Model of communication

- Their norms, i.e. the norms of the society in which they live.
- Their assumptions, i.e. what is taken as a fact or believed to be true.

Communication filters

Where the sender/receivers do not share the same culture, the particular filters through which the messages pass can lead not just to incomprehension of the messages, but also to their distortion and misunderstanding. The elements that act as barriers to communication will be examined in Chapter 14. Suffice for the moment to outline/define the filters involved.

Use of language: verbal and non-verbal

Language can be seen as part of the social process, a systematic framework for handling events. As such, its use allows entry into a social organization, which is at the same time a sort of language community. Its members share certain language habits that are formalized in grammars and dictionaries.

Cultural groups can differ in the way they distribute the total information involved in an interchange between verbal and non-verbal language. The **verbal** use of language has to do with sounds, intonation, idiom, grammar and dialects, both regional and occupational. It also has to do with the assumptions of the language community with regard to the meaning of words and idioms it uses, the connotations attached. The use of **non-verbal** language is a necessary concomitant of any spoken interchange. Although determined by the social groups using it, non-verbal language may cut across the boundaries of language communities. Non-verbal language has visible elements, such as gestures, facial expressions and eye contact, as well as body posture and physical distance between those involved in conversation. Non-verbal language has also audible elements such as the tone of voice and (the nature and frequency of) interjections. The assumptions underlying the various elements of non-verbal language may differ from one language community to another, even if they look or sound the same. Particular attention is given to non-verbal language and differing cultural contexts in Chapters 13 and 14.

Styles of thinking and communicating

How people think and how they express their thoughts appears to be determined not just individually but also socially. Patterns of thought involved in discussing the fortunes of a company, for example, may be problem-solving in approach, using a cause/effect analysis. Equally, the subject can be approached without the idea of a 'problem' being in mind, but rather the contradictions and complexities inherent in running a concern.

The way such thoughts are communicated depend on a number of factors, including:

- **Context** – the spoken word may or may not be the primary means of communicating. As we saw in Part One, high-context and low-context styles of communication (Hall and Hall, 1990) show the importance or otherwise for the interlocutors of the situation they are in and their relationships. Here is an example from life at home which shows how, within the given context and the relationship between partners, very few words can convey a lot of meaning.

> The husband is reading his newspaper and his wife is having a bath. The doorbell rings.
>
> The wife shouts 'Darling!' and the husband, getting up from his chair and heading for the door shouts 'OK!'
>
> Only a couple of words have been spoken, but a lot has been said.
>
> When the wife says 'Darling!' she probably means 'The door bell has rung, I'm in the bath, so I can't answer it. Please could you go to the door?' When he replies 'OK!' his message is probably 'I realize you're in the bath and can't go the door, so I'll go.'

Whenever something is said, an act of communication is being performed. But is the act always understood by the other? Is the intention behind the spoken word always clear to the other party?

This matter of context is in turn is related to:

- **Directness** – the extent to which communicators wish to 'get to the point'. Do they cut straight to the perceived 'truth', or do they imply, suggest, understate matters? Is assertiveness seen by the other as aggression, indirectness as being submissive?

- **Face** – is related to the previous two aspects: is exchange of information and opinions the primary goal of a conversation, or is it more to do with saving face, maintaining the relationship, showing respect for an elder or superior, avoiding confrontation and promoting harmony?

These elements will be dealt with in various chapters, particularly Chapter 14 on communication barriers and Chapter 17 on dealing with conflict.

Stereotypes

Stereotypes are beliefs based on generalizations made about another group of people or their individual members. Such generalizations can be true, but they are often wrong because they are based on inaccurate information and resistant to change. As such, they reflect one or more prejudices, a prejudice being an attitude that is often negative towards another social group.

The source of prejudice, according to social identity theory, is to do with the idea that a person's identity is created primarily through their membership of a group (the in-group). Group members tend to regard their own group as superior, have prejudicial attitudes towards other groups and may be prepared to discriminate against out-groups, even though there are no obvious reasons extrinsically.

Chapter 14 will deal further with stereotypes as one of the main barriers in intercultural communication.

Management of relationships

This has to do with how those communicating perceive each other's social standing. A range of factors may be involved, including the degree of (in)formality, respect and intimacy considered appropriate by one or the other, and the way this is reflected in the interactional behaviour. Hierarchical considerations can also come into play: when employees from different hierarchical levels and cultural backgrounds have to work together, status may be a barrier in communication between them. However aware interlocutors may be about the question of managing working relationships, there are unconscious behaviour elements that can support or contradict spoken communication, such as (lack of) eye contact, or tone of voice.

Aspects of relation management will be dealt with in various chapters, including Chapters 13, 15 and 16.

As stated earlier, Part Three is by no means comprehensive. Readers who wish to go into more depth on the areas chosen, should turn to the list of further readings. This introduction also contains a selection of literature on the general area.

Chapter and concept overview

Chapter 13 Business communication across cultures

This chapter introduces the concept of communicating in and between cultures. In dealing with people from other cultures within a company, or with cross-border business clients, a manager will use the normal channels of communication. However, in this communication process the identities of the cultures in question, and the resulting interactions, will play an important role. A number of factors can affect the process of communication.

The concept is divided into four sub-concepts:

- A model of communication.
- Forms of communication in business practice.
- Language during business encounters.
- Face-to-face management relations across culture.

Chapter 14 Barriers to intercultural communication

Perception is the key word in communication and is largely determined by culture. When business is being done with other cultures, communication is the most important cause of misunderstandings. The filters mentioned in the introduction will now be regarded more closely in terms of barriers to cross-cultural communication. Particular attention is paid to stereotypes because of their important role in relations between cultures. This applies across the board – from one-to-one encounters to marketing campaigns. It is important to know where stereotypes come from and how best to deal with them.

The concept is divided into four sub-concepts:

- What are communication barriers?
- Non-verbal behaviour as a barrier.
- Assumptions and culture.
- Perceptions and stereotypes.

Chapter 15 Negotiating internationally

This chapter introduces the concept of approaches to negotiating in an intercultural context. The concept is divided into three sub-concepts:

- The nature of negotiating from both a Western and non-Western perspective
- Key facets of negotiation in an international business context and the various types of interaction that may result.
- The issue of strategy adaptation when negotiating with counterparts from other cultures.

Chapter 16 Working with international teams

This chapter introduces the concept of groups processes during international encounters. After defining the word 'team' and the elements involved (types and roles), this concept will focus on a common phenomenon of global business, namely international teams and their functioning. The final part of the concept will deal with the management of multicultural teams, with particular reference to Afro-Western teams.

The concept is divided into three sub-concepts:

- Teams in organizations.
- Team processes.
- The management of multi-cultural teams.

Chapter 17 Conflicts and cultural differences

This chapter introduces the concept of understanding and dealing with conflicts. This concept will first give a general overview of conflicts and their sources before looking at the role emotions can play in different cultures. It will then examine the management of conflicts, particularly the different approaches used in Eastern and Western cultures.

The concept is divided into five sub-concepts:

- The nature of conflict: when conflicts happen and factors involved.
- A model of conflict styles: how modes of communicative behaviour during conflict can be classified.
- Culture, emotions and conflict: how different cultural values influence the role of emotions in conflict situations.
- Management of conflict: the culture-based views of effectiveness and appropriacy in conflict resolution.
- Mediation and cultural transformation: how third party intervention and/or the practice of mindful communication skills can transform the perception of conflict and the attitudes of those involved.

Chapter 18 Developing intercultural relationships

This chapter examines how an individual can meet the challenges involved in communicating with different cultures through developing an intercultural communication competence. It has the concept of becoming a competent intercultural communicator at its core. This concept is divided into four sub-concepts:

- The main components involved in adapting and developing communication skills appropriate to a cultural context.
- How intercultural competence can be achieved through collaboration between those communicating interculturally.
- The ethical component as a component of intercultural communication competence.
- Developing a third culture between parties to allow the emergence of a shared system of values.

Final activities

Part Three contains two extra activities:

1. **A role-play simulation:** *Working internationally.* You will be taking part in a meeting of department heads within a newly-merged company. You are required to decide on company policy, particularly with regard to the location of production facilities.
2. **A case study:** *Vechtel: adapting an international approach to a local market.* This presents a series of events in the recent past of a company on the international takeover path and describes the perceptions of those involved.

What you will gain

After working through Part Three you will gain more insight into:

- How culture affects communication.
- How intercultural communication can be affected by the cultural differences between those involved.
- How intercultural communication can be made more effective.

References

Beamer, L. and Varner, I. (2001) *Intercultural Communication in the Global Workplace,* New York, NY: McGraw-Hill.

Gudykunst, W.B. (ed.) (2004) *Cross-Cultural and Intercultural Communication,* Thousand Oaks, CA: Sage.

Guirdham, M. (2005) *Communicating Across Cultures at Work*, 2nd edn, New York, NY: Palgrave, Macmillan.

Hall, E.T. and Hall, M.R. (1990) *Understanding Cultural Differences*, Yarmouth, ME: Intercultural Press.

Lewis, R.D. (1999) *Cross Cultural Communication: A visual approach*, Winchester: Transcreen.

Samovar, L.A. and Porter, R.E. (1994) *Intercultural Communication,* 7th edn, Belmont, CA: International Thomson.

Ting-Toomey, S. (1999) *Communicating Across Cultures*, New York, NY: Guildford Press.

Chapter 13

Business communication across cultures

As seen in Part Two, the development of globalization in business has compelled managers, employees and customers to take increasing account of intercultural relations. The increasingly global nature of business and the growing interaction between cultures is adding to the complexity of doing business.

The composition of staff and clientele is changing as companies start up operations in countries across the globe. Managers in such companies must therefore be able to operate on an international level and deal with other cultures. It is no longer enough for them to be aware of the existence of cultural differences; they must also be able to communicate, negotiate and work together with business partners from other cultures.

These requirements go far beyond the standard recipes for management from early business studies where the emphasis was very much on a universal approach, one taking no account of relativity or diversity. New management skills are necessary, particularly in the area of communication skills.

The concept in Chapter 13 first examines the elements involved in inter- and intracultural communication before looking at communication in business. Chapter 14 follows on with an analysis of a number of barriers, both verbal and non-verbal, to intercultural communication.

Learning outcomes

After reading this chapter you will gain an understanding of:

● The different components which have an influence on the process of communication;

● The role of communication in business practices.

Concept 13.1 Communicating in and between cultures

As discussed in the introduction to Part Three, intercultural communication comprises all forms of communication both within and between cultures. This concept should be considered not just in terms of comparisons between cultures, but also in terms of the process of interaction and exchange between different cultures. As Ladmiral and Lipiansky (1989) indicate, the term 'intercultural communication' could imply that it is the cultures and identities that are in contact. This is not really the case. Instead, it is individuals who are interacting and it is they who bring their culture's way of thinking, feeling and living into the interaction. This book therefore considers that intercultural communication can be seen as a 'fabric of relations', a fabric created by the individuals or groups from different cultures and woven from the perceptions they have of each other, as well as the values, codes, lifestyles and thought processes belonging to their respective cultures.

Intercultural communication can be better defined as an interactive phenomenon rather than one involving comparisons between cultures. These cultures are non-homogeneous social groups that are forever evolving. Their interaction should not just be seen in terms of a set of relations between the cultures, but also as a dynamic process (therefore one implying change) whereby the cultures are defined both through their own characteristics as well as through their interaction with each other. This definition therefore takes both a systemic perspective (involving sets of interrelations between individuals) and a dynamic one (whereby the interrelations can change).

This approach to communication brings us to the model which we presented in the introduction.

A model of communication

The schematic representation of the model in the introduction emphasizes the actors involved in the communication, namely the addresser and the addressee. When they communicate, they unconsciously make use of a frame of reference which, in general terms, consists of:

- knowledge (about the subject under discussion);
- experience (in professional or individual terms);
- norms (i.e. the norms of the society in which they live); and
- prejudices (with regard to each other).

However, according to a model proposed by researchers known as the Palo Alto Group, human communication does not emphasize the addresser and the addressee. These researchers, who were based at the Mental Research Institute in Palo Alto in the US, collaborated in the 1950s and 1960s on the theory of communication and the relationship between the individuals. They maintained that since both addresser and addressee are in perpetual interaction, they cannot be isolated. The emphasis is not on the message, but on the whole system of communication involved, including a network of relations that cannot be broken up. Everybody is involved in a network of relations woven by the cultural group (the ethnic group or society in question). Communication does, of course, require a message (form and content), but more important than the message in the exchange between protagonists is the interaction, i.e. the relation between the persons communicating and the context of the communication. This determines the information exchanged. Furthermore, the information in the message does not have an absolute value; it is subject to interpretation due to the interaction itself. That is why in human communication – and even more so in intercultural communication – the question of interpretation remains crucial (Donnadieu and Karsky, 2002).

Without going more deeply into the concepts of the theory of communication, it can be concluded that not only are the relations between those communicating an important factor, but also the role of context. It is this role, already referred to in Part One, to which this chapter now turns, with particular reference to the business environment.

The role of the 'context' in communication

Context can be defined as the environment in which the communication process takes place and which helps to define the communication. Knowing the physical context, one can predict to a high degree of accuracy much of the communication. The choice of the environment, the context, helps assign the desired meaning to the words communicated. Culture is also context. Every culture has its own world view; its own way of thinking of activity, time and human nature; its own way of perceiving self; and its own system of social organization. Knowing each of these helps people assign meaning to the symbols. The component of context helps identify the extent to which the source and receiver have similar meanings for the communicated symbols. Similar understandings of the culture in which the communication takes place is critical to the success of the communication.

Hall and Hall (1990) established two groups of cultures, called *high-context* and *low-context*. The difference between them was the degree of importance attached to the context of any message. In low-context cultures, the information of any message is contained in the message itself, i.e. in the words used. The message is explicit. In high-context cultures, most of the information is contained in the context where the message is being sent, i.e. in the relationships between the people involved and the situation where people are communicating. The message is implicit.

When representatives of high-context and low-context cultures are doing business, the one may have a very different idea as to what is important in their communication. For example, when the Swiss and the Japanese meet, the former may prefer to come quickly to the point and get down to business. The Japanese, on the other hand, prefer not to talk directly about the business at hand; they are inclined to talk generally about this and that, about life in general, and to do so to get to know each other.

As Figure 6.2 shows, Hall and Hall place the Swiss in the low-context group and the Japanese in the high-context group. These two cultures lie at the extreme ends of a continuum.

Another aspect of the process of communication raised by Hall, one often neglected but also important in the relation between cultures, is what he called 'proxemics'.

Proxemics and cultures

The term **proxemics** was coined by Hall (1966) to describe the study of how people perceive their social and personal space. Hall maintains that awareness of the differences between cultures with regard to proxemics is indispensable when interacting with other cultures. This entails being able to work out the 'silent' messages being communicated through the distance separating people when they are interacting, as well as in terms of the senses (touch, smell, sight and sound). Different cultural frameworks define the information received by our physical senses, not only in terms of what can be perceived, but also in terms of what can be eliminated. According to Hall, individuals learn from childhood which types of information they need to retain and which they can dispense with. As soon as these perceptive models have been developed, they appear to be fixed for life.

Personal space is characterized by an invisible zone with distinct boundaries. When an intruder enters this zone, people may feel uncomfortable. This space is a sort of personal territory, a zone of protection or even of defence. The main factors influencing personal space are: gender, age, personality, the degree of sympathy towards the individuals concerned, the situation in which the individuals are confronted and also the culture(s) involved.

Corraze (1988) reports on investigations made by Hall (1966) and Watson (1970) into the differences between cultures with regard to the notion of 'personal space'.

Hall postulates that the distance between individuals is related to the preferences each culture has with regard to the sensory inputs used. Each culture has a preference for certain sensory receptors. Take, for example, the differences in personal space between Arabs and Americans: Arabs, it seems, prefer a smaller personal space than Americans because the former are more susceptible to the olfactory dimension, including skin odour. Hall, in fact, makes a link between smell and a person's disposition in the Arabic-speaking world. A prospective bride, for example, may be rejected if she gives off an unpleasant odour:

> When couples are being matched for marriage, the man's go-between will sometimes ask to smell the girl, who may be turned down if she doesn't 'smell nice'.
>
> Hall 1969: 149

Watson compares the distances between people in conversation in different cultures and makes a ranking according to the differences in the size of their personal space. The ranking, from small to large is illustrated in Figure 13.1. Research supports the hypothesis that if someone's personal space is violated, this can impair communication because of an increase in anxiety.

Small personal space					Large personal space
Arabs	Indians and Pakistanis	South Europeans	South Americans	Asians	North Europeans

Figure 13.1

Proxemics also relates to the places where people move and the places where they work. If tables in a restaurant are placed in a way that does not respect personal space, the occupants may well apologize to their neighbours for sitting so close, or display non-verbal behaviour (such as deliberately looking away). If managers do not take the concept of personal space into account when seeing to the organization of offices and arrangement of desks, the ensuing anxiety among staff can hamper communication and thus the efficient running of a business. This is a non-verbal aspect of communication in the working environment to which managers pay little attention.

Communication also refers to the meaningful exchange process by which verbal and nonverbal information is shared through messages, and it can take many forms. Even if managers use all these forms in their business practices, they each have different perceptions of the effectiveness of these forms of communication and may therefore prefer some over others. The question of which forms of communication to use is one that should receive more attention in business as well as in research into communication generally.

Forms of communication in business practice

Many channels of communication are available to managers. Electronic mail, for example, is becoming the most common form of written communication within many companies. It is used for many purposes, both externally and internally: managers use email to call a

Table 13.1 Channels of business communication

Medium	Oral	Written	Electronic
(Telephone) conversations	x		
Conference calls	x		
(Online) meetings	x		x
Voice mail (asynchronic)	x		x
Video teleconferences (synchronic)	x		x
Electronic mail (asynchronic)		x	x
Messaging (synchronic)		x	x
Training sessions	x	x	x
Presentations, speeches	x	x	x
Press conferences	x	x	x
Press releases		x	
Memos		x	
Proposals		x	
Letters		x	
Reports		x	
Fax		x	
NB: any of the written documents listed above, if attached to emails, could also be considered as using an electronic channel.			

meeting, or give their colleagues and subordinates feedback and instructions, or correspond with customers and clients. Some managers, however, prefer to communicate by talking face-to-face in a meeting or informally, by making phone calls (including conference calls), or by using video teleconferences. These ways of communicating in turn involve the use of some or all of the non-verbal elements of communication, such as gestures, tone of voice, facial expressions, and body language generally.

Table 13.1 summarizes the main channels of business communication.

Culture and choice of communication mode

The choice of communication mode can be influenced by cultural factors. Mead (1990: 84) gives an example with regard to telephoning. A US businessman would consider it quite normal to make a 'cold call', to phone a stranger with whom he thinks he could do business. A Japanese businessman, on the other hand, would consider this to be intrusive or aggressive, preferring instead to find a third party who can 'vouch for your credibility and make a formal introduction'.

This is, of course, related to the cultural dimensions discussed in earlier chapters. A business from an 'individualist' culture, for example, may be intent on what it considers 'efficient' communication when dealing with a business in a 'collectivist' culture. It puts forward a comprehensive business proposal and expects a similar response. If the company asked to respond is not accustomed to such direct approaches, it may well decide not to deal with the proposal directly in writing, but to request instead a face-to-face meeting with representatives of the company concerned. In this way, a good relationship can be established before any discussion of the proposal is entered into since, in the eyes of the possible business partner, efficiency and speed are in their eyes less important than establishing trust and confidence. The oral mode is used to set the conditions for co-operation, whereafter the written mode can be considered as a means of communication, provided the relationships established are scrupulously maintained.

Computer-mediated communication (CMC)

Electronic mail is being increasingly used as a way of sending documents, requests and information generally to colleagues and (potential) clients. However, even though it offers many advantages in terms of speed and efficiency, it can also contain many pitfalls when used interculturally. Problems of comprehension may arise, of course, through inaccurate language and poorly structured text. (These points are discussed in the next sub-section with reference to using English as the medium of communication.) Also, cultural issues can lead to misunderstanding and even antagonism. The recipient of an email may consider its style too formal or informal depending on what their expectations are. They may take offence, for example, if they are not addressed at the start of the email or if the style of the message is too direct or casual, particularly if it contains careless language. Others who consider emails to be more conversational in nature may dislike the distancing effect of a formal written style and the lack of explicit information or opinion, particularly if direct answers are not given to direct questions. As with any written form of communication, there are no facial expressions to mitigate or clarify messages.

It could be argued that the use of email, just as other forms of computer-mediated communication (CMC), blurs the distinction between the oral and written messages for many of its users. A sender or recipient may expect an email to be the equivalent of a letter or memo, meeting the formal requirements of language accuracy and text cohesion of written text. Another sender/recipient, however, may regard the message sent as being the start (or continuation) of a conversation in writing, of a thread of messages. The style will reflect more the spoken word with its slips of the tongue, false starts, hesitations and inaccuracies. Any resulting misunderstanding or incomprehension can be communicated and dealt with in later messages.

Such differing expectations, be they intra- or inter-cultural, need to be recognized and managed by the communicating parties. However, CMC can help to alleviate discrepancies because both sender and receiver have, in theory, time to reflect upon and discuss the process as they are communicating.

Differences in expectation and resulting behaviours in both the intra- and inter-cultural context are discussed in a literature review, in which the author found that many of the gender differences in face-to-face interaction were carried over into CMC and even accentuated:

> There is evidence that women and men communicate in different ways on the net. A study of two academic groups conducted by Herring (1996) reveals that 'Both men and women structure their messages in an interactive way and that for both, the pure exchange of information takes second place to the exchange of views. Significant gender differences are found in how electronic messages are oriented . . . Although messages posted by women contain somewhat more interactional features they are also more informative, in contrast with male messages which most often express (critical) views.'
>
> Herring found that while women value politeness, men operate in accordance with competitive values which result in violations, including flaming, of conventional politeness norms. Men dominated the 'talking' time. They participated at a higher rate than their

numerical representation justified, and their messages were considerably longer. They took little interest in what women had to say, which seems to have resulted in a decline of female participation. In this supposedly liberal academic environment, CMC was found to be male-dominated, power-based and hierarchical.

Waldvogel, 2001: 7–8.

Language during business encounters

The previous discussion assumes that the two business representatives are able to communicate even though their native languages are different. When this is not possible, a number of options present themselves:

- Both sides could insist on using their native language when communicating, necessitating the use of an intermediary to translate. This may remove the obligation of managers to learn their counterpart's language and ensure that communication runs efficiently. However, apart from practical problems (including the availability of interpreters and the cost involved), there is always the question of reliability: Is the translation accurate? Is the interpreter able to convey the full nuance of what is being said? Moreover, the presence of an intermediary hampers the establishment of a relationship between the parties. Interaction is necessarily delayed and the role of non-verbal communication reduced. The focus of interaction may well become the interpreter who, in a way, is controlling the whole exchange without bearing the responsibility for the outcome.

- One interlocutor uses the mother tongue of the other. Many regard this as the best solution: by becoming truly bilingual, the manager is able to 'tune into' the other's culture, pick up all the nuances, understand the cultural references and respond appropriately. An 'expat' manager who has worked and lived for a long time in one country or region may well be in a position to perform this role optimally. However, managers who are operating across many cultures and making forays into new countries cannot be expected to acquire the language of every culture with which they are (about to be) involved.

It is worthwhile mentioning here problems experienced by interlocutors who share the same language, whether they come from different cultures or not. Within an English-speaking country, such as the UK, there can be enormous differences in the level of expression in both written and spoken language, and this can affect communication generally. Between English-speaking countries, such as the UK and the US, there may be a shared language, but British and US managers must sometimes check the meanings of words that their counterparts use. Differences in pronunciation can also add confusion. This goes also for speakers of other dialects of English such as Indian English, Singapore English and South African English.

Exhibit 13.1 shows how native speakers of English in the UK can be confused by the plethora of business terms taken from American English.

English: a neutral language?

A third possibility for managers who cannot communicate with each other through their mother tongues is for them to share a neutral foreign language. History shows how the use of a 'lingua franca' (common language) has been indispensable to the development of

Exhibit 13.1

Meeting-room jargon: just fuel for buzzword bingo?

By Michael Quinion

If you can't understand half of what your colleagues are saying in meetings, take heart – you are not alone.

A survey of a thousand office workers in Britain was published last week by the firm of recruitment consultants Office Angels. It reported that two-thirds of office staff used unnecessary jargon terms, for the usual reasons of wanting to confuse opponents and seem superior. But 40 per cent of those surveyed found it irritating and distracting, and 10 per cent thought it made the most frequent users sound pretentious and untrustworthy.

Nothing very new or startling so far. But the list of buzz phrases that were reported as being at the same time most common and least understood was intriguing:

Low-hanging fruit, e-tailing, talk off-line, blue-sky idea, win-win situation, think outside the box, holistic approach, level playing field, sanity check, put to bed, whole nine yards, helicopter view, gap analysis, touch base, rain check, sing from the same hymn sheet, finger in the air, get in bed with, big picture, benchmark, ball park, ticks in all the right boxes, strategic fit, bread and butter.

It's clear that jargonisers in British offices are picking up terms from American English, some from the standard language, but mostly from business jargon. The survey suggests they are doing so because more business people have access to the American-dominated internet.

You can see that phrases like rain check, ball park and touch base could confuse hearers in Britain, because we literally don't play the game. (But one supermarket in Britain uses rain checks as its name for the vouchers it gives out when special offers are in short supply, so some of us have been exposed to it.)

Some terms are odd and would stop almost anybody for a moment – low-hanging fruit, for a target that's easy to reach, helicopter view, for an overview, and gap analysis, for assessing untapped opportunities. But several – such as level playing field, benchmark, and blue-sky – have been in British English for many years. And are strategic fit or bread and butter really so hard to figure out, in context? It would seem so, from the survey.

Jargon is all right in its place. But what the survey shows is that people are easily confused by the unfamiliar, good enough reason for sticking to plain English the rest of the time. Giving bored attendees at meetings the chance to play buzzword bingo is hardly a substitute.

Source: www.worldwidewords.org/articles/jargon.htm

trade in many parts of the world. Nowadays, English frequently serves as a means of communication between companies whose managers have acquired the language as part of their education and have been exposed to it through various media. This language is often referred to as 'international English', but is difficult to define exactly because it has evolved organically on the basis of how non-native speakers use English. It is said to contain words and phrases that are generally understood across the world. It appears to be devoid of complex grammar constructions and of all but the most common idiomatic phrases. Those using it may often need to readjust their use of the language while using it to accommodate differences in knowledge and understanding between the speakers concerned. The differences in pronunciation may also need to be considered, especially when it is heavily influenced by that used for the mother tongue.

Even here, however, there are problems. A speaker using English as a neutral foreign language may well suffer similar problems to native speakers using English to communicate with non-native speakers. This is particularly the case when the speaker in question is from a country where English is used as the second language of communication in, for example, education and business. The speaker may not be aware of the breadth of his vocabulary compared with that of his counterpart, and may be unable to modify his pronunciation since it is part and parcel of the way English is used in his country of origin.

Some observers regard international English as a move towards cultural neutrality, a way of shedding the cultural connotations of British or American English. However, as a sort of default language, it has considerable limitations: discussion can be superficial and communicating thoughts difficult. The basic problem is that language is the very expression of a culture, be it Canadian English, Hong Kong English, Caribbean or African English. Stripping culture off any language, let alone a particular sort of English, can impoverish the semantics of the language and reduce its whole power of expression. There may be less room for nuance and subtlety, for saying something that expresses much more than the words used. The language can be deprived of its deeper meaning.

This goes equally for written English. A report in writing in a 'stripped down' English – particularly one using 'bullets' of information – may not in itself prove easy to understand by a non-native speaker of English. A noble attempt to simplify English may cause more problems than those it was intended to solve. The connections between thoughts, ideas and information may become more diffuse or even non-existent. Deprived of proper cohesion, clear context and any oral explanation, the adapted text may have lost a good deal of the intended meaning of the original. Such problems frequently occur during exchanges of emails when messages sent in simplified telescopic form can result in misunderstandings or incomprehension. This goes particularly for emails written in idiomatic, telegram-style language that may be appropriate for an office colleague, but not for a client in Bangladesh.

Over and above such problems, there is, of course, the question of language as a potent way of expressing cultural identity. How motivated are people to use a language that is not theirs and which does not allow them to assert their own personal or cultural identity? Exhibit 13.2 shows what can happen when a company, which was once a Chinese state-owned enterprise, adopts English as its official language.

Face-to-face management relations

This brings us to the question of face-to-face business encounters. Whatever the language chosen, encounters occur in situations and contexts where the expectations of the interlocutors may be very different, where the pressure of differing social norms can disturb the communicative relationship.

The first encounter

The way different cultures pursue the formality mode indicated earlier reflects tendencies within the cultures concerned. The very start of an encounter can indicate clear differences, even if it takes place in a shared language. A formal first meeting between a US manager and a German manager, for example, may show how the one is intent on

Exhibit 13.2 FT

Straight-talking, English-speaking culture brings communication problems

By Justine Lau

When a Hong Kong-based analyst recently called computer-maker Lenovo's Beijing office and asked for an employee by the English first name on her business card, he got a puzzling response. The operator told him the person did not exist.

Baffled, he called back and asked for the same person in her Chinese name. He was put through to her office immediately.

What the analyst encountered was a Lenovo in flux where the transformation of a corporate culture has yielded occasional moments of confusion even within the company.

Some employees at Lenovo, which acquired IBM's PC unit last year, now receive internal emails from a 'John' or 'Mary' whom they struggle to identify until they find out their Chinese names.

'In the past, we used to call each other by Chinese names. But now since a lot of our communications involve our US colleagues, some people may find it easier to have an English name,' says one Lenovo employee.

The spontaneous move by staff to adopt English names may be causing slight confusion, but it underlines broader changes in the company's culture that analysts see as key to its success in managing the acquisition of the IBM unit.

Shortly after the deal, Lenovo hired Bill Amelio, a former Dell executive, to be its chief executive. It moved its headquarters from Beijing to North Carolina and changed the official company language from Chinese to English. It is also establishing a straight-talking culture inside the company.

'Lenovo used to behave like any state-owned enterprise. [But] it has realised that in order to become a true global company, the first step is to drop some of the old habits,' said Randy Zhou, an analyst at Bank of China International.

Source: *Financial Times*, 9 November, 2006: 31

Questions

1. How do you think the adoption of English by the company would help establish a 'straight-talking culture'?

2. What else do you think would need to be done for this new culture to be established?

establishing an open, friendly and eventually informal relationship whereas the other is more reserved in exchanging information, particularly with regard to their respective positions and responsibilities. The very exchange of names ('Hi! I'm Ron Smith.' – 'Hello. Stoldt, Dr Peter Stoldt.') can be the start of a precarious scenario, particularly when English is being used: using 'you' goes hand-in-hand with informality for the American, whereas the German may use 'you' as the equivalent of 'Sie', the formal version of 'you' in German which establishes a certain distance between speakers. Two conflicting functions of the meeting (cultivating social ties and exchanging information) may well be pursued with growing unease by the two parties. The German possibly does not share the optimism and (superficial) friendliness of the other; he is more intent on establishing the other's credentials and clarifying the potential of a business deal. Any attempt by the

American to break through what he considers to be the rather cold reserved manner of his counterpart could have an adverse effect, with the German developing an antipathy towards persistent affability.

The context of meetings can determine the nature of such encounters. For example, it will become apparent to any foreign visitor in a Japanese setting that addressing a Japanese manager by his first name is inappropriate: office relationships retain a formality not experienced in many Western business cultures. Any attempt to counter this can result in extreme embarrassment for the Japanese manager and his colleagues. In another (Western) setting, however, first-name terms may be the norm and insistence on using a title and surname may prove a barrier to establishing trust and confidence in that setting.

Conversational styles

If a business relationship develops, some kind of negotiated communication mode may be established, whereby the context involved plays a decisive role. Once the Japanese manager has deemed it appropriate for business with his Western counterpart to be pursued, then he may be prepared to drop his guard and enter into a less formal style of communication. However, if other, less involved, Japanese colleagues are present, the more formal style will be retained, and the American will adapt his (verbal) behaviour correspondingly. On the other hand, the Japanese may well be prepared to communicate (and possibly behave) more informally in a Western setting – as long as his authority is not questioned.

Once the relationship between managers from different cultures has been established, the maintenance of such a relationship can be fraught with difficulty, particularly when different styles of conversation are used. One interlocutor may expect those involved in a meeting, for example, to be able to take turns when speaking, the other may assume it is his right to interrupt as and when necessary; one interlocutor may be focused on his particular take on matters, the other may involve his 'ego' much less; one may tend to make assertive, conclusive statements, the other may prefer to make more negotiable contributions and be less conclusive; one may consider pauses in the conversation to be appropriate for reflection, the other may shy away from silence and fill up a gap as soon as it appears.

Listening is, of course, a crucial element of any conversation: understanding not only what is being said but evaluating the meaning of what is being said. Taking turns to speak, rather than interrupting each other, may certainly ease the process of understanding, as will asking questions to check on understanding. The use of a shared second language will probably necessitate a check on the intended meaning of words or phrases used, and possibly a rephrasing of statements to clarify understanding. Listening carefully to what is not said is just as important. As Mead (1990: 118) indicates in his list of habits a good listener needs to develop:

> Listen for what is *not* said; that is, for what the sender thinks is so obvious as to be redundant or what is so new as to be outside his or her experience. This means processing the message in terms of the differences between your and the speaker's personal and cultural priorities.

Another element to take into account when evaluating the contributions of other interlocutors is their facial expressions.

Facial expressions during interaction

Facial expressions have been analysed more frequently in terms of the emotions expressed than in terms of their effect on human relations. However, such expressions give important signals in social and business interaction. They are totally linked to the context and differ according to whether the context is clear or ambiguous. A persistent look can make the interlocutor feel like escaping or responding with signals of aggression. Such looks are therefore often associated with feelings (unease, embarrassment) which, according to the context, will express attitudes that are diametrically opposed (such as aggression and friendliness).

Facial expressions are also connected to the status of the interlocutors. In social and business encounters they can play an important role when expressing the degrees of dominance between people with different levels of status. Any perceived degree of status can, however, have causes unrelated to a person's actual social position. We sometimes arbitrarily attribute a dominant status to someone because they are able to talk very fluently and knowledgeably during a discussion.

Cultural differences can play a significant role in the way facial expressions function. The length of visual contact, for example, depends to a great extent on the cultural origin of the interlocutors. When someone actually averts their gaze, this can be interpreted differently. In some cultures this act can have a negative connotation, but in others it may be seen simply as a sign that the speaker is changing direction in the discussion. The act of smiling might be assumed to have a similar function across the world as a signifier of happiness. Trumble's book (2004) *Brief History of the Smile* reveals many of the nuances attached to this physiological process. Through his enlightening account Trumble shows that smiling intersects not just with happiness, but also with piety, sex and corruption. Here is an account of how a Russian smile can be interpreted (Sauer, 2007: 13):

> Anyone who has been to Russia knows how unbelievably sullen the people look. They hardly ever smile but instead give all the signs that life for most Russians is just hell. I maintain that a smile actually has another function – an observation that has been scientifically corroborated. My teacher of Russian, Maria, obtained her doctorate from Moscow University with a dissertation entitled: 'A comparison between the function of the smile in Russia and its function in Western cultures, together with the historical background.' My teacher spent over three years researching the subject and interviewed hundreds of Russians and non-Russians. A smile in Russian culture, sends a totally different message to that sent by a smile in the West. According to Maria, a smile in Russia – when shown to a stranger – has a negative connotation: 'He's pulling my leg!', or 'He's criticising me!' In Russian, the word 'smile' often evokes a negative feeling. Maria: 'We use the phrase "Enough smiling!" meaning "Cut it out!", while in English you say "Keep smiling" – which means the opposite.'

This concept has presented the main forms of communication exchange and addressed some of the issues involved in the choice of language in business encounters. The management of relations during such encounters has also been examined and this has shown the many facets of communication that people from different cultures need to be mindful of during face-to-face meetings.

The dangers of stereotyping are also ever-present during such encounters and these will be discussed in Chapter 14. The question of interaction between people from different cultures will be examined further in Chapter 18.

ACTIVITY 13.1

English names catch on among Chinese: Young bridging a gap with West

By Jehangir S. Pocha

Di, Chao, Xu, and Wentao now answer to Eddy, Super, Promise and Wendy.

For pragmatic Chinese, adopting English names has long represented a way for them to bridge the linguistic and cultural gap. Now, as China widens its reach abroad and as the number of foreigners living in mainland China swells, picking an English name has become a rite of passage for most young, urban Chinese.

When students enrol in Chinese universities, they routinely are required to pick English names as a way to prepare themselves for life in their increasingly Westernized world. Students race to snap up the 'best' English names on a list the schools circulate.

'Popular names like Michael and Alex go quite fast, and Eddie was already gone before I could choose it,' said Eddy Wu, 19, a student at Beijing Forestry University, explaining that he wanted the name because it sounded like his Chinese name, Di. 'So I said "OK, let me take Eddy with this other spelling." '

People usually adopt only English first names and retain their Chinese family name. The practice is informal and has no legal significance. Sometimes, the results can be quirky, with Chinese names that potentially mystify foreigners often being replaced with English aliases that amuse them.

Super Zhang, 25, a paralegal in Beijing, said he chose his English name because it is a literal translation of his Chinese one, Chao. 'I like to see myself as a great and extraordinary person,' Super said. 'People wonder about my name all the time and are always asking me to explain it. But I still enjoy having it.'

Most Chinese take their English name – its meaning, its sound, and its associations with historic figures – very seriously. Promise Hong, a 30-year-old writer in Beijing, said her English name was a rough translation of her Chinese one, Xu, and that she saw a philosophical connotation in it.

'Promise has more profound meanings especially with the biblical background of the promised land,' she said. 'I began to use it when I was a freshman in college, twelve years ago, and some people I've met have expressed their kind appreciation and curiosity about my choice.'

In nineteenth-century China, choosing an English name was the privilege of only a handful of elites. Possessing one was a status symbol indicating that a person had been to college and rubbed shoulders with the 'laowai', the Puntonghua word for foreigner. The process of picking the name often involved weeks of discussions between the person, English tutors and foreign friends. Chinese sages would then vet the short list of names for their tonal qualities and astrological powers.

That English names are now ubiquitous in urban China is a sign of the country's progress, Eddy said. 'My parents tell me how once any foreigner on the street would be stared at, they were so unusual,' he said. 'Now, China is developing very fast and Chinese are becoming very modern.'

While most Chinese with English names reserve their use for times when they are in the company of foreigners, Eddy said more people, especially young women, prefer using their English names. This is particularly true for Chinese immigrants in the US and other English-speaking countries, who use their Western names to help them fit into their new world.

Wentao Zhang, 40, began calling herself Wendy while living in New Jersey for 15 years. 'It just makes things easier,' she said. 'People (in the US) used to find it really hard to say my name, so I began saying "Just call me Wendy" and it worked really well.'

This phonetic approach, picking a new name that sounds like your original one, sidesteps the pitfalls of trying to find English translations of Chinese names.

Of course, not every Chinese person has an English name. In the sleepy hamlets that dot the countryside, farmers and workers look surprised at the thought of taking an English name. And sometimes, name-changes alone are not enough to bridge the cultural gap.

Apple Li, 21, a travel agent in Beijing, said she chose her English name because her Chinese name is Ping and the Mandarin word for apple is 'pingguo'. But one problem remains: her business card reads Li Ping, since the Chinese write their family name first and given name second.

→

Many foreigners accustomed to the Western format assume that Li means apple in Mandarin, she said. Adding to the confusion is that Li, when written using a certain character, means pear.

Source: *Boston Globe*, 1 October 2006 (www.boston.com/news/world/asia/articles/2006/10/01/english_names_catch_on_among_chinese)

Questions

1. What are the reasons given for young Chinese adopting an English first name?

2. Do you think that this custom can help to improve communication between China and Western countries? Explain why.

3. What changes, if any, do you think the use of English names brings to the Chinese way of doing business? Explain your point of view.

ACTIVITY 13.2

The text below highlights the problem of cultural identity by describing developments in France, a country proud of its language and of the historical importance of French as the language of politics and culture.

Why English is de rigueur in many French boardrooms

By Tom Braithwaite in Paris and Chris Smyth

When Jacques Chirac stormed out of a meeting at the European Union summit, he said it was because he had been 'profoundly shocked' to hear a French industrialist speaking in English. On this basis, the French president may wish to stay away from a number of his nation's boardrooms.

Mr Chirac's outrage was all too visible on Thursday night when he heard Ernest-Antoine Seillière, the head of the Unice employers' organization, explain he had decided to deliver his speech in English because it was 'the language of business'.

But in the boardroom of Air Liquide, the French industrial gases group, meetings are usually held in English. So too at the media group Thomson, once chaired by Thierry Breton, the French finance minister, who joined his president in boycotting Mr Seillière's meeting. At France Telecom – where Mr Breton was also once chairman – English is commonly used in internal memos.

French companies choose English because they do most business outside France and because of an increased foreign presence on their boards. Meetings at Total, the oil group, regularly take place in English, even when only Frenchmen are present. 'It's the language of the oil industry,' explains a spokeswoman. English is also the lingua franca at Thales and EADS – the French government has stakes in both defence groups.

Air France-KLM holds meetings of 'le strategy management committee' in English, while competence in the language is compulsory for managerial recruits at Renault. Mike Quigley, the chief operating officer and heir apparent at the telecoms equipment maker Alcatel, is an Australian who does not speak French. 'The English language has connotations of liberalism,' said Jean-Louis Muller, the director of Cegos, a management training school. 'The defence of the French language by politicians and unions is the defence of the French social model.'

Mr Muller said the rise of English in French boardrooms appeared unstoppable: 'I witnessed a meeting at [engineering group] Alstom where there were only French managers in the room but English was still the language.'

Source: *Financial Times*, 25, March, 2006: 8.

Questions

1. What may explain the sudden departure by the president of France when a French industrialist used English to address the summit meeting?

2. Why, according to the interviews, is English used more and more in French boardrooms?

3. What, according to Jean-Louis Muller, do French and English seem to represent in terms of cultural identity?

Conclusion

This chapter gives a brief outline of the theory of communication, which is indispensable to a better understanding of intercultural communication. Even if language remains the dominant factor in communication situations, there are other elements which come into play, including the context, proxemics and facial expressions.

Even if they share a common language (English being increasingly used in business by non-native speakers), interlocutors may still experience problems because of their cultural backgrounds. Developments in computer-mediated communication in particular are changing forms of communication. The numerous examples given in this chapter allow a better understanding of the new framework of intercultural business communication.

Points for reflection

1. The concept examined three possibilities with regard to the use of language during a business encounter. A fourth possibility is for the manager in question to learn the target language and employ translators.

   What advantages does this combination afford those involved?

2. When two people from different cultures meet in a business situation, the interaction, which is specific to each situation, does not allow the protagonists to be certain of the outcome of their encounter.

   What, in your opinion, are the factors which can influence the outcome of an intercultural interaction? Explain how these factors can influence the outcome.

Further reading

Gudykunst, W.B. (ed) (2004) *Cross-Cultural and Intercultural Communication,* Thousand Oaks, CA: Sage. In his role as editor, W.B. Gudykunst has chosen to classify the contributions from experts in the field into two distinct categories: cross-cultural communication and intercultural communication. The difference lies essentially in the subject area being researched. Intercultural communication includes all aspects of the study of culture and communication. Cross-cultural communication research tends to be comparative and focuses on cultural communication – the role of communication – and cultural identities. The book covers such topics as: language and verbal communication across cultures; non-verbal communication across cultures; cultural influences on the expression and perception of emotions; identity and inter-group communication; communication in intercultural relationships; and adapting to an unfamiliar culture.

References

Corraze, J. (1988) *Les communications non-verbales*, 4th ed, Paris: Presses Universitaires de France.

Donnadieu, G. and Karsky, M. (2002) *La systémique*, Rueil-Malmaison, France: Editions Liaisons

Hall, E.T. (1966) *The Hidden Dimension*, New York, NY: Bantam Doubleday Dell.

Hall, E.T. (1969) *The Hidden Dimension: Man's use of space in public and private*, London: Bodley Head.

Hall, E.T. and Hall, M.R. (1990) *Understanding Cultural Differences*, Yarmouth, ME: Intercultural Press ANC.

Herring, S. (1996) *Computer-Mediated Communication: Linguistic, social and cross-cultural perspectives*, Amsterdam: John Benjamins. Quoted in: Waldvogel, J. (2001): 7–8.

Ladmiral, J.R. and Lipiansky, E.M. (1989) *La communication interculturelle*, Paris : Armand Colin.

Mead, R. (1990) *Cross-Cultural Management Communication*, Chichester: John Wiley.

Sauer, D. (2007) 'Gimlach', *Het Parool*, 16 June: 13.

Trumble, A. (2004) *A Brief History of the Smile*, New York, NY: Basic.

Waldvogel, J. (2001) 'Email and workplace communication: a literature review,' Wellington, New Zealand: Victoria University of Wellington (www.vuw.ac.nz/lals/research/lwp/docs/ops/op3.htm).

Watson, O.M. (1970) *Proxemic behavior*, The Hague: Mouton. Quoted by Corraze, J. (1988) *Les communications non-verbales*, 179.

Chapter 14

Barriers to intercultural communication

Apart from the framework of reference examined in Chapter 13 and the context of the communication, other elements play an important role. These are essentially barriers to the communication process, as described in Figure III.1 when the sender and receiver in the diagram are from different cultures, communication may prove to be ineffective through misunderstanding that may even cause a breakdown in the process. These barriers will be examined in the concept of this chapter.

Concept 14.1 examines the obstacles preventing the effective flow of information within an organization. These obstacles relate to either the failure of individuals to communicate effectively, or the failure of systems to make effective communication possible. The breakdown in communication is often to do with either too much information (information overload) or too little information, or it can be caused by communication that is misplaced, inaccurate or incomplete. It may also involve the context: personal and environmental factors can impair the quality of the information received. The context of communication is often complicated by the question of culture, with misunderstandings occurring when the sender and receiver do not share similar meanings for the communicated symbols.

Learning outcomes

After reading this chapter you will gain an understanding of:

- Those components of communication that can create obstacles in intercultural communication.
- The importance of the effects that barriers have on communication in business.

Concept 14.1   Barriers in cross-cultural management communication

What are communication barriers?

Ideally, for communication to take place, the frameworks of reference being used, with regard to norms, for example, should not be in conflict. However, since a framework of reference is to a considerable degree culturally determined, it is to be expected that the communication between individuals from two different cultures will be disturbed.

Some problems of this nature can occur when doing business with foreign partners, working with foreign colleagues in the same company, or within a joint venture with a foreign company. Communication problems may happen not only during meetings or negotiations but also during informal situations: a barrier can lead to a missed business opportunity and/or a business relationship ending on the rocks.

Such disturbing factors between cultures are many in number and nature (see Figure III.1). Breakdowns in communication commonly occur when the context of the message being communicated between the sender and receiver is unclear. Some barriers to communication originate from cultural misunderstandings between the speaker and receiver and these can clearly be of great importance for communication in business. Before looking at these barriers in detail, this chapter will discuss some notions that offer insights into the causes of misunderstandings in communication between cultures.

Non-verbal behaviour as barrier

Is non-verbal behaviour natural or cultural? Is it productive (monologue) or communicative (dialogue)? Is it done voluntarily or spontaneously? We know from the many researchers who have investigated this phenomenon that antiquity was also fascinated by it and, moreover, that non-verbal communication plays an important role in communication as a whole. What this term encompasses is so large that this discussion must confine itself to gestures, facial expression (including affective expressions such as laughter or showing anger), posture and the distance between sender and receiver. These are all closely allied to or indeed replace verbal communication in terms of producing messages. They may even contradict the accompanying verbal messages. In short, all these also have a communicative value over and above verbal communication.

Meta-communication and verbal behaviour

In its basic form, a meta-communication is an act of communication between two agents that also communicates something about the communication itself, or about the relationship between the two agents, or both.

In terms of non-verbal behaviour, meta-communicative functions can also include:

- making gestures to complete messages when information is missing (e.g. when gesturing to indicate someone's height or size);
- making hand gestures and modulating the voice to reinforce the verbal message by adding rhythm and emphasis;
- replacing spoken language when it is impossible for some reason (physical barriers, the dominance of other sounds).

The nature of this meta-communicative behaviour is determined by personal, social, relational and cultural factors. The nature of the interaction itself may be modified on the one hand by the intended character of the non-verbal signal of the sender and on the other hand by the way the receiver reacts to the signal.

The cultural dimension of non-verbal behaviour is apparent once the body language used by interlocutors from different cultures is compared and contrasted. The interactional nature of face-to-face communication therefore takes on an intercultural dimension. All cultures use forms of body language to communicate, but the meaning of these forms is subject to different interpretations according to the cultural background of the interpreter.

Non-verbal interaction

Although facial expressions communicating anger, sadness and fear are considered to be universal, the causes of these expressions may be different. Other gestures, however, may not be so universal: a nod of the head may well be expected to indicate affirmation and a shake negation, but some cultures nod to negate and shake to affirm (for example the Greeks give a shake of the head to say 'yes'). When a speaker raises his shoulders, this could convey indifference, resignation or ignorance, depending on the cultural context. On the other hand, to convey the idea that someone is stupid can be conveyed in several ways, depending on the cultural context. If the gesture or expression made is unknown in another culture, then its meaning will not be understood. Communication could be interrupted or, if an incorrect meaning is applied by the 'receiver', diverted.

When those interacting come from different cultures, the non-verbal signals used in a certain context may therefore not only differ but also necessarily influence other consequent non-verbal signals. Furthermore, the question of the intention behind non-verbal language must also be addressed. How is it possible to determine whether the sender (if from another culture) has intentionally chosen to transmit a non-verbal message with an exact purpose or whether he is pretending to do so? The receiver is expected to respond to the signal given by the sender who in turn may need to re-adjust his communicative goal, vary the non-verbal messages so that the desired goal is eventually reached. Non-verbal behaviour can therefore be crucial in face-to-face interaction.

Those communicating across cultures must therefore be careful not to assume that certain gestures have the same meaning as in their own culture. In France, for example, pulling one's eyelid down with the forefinger means 'I don't believe you!' In Italy, however, the same gesture means something very different: 'I'm keeping an eye on you!'

Since gestures are a purely cultural acquisition, they also reveal certain characteristics of a culture's collective mentality. Let us compare the expression 'to be fed up with...' or 'have had enough of...' in France and the Netherlands (Figure 14.1).

Figure 14.1 'I've had enough!'

The gesture for these words is made in the same way by raising one's hand to the head. However, there is a crucial difference as to where the hand movement stops. In France, the hand stops at the top of the head but in the Netherlands it stops earlier – at the neck. Therefore, in this example, it is more than only a difference of gesture: the gesture represents a cultural attitude that here expresses either the limit of exasperation or loss of patience.

We can only make tentative explanations about how certain gestures and body language generally came into being. This is due to the unstable nature of the values of gestures associated with a language. If, for example, we look at the past with Cresswell (1968), he reminds us that in the eighteenth century there was disapproval of the tendency of the English to use gestures when speaking. A century later, however, the English were characterized for their 'phlegm', their calm self-possession.

Non-verbal communication barriers in business

Verbal communication is essential in business contacts. Language differences can therefore be a dominant factor in any communication barrier and can even be an insurmountable one. Just as with translating from one language to another, it can be difficult to convey the full meaning and nuances can be lost. As seen in Chapter 13, using English as a means of communication can make the situation easier when doing business, but this does not mean, of course, that misunderstandings do not occur. This applies even to native speakers of English who come from different countries.

Non-verbal communication can also be a source of misunderstanding and irritation. For example, research carried out into the use of body language by Dutch and French people from a similar business environment showed how great the differences were. When using gestures, for example, the French are very expressive and use the whole upper part of their body. The Dutch, on the other hand, usually limit gestures to the use of their arms – or just one arm – to emphasize the rhythm of their speech. When the Dutch are interacting with the French they can easily come to the conclusion that their interlocutors are very emotional and excited since, in their culture, such 'exaggerated' use of gestures is only witnessed when very strong emotions are at play.

Silence can also be a cause of misunderstandings, particularly between Western and Asian cultures. In Western cultures, silence marks pauses in a discourse. These pauses must not last too long, unlike those in oriental cultures where any time without a word being spoken is an integral part of communication. In Thailand, for example, silence is not only a sign of respect, of agreement or disagreement, but it is also highly appreciated as a style of discourse. Asian cultures discourage verbalization since it contradicts the principle of modesty. In Korea, silence is preferable to the improper use of words. Japan, however, appears to be the exception: even if silence is preferred to verbalization, it can also be considered as being impolite in situations where active participation by the interlocutors is expected. This is especially the case where an interlocutor is a stranger; remaining silent 'is considered more negative than it is in America' (Tae-Seop Lim, 2003: 62).

It should be said at this point that such examples of non-verbal communication are simply styles of communication and do not indicate that a particular culture experiences more or less emotion. However, the way all sorts of feelings are expressed can be so different between cultures that it can result in representatives of one culture having negative feelings towards another. The creation of such prejudices is not the differences in themselves but the way in which the differences are interpreted.

Assumptions and culture

Cultural assumptions evolve as basic human responses to fundamental problems. Usunier and Lee (2005) provide a framework for the evaluation of the problems and combine three dimensions. Assumptions may have: a cognitive dimension, related to presumptions as to how people think that things work; an affective dimension, related to the presumed likings of people; and a directive dimension related to the presumed choices of people.

Cultural assumptions can be related to time, space or identity. Time-related cultural assumptions relate to four common questions:

- Is time considered as a scarce good (economy of time)?
- Are tasks performed simultaneously or one after the other (monochronic versus polychronic)?
- Is life seen as a continuity or as cyclic episodes?
- Is the orientation in time towards the past, the present or the future?

Cultural assumptions that are space-related have to do with being 'in' or 'out'; being a member or not; belonging or not belonging. The strict opposition defines the content of the 'out-group' and 'in group' whereby the group space includes – or excludes – families, nations and cultures. Out-group orientation is based on the assumption that there is a unity of mankind beyond the borders of in-group spaces. In-group orientation does not completely exclude out-group orientation as can be seen in, for example, Nordic European cultures, where a strong sense of national identity goes along with a strong commitment to the development of the poorest nations and international organizations.

Identity-related assumptions relate to self and others and are about the ideal conduct in certain social contexts. They are related to the main socio-demographic categories (age, sex, social class), as well as to particular roles in society (such as the perfect politician, or successful businessman).

Cultural assumptions are difficult for foreigners to detect because they are not easily expressed and are for the most part hardly understood by the insiders. As seen in Part One, statements may be given about values and ideas, but the underlying assumptions are generally unclear. There is a gap between the explanations people give for their behaviour and the real motives for the behaviour. In the same way, there is a difference between what people say and what people want to say. (Schneider and Barsoux, 2003). That is why assumptions can generate a lack of understanding and misunderstandings when people from different cultures are communicating.

Barriers

Apart from a system of values, every culture has assumptions that are seldom tested for their justifiability. These are affirmations, which are mostly normative in nature, about what is true and what is not. To be accepted in a culture or subculture, one has to respect this system. What 'should be done' is generally close to what is believed to be the 'nature of things'. However, assumptions about 'how things are' are often disguised suppositions about 'how they should be'. Moreover, once the values of a group are institutionalized and assimilated, they acquire a kind of existential validity for the members of the group. Sometimes, a value acts as a self-fulfilling prophecy and causes behaviour that complies with the idea, e.g. 'men don't cry' (Oomkes, 1987).

As such, assumptions can create all kinds of problems. A simple example from the business world shows how they can even lead to conflict (Case study 14.1). Imagine you receive an order confirmation from a supplier stating that the delivery date of the order will be two weeks. The question is: what does a Dutch supplier mean by delivery date compared with a French supplier?

Case study 14.1

Delivery date: two weeks

Paul had recently begun working as the purchasing manager of a French-owned company in the Netherlands. He was in a bad mood because of a delay resulting from a bottle-neck. His mood worsened when he read a memo on his desk. The memo informed him that an order to be supplied by the parent company had not yet been delivered, although it should have arrived two weeks previously.

Delivery delays had almost become a routine problem in his dealings with the parent company. He sent a very business-like reply stating briefly, in English, that he had not yet received the goods on order and that they must be delivered as soon as possible, otherwise he would have to turn to an outside supplier.

The reply came by email, three pages of it, written in French by Jacques, the production manager. His tone was friendly:

> We have done everything possible but you see, what with the renovation of the production area and the holiday period, as well as the specifications of your order, there has been a delay. But don't worry: it's only a question of time now - a little patience and all will be fine.

Paul was flabbergasted by what he considered to be French arrogance. His reaction was as follows:

> Firstly, I don't understand French, and secondly, the delivery date had been clearly indicated in the order, namely in two weeks' time. The two weeks have elapsed and now it's a simple matter of whether the goods are here or not. That's the only thing that counts here.

A Dutch supplier will in all likelihood think that the product must be delivered within two weeks: he feels contractually bound to this delivery time. A French supplier, however, may well think that he will do everything he can to dispatch the goods by the date given. For him this date is a promise that is still subject to negotiation.

This problem of interpretation is not a language issue but a cultural one. The words are clear, but the assumptions underlying the words may differ from culture to culture. This can also be seen in the use of words describing time such as 'soon' or 'straightaway'. Does that mean in one minute or an hour? These words can have a very different meaning in Indonesia than in Germany.

Perceptions and stereotypes

Table 14.1 is an example used in Europe as an introduction to the question of stereotypes. In the hand right-column is a list of stereotypical remarks made by or about a number of Western cultures given in the left column. Can you work out which nationality says what about whom?

Table 14.1 Who is saying what about whom?

Who/About whom?	What?
Germans	*They're pretentious*
British	*They've got no sense of humour*
Americans	*They're chauvinist*
Spaniards	*They're hypocritical*
Dutch	*They're arrogant*
French	*They're individualistic*

Source: Gruère and Morel (1991).

The French could be the subject of all the stereotypical remarks in Table 14.1. The Germans consider the French to be showy, the Americans see them as chauvinistic, the Spanish as hypocritical, and the Dutch view them as the embodiment of arrogance. The British may even see them as having no sense of humour. And the French see themselves as individualistic.

However, all the comments given on the right could be applied by the nationalities in question to each other. Some generally perceived stereotypical characteristics could emerge: the British could well consider that the Germans have no sense of humour. They are very serious and any humour a German displays does not fit into the British concept of what is funny. The Dutch could well consider the French as chauvinist. They see themselves as being much more tolerant of other nationalities than the French and do not so readily express their feelings of superiority. All the European nationalities could well consider the Americans to be arrogant. In their eyes the Americans may come over as people who wish to impose on others what they think is best for them. Europeans may consider themselves superior to the Americans, but do not express their feelings of superiority so crassly.

Every culture sees its own system of values in a positive light. So when asked to apply a stereotypical characteristic to itself, every culture listed above could, for example, refer to itself as being individualistic because in the West this is generally considered to be a positive trait.

However, if individuals of a specific nationality within a multicultural group are confronted with negative rather than positive stereotypes of themselves by other nationalities, these individuals will, according to Lipianski (1992), not recognize themselves in the profile made. They will react strongly because they feel personally under attack and deny belonging to the group being characterized. They will defend their own personal identity and see their national identity more in terms of 'them' rather than 'us'.

Identity and communication

National identity therefore appears first as a compulsory image imposed by the outside world. It may characterize people with the same nationality, but it is an identity which the people may not recognize in themselves. In intercultural encounters, this identity dimension influences communication. Indeed, there is no communication without identity and identification of the persons present. According to Ladmiral and Lipianski (1989: 145), when people meet for the first time it is difficult to avoid asking and answering questions to do with identity (Who are you? Where do you come from?). For these authors: 'It is a question of knowing at the same moment the identity of my interlocutor and what elements of my own identity (sexual, social, professional, national, ideological) are going to be required during our exchange.'

However, identity can also appear as an obstacle to communication because the identity of both interlocutors defines and sets the limits of the exchange. The conflicts of ideas, opinions, and interpretations – also in the interpersonal relations between individuals of different nationalities – refer to identity conflicts: on the one hand, the alter ego – the double who reflects our own image – and on the other hand, the opponent for whom we feel aversion. (Ladmiral and Lipianski, 1989). The perception of the other always has a projective nature and can only have one's own culture as base and reference. This phenomenon is called **ethnocentrism** and refers to the values of one's own culture even when dealing with others who cannot share these values.

> Likewise, the tendency exists to describe and judge the value systems and dominant practices of other cultures from the standpoint of one's own. Such an attitude has connections with the stereotyping of others.
>
> Edgar and Sedgwick, 2002: 133

Ethnocentrism is inherent to any membership of a socio-cultural, ethnic or national group. It is the intrinsic mechanism of distinction separating mine from yours, relatives from foreigners, people here from people elsewhere. Ethnocentrism is both a cultural feature and a psychological phenomenon. It leads to any perception being made through a barrier that is unconsciously made up of our own values. Ethnocentrism, in its most simplified and elementary form, is responsible for forming prejudices and stereotypes – 'ready-for-use judgments' (Ladmiral and Lipianski: 138).

Stereotypes can be a disturbing factor not only in communication, but also in other areas of management. As seen in Chapter 11, it is advisable in marketing to tread very carefully when it comes to stereotyping across consumer nationalities.

Exhibit 14.1

'Unleash the power of the Hispanic market by avoiding these pitfalls'

By Mary Baroutakis

While writing this article, I tried to narrow down the number of pitfalls that marketers encounter when advertising to the Hispanic market. There are many, but for the sake of brevity, I will address the three that I come across most frequently:

- overusing Hispanic traits in ads;
- cloning a general market strategy for use in the Hispanic market; and
- keeping Hispanic advertising less ambitious and far more conservative than that aimed at the general market.

Overusing Hispanic traits

We have all heard again and again that Hispanics are very family-oriented; that they are very close to their extended family; that they take care of their elders; that children tend to live at home after they reach 18. We've also heard that Hispanics tend to be emotional and sentimental. They listen to their hearts a lot and value relationships.

This brings me to the first common mistake: the overuse of the above traits in Hispanic advertising and how this can sometimes weaken or cloud a selling message.

A few years ago, a telecommunications company aired a commercial introducing a new plan for international callers to Latin America. The commercial was absolutely beautiful. It was shot on location in many parts of Latin America and the scenery was breathtaking. It showed vignettes of people abroad receiving calls from their family in the US. The background music score was very nostalgic.

The research company that pre-tested this commercial uncovered very positive findings for the client. After a couple of months on the air, however, the amount of calls to the free phone number in the commercial seeking more information was very disappointing. The client was perplexed. What happened? Why was there was so little interest?

The client contacted us because they wanted another firm to re-test the spot. We did so and found, to the client's and agency's amazement, that the first research company had misread the results. Even though the target audience understood the main message and liked the spot, all they retained were the bittersweet images of the people back home, the beautiful scenery and the feeling of nostalgia for their family and country. The execution had gone overboard using warm-and-fuzzy family scenes and nostalgia to sell its product. After people saw this commercial at home, they made a call – but not to the free number to inquire about the calling plan. Instead, they called their mother, or their grandmother or their sister in Latin America. They had been distracted by these warm scenes and completely forgot about the calling plan!

Our client decided to start from scratch. A new commercial was shot based on our findings and recommendations. In this new spot, the calling plan was 'the hero' – not the family or the scenery. It was a happy commercial but also one that provided factual information about the calling plan. This new commercial broke all previous records in number of calls received and new subscribers to the plan.

Cloning the general market

The next pitfall is using a general market strategy for the Hispanic market. Generally, marketers like to do this because it keeps everything nice and organized. It is also the path of least resistance: upper management will buy into their plans faster and it's easier to deal with one strategy.

Using a general market strategy may be effective but this can only be determined after testing various options.

I can't count the number of times that marketers have decided to use a general market approach before any testing has been conducted among the intended Hispanic target.

Before taking this step, advertisers must be sure that this will be the most compelling strategy. It isn't that the general market strategy is plain wrong, it's just not the one that will attract most Hispanic consumers. An even worse scenario is forcing the use of a general market commercial (re-shot with Hispanic actors) to target Hispanics.

Here's an example of both pitfalls. A while back, we tested a commercial for a drink that was being sold as 'offbeat and wacky' in the general market. The client wanted to define the brand the same way in the Hispanic market, so a number of commercials were produced using this strategy. By the way, this was the first time this client had advertised to the Hispanic market and this was the first piece of Hispanic research it had conducted. In other words, without knowing if this wacky, offbeat personality would sell in the Hispanic market, the client and the agency had already produced five radio commercials, which we were going to test.

The focus group participants rejected this strategy. Unfamiliar with this drink's general market spots, Hispanics had their own image of the product – they saw it as fun and friendly – and what was being presented went against that perception. They felt that this product, as presented in the radio executions, was for weird, confused people!

We also tested a commercial for an ice-cream brand that was a word-for-word adaptation of the general market spot. In this case, the spot used humour to make its point – American humour translated into Spanish.

The spot features a couple of vignettes. One tested well, the other did not. It shows a little boy telling his father that he's going to wash the family car. What he neglects to say is that he intends to use a scouring pad. When the father finds out, the announcer comes on and tells him: 'Relax, and enjoy some of our ice cream.' No one saw the situation as funny. And, everyone agreed that this would not be the right time to enjoy this product.

Inordinate caution

Another mistake advertisers make quite frequently is 'holding back their horses', in other words, running more 'in-the-box,' less ambitious advertising in the Hispanic

263

market. Hispanic consumers complain about this phenomenon all the time.

Why does this happen? Many reasons are cited. The one we hear most often from Hispanic agencies is that Hispanic production budgets are much lower than those allocated for the general market. But we all know that big budgets don't always lead to great commercials nor do low budgets result in poor advertising.

There is another possible reason, however, for creating less-ambitious Hispanic ads – the idea that simplistic, innocuous commercials are good enough for the Hispanic market or even worse, that 'out-of-the-box' commercials do not appeal or are not understood by Hispanic consumers.

How many times have we heard the phrase 'Hispanics take everything literally'? This is generally true in instances where the audience is looking for concrete information. It should not be used as an excuse, however, to lower standards in the Hispanic market.

Less ambitious, more run-of-the-mill advertising falls short of achieving goals, especially with Hispanic teenagers and young adults who are bilingual and also watch American TV and tend to compare the Spanish with the English language ads.

For example, we tested some commercials for a sports drink that strongly appeals to Hispanic male teens and young adults. They complained that the Hispanic commercials for this product constantly showed young males like themselves playing different sports (basketball, soccer, baseball) in different venues (the park, the beach, the gym). These commercials may be new but they always come across as old and tired. These consumers couldn't help comparing them with the general market commercials, which they described as cutting-edge. And the question remains: why does a leading-edge product use tired, run-of-the-mill commercials to attract its Hispanic target?

Unfortunately, the root of many of these marketing mistakes is the result of preconceived notions or impressions about ethnic markets. When it comes to the general market, no client expects its agency or researchers to be experts on Americans and the American way of life.

Think for example what you would say as an American if someone asked you 'What are Americans like?' You probably wouldn't even know where to start or what to say. The American market is not a static market. New things happen all the time and that's why studies are conducted every day. You would never ask such a general question of your agency or researchers. Yet this question is asked every day of Hispanic agencies, consultants and primary researchers. What is odd is that there are people who answer this question, ignoring the fact that things are constantly changing in the Hispanic market as well.

Recommendations

What can be done to correct these problems and avoid these pitfalls? Stick to a few principles:

- Watch Hispanic TV once in a while. It's not enough to know what your competition is doing – you need to see what other advertisers are doing as well. For instance, if you see that too many commercials are similar in style to yours, then your commercial may not be working as hard for you as it should.
- Be bold in your Hispanic ads. Don't be afraid to try something new. Get out of that box!
- If possible, view some ads currently running in Latin America – any ads, not necessarily the ones for your category – and remember that these are the ads that the more recent immigrants have been accustomed to before coming to the US. You might be surprised!
- Be as demanding of your Hispanic agency/consultant as you are of your general market agency. Ask for evidence, not opinions.
- Finally, after you've worked with a Hispanic researcher, ask yourself: 'Is this person or organization just as good as my favourite general market supplier?' If the answer is no, then you may be getting less than excellent work when you conduct Hispanic research.

Source: *Quirk's Marketing Research Review,* April 2000, article 20000402 (www.quirks.com/articles/a2000/20000402.aspx?searchID=2071341).

Consumer attitudes and perceptions about foreign products are highly influenced by ethnocentrism, the belief in the superiority of one's own ethnic group. Usunier and Lee (2005) report that highly ethnocentric consumers, who are usually elder people, are likely to believe that purchasing imported products harms the domestic economy and causes unemployment. Younger consumers, they found, were less affected by ethnocentricity. This means that domestic companies may benefit to a certain extent from ethnocentrism, but also that the resistance that foreign companies may meet to their products will depend on the product category (e.g. wine, cars) and the consumers targeted.

Having seen how stereotypes can be a disturbing factor in marketing as well as communication, we need to examine the way stereotypes are formed.

Building stereotypes

In specifically cultural terms, the starting-point for building stereotypes is the norms and values of the culture concerned. When someone from that culture judges someone from another culture, the tendency is for that person to do so using these norms and values. If the person being judged does not conform to these in some way through their behaviour – or simply appearance – then a negative judgement will probably be made.

A stereotype is a series of images created in our minds with regard to a group or groups of people, in this context: cultural groups. These images are over-generalizations made through selective perceptions (self-perceptions) and information that corresponds with our beliefs. A stereotype is therefore a confirmation of prejudices rather than the result of accurate observations of reality.

The development of prejudices, which are a 'distinct combination of feelings, inclinations to act and beliefs' (Myers, 2005: 333), is supported or provoked by our cultural environment: family, friends and the media can fill us with stereotyping images of all kinds. Comments, jokes, commercials and anecdotes can create and perpetuate stereotypes, categorize nationalities in a way that sustains a culture's norms and values.

Case study 14.2 illustrates how a prejudice can lead to unjustifiable behaviour of one group towards another.

Case study 14.2

The misunderstood marketing manager

A Dutch company wanted to introduce a new product into its range. On-site production would be too costly and, besides, there was a US company already manufacturing this product.

The marketing manager decided to phone this supplier. 'Yes' was their reaction, but only if a large quantity were to be ordered. The minimum amount they stated was much more than the Dutch market would warrant. When told this, the US manufacturer suggested the Dutch company contact a partner of theirs operating in France.

So the marketing manager phoned the French company. Talking in French to the manager of the production department, he gave the name of this company in the usual way, explaining that he would like to buy this product because the US company was unable to supply the small amount which they required. The Dutchman was told to put his request in writing.

The Dutchman was really shocked by this reaction and accused the French of being odd. Why could they not simply give him the information he required over the phone?

The French manager had asked for a request in writing because the Dutch marketing manager had put forward his query without any preliminaries, and had not fully introduced his company. The Frenchman could not therefore 'place' the person on the other end of the phone. He needed to know exactly which company he was doing business with, and the identity of the man proposing the co-operation in the first place.

After he had put down the phone, the Frenchman wondered: 'Who the hell was this guy with the funny accent?'

Case study 14.3

Delete stereotypes!

ICT is a male profession! In Malaysia, such a statement raises smiles. In the faculty of information technologies of Kuala Lumpur, the capital, all those in positions of responsibility in the department are women, including the dean. In Penang, 65 per cent of the ICT students and seven of the ten ICT professors are women, as well as the dean. The head of the department says she has never considered ICT as a male discipline: 'I do not see anything male in ICT!'. The reasons she gives are that ICT is clean work, does not require much physical strength, is an activity exercised in the service sector, and allows those employed in it to work at home. In contrast, outside Malaysia, ICT is a very masculine sector. In France, it is the only scientific profession where there has been a very large fall in the proportion of females employed.

Source: Extract from Isabelle Collet (2007), 'L'informatique a-t-elle un sexe?' *Le Monde Diplomatique*, June: 3.

To summarize the building process of stereotypes, it can be said that prejudices, which may be positive or negative in nature, are basic, irrational reactions that depend simply on how someone views the group in question in terms of their own cultural preferences. People may be classified in some way socially on the basis of a perception of common attributes: people may perceive them as members of an 'in-group', sharing a system of values or as members of an 'out-group' whose values counter theirs in some way. As prejudices are confirmed over and over again through such selective perceptions, people develop stereotypical images that come quickly to mind and which serve to legitimize the statements people make about another culture. However, as indicated earlier, cultural stereotypes may also display positive traits, particularly when people perceive that there are aspects of another culture's norms and values that reflect their own and in an exemplary way.

This issue of prejudices and stereotypes is illustrated in Case study 14.3. Most people regard the information and computer technology (ICT) sector to be a male preserve. This is indeed the case, since the majority of ICT workers in most countries are male. Malaysia, however, is an exception. This may seem surprising for a country where the government has resorted to aggressive social policies such as the 'Islamicization' of Malaysian institutions (Fontaine and Richardson, 2003).

However, stereotypes are not always based on prejudices. A stereotype may have an intrinsic quality as shown in the passage below on the perception of Confucianism in the world of business.

Stereotypes in the Confucian business world

Cazal (1993) raises the question of stereotypes in business relating to Confucianism. This system of thought was referred to in Chapter 2 when the importance of loyalty in Chinese business relations was being discussed. Cazal wonders how present-day Confucianism, which he defines as 'a specific discourse constructed to maintain the economic development and performance of [Asian-run] companies' (Cazal, 1993: 188) is perceived in the West and in Asia. He reminds us of an important characteristic of Confucianism whereby formal value is attached to status in the sense that a person in a subordinate position must behave in a way that conforms to that of his interlocutor. Nowadays, however, a subordinate is not expected to adhere to these Confucian principles.

Foreigners, especially those who have lived in South Korea, observe that Confucianism still survives in social relations, such as those within the hierarchy based on age, gender and qualifications. Although these people still see that it reflects a philosophy which rests on the principle of harmony, they consider the majority of the stereotypes resulting from it as being negative in nature. Some Asians are critical of Confucianism, seeing it as a 'cultural alibi for political, social and managerial abuses' (Cazal, 1993: 190). Cazal ends up by questioning whether present-day Confucianism is itself a stereotype since its principles are far from the founding precepts in the teachings of Confucius. Even if classic Confucianism serves as a reference, this doctrine as applied in countries such as China, South Korea and Japan lacks unity and homogeneity.

Several articles have commented on and misrepresented Confucian thought. And that explains why doubt can be cast on the unity of Confucianism as a doctrine in countries such as China, South Korea and Japan, even if this unity is to be found at a practical level.

Dealing with stereotypes

The question remains: what is the best way of dealing with prejudices and stereotypes? Is it best to try and suppress them, fight against them or simply ignore them? The best route may lie in the views of those anthropologists (including Caroll (1987) and Hall (1983)), who approach the question of cultural differences without battling against stereotypes or without creating stereotypes to replace the old ones. It is better when dealing with other cultures not to fight against stereotypes and prejudices. A stereotype is, after all, the first stage in the process whereby the existence of another culture is acknowledged.

Furthermore, it can be argued that stereotypes are a necessary way of establishing one's own cultural identity. If a cultural group cannot compare itself with other groups then it cannot become aware of what it is. All its characteristics must be perceived in terms of those characteristics of others. In this context, a stereotype can be seen as an articulation of this differentiation, even though it is based on prejudices and imperfect information.

Moreover, if stereotypes were to be somehow set aside, the vacuum created would inevitably be filled by those who had set them aside. In other words, the culture of these people would be perceived as the one and only culture in the world – the worst of all prejudices.

Nevertheless, cross-cultural researchers are attempting to find perception areas that cultures share, rather than the differences. In the best of all possible worlds, people would be able to place another culture in its own context and so avoid judging a culture on the basis of their own 'system'. Only then would stereotypes eventually disappear.

Finally, it should be noted that there is a dynamic element present when two people are communicating, namely interaction. Not only do the specific characteristics of the speakers play a role, but also the structure of the situation and the context, as well as time and space (see Chapter 13). If you are aware of the barriers when communicating with your interlocutor, this does not mean that you are unable to conduct the conversation well. The variable nature of the interaction makes every communicative situation unique and therefore unpredictable.

Every culture proposes a structure which, even if it is not unchanging, forces its members to conform to it, and it is by the process of communication that it succeeds in doing so. Furthermore, as seen in this chapter, the encounters between cultures often destabilize the process of communication, create barriers and lack of understanding between the interlocutors. At the same time, thanks to these intercultural contacts, the expression of a culture evolves – and thereby the way it communicates – without any loss of identity.

On the contrary, this identity is maintained because, according to Todorov (1986: 16), 'the relations between cultures is per se an element of culture'.

The concepts described in Chapters 13 and 14 can be used as a basis for any form of communication in the professional domain. The following chapters will deal with the application of these concepts in specific domains such as international negotiation and international teamwork.

ACTIVITY 14.1

FT

Read the text below and answer questions which follow.

Germans aim to spring a World Cup surprise: they're fun

Soft power: The nation long seen as dull is plotting an image overhaul that could help it punch its weight on the international stage

By Hugh Williamson

For the host country Germany, next month's football World Cup is about a lot more than its (pretty slim) chances of lifting the trophy. An image overhaul for Europe's largest economy is the prize in its sights.

Robert Rode, a Berlin bus driver, understands the scale of the challenge. A stocky man with a strong local accent who speaks little English, he was one of 4,000 drivers who recently struggled through a 'World Cup language course'. Taking a break from learning how to guide fans through Berlin, he says that, despite the tongue-twisting, the course was worth it. 'When people arrive in Berlin, say at the airport or main station, and the first German they talk to is a bus driver who either cannot understand them or tells them to go and ask someone else, then that doesn't create a very good impression.'

Mr Rode is in good company. True to the tournament motto 'A time to make friends', chancellor Angela Merkel and her government, leading companies and cultural organizations and dozens of local authorities, have planned thousands of initiatives in the most ambitious attempt by a country to alter the way it is viewed. Ms Merkel heralded the tournament as 'a unique chance for Germany to present itself as a welcoming, tolerant and modern country, bursting with ideas'.

But as teams arrive in Germany this week ahead of kick-off on June 9, a senior German official is disarmingly candid. 'The world generally sees us in a positive, but one-sided way. A bit like the cars and household goods for which we are famous, Germans are seen as efficient, reliable but a touch boring. We need to show we are more than this: friendly, surprising and fun.' At stake is more than national *amour propre*. The transformation is seen as vital if Berlin is to maximise the country's post-reunification potential on the world stage.

The business community alone has invested more than €10m ($12.8m, £6.8m) to promote Germany as a 'Land of Ideas'. 'An opportunity of this kind will not return for another 50 years,' says Franz Beckenbauer, president of the German tournament organising committee.

Since 1990, Germany has stepped up its public diplomacy, as it has increased its role in international peacekeeping operations and intensified efforts to gain a permanent United Nations Security Council seat. Its World Cup campaign marks not only a new milestone in its engagement with the world but also a form of laboratory experiment in whether image offensives work.

Many are sceptical. A German ambassador, who declined to be named, argues: 'You can't market a country like a washing powder. To believe you can just tell others that, all of a sudden we [Germans] have become funny and good looking, is wrong. You can't deceive people.'

Germany's endeavour, which started three years ago, includes a €30m arts programme linking soccer and culture: a 'friendly service campaign' involving handbooks on how to welcome foreign guests; and giant sculptures in Berlin of football boots and aspirins to illustrate the wonders of German creativity.

Attempts to stir national pride raise some discomfiting parallels, however. 'You can't conquer history, or wash it away by just being happy,' says Ulrich Maly, mayor of Nuremberg, the city infamous for Hitler's Nazi party rallies where England is due to play one of its games.

Meanwhile, Volker Perthes, director of Berlin's Institute for International and Security Affairs, points out that in twenty years, West Germany went from post-war international pariah to economic beacon – only to see its attempt to present a more open face to the world go 'terribly wrong' when Israeli athletes were murdered at the 1972 Munich Olympics.

Germany's campaign is part of a broader debate on the value of public diplomacy and 'soft power' – the tools increasingly used by national governments to deepen their influence without resorting to economic and military might.

Joseph Nye, a Harvard professor and author of *Soft Power: The means to success in world politics*, argues that it can be used to complement traditional diplomacy. 'Tangible threats or payoffs' are replaced by initiatives to influence stereotypes about a country, for example.

According to an internal German government strategy paper seen by the *Financial Times*, this approach was partly behind the decision to use the World Cup to alter Germany's image abroad. 'States are increasingly in competition for markets, tourists . . . value systems and political influence', and in this context 'Germany must take a position', the paper argues. It notes that foreigners' images of Germany often 'lack emotion' and 'exclude the [country's] more dynamic developments over the last 20–30 years'. 'Emotional aspects, such as street cafes in Munich . . . [German] lifestyle brands such as Adidas and Boss, and the happiness of reunification in 1989/90' need to be emphasised, the paper concludes. In a section on 'Germany's Image Abroad', Michael Reiffenstuel of the foreign office enthuses that the World Cup provides a 'unique communications opportunity'.

Germany is not the first country to attempt a national makeover. Britain tried – with limited success – to repackage itself as 'Cool Britannia' early in Tony Blair's premiership. Japan, co-host with South Korea of the 2002 World Cup, ran a less elaborate image campaign than Germany's. But visitors were surprised to find a country more vibrant and accessible than many had expected. The Japanese government has since deployed 'soft power' to exploit the popularity of manga cartoons and Japanese design and fashion. The number of tourists has noticeably increased – in part the result of an official tourism campaign but also reflecting a 'word-of-mouth' effect from the World Cup.

In Germany the jury is out on the campaign's impact. Nathalie Thiemann-Huguet, of the business-led Land of Ideas programme, says the giant sculptures in Berlin have become a 'major tourist attraction', while about 2,000 foreign journalists have registered to use pictures and TV footage on 'positive aspects of Germany's economy and society'.

Yet a series of organisational and other problems that have blighted tournament preparations have brought negative media coverage. Most recently, Ms Merkel was forced to allay concerns in the United States Congress that Germany was ignoring an alleged rise in illegal trafficking of prostitutes for the tournament. Worst of all was last month's apparent racist attack that left a young Ethiopian man in a coma. Experts argue that such incidents are unlikely to undermine Germany's broader campaign, but that this must in turn be seen as only one element in reshaping its image. Ulrich Sacker of the Goethe-Institut, Germany's overseas cultural agency, says the World Cup will remain in the minds of tens of millions of global television viewers. 'We have to surprise people, make them think: "Germany is different to the country I imagined",' he says.

Mr Perthes believes government campaigns can only ever have a modest impact, given the post-Cold War complexity of public diplomacy. But rhetorically posing the question 'will the country's image after the World Cup return to the cliché about the ugly German?', he provides his own, upbeat answer: 'I don't think so. At least something from the campaign will stick.'

Source: *Financial Times*, 22 May 2006: 19.

Question

Referring to Concept 14, comment on the statement made in the text: 'You can't market a country like a washing powder.'

ACTIVITY 14.2

Read the following account of an Indian's experiences when inspecting a local bank in India. Then answer the question below.

Meeting a brick wall

I was working in the inspection department of the Central Bank of India and was given an assignment a few years ago to inspect a branch of a private commercial bank. I was assisted by a junior officer. One of our main tasks was to get some important information about a fraud, determine the chain of events, establish accountability and pass on the information to the team which was inspecting the head office of the bank.

The branch was in a small town which was very different to what I was used to: they spoke a different language there, ate different food and enjoyed a very different climate. The people working there were very old compared to employees of other banks I had visited and they behaved towards me in an indifferent and uncooperative manner. They claimed they had no idea how the fraud was committed and were reluctant to show me the relevant records.

Many of the staff members had been working in the branch for decades and had developed close relationships with each other. Their former branch manager had already been suspended for his suspected involvement in the fraud. My colleague, who was from the same region and of a similar age, managed to mix with the staff but was unable to get hold of the information needed. Eventually he also became rather reluctant to get items of information requested, giving delays and unavailability as reasons for their non-appearance.

I was proud of my experience in inspections, my analytical skills, my management education and my past success in meeting deadlines. I followed the code of behaviour expected of someone in my position and kept the staff at a distance. I declined offers of lunch or even tea or coffee so that these should not be considered as some sort of bribe. I felt that the local staff were making one excuse after another not to come up with the right information. Were they perhaps trying to protect their colleagues, or were they afraid of being reprimanded by their bosses? The information I needed was crucial and could be obtained only from this branch. The days passed, but nothing substantial emerged. Time was running out.

Source: adapted from Browaeys and Trompenaars (2000): case 11.

Questions

1. To what extent is the problem presented in the case a communication problem?

2. How do you think the author could try to get hold of the information needed?

Conclusion

This chapter has elaborated the model of communication given in the introduction by looking at barriers to intercultural situations in general and in those in business in particular. The culture of the interlocutors filters the information and interprets it according to their own reference framework. Barriers can build up at various levels: badly interpreted gestures, a smile expressing the opposite of satisfaction, concrete words having an implicit meaning. Stereotypes, however, remain the most important barrier in communication. They are very difficult to deal with since they are formed by the identity and the perceptions of individuals.

Points for reflection

1. Stereotypes appear in all cross-cultural situations. When you are doing business with other cultures, stereotypes particularly arise in meetings and negotiations. If you are aware of the stereotypes of the group you are dealing with, it may help you at the beginning of the interaction.

   What is your opinion of this statement?

2. You have just read about barriers to communicating with other cultures. Some of these can lead to misunderstandings, others can degenerate into conflict.

   Which of these barriers, in your opinion, can lead to misunderstandings and which of them can lead to conflict? Explain your choice.

Further reading

Mead, R. (1990) *Cross-Cultural Management Communication*, **Chichester: John Wiley.** This book explores the many aspects and problems of cross-cultural communication encountered by managers. It focuses on understanding management cultures, and explores how situations within the context of different cultures and markets can be interpreted accurately. The author shows how management priorities are decided and communicated in different cultures and examines the organizational problems managers may face when operating in other cultures. Despite its age, this book remains a useful reference.

References

Browaeys, M.-J. and Trompenaars, F. (eds) (2000), *Cases Studies on Cultural Dilemmas,* Breukelen, Netherlands: Nyenrode University Press.

Browaeys, M.-J. (1989) *Les gestes conversationnels et les différences culturelles en France et aux Pays-Bas,* Amsterdam: Universiteit van Amsterdam.

Caroll, R. (1987) *Evidences invisibles*, Paris: Editions du Seuil.

Cazal, D. (1993) 'Ethique et management interculturel: le cas du confucianisme d'entreprise' in Bosche, M. (ed), *Le management interculturel,* Paris: Editions Nathan: 181-192.

Cresswell, R. (1968) 'Le geste manuel associé aux langages,' *Langages,* 10: 119-127.

Edgar, A. and Sedgwick, P. (eds) (2002) *Cultural Theory: The key concepts,* London: Routledge.

Fontaine, R. and Richardson, S. (2003) 'Cross-cultural research in Malaysia', *European Management Journal,* 10(2): 75-89.

Gruère, J.-P. and Morel, P. (1991) *Cadres français et communications interculturelles*, Paris: Editions Eyrolles.

Gudykunst, W.B. (ed) (2003) *Cross-Cultural and Intercultural Communication,* Thousand Oaks, CA: Sage: 53-71.

Hall, E.T. (1977) *Beyond Culture*, New York, NY: Anchor Press/Doubleday.

Hall, E.T. (1983) *The Dance of Life*, New York, NY: Anchor Press/Doubleday.

Ladmiral, J.R. and Lipianski, E.M. (1989) *La communication interculturelle,* Paris: Armand Colin.

Lipianski, E.-M. (1992) 'Identité, communication interculturelle et dynamique des groupes' in *Interculturel: groupe et transition,* Toulouse: Editions Erès: 59–70.

Myers, D.G. (2005) *Social Psychology,* 8th edn, New York, NY: McGraw-Hill.

Oomkes, F.R. (1987) *Communicatieleer,* Amsterdam: Boom Meppel.

Tae-Seop Lim (2003) 'Language and verbal communication across cultures' in Gudykunst, W.B. (ed.), *Cross-Cultural and Intercultural Communication,* Thousand Oaks, CA: Sage: 53–71.

Todorov, T. (1986) 'Le croisement des cultures,' *Communications,* 43: 5–24.

Usunier, J.-C. and Lee, J.A. (2005) *Marketing across cultures*, 4th edn, Harlow: Pearson Education.

Chapter 15

Negotiating internationally

Having given some attention to theories concerning cross-cultural communication, the following two chapters will examine two activities in intercultural communication – negotiating and team-work. Each chapter will then consider some cross-cultural aspects of each activity.

This chapter examines a crucial aspect of international business dealings – negotiating. First the nature of negotiating from a Western perspective is considered and compared with a non-western viewpoint. Thereafter, facets of cross-cultural business negotiation are described and applied to an examination of possible problems in the interaction between two negotiating parties, one from the US, the other from China. The chapter then moves on to examine a framework to address the issue of strategy adaptation when negotiating with counterparts from other cultures. Finally, the question of an international negotiating (meta-) culture is briefly discussed.

Learning outcomes

After reading this chapter you will:

- Understand how the perception of negotiating can differ from culture to culture.

- Be aware of how these different perceptions can affect the negotiating process between parties from different cultures and the eventual results.

- Be familiar with strategies of negotiation that are culturally responsive and which, at the same time, take account of the skills of the individuals involved.

Concept 15.1 Approaches to negotiating in an international context

The nature of negotiation

Negotiating is essentially regarded in the West as a problem-solving exercise. It is seen as a process whereby a problem is deliberated, ideas are put forward for resolution and where a solution of some kind is eventually reached. As Fisher (1980) indicates, the literature on negotiation, most of it emanating from Western academics and practitioners, is preoccupied with tactics and strategies that can be applied universally to achieve a result. Implicit in these works is the assumption that the participants share similar approaches, attitudes and principles.

The Western approach focuses on what happens between parties. This is evident in the way negotiating is dealt with by D. Whetten et al. (2000). The authors address the subject in a chapter on constructive conflict management whereby they distinguish two types of negotiation strategy predominant in Western culture: the distributive and integrative strategy. The distributive approach involves trying to get a piece of what they call a 'fixed-sized cake'. The negotiators are adversaries, trying to gain the best deal for themselves, which usually means that others lose out in some way (i.e. the result is 'win-lose'). Those adopting integrative strategies are trying to expand the 'cake' by collaborating in a problem-solving approach to try and get a 'win-win' result.

However, if negotiations are taking place between societies/cultures, rather than between groups from the same culture, then those involved need to try and work out what is going on in the minds of their counterparts. Negotiators in an international context are participating in a communicative event where assumptions and expectations may not be shared. Participants cannot assume that the 'opposite party' will have motives which chime with their view of the world, or that the behaviour displayed by both parties – even if similar in nature – reflects similar motives.

As Fisher (1980) points out when recounting the words of a Japanese business executive, even the very act of negotiating can be an alien concept to other cultures. He makes it clear that the Japanese do not have in their culture the idea of a meeting where a conflict is resolved through a compromise acceptable to all sides, where the persuasive delivery of rational arguments is all-important. For the Japanese such a meeting of parties is a ceremonial occasion where a seal of approval is formally applied to what has been put together in a patient consensus-generating process 'behind the scenes'. This contrast of views reflects the possible perils of negotiating across cultures.

Facets of negotiation

This section aims to outline some key aspects of negotiating in an international context. First, though, some facets of negotiating need to be established as a framework of reference. Usunier (2003: 104) sees three facets of cultural differences affecting international marketing negotiations. These facets incorporate all the variables given in the 'Model of Culture' introduced in Part One of this book. They are presented here in a way that allows the cross-cultural process of negotiation to be more clearly perceived. An overview is given in Table 15.1, followed by a brief examination and exemplification of each facet.

Behavioural predispositions of the parties

- *Interpersonal orientation*. A fundamental issue is to do with how the negotiating parties relate to each other and to the context of the negotiation. The individualism/collectivism dimension, referred to in Chapter 2, is an appropriate method of analysis in this respect. Negotiators from cultures deemed to be 'collectivist' tend to avoid open conflict and prefer to maintain formal harmony during negotiations. Those from cultures deemed to be 'individualist' are expected to act more in self-interest and will not shy away from being overtly competitive and confrontational. With the former, the focus is on establishing good relations with negotiating counterparts, developing mutual

Table 15.1 Facets of negotiation

Negotiation facet	Elements	Concepts
Behavioural predispositions of the parties	Interpersonal orientation	Harmony, self-interest
	Power orientation	Formal power (informal) influence
	Willingness to take risks	Negotiating party's degree of delegated decision-making, and (lack of) uncertainty
Underlying concept of negotiation	Negotiation strategies	Trust or mistrust as basis
	Strategic time-frame	Logical, finite process or ongoing dialogue
Negotiation process	Styles of negotiation	Work towards specific, concrete goals, or more towards principles, concepts
	Outcome orientations	Iron-cast deal or less explicit agreement

Source: Usunier (2003).

respect and trust as a basis for a deal. With the latter, relationships certainly play a part, but respect may tend to result from the skills shown in reaching a good deal. Coming to a satisfactory conclusion – the deal – is for them the main objective.

- *Power orientation.* Also examined in Part One, this dimension relates to the question of who has formal influence and who has actual influence on the negotiating process. Are the people involved able to negotiate, how are they chosen and what is their role in the company? What qualities are attributed to the person in that position, and who is actually calling the shots?

- *Willingness to take risks.* This is in one sense closely related to power orientation. Negotiators from strictly controlled bureaucracies, where approval for any deal involves the approval of a number of bodies or committees may well be reluctant to take as many risks as negotiators who need to consult their superiors less often, having been delegated negotiating power and a certain room for manoeuvre. This has clearly to do with the (lack of) uncertainty avoidance tendencies of certain cultures.

However, it should be noted that uncertainty and risk avoidance do not necessarily go hand-in-hand. Chapter 8 referred, for example, to Japan's high position on the index of uncertainty avoidance but made clear that the country is not averse to taking risks. What distinguishes it from cultures that are more willing to face risk and the consequent ambiguity is that it pays considerable attention to risk-management. Rather than dealing with risk in a cavalier fashion, Japan takes very well-calculated risks and its industry has benefited considerably as a result.

Underlying concept of negotiation

- *Negotiation strategies.* The integrative approach, described earlier whereby negotiation teams collaborate to get the best result, may be regarded as the most effective form of negotiating in Western business literature. The context, however, is implicitly an intra-cultural one, whereby both sides agree to work together to get a so-called 'win-win' result. In an inter-cultural situation, however, the oppositional nature of negotiating may come to the fore if one or both sides do not trust their counterparts, or if the so-called best deal is not felt to be necessarily the best deal for their side. The establishment of trust may precede any discussion of details, with principles being established by which an agreement is eventually reached.

- *Strategic time-frame.* The idea of following a 'logical' process, starting with orientation, then coming to a series of agreements, possibly in some form of package, and then closing a deal within some agreed-on time-limit, will contrast strongly with what could be called the dialogue approach. Negotiating is considered to be just part of a dialogue between business parties whereby any deals made are not necessarily regarded as immutable, but as a reflection of the wish to initiate or continue cooperation. Changes may well be needed later on to improve the situation for all those involved. The establishment of trust as the starting-point enables such flexibility and improves the nature of the collaboration.

Negotiation process

- *Styles of negotiation.* With different concepts of negotiation come different styles. This is where the universalism–particularism dimension referred to in Parts One and Two can be reflected in the way negotiations are made. Is the focus on general issues or is there a concern for dealing with (a range of) specific issues? Is negotiating more to do with feelings than facts, opinion rather than evidence? If present in a negotiation, this stark opposition of styles can cause both sides headaches, with the 'universalists' frustrated by the concern for details rather than the more important principles and concepts, and the 'particularists' frustrated by the very broad approach taken by their counterpart which, in their eyes, makes it difficult for practical decisions to be taken.

    The high/low context dimension, covered in Chapter 8, plays a key role in the style of communication during negotiations. Low-context negotiators are more explicit, exact and direct than high-context negotiators. Their outspokenness will not necessarily be appreciated or accepted and the reciprocity they may expect from being explicit in their dealings is unlikely to be realized. Low-context negotiators tend to infer, allude and do not always feel compelled to take turns in the discussion. The long pauses or silences which they bring to the discussion allow for consideration of what has been said and of the circumstances surrounding the discussion. A concrete decision or statement, however, is unlikely to be made as a result of their reflections.

- *Outcome orientations.* It will come as no surprise that the polarities described above are reflected in two types of outcome: a rather vague statement in which the parties involved express their mutual trust and desire for mutual co-operation, or a detailed account of the agreements reached and the ways in which these are to be implemented. Between these extremes lie agreements that will vary in terms of detail and explicitness.

    However detailed a conclusion, the interpretation of the 'document' may well differ since the wording will not necessarily refer to all the assumptions underlying any agreement. Moreover, the status of the document for negotiators may vary: it may be seen either as a cast-iron document determining exactly how matters should proceed, or as a statement of good intentions, which may not be realized. The very idea of preparing some sort of final document following on from a negotiation phase concept of an outcome may even be seen as superfluous. Any business relationship involves continuing negotiation at all levels: a statement of some kind after a negotiation phase is not the end of the story.

Cross-cultural negotiation in practice: the US and China

The facets of intercultural negotiating outlined above will now be used to profile two contrasting cultures. Imagine them facing each other across the negotiating table (an image that is itself culture-determined!) and imagine how they are likely to react to each other's approach to the task at hand.

Predispositions

Interpersonal orientation

In the US, the deal is seen as the objective of any negotiation while for the Chinese a negotiation is just part of the process of forming a life-long relationship. A focused, bottom-line approach is at odds with the Chinese need to establish a good rapport before talking of a deal. However, Americans might feel that the wish by their Chinese counterparts to establish friendship is one way to get a better deal later on in the negotiation(s).

Power orientation

It is usually clear where the power lies in a US negotiating team. The hierarchy is usually clear, with subordinates and experts accompanying the boss making it clear in the deference they show, even if the language used between them is informal. The boss will probably have been delegated considerable leeway in the negotiating process, although this will have been carefully discussed with headquarters beforehand. Risk-taking is part of the game and seen as inherent to getting the best deal possible.

The US team may find it difficult to determine who is leading the negotiation on the Chinese side, particularly if there are a large number of people in the delegation. For the Chinese, the consensus-building process is undergone not only between the negotiating teams but also within the Chinese team where a number of interested parties both from within the company as well as outside the company (essentially government bureaucrats) are involved. Pressure from the US side to get a deal will be stonewalled until all interested Chinese parties are satisfied. This dependence on consensus within the negotiating team means that any risk-taking behaviour within or before negotiations needs to be carefully orchestrated.

Underlying concept of negotiation

Negotiation strategies

There are two main approaches used in the US towards negotiations: the competitive ('win-lose') approach and integrative ('win-win') approach. The former approach involves taking up an initial position and then making concessions if necessary to reach a compromise agreement. The latter approach involves both 'sides' focusing on mutual interests rather than pre-determined positions, achieving joint profits using an objective standard. Both approaches, however, should lead to a definitive contract to which both sides are expected to adhere.

The Chinese will probably find it difficult to take such a linear approach. For them, a negotiation is just one of many encounters whereby the principle is to build a business partnership for the long term. Establishing a relationship entails getting to know your partner well. Hence a lot of questions will be asked to do with the interests and personalities of the other team rather than dealing directly with the details of any deal or joint project. Detailed terms of any agreement need this strong consensual basis. However, observers, including Faure (1998), note that there is also another side to their strategic behaviour, namely a persistency whereby the negotiator does all he can to exploit his opponent to the maximum. The style is therefore a combination of what Faure calls 'joint quest' with 'mobile warfare' where they are trying to outflank their opponent (a reference to the tactics of Sun Tsu, the notorious ancient Chinese warrior). In US terms this could be seen as a combination of affiliative, integrative behaviour (the affective dimension) and competitive, forcing behaviour (the cognitive dimension).

Strategic time-frame

For the Chinese, therefore, a negotiation is not a one-off event but a step along the path to a harmonious and mutually beneficial relationship in the long-term. A deal made at the end of a negotiation remains in their eyes negotiable in the long-term since both parties could benefit more from an improvement of some kind in an agreement made. Moreover, all agreements are based on trust and goodwill, so a firm contract is superfluous. This attitude can be frustrating for Americans: time is of the essence.

Negotiating process

Style of negotiation

US negotiators will be concerned with specifics, eager to get a lot of information to enable them to pursue their way of negotiating. Only when they have sufficient input can they gain a clearer idea of the other party's concerns and interests and so establish or modify their negotiating goals. They, in turn, are willing to give a lot of information as long as this is part of an exchange. The Chinese reluctance to give information is noted in the literature on this area, and the resulting frustration amongst Western negotiators. However, as Kumar discovered during research on business negotiations with the Chinese, the majority of their Western respondents noted that their Chinese negotiating partners were willing to disclose information – provided they had it! As another respondent remarked: 'Chinese firms are not accustomed to collect(ing) information' (Kumar and Worm, 2003).

This raises two interesting issues in relation to the negotiating process. First, the importance of face to the Chinese: asking for information they do not have could be seen as an unintentional way of causing the Chinese to lose face. Second, times are changing in China: a freer exchange of information is now being applied in negotiations, presumably because a more systematic collection of information has been developed in Chinese companies.

Having said that, however, co-operation with the Chinese still has trust as its bedrock. However successful information exchange may be, the process of gaining trust and confidence remains, for the Chinese, of greater import than facts and figures.

A word of reservation is appropriate here. On the basis of a finding made by Kumar and Worm (2003) in their survey, younger managers who are involved in negotiations are more in tune with Western behavioural norms. One implication of this (although it is not tested in this study) is that Western managers may be able to conduct their negotiations more effectively/efficiently when dealing with Chinese who are younger.

Perhaps younger Chinese are also more comfortable with a lower position on the high/low context dimension referred to earlier. Although the explicit, direct, fact-oriented, cause-effect nature of discussions as favoured by the Americans contrasts strongly with the generally consensus-focused, relationship developing nature of the Chinese, some younger Chinese may be more comfortable than their older colleagues in the American company.

Outcome orientations

For the US negotiators a detailed contract is the ideal conclusion to a negotiation, signed, sealed and delivered. Detailed points are hammered out in the final phase of the negotiation, particularly with regard to the implementation of the deal. The legal aspects are also given considerable attention.

The Chinese tend to avoid getting tied up in what they may consider to be Western legalistic details, preferring short, vaguer contracts that signify the willingness of both sides to commit to a joint project of some kind. Rather than being the last word on the deal, a contract is a formal moment in the development of a relationship; further negotiations will take place on the basis of the goodwill and friendship established.

All in all, therefore, the Chinese and Americans face innumerable difficulties around the negotiation table. The opposition in expectations and attitudes are clear, the expected frustrations and irritations evident. How can both sides resolve this dilemma? A framework for dealing with apparently conflicting cultural values is presented in the next part of this concept.

When in Rome, do as the Romans do?

Much of the international literature tends to focus on the rituals of negotiating in other countries and, particularly in the case of non-Western countries, gives a convenient outline of the systems of values they embrace. Little attention appears to be given to the question of the extent to which a negotiator should adapt to the cultural values of the other party. Are international negotiators expected to adapt totally? Is the maxim 'When in Rome, do as the Romans do' appropriate?

The simplistic nature of this approach raises issues. First, it does not take account of the dominant role of one or the other partner: the Rome in question may well yield culturally to its counterpart. Second, is it ever possible to 'do as' the Romans? However much we try to behave as the other party does during negotiations, will they ever really consider us to be a member of their culture? Try as people may, behaving as the Romans will not make them Roman. Finally, there is a questionable assumption underlying this maxim – that a 'Roman' will always act as a Roman with a non-Roman in Rome!

This last point is one of a number put forward by Stephen Weiss (1994) when examining cultural aspects of negotiating. He sees that international negotiators in today's global business cannot resort to a 'one-size-fits-all' approach when confronted with a variety of situations and individuals. Weiss advocates instead approaches that reflect the skills of the individuals involved. He proposes strategies which, while being culturally responsive, reflect the negotiators' own skills and the circumstances in which they are working.

In any communicative situation between two parties, one aim is to make sense of the interaction. In negotiations this means that the least both parties must be able to do is:

- recognize each other's ideas and the types of behaviour that form an international part of the negotiating process;
- interpret these in such a way that they can detect common and differing standpoints as well as changes made to these during the negotiating process;
- ensure that communication is maintained as the negotiation proceeds.

However, as indicated earlier, the knowledge and skills required to perform these crucial acts is often limited. What is needed, Weiss says, is a strategic framework allowing the parties to make sense of the negotiating process as best they can, using their own attributes and, where necessary, the skills of others.

The Weiss strategic framework

The framework Weiss drew up is given in Figure 15.1. It shows in an organized form culturally responsive strategies that can be adopted according to the level of familiarity which each negotiator has with the other's culture. The strategies in brackets reflect a co-ordinated approach between the parties involved.

Before briefly examining the strategies, note that:

- 'Familiarity' is the term Weiss uses to denote not only one party's knowledge of the other party's culture, but also the ability to apply this knowledge effectively to the interaction. High familiarity entails fluency in the predominant language, extensive exposure to

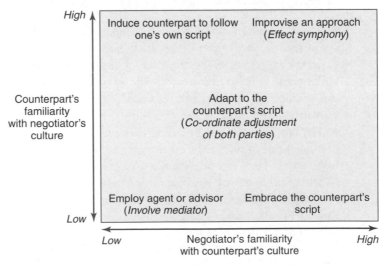

Figure 15.1 Strategic framework for negotiating
Source: Weiss (1994a): 54.

the culture concerned and previous successful social interactions with those from the culture in question.

- 'Script' is the term which Weiss uses to denote a standardized sequence of behaviour expected by the person concerned.

According to Weiss, negotiators may consider using not only the strategies appropriate for their degree of familiarity, but also any strategies that correspond to lower degrees of familiarity.

The strategies proposed by the framework are:

- If a negotiator has *low familiarity* with the counterpart's culture, a third-party of some kind can be introduced to help out. This can be an agent who takes over the negotiating role (thus creating other possible problems, especially with regard to accountability and trust), or an adviser to help in preparations and during the process. The negotiator may also explicitly persuade the counterpart to adapt his approach, pleading ignorance with the other's culture and language, but every respect for them. The result may be further hindrance to agreement if the counterpart regards this as arrogant behaviour that results in a disadvantageous situation.

- If the negotiator has a *moderate familiarity* with the counterpart's culture, then the negotiator has two other options, provided the counterpart shares a similar familiarity. The negotiator can go some way to a compromise by altering his usual negotiating approach. This could include, for example, following the etiquette used by the counterpart, modifying the usual time frame, or being more 'upfront' with providing information. Tinkering with just part of the process, however, may create more confusion – and it may be exacerbated if the counterpart finds this half-hearted approach unacceptable. More promising is the idea of *co-ordinating adjustment,* whereby both parties negotiate as to how the negotiating is to proceed. This can be done explicitly at the start, or implicitly through a gradual blending of elements from the respective cultures. Weiss refers in particular to the medium of discussion and gives an example of a third language being used (presumably with some of its cultural baggage) in a high-level negotiation.

- Those parties that are *highly familiar* with each other's culture may improvise during the negotiating process, focusing on each other's attributes and skills as well as the circumstances. Weiss is careful to point out that this does not allow an impromptu free-for-all, but rather a sensitive dialogue whereby both parties take account of each other's individuality as well as culture. It allows aspects of each other's culture to be brought to the foreground or pushed into the background as appropriate, pushing stereotypes aside and encouraging the development of a relationship that is not just based on the deal. Weiss takes this approach further by talking of *effecting symphony*. Here, both parties go beyond their home cultures and create their own approach, which may draw on their familiarity with both cultures but is unique to their relationship.

This final strategy takes further the idea of a synergistic approach to negotiating as proposed by Adler (1991). She saw the limitations to what she terms 'principled negotiating' in complex international business negotiations and called instead for a collaborative, synergistic style of negotiating. While recognizing the extra problems caused through cultural differences, she argued that the very diversity of culture could help to increase the search for creative options for mutual gain. This collaborative approach is considered further in Chapter 18.

In his follow-up article to the one already outlined in the concept, Weiss (1994b) presents a step-by-step procedure for deciding which of the strategies put forward is:

- the most feasible, i.e. the extent to which it will fit with the counterpart's possible approach;
- the most appropriate in terms of the relationship and circumstances surrounding the interaction;
- the most acceptable in terms of the manager's own values.

This involves considerable reflection on one's own culture as well as careful investigation into the counterpart's culture. Moreover, it calls for both parties to consider their relationship as individuals as well as members of different cultures. Finding a balance between culture group and individual considerations is difficult, particularly as the degree of variation within a particular culture group can be considerable. The five steps Weiss (1994b: 86) proposes for selecting a negotiating strategy take account of these complexities.

1. Reflect on your culture's negotiation script.
2. Learn the negotiation script of the counterpart's culture.
3. Consider the relationship and circumstances.
4. Predict and influence the counterpart's approach.
5. Choose your strategy.

This approach highlights a regular message in this book: reflect carefully on your own culture while investigating others. The concept in Chapter 16 takes this approach further when considering international team-work.

ACTIVITY 15.1

Negotiating with the Japanese

Table 15.2 is a brief description in note form of the typical approach by the Japanese to negotiating, using the framework given in the concept.

Questions

1. Choose another culture with which you are familiar and note what you consider to be the similarities or differences with regard to the Japanese approach to negotiating.

2. Imagine how a Japanese party and a party from the other culture chosen would react to each other over the negotiating table.

Table 15.2

Behavioural predispositions	
Interpersonal orientation	Wish to establish personal rapport: essential for building trust – the basis for doing any business. Time-consuming entertainment as part of that process. A negotiation is a face-to-face ceremonial and very formal moment when a stage of partnership development has been rounded off.
Power orientation	Any decision requires consultation and support at all levels of the company. The leader of the negotiating team will probably be the motor behind this consensus-building. Others will be experts who have talked in great detail to the counterpart.
Willingness to take risks	The concern for consensus will make the Japanese unwilling to take risks: intensive pre-negotiation preparation, reviews before and during the negotiation, No impulsive response to proposals from the other side.
Underlying concept of negotiation	
Negotiation strategies	Doing business is a continuing affair, based on mutual trust and confidence. A negotiation is part of the process of developing a relationship. Once the base for the relationship has been established, details can be discussed and agreed upon, often before formal meetings between the two sides where the focus is less on problem-solving and, as Fisher calls it (Fisher, 1980: 32), 'direction-taking'.
Strategic time-frame	Patience is the key. Considerable care in preparation of a deal will allow its implementation to take place quite quickly.
Negotiation process	
Styles of negotiation	No confrontation, disagreement or haggling involved – face-saving a key requirement. Highly indirect, highly formal communication. High-context negotiators: many allusions and inferences to the situation.
Outcome orientations	Prefer a short written agreement to a definite, detailed contract. The establishment of a (further) stage in the relationship is what really counts: inevitable changes in the circumstances of both companies will necessitate later amendments anyway.

ACTIVITY 15.2

Selecting a negotiation strategy

The aim of this activity is for you to use the five steps Weiss puts forward as a way of selecting a strategy for a particular negotiation with counterparts from another culture. For ease of reference these steps are given again below:

1. Reflect on your culture's negotiation script.
2. Learn the negotiation script of the counterpart's culture.
3. Consider the relationship and circumstances.
4. Predict and influence the counterpart's approach.
5. Choose your strategy.

→

Imagine that you are about to take part in an international, cross-cultural negotiation. You represent a company from your own country and are about to meet either a US or a Japanese negotiating team.

Questions

1. Sketch out the scenario for the negotiation that allows you to determine the degree of familiarity which both sides may have with regards to each other's culture. You will need to:
   - Describe the circumstances of the negotiation (including the experience of both teams in international business and the nature of any possible agreement).
   - Describe the relationship, if any, that you have developed with your counterparts.

2. Using the information from your response to question 1:
   - Choose one negotiating strategy from those proposed by Weiss in his strategic framework (referred to in this chapter's concept) that you believe to be appropriate.
   - Describe the negotiation process as you envisage it, using the strategy chosen.

Conclusion

Chapter 15 has examined three facets of cultural differences in international negotiations. One very important facet is the concept of negotiating: do people consider it to be more to do with problem-solving within a given time-frame, or is it just one aspect of a continuing dialogue between parties who are beginning or continuing a harmonious, mutually beneficial relationship? People's perception of negotiating colours their style of negotiating, as well as their expectations about the outcome. And, of course, it influences the way they tend to behave during the negotiations.

This chapter has also addressed the question as to what international negotiators should do when having to contend with such differences. The strategic framework of negotiations presented is a culturally responsive instrument, taking account of the negotiators' own skills and the circumstances of the negotiation.

Points for reflection

There are many books, articles and websites on international negotiations that offer 'dos and don'ts' on how to negotiate with parties from different cultures. For example, negotiators in China are urged not to say or do anything to embarrass the Chinese participants, or point at anyone, or to raise their voice. Another guide to negotiating suggests that those negotiating in the US should be prepared to partake in preliminary small talk with their counterparts at the start of a meeting, and not be surprised if a gift cannot be accepted.

1. To what extent do you think such prescriptive advice is useful?

2. What other ways of preparing for a cross-cultural negotiation do you consider to be (more) useful?

Further reading

Fisher, G. (1980), *International Negotiation: A cross-cultural perspective*, **Yarmouth, ME: Intercultural Press.** This focuses on the factors which affect the negotiating process between parties from different cultural and national backgrounds, with particular reference to Japan, France and the US. Fisher puts forward a conceptual framework for the negotiating process and allows negotiators to manage the process more effectively.

Ghauri, N. and Usunier, J.-C. (eds) (2003) *International Business Negotiations*, **2nd edn, Oxford: Elsevier.** Aims to enhance understanding of the effect of culture and communication on international business negotiations. It explores the problems faced by Western managers while doing business abroad and provides guidelines for international business negotiations. In particular, the book discusses negotiations for different types of businesses, using examples from different parts of the world.

References

Adler, N.J. (1991) *International Dimensions of Organizational Behaviour*, 2nd edn, Boston, MA: PWS-Kent.

Faure, G.O. (1998) 'Negotiation: the Chinese concept', *Negotiation Journal*, 14 (2): 137–148.

Fisher, G. (1980) *International Negotiation: A cross-cultural perspective*, Yarmouth, ME: Intercultural.

Kennedy, G., McMillan, J. and Benson, J. (1984) *Managing Negotiations*, 2nd edn, London: Hutchinson Business.

Kumar, R. and Worm, V. (2003) 'Social capital and the dynamics of business negotiations between the northern Europeans and the Chinese,' *International Marketing Review*, 20 (3): 262–285.

Whetten, D., Cameron, K. and Woods, M. (2000) *Developing Management Skills for Europe*, Harlow: FT Prentice Hall.

Usunier, J.-C. (2003) 'Cultural aspects of international business negotiations' Ghauri, N. and Usunier J.-C. (eds), in *International Business Negotiations*, 2nd edn, Oxford: Elsevier: 91–1180.

Weiss, S.E. (1994a), 'Negotiating with "Romans"': part 1 *Sloan Management Review*, 35 (2): 51–61.

Weiss, S.E. (1994b), 'Negotiating with "Romans"': part 2 *Sloan Management Review*, 35 (3): 85–99.

Chapter 16

Working with international teams

Having considered communication barriers in cross-cultural management and aspects of negotiating internationally, attention now focuses on an increasingly common phenomenon of global business, the international team. Knowing that cultural backgrounds have an enormous influence on how people behave, how do teams composed of people from different cultures operate?

After defining the word 'team' and the elements involved (types and roles), this concept will focus on global teams, their processes and the effect of cultural differences on these teams. The final part of the concept will deal with the management of multicultural teams, with particular reference to Afro-Western teams.

Learning outcomes

After reading this chapter you will gain an understanding of:

- The cultural factors that influence teams working in organizations.
- The importance of communication in the management of teams.

Concept 16.1 Groups processes during international encounters

Teams in organizations

The word 'team' can be defined as a small number of people who work together for a common purpose and hold themselves collectively responsible for what they do. Senge et al (1995: 354–355) define the word as 'any group of people who need each other to accomplish a result'. The word 'team', which comes from the Indo-European *deuk* (to pull), has always been understood in terms of people 'pulling together'. It was not until the sixteenth century that the word took on its modern meaning of 'a group of people acting'.

This recent definition includes all those who are working both inside and outside the organization, even if they are not regular participants. Senge et al (1995) give us the example of large, technologically-oriented organizations that have learnt to design their infrastructures on the basis of this broad definition of a team. This is because a team can also be a global network of specialists who email and telephone each other, or occasionally meet.

The teams found in organizations can differ in kind according to their objectives. Robbins (2000: 106) proposes four types:

- *Problem-solving.* Such teams meet regularly to discuss and put forward suggestions such as to how to improve work processes and methods.

- *Self-managed.* Such teams have no supervisor. Employees in these teams are directly involved in the decisions made concerning work.

- *Cross-functional.* The members of these teams come from different departments and work together to complete a task. Their position in the hierarchy is usually the same, even if they come from different domains.

- *Virtual.* These teams can do the same as the other types mentioned – exchange information, take decisions, accomplish tasks – but can also increase in size by co-opting members from other organizations such as suppliers or joint partners.

In business, companies are depending more and more on virtual teams. Most international virtual teams exist only through necessity, to overcome geographic distance or time differences. Although there seem to be fewer problems nowadays on the technical front, this modern way of working in international teams has generated other problems, or at least amplified them. Consider Exhibit 16.1.

Exhibit 16.1   FT

'Virtual teams' endeavour to build trust:

Global communication: Alison Maitland looks at how companies create corporate harmony between colleagues in different parts of the world.

Jenny Goodbody's team of six people is spread across six continents. Once a week, they meet through a teleconference, which means that she must be wide awake by 6.30am in New Jersey while her colleague in Sydney, Australia, has to stay in work mode until well past 8.30pm. This would mean that at least two of the team would be less tired. On the other hand, some of them might feel more isolated if they had fewer opportunities to talk as a group.

It is the kind of dilemma that faces any geographically dispersed team that has to communicate through email, telephone calls or video conferences rather than face-to-face. While trust is crucial for every team to operate effectively, it is harder to build that trust among people who rarely, if ever, see each other.

Part of the problem is that people working in a virtual team often assume that trust will come about automatically. 'The teams that were more successful put in an effort to try and build trust,' she says. 'They had short-term activities for people to work in pairs or threes, getting to know each other in smaller groups.'

A face-to-face group meeting at the start is important. 'The teams that got together once could kick off that trust-building much more quickly. With the ones that didn't meet face-to-face, it was slower.' 'An important aspect of management behaviour, identified as supporting the development of trust, is consistency and its encouragement among other team members,' they add. 'Managers can also act in a sensitive way to the stage of development of team trust.'

Ms Goodbody found that the first stage, when the team is actually formed, is the most important in determining success. Team leaders can help to build relationships in different ways. 'They can try and get people to share some level of social information, for example about their country or their family.' As team co-ordinators, they also need to know how to summarise relevant information from the conversations that they have with individual members for the rest of the group. 'There's a fine line between making sure everybody is aware of what's going on and inundating people with emails they don't need,' she says.

Virtual teams need a strong 'sponsor' from the start – someone who is not involved in everyday team activities but who represents their interests at a senior level in the parent organization. 'One of the key things for the sponsor is to show interest in the team's progress and be involved in solving major issues.'

Source: *Financial Times*, 9 September 2004: 13

Exhibit 16.1 makes it clear that trust is a prerequisite for working effectively in a team, but also shows that developing a climate of trust is a challenge for multicultural teams. To establish trust, team members must have an attitude of co-operation, which includes sharing common norms and values. But, as Schneider and Barsoux (2003) point out, this condition is difficult to realize because people from different cultural backgrounds seldom have common norms and values. Moreover, the concept of trust – and ways of developing it – vary from culture to culture. Such variations rest on differing cultural assumptions about relationships to nature, the environment and to other people. This explains why people from some cultures react more positively than those from others when they are asked if they trust other people. According to Inglehart (1997), 70 per cent of the Scandinavians interviewed said they did, compared with 50 per cent of the Americans, Chinese and Canadians and only 20 per cent of the Romanians, Turks and Brazilians (Schneider and Barsoux, 2003: 246).

Cultures also have different assumptions as to the purpose of groups and teams: either these are to enable the dissemination of information and discussion of problems, or they enable decisions to be made and action to be taken or, lastly, they enable the creation of social relations. These assumptions will in turn determine the frequency of the meetings and contacts and the time needed for the group to function, as well as determine whether the meetings will take place face-to-face or by telephone.

When the members of a team display complementary skills to achieve a certain goal, then we can talk of teamwork. That is the reason why the concept of the 'team' goes further than that of the 'group'. While the term 'group' usually refers to two or more individuals who share a collective identity, and have a common goal, the term 'teamwork' implies a synergy from working together which increases the performance of the work being done collectively.

Team roles

What types of roles need to be performed within a team? There are two roles for each member of a team. First, as representative of a profession, a team member must show his professional aptitudes as a *specialist* in his area, such as a personnel manager or sales manager. Second, each member should also demonstrate personal characteristics, thereby performing an *interpersonal* role within the team. This should reflect the style in which each member works.

For Senge et al (1995), it is also important for the team itself to clarify how decisions are taken and by whom. A *facilitator* could play an important role in this, thereby improving the team's whole performance. This facilitator should preferably come from outside the team and be someone who is trained in techniques for developing the team's reflection and inquiry skills while stimulating dialogue among its members. The authors argue that the members of a team 'often collude to misrepresent reality to each other' in a deceitful way, and do so without being aware of what they are doing. Only a facilitator who is not part of the team can see the team's shortcomings clearly and get the team to work on their behaviour. That is why a member of the team, even if competent to take on the role, is not the most suitable facilitator.

The role of team members and their performance as a team brings us to the Belbin model (1981, 1993). This is used by many organizations to measure the influence of team member diversity regarding the different roles played in a team at work. Aritzeta et al (2007: 99) emphasize that Belbin's team role model mainly concerns the way the roles evolve and that it defines the team role as a 'pattern of behaviour characteristic of the way in which one team member interacts with another to facilitate the progress of the team as a whole'.

Besides the stages of development of the team – identifying needs, finding ideas, formulating plans, executing ideas, establishing team organization, following through – this model highlights the team roles (Table 16.1) which should each dominate in a particular stage of development. In addition, a good representation of all team roles is a guarantee of a team performing well (Aritzeta et al, 2007).

Cultural background may have an influence on the choice of role in teams. Schneider and Barsoux (2003) suggest that some cultures may also have a preference for certain roles. They mention a study from which it appears that bringing up good ideas would be the domain of the French, structuring tasks would be that of the Germans, and obtaining the necessary means to perform would be the task of the Swedes.

These preferences for team roles could have important implications for multinationals where managers with different cultural backgrounds form teams to help run their global business.

Table 16.1 An overview of team roles

Team role	Descriptors and strengths
Completer-finisher	Conscientious, introvert, delivers on time
Implementer	Conservative, reliable, turns ideas into practical actions
Team worker	Extrovert, co-operative, avoids friction
Specialist	Serious, provides knowledge and skills in rare supply
Monitor evaluator	Introvert, open to change, judges accurately
Co-ordinator	Dominant, good chairperson, delegates well
Plant	Trustful, creative, solves difficult problems
Shaper	Emotional, impatient, has the drive to overcome obstacles
Resource investigator	Diplomatic, persuasive, communicative, develops contacts

Source: Belbin (1993): 22.

Global management teams

This term refers to a group of managers from different countries who work together to achieve common goals of an international enterprise. Deresky (2003) gives the example of a US–Dutch joint venture whose headquarters are in Italy. This company is managed by a Swede and has a management team composed of six people from Sweden, Italy, the Netherlands, the US, Belgium and Germany. To realize the goals the enterprise has set itself, the international teams must develop a global perspective and communicate a corporate culture while paying attention to the needs of the local market.

While the work of cross-cultural teams in domestic companies is restricted to internal activities and a few external contacts, the role of a multicultural team in an internationally operating company is important in establishing and maintaining relations with suppliers, sales people and other intermediaries. This goes also for multinationals, which have teams composed of managers and technical people who work together in local operating companies in different parts of the world. The ability to work together is vital to the company's success.

For global organizations, internal interactions at all levels go on at the same time as interactions with the external environment. That is why it is vital for an organization to have not only global teamwork but also what Deresky calls 'pockets of cross-cultural teamwork and interactions that occur at many boundaries'. These allow account to be taken of the organization as an entity and local operations and their markets at one and the same time.

On an individual level, the members of a global management team share a multitude of identities derived from their national and professional cultures. Culture influences, for example, the way members see the role of the leader, the relations between superiors and subordinates, participation in meetings, the use of deadlines, as well as decision-making and problem-solving generally.

Team processes

The next part of the concept focuses on the human dynamics of group behaviour, particularly the roles and contributions made by group members in the process of team interaction. Group members display many kinds of behaviour and the group itself will develop properties that are more than the average of the properties of the individuals composing it. Individuals influence group and team life but their behaviour in turn is changed through the dynamics within the group.

Cultural differences can be seen in terms of what the organization expects from a group, as well as how a group is expected to operate. Some of those expectations are related to *task strategies*: how the tasks are planned, who does what and when, how decisions are taken. Other expectations are related to *process-group building:* language, participation, ways of managing conflict and group evaluation. These expectations have to be negotiated in terms of both task and process.

Differences between task-oriented cultures (such as Germany, Switzerland, the US) and relationship-oriented cultures (such as Latin America, the Middle East and Southern Europe) were noted by Adler (2002). During the initial stage of team formation, the time when team members get to know each other and start building a long-lasting relationship, it was observed that those from task-oriented cultures spent little time getting to know each other before getting down to business. Whereas those from relationship-oriented cultures spent much more time establishing a personal relationship. It is not surprising, therefore, that when members of two such cultural groups meet together as a team they may find it more difficult to build strong relations with each other than single-culture teams.

Process strategies for global teams

Whatever type of global team an organization wishes to create, these teams face a complex task to reach their objectives. Gluesing and Gibson (2004) classify these in terms of:

- task;
- context;
- people;
- time (the amount of time which the team has to work together); and
- technology (information sharing and collaboration).

Task and context may be closely linked when the contexts in which the members of a team are working – such as climate, nationality, education, political and economic systems – are the same or very similar. Global teams, however, are based on the complexity of different contexts. Therefore, cross-cultural competence and the ability of the team to adapt appear to be just as necessary as professional expertise for the realization of its task.

Before examining the effect of differences on global teams, it is useful to review the elements that are essential to team dynamics. Davison and Ekelund (2004) describe three aspects:

- *Task and social processes are closely linked.* The task process directly influences the performance of the team while the social process is related to the ability of the team to work together over a longer time.
- *Emergent states.* Through interacting, members of a team create a collective mental environment in which the predispositions and assumptions of each member 'sets the stage for the dynamics'. The most important emergent states are: 'mutual trust, collective team identity and confidence in the team's ability to achieve its tasks'.
- *Co-ordinating mechanisms.* The mechanism most frequently used by teams for co-ordination purposes is the face-to-face meeting. Thanks to developing technology, online meetings are also becoming increasingly important.

Differences between team members, particularly in global teams, can be seen at several levels: profession, culture, personality, style and role, as well as organization. These differences can help improve the performance of the team, but can also be the source of conflict, depending on the way the team deals with these differences. Davison and Ekelund (2004) have compiled an overview of the ways in which differences can affect global teams (Table 16.2). The possible sources of difference are listed, together with the opportunities they may offer, where the differences may have an effect and how they may be experienced within the team. The final column describes ways in which the whole group must integrate to choose a process which it considers appropriate as a response to the source of difference given. This can be negotiating the problem, finding a compromise, achieving consensus or just voting – whatever the team agrees on.

Table 16.2 The effect of differences on global teams

Source of difference	Opportunity presented	Effect on	Experienced as	Integrated mechanisms
Preferred leadership styles	To make leaders and members actively search for the most effective leadership role(s) and style where both adjust and align their expectations	Effective leader/team member interaction, decision-making, levels of satisfaction	Frustrations, disagreements on form. Disappointment due to failed expectations	Openness about leader style and leader-team member expectations. Identification of conflicts and the best ways to handle them
National and organizational culture of origin and leadership of the organization	Can give core identity and sense of cohesion that can be adjusted/improved through experience in other cultures	People who share the nationality of the organization and its leadership are perceived as more influential than others	Perceived bias in accepted norms and levels of influence and access to resources. Glass ceiling based on nationality	Well-structured participative processes and inclusive policies
Preferred ways of resolving conflicts	Confronts team with need to find synergistic solutions	Ability to address difficult challenges and conflicts	Denial of conflict. Displaced frustrations. Lack of trust. Lack of group efficacy	Joint definition of which conflicts need to be addressed and how. Also which conflicts are to be avoided
Preferred ways of making decisions	Creates variety; highlights need to make decision-making processes explicit and suitable for different contexts	The quality of, involvement in, and follow up/implementation of decision-making processes	Lack of loyalty to decision and team. Dissatisfaction and lack of respect	Collective training on which type of decisions
Different languages yet working in one (often English)	May force native speakers to improve communication styles. May be a hindrance for second-language speakers	Interruption patterns. Use and interpretation of silence. Meaning of gestures and body language. Use of in jokes/humour. Dominant patterns of logic	Inability to participate. Frequent misunderstandings. Exclusive patterns of humour. Translation can be clumsy when building relationships	Choosing a working language and/or translators; maintaining steady rhythm and active listening skills
Different professions	Brings requisite variety of knowledge, skills, and approaches to complex problems. Speeds things up. Improves quality, relevance of output	Values and where to focus. Common professions can act as a large integrating factor	Power struggle. Ignorance. Misunderstanding	Definition of the uses of different functions in relation to the goal. Respect and positive acknowledgement
Expectations and values around interaction and team behaviour	Forces awareness of differences, assumptions, the tensions that they bring and the need to acknowledge and work with them	Levels of participation. Misunderstandings	Missed timing, anger at inappropriate reciprocity. Feeling misunderstood. Things not happening 'in the right way'	Value checklist-type exercises to make differences explicit and legitimate and then negotiate them

Table 16.2 (*continued*)

Source of difference	Opportunity presented	Effect on	Experienced as	Integrated mechanisms
Cultural preconceptions	Increased awareness of these. Approaching them with humour, not acting on them. A learning opportunity that there are many ways of seeing the world	Preconceived perceptions of more or less relevant experience, education	Stereotypical comments or implicit behaviour toward 'disadvantaged' people or about those 'in charge'	Highlighting team members' strengths and relevant experiences up front and using the strengths
International experience	Can bring empathy, flexibility, humbleness, self-reflection. People with international experience can act as bridges between core and local sites	Ability to understand implicit rules and working norms. Ability to speak different languages. Ability to empathize with other team members	Bias that wide International experience and linguistic skills are more essential for people from 'other' nationalities than for those whose mother tongue is the working language of the firm	Insist on international experience as part of international career path and selection criteria for international team leaders
Different geographical locations	Allows global efficiencies, local responsiveness, and knowledge transfer and learning across the organization	Who meets face-to-face and who does not. Co-ordination, timing understanding of importance of required actions	Impenetrable in groups in certain locations. Lack of loyalty, invisible agendas	Stress integrated team model spread across geography, not hub and spoke. Create hyper-attractiveness and virtual team visible locally and globally

Source: Davison and Ekelund (2004): 232–234.

Den Hartog (2004) suggests that teams whose leaders encourage reflective processes (i.e. discussions on subjects such as the work of the team and who is more likely to come forward with suggestions) will function better than teams where such processes are not to be found. Other aspects of the team context can reinforce such processes when the team is working as a virtual one, with members who come from diverse cultures. Such members may have different rules and expectations in communication. Seeking harmony, using implicit (high context) communication and saving face are the norms for certain cultures while other cultures consider open criticism and disagreement with their superiors to be the norm. The degree to which the communication process is expected to be structured and formal is also influenced by culture.

However, some writers think that the importance of the cultural dimension in the management of multicultural teams is over-stated. They believe that having clear objectives and a good allocation of roles and responsibilities among individual members of the team is enough to create teams that can work together. The synergy may not be present, but such teams do not create problems, and even produce good results.

The management of multicultural teams

For Chevrier (2000), managing teams composed of people from several cultures is the essential task of intercultural management. This type of management has become necessary as a consequence of the development of transnational companies and the globalization of economies.

The way management deals with the cultural diversity of these teams can vary. Some managers will appeal to the professional culture of its members to bring an international team together. (This appeal is not part of a Japanese manager's strategy since Japan does not attach the same value to professional culture as the West.) Other managers lay stress on the communication between the actors, such as making the unspoken, rules explicit, or using an approach that conforms either to what Chevrier calls American culture – or to the corporate culture.

Multicultural groups with the most harmonious relations are those whose members:

- have the same status;
- do not have contradictory interests;
- do not feel that their identity is threatened.

However, 'the absence of detailed understanding of other cultures, even if it creates irritations and causes other difficulties, including loss of time, will not prevent a team from reaching its goals' (Chevrier: 202).

Another characteristic of multicultural teams is their potential to be creative. Adler (2002) argues that, thanks to their diversity, such teams can work in a more creative way than homogeneous teams. Although multicultural teams encounter more process problems, they produce more divergent ideas, so favouring creativity, and propose more solutions for problems. Thus, it remains the challenge for the leaders of these teams to balance 'creativity (divergence) and cohesion (convergence)' (Adler, 2002: 146).

The word 'multicultural' can also refer to the issue of multiculturalism, observable in the working relations between members of a team composed of people who come from countries (large or small) or companies (large or small) or of people with unequal power. This is explained by Mutabazi and Deer when referring to Afro-Occidental teams (2003).

Afro-Western teams

In their study of Afro-Occidental teams, Mutabazi and Deer (2003) show that the problem associated with multiculturalism 'comes from pre-existing attitudes about relations between Africa and the West'. The dominant partner is the West, with its ideals and concepts of the world. This has repercussions on the relations in a team where one notices the indifference towards the values and perspectives of the other members, as well as the inability to have spontaneous interactions. Perfect integration between Western expatriates and local executives also appears to be impossible.

However, when the conditions regarding multiculturalism disappear, it is possible to achieve a high degree of integration, to go beyond the superficial relations work requires. This integration results in a mutual commitment that allows skills within the teams to be developed rather than just what Mutabazi and Deer call 'the opportunist addition of know-how techniques'.

One particular point in the authors' conclusions to their research on the African experience of intercultural team management deserves particular mention, the importance of time. According to Mutabazi and Deer (2003: 11–12), time is needed for a group composed of people from different national and professional cultures to develop a real team spirit. Without it, the manager of the team loses his credibility and the ability to mobilize all the team members. Enough time also needs to be given to the members of a cross-cultural team to gain a clear perception of the project they are undertaking. This will help them individually to grasp exactly what the purpose of their work is, to understand how it is to be achieved and in what period of time. All these elements can then be incorporated into their own particular reference system.

Working in a team implies change not only in the way of doing but also in the way of thinking. This teamwork pre-supposes the creation of common values and ideas, a delicate process in multicultural teams and organizations. This will be developed in Chapter 18. Teamwork also involves learning to deal with conflicts. This is what Chapter 17 will cover.

ACTIVITY 16.1   FT

Before reading the case study and answering the questions, read through the concepts of Chapters 13 and 14 again.

Global harmony is their dream

Virtual teams: Sarah Murray considers collaboration between dispersed staff of different cultures

If managing diversity in the workplace is a tough task for business leaders, the challenges of keeping executives from different backgrounds working together efficiently in various parts of the world is even more difficult.

However, virtual working presents some unexpected benefits to teams whose members come from a variety of backgrounds. For executives whose first language is not English, for instance, working by means of email or online chat rooms can eliminate many of the communication inequalities that might exist were the group to be working together face-to-face in the same location. People tend to be more comfortable reading and writing in their second language than speaking it, and email technology provides those less sure of the language with an opportunity to reflect before communicating.

'It certainly suggests that one of the things you should take into account is whether your team includes members who don't speak English well,' says Joanne Yates, a professor of management at MIT Sloan, who has studied the use of communication and information systems in companies. 'Any good virtual team has a communication plan that includes weekly conference calls or email check-ins, but with a virtual team where not everyone speaks English well, the regular report-ins should be in written mode rather than by phone or conference call.'

The other advantage of email communications is that, for those working in different time zones, group messages can be responded to when it is convenient, reducing the need for early morning or late night calls.

At the same time, using email for work exchanges can remove much of the hierarchy of professional communications, since many executives find it far less intimidating to send an email to someone in a senior position than to telephone them. 'In many organizations that are fairly hierarchical, the lower and middle management executives often won't communicate with senior managers if it means picking up the phone,' says Emma Kirk a psychologist at Pearn Kandola, a UK-based research business and consultancy of occupational psychologists. 'Email removes that barrier because of its informality and immediacy, so it encourages people to communicate that might not otherwise,' says Ms Kirk. 'And it's now accepted that people will send off ideas to each other via email.'

However, cultural or behavioural differences that can manifest themselves in face-to-face working situations can be exacerbated in virtual team working, particularly when the group has members from different backgrounds. One reason for this is that, when one is physically immersed in a new culture, it takes less time to adapt to the social norms and become aware of cultural sensitivities. So those trying to do this at a distance may find it tougher to fit in, increasing the potential for misunderstandings between team members. 'You don't build the relationships in the same way as you do working face-to-face, and you don't have those water cooler chats,' says Martin Galpin, a psychologist at Pearn Kandola.

He argues that the differences can become more problematic when people are not working in the same location. 'When you have a group of people who are more diverse, there's a danger of increasing the chances of conflict if you don't manage it effectively.' For this reason, experts advise that those managing virtual teams organize face-to-face meetings at the start of a project or the formation of a new team of executives who will be working together remotely.

While this is true for all virtual teams, it is even more important for those with cultural differences. 'If a team is newly formed, there's huge value in bringing that team together,' says Mr Galpin. 'Or if a new person joins the team, they need to be able to build new relationships. There's always a need for the social side – even if that's just setting aside time for more informal chats during the conference calls.'

Prof Yates points out that, when people in professional groups come from different backgrounds or cultures, it is often useful to appoint someone in the team who knows both cultures as the person responsible for setting the norms of working behaviour during a project that is being carried out from different locations.

And virtual working certainly does not eradicate the sort of cultural misunderstandings that can arise in a face-to-face situation. Prof Yates cites an online mini-conference she recently observed that took place between a group of US and Japanese executives working in the research and development unit of a Japanese company. 'A Japanese executive was putting text into a window for instant messaging when one of the Americans started asking questions in the middle of the presentation,' she explains. 'That was not culturally familiar and required an instant response, which caused real problems. So [virtual communications] have a cultural element as well.'

Source: *Financial Times*, 12 May 2005: 8.

Questions

1. According to the article, what are the advantages of virtual communication compared with working face-to-face in with people from different backgrounds? What other advantages can you think of?

2. The text does, however, suggest that virtual working groups should meet at the start of a project or when a new team of executives is to work together remotely. Why is this thought to be necessary?

3. What are the specific problems multicultural teams experience when they are communicating with each other virtually?

ACTIVITY 16.2

The following case study illustrates what may happen in the first meeting of a team that has been brought together to improve a company's fortunes.

A meeting of minds?

The Indian owners of an agricultural machine company, with a growing number of subsidiaries around the world, were determined to improve the productivity of their operations in Europe. To this end they sent a managing director (MD) from its headquarters in Bombay to head its recently acquired company in Italy and to spearhead changes in the running of the European operations. Before his departure, the MD had persuaded the owners that a cross-subsidiary team of key managers needed to be created which, under his leadership, would harmonize the decisions made by the two European companies they owned (one in Italy and another in Lithuania). This team would eventually serve as a basis for integrating decision-making across all of the company's operations in Europe and Asia.

The initial team was to consist of managers from the technical, production, quality control and client relation departments of the Italian and Lithuanian subsidiaries. The team would have its first meeting in Rome, with later meetings in

Vilnius and Bombay. The company's infrastructure would be updated to allow the team to meet virtually between their regular face-to-face meetings.

The MD regarded the first meeting as an opportunity for the team-members to get to know each other and to share information about day-to-day operations. Once he had explained his aims to his Italian management team, he left them to organize the meeting.

This get-together was conducted in English, which was the operating language of the concern. After the MD had explained his plans and the importance of the team in improving the company's fortunes, he asked the individual members to take it in turns to introduce themselves. The Lithuanian members each talked very briefly about their positions and responsibilities. The Italians, however, found it difficult to restrict themselves to introductions and started talking in detail and with great eagerness about all the machinery they were producing. There was only an outline agenda for the meeting, so the introductions quickly became a disorganized discussion dominated by the Italians. They talked about the manufacturing process ('We were the leaders in automated production ten years ago, but now we are a long way behind our competitors'), and complained vociferously about the working conditions ('Our main priority must be to renovate the factory. We cannot go on like this!'). They deplored the motivation of the employees ('Absenteeism is a terrible burden . . . but you people must have the same problem in your country'), and speculated about future products ('We wonder whether the company is going to continue with tractor production').

Unable to get a word in edgeways, one or two Lithuanians in the team now and again asked the MD if they could add to the discussion, but their requests were frequently drowned out by the loud comments of the Italian participants. All the Lithuanians really managed to do was to ask occasionally questions about certain products that they were also making.

Afterwards, when the team-members were drinking an aperitif before dinner, the MD wandered among the rather quiet Lithuanians on one side of the room, and asked them how they felt the meeting went. They were rather reluctant to respond at first, but eventually volunteered a few comments that showed their disappointment. One of them had this to say: 'We didn't really get the information we needed. We didn't find out enough about what is going on in your company – certainly not enough to write a decent report. Our management will wonder what we actually achieved here.' The MD then went over to the Italians on the other side of the room who were still continuing the discussion they had had during the meeting. When he asked one manager for his impression of the meeting, he was deluged with comments by everyone standing nearby. The reaction of one Italian participant reflected the general feelings of his fellow-countrymen: 'I don't understand why the visitors are so cold; they really didn't want to know anything about us and told us nothing about themselves. It should have gone much better – after all we speak the same technical language!'

Questions

1. Using the information given in the case study, as well as Table 16.2, make an analysis of the situation. Use the following questions as a guideline:

   - What are the 'sources of differences' in this case?

   - Which responses – appropriate or inappropriate – to the sources of these differences were used during the preparation for the meeting as well as the meeting itself?

2. How could the first meeting of the team have been more successful? Consider the suggestions below and add any ideas you may have.

   - The new managing director of the Italian subsidiary could have asked the Italian participants to organize a meeting some days before the one planned with their Lithuanian counterparts. This internal meeting could have functioned as a rehearsal for the 'real' meeting, with the managing director (as chairman) allowing the participants to speak as they wanted and not organizing the discussion in any way.

   - Those who were to attend the first meeting of the team could have been required to get to know each other beforehand, either through some kind of social/team-building event, or through telephone (conference) calls to each other, or even through video conferences.

Conclusion

After giving Senge's definition of the word 'team', this chapter presents the range of roles that, according to Belbin, individuals can play in a team. When considering how teams work in an international context, it can be seen that the culture of each individual involved not only influences their role, but also the dynamic process within the team. The 'culture' variable therefore can increase the difficulty of managing global teams, which may be composed of task-oriented and relationship-oriented cultures, high-context and low-context cultures, or even different ethnic groups, such as Afro-Western teams.

The success of teamwork is crucial to all international organizations. Whether they meet face-to-face or online, teams must address problems that go far beyond the field of communication. Creating common ideas and defining one's own values remains a challenge for those working in cross-cultural teams

Points for reflection

1. To what extent is it necessary for the leader of a multicultural team to be very familiar with the culture of each team-member?

2. To what extent do you think the leader of a global team can ensure its success by just resolving any communication problems within the team, such as the choice of language?

3. Some researchers in team dynamics argue that cultural differences have less influence on the effective functioning of a multicultural team than a good combination of team members. They maintain that the effective distribution of roles within the team is more likely to ensure its success. Discuss this standpoint.

Further reading

Lane, H.W., Maznevski, M.L., Mendenhall, M.E. and McNett, J. (eds) (2004) *The Blackwell Handbook of Global Management: A guide to managing complexity,* Oxford: Blackwell. This has been written for global executives and managers who are dealing with global complexity. The most important findings in the field – and their implications – are given in five areas: people and context, global competencies, leading and teaming, executing strategic initiatives globally, and special issues in developing and transitioning economies. The section on leading and teaming is of particular interest because the articles consider the importance of global teams, a relatively recent phenomenon in the world of business. Their diverse nature, in terms of function, organization as well as cultural composition, necessitate the development of both relational and cross-cultural competences among its members and those managing such teams.

References

Adler, N.J. (2002) *International dimensions of organizational behavior,* 4th edn, Cincinnati, OH: South-Western.

Aritzeta, A., Swailes, S. and Senior B. (2007) 'Belbin's role model: development, validity and applications for team building', *Journal of Management Studies,* 44 (1): 96–118.

Belbin, M. (1993) *Teams Roles at Work*, Oxford: Butterworth-Heinemann.

Chevrier, S. (2000) *Le management des équipes interculturelles,* Paris: Presses Universitaires de France.

Davison, S.C. and Ekelund, B.Z. (2004) 'Effective team processes for global teams' in Maznevski, H.W., Mendenhall, M.L. and McNett, J.M.E. (eds) *The Blackwell Handbook of Global Management,* Oxford: Blackwell: 227–249.

Den Hartog, D.N. (2004) 'Leading in a global context: vision in complexity' in Maznevski, H.W., Mendenhall, M.L. and McNett, J. M.E. (eds) *The Blackwell Handbook of Global Management,* Oxford: Blackwell: 175–198.

Deresky H., (2003) *International Management*: *Managing across borders and cultures*, 4th edn, New Saddle River, NJ: Prentice Hall.

Gluesing, J.C. and Gibson, C.B. (2004) 'Designing and forming global teams' in Maznevski, H.W., Mendenhall, M.L. and McNett, J.M.E. (eds) *The Blackwell Handbook of Global Management,* Oxford: Blackwell.

Inglehart, R. (1997) *The Silent Revolution: Changing values and political styles in advanced industrial society,* Princeton, NJ: Princeton University Press. Quoted by Schneider, S.C. and Barsoux, J.-L. (2003) *Managing Across Cultures*, 2nd edn, Harlow: Pearson Education.

Mutabazi, E. and Deer, C.B. (2003) 'The management of multicultural teams: the experience of Afro-Occidental teams in Africa', *Cahiers de recherche*, 13.

Robbins, S.P. (2000) *Essentials of Organizational Behaviour,* 6th edn, Upper Saddle River, NJ: Prentice Hall.

Schneider, S.C. and Barsoux, J.-L. (2003) *Managing Across Cultures*, 2nd edn, Harlow: Pearson Education.

Senge, P.M., Kleiner, A., Roberts, C. Ross, R.B. and Smith, B.J. (1995) *The Fifth Discipline Fieldbook,* London: Nicholas Brealey.

Chapter 17

Conflicts and cultural differences

Chapters 15 and 16 examined intercultural communication in negotiating and working in teams. This chapter examines an aspect of intercultural communication that is often a feature of both these activities, as well as of interaction between cultures generally, and that is conflict. Cultural differences can be a cause of conflict, and the way conflict is dealt with is influenced by the cultural background and experience of those involved. The ambiguous nature of intercultural conflict may compel those in dispute to deal with the situation by using approaches – or styles of communication – learned from their own culture; these may only serve to exacerbate the conflict.

Concept 17.1 will first look at the question of the styles of communication in conflict situations and the tendencies displayed by certain types of culture. It goes on to examine emotion in conflict and its role in different cultures. Approaches to the management of conflicts will then be surveyed, with examples taken from conflicts between Eastern and Western cultures. Finally, a more radical approach to managing conflict, the concept of conflict transformation, will be addressed.

Learning outcomes

After reading this chapter you will:

- Be aware how culture influences the way people communicate in conflict.
- Understand how different cultural values affect the way people perceive and manage conflicts.
- Realize how particular communicative skills can transform the way people perceive the nature of conflict and the attitudes of those involved.

Concept 17.1   Understanding and dealing with conflicts

The nature of conflict

To gain a clearer insight into what conflict entails, it would be useful to define the very term in relation to managing and resolving disputes, whether within or between cultures. Yet, as Saphiro and Kulik (2004: 177) indicate, there seems to be no comprehensive definition of conflict because the many disciplines involved – psychology, sociology, anthropology and communication – each have their own. However, these definitions all agree on the moment when a conflict appears. This is when people with differing needs or goals are prevented – or perceive that they are being prevented – by others in achieving these needs or goals.

Incompatibility of goals in terms of material resources is referred to in relatively recent social psychology theory as the source of inter-group conflict. As Liu (2004) indicates, this realistic group conflict theory sees struggles over (limited) structural resources such as land, oil, gold and labour as the source of inter-group conflict, not personal characteristics. These insights were developed by social identity theory, whereby conflict between groups is seen to be the result of perceived identities. As noted in the introduction to Part Three, if one group perceives itself as being different to another, then prejudicial attitudes and discriminatory behaviour can result in favour of the in-group against the out-group. Both theories, however, stress that it is the situation that causes the conflict rather than the personalities of those involved.

Ting-Toomey (1999) also sees conflict as involving (cultural) groups protecting their own self-image, as well as intercultural perceptions, which are coloured by ethnocentrism and stereotypes. However, she sees conflict as involving not just the situation but also communicative behaviours, which are profoundly shaped by the way individuals in a culture conceptualize the sense of self. Those who regard themselves as having an *independent sense of self* 'value individualism, personal achievement, self-direction, and competition.' Those who see themselves as having an *interdependent sense of self* 'want to fit in with others, act appropriately, protect others' goals, and value conformity and co-operation' (page 77). Ting-Toomey maintains that both types of self-construct are to be found within each culture, but that the independent self-concepts are to be found more often in individualist cultures, and interdependent self-concepts are more prevalent in collectivistic cultures.

Those with an independent sense of self will view communication in the conflict process as welcome, provided both parties address the issues in an open, honest manner. In this way, the chance to talk openly about thwarted needs or goals may prove very productive, with tangible results, even creative solutions. Those with an interdependent sense of self tend to see conflict as negative and unproductive, particularly if the other party is assertive and does not properly address issues or relational feelings. A conflict process is only satisfactory if the 'faces' of both parties have been saved in addition to a productive agreement.

A model of conflict styles

Several models have been proposed to predict and explain communicative behaviours during conflict. Reference is often made to a person's conflict style, which Hocker and Wilmot define as 'patterned responses or clusters of behavior that people use in conflict' (1985: 96), 'style' being used to denote a way of communicating that reflects not only a person's cultural traits and personality, but also the situation in which the conflict takes place.

A number of these models emanate from a typology proposed by Blake and Mouton (1964) based on two dimensions defining the negotiators' concerns: 'concern for production' and 'concern for people'. This dual concern model was originally prescriptive in nature, but through it being validated by many empirical studies it is now considered to be descriptive. Other researchers have re-labelled the two orientations, but maintained the original opposing notions of concern for self and concern for others, echoing the distinction made earlier between independent and interdependent sense of self.

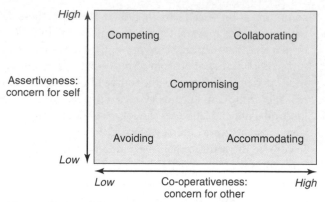

Figure 17.1 Two-dimensional taxonomy of conflict handling modes
Source: Thomas and Kilmann (1974): 11.

Consider the model in Figure 17.1 devised by Thomas and Kilmann (1974). A questionnaire based on this model (see www.pyschometrics.com) is used extensively by consultants to assess how conflict-handling styles affect personal and group dynamics. The model allows individuals to be placed in five categories on the assumption that there are two factors in a person's conflict style defined as follows:

- assertiveness – the degree to which a person is concerned with his or her own interests; and

- co-operativeness – the degree to which a person is concerned with the interests of others.

If someone is low on both dimensions, then that person is an avoider, unassertive and unco-operative, rather withdrawn, preferring instead to put off an issue (possibly to save face). Someone who is high on the assertiveness dimension but low on the co-operative dimension is competitive, preferring to pursue their self-concern rather than the concern for others. An accommodating person, low on assertiveness but high on co-operativeness will be concerned more with others' needs rather than their own. Those in the middle 'box' will try to compromise between their own needs and those of the other party, trying to find a solution which, although not fully satisfactory, may resolve the issue in the short-term. A person high on both the assertiveness and co-operative dimensions works actively to develop a solution to a conflict to satisfy the needs of both parties. This collaborative, or integrative, approach involves attempts to reveal the underlying concerns of the other party.

Apart from the 'avoiding' style, the strategic choices imply willingness to make concessions by at least one of those involved in the dispute. The collaborating style is seen as being the most beneficial for those concerned. Unlike 'compromising', it is about working out a problem together, often by brainstorming, a method that responds best to the needs of both parties. The avoiding style means that those involved in a conflict do not overtly recognize that there is any dispute.

Originally, the model was to be seen as predictive, and experimental studies appear to support its predictions. However, one of the original designers of the model, Thomas, has downplayed the predictive nature of the model by referring to it more as a classification of modes (Thomas, 1992).

The effectiveness of such a model is questioned by some researchers. Saphiro and Kulik (2004) doubt whether it can be applied to the increasing complexity of modern-day disputes. Such a model needs to take account of the following elements:

- The parties in dispute do not always know each other. This applies particularly to situations where organizations rather than individuals are in dispute. If it is impossible for one to identify the other in some way, then taking action to resolve differences can be very difficult.

- The strategic choices for the disputing parties are not always 'free'. Circumstances such as previous dealings with the parties concerned, government legislation and financial restrictions could narrow any room for manoeuvre.

- Modes of communication used during conflict: the model assumes that communication between the parties is direct. A number of modern-day disputes, however, take place over large distances, without any resort to face-to-face resolution.

Another objection is that raised by Leung et al (2002). They point to the fact that a dual concern model such as this is focused solely on instrumentality because conflict behaviours are driven by concerns for the outcome of the conflict, either in terms of concern for self or concern for the other. They propose the introduction of harmony into the model. As a goal in itself, rather than a means to an end, harmony can be seen as a value perspective concerned with the relationship between the self and the other rather than focusing on concern for self or the other. At the same time harmony can be an instrumental perspective whereby the focus is on using a conflict-free relationship to achieve a goal.

The proposal by Leung et al (2002) to introduce harmony into the dual concerns model is made in the light of their investigation into conflict avoidance, a feature common in East Asia, and one associated with collectivistic cultures. Conflict avoidance can in the end be just as dysfunctional in the long run, they argue, as competing (or dominating) behaviour. The harm caused by the competing style to relationships may be more apparent and given more attention in conflict management literature, but an avoiding conflict style can cause equal harm to relationships in a more subtle manner by replacing genuine problem-solving with superficial harmony.

These considerations invite an examination of conflict management in Eastern cultures where the conflict styles used are not fully accounted for in dual concerns models.

Before this, however, some attention will be given to one particular element that affects all types of behaviour relating to conflict management.

Culture, emotions and conflict

The culture value systems examined in this book have a profound effect on the ways in which emotions are experienced, expressed and controlled.

Kumar (2004) has investigated the theme of culture and emotions in intercultural negotiations, but his findings are relevant to conflicts generally between cultures for which a resolution of some kind is needed. He has adopted the definition of emotions as 'high-intensity affective states that stem from the focal actors' ability or inability to achieve their goals' (2004: 96). The nature of the goals pursued, however, varies across cultures according to the value systems of the cultures concerned. The greater the distance between cultures and their value systems, he hypothesises, the more likely it is that perceived dissimilarity will cause negative emotions to emerge, particularly when cross-cultural encounters are ambiguous and unpredictable.

Kumar uses the individualist/collectivist cultural dimension to put together the findings of research as to typologies of emotion. 'Ego-focused' emotions such as anger, frustration, pride and guilt are linked to the (non-)fulfilment of individual goals, whereas 'Other-focused' emotions such as shame, anxiety and fear are related to the (in-)ability to promote the interdependent self, to show oneself as belonging to the social context. The difference is essentially that ego-focused emotions reflect the need for individuals to show their particular identity whereas other-focused emotions reflecting the need to 'fit in'. Although some research findings do not always confirm this hypothesis (possibly because of contextual factors in the measurement process), the distinction is an appealing one.

As for the behaviour associated with emotions, clear individualist/collectivist differences can be discerned. Individualist, ego-focused emotions can cause individuals to try harder to reach their goals. Collectivist, other-focused emotions can cause individuals to repair the damage done to relations. As Kumar (2004: 102) points out, the association between certain emotions and certain actions has important implications for intercultural interaction, particularly the discovery that 'different negative emotional states have different motivational implications'. In negotiation conflict, for example, those undergoing negative ego-focused feelings will put pressure on their opponents to make concessions, whereas those experiencing other-focused feelings may adjust their expectations to get an agreement. However, in some cultures, it seems that those experiencing other-focused emotions will be very reluctant to take any action. Kumar recounts his own finding that Japanese negotiators do not feel any compulsion to come up with new proposals if the negotiation process has hit a roadblock.

This last observation from Kumar (2004) reflects the first of three points he has to make concerning the extra dynamics which can arise during an encounter between disputants from different cultures:

- People from individualistic cultures are less constrained in their ability to overcome an impasse than negotiators from collectivist cultures. The latter are more likely to share the same perception of a given event and unlike their individualistic counterparts will find it difficult to suggest a way round an obstacle.

- This unanimity goes also for the way those from collectivist cultures respond overtly to emotion. Their obligation to maintain group harmony and conform with its ways may not allow them to express their frustration openly or make emotional individual responses. Expressions of strong feelings provoke unseemly attention to a person's individuality and distinctness. They must be countered with attempts to restore personal composure in a way that restores harmony and prevents embarrassment.

- People from collectivistic societies are more sensitive to emotions that arise from a contravention of relational norms than from failure to attain desired goals. If emotional behaviour within such a society is felt to threaten harmony, the person exhibiting that behaviour tends to be regarded as unreliable and untrustworthy. Should a person who is not from the 'in-group' behave in such a way, collectivists may be less reluctant to respond aggressively.

This final point raises the issue of behavioural incompatibility. What if conflict occurs between people from individualistic and collectivistic cultures? Emotions could drive them further apart, with one side attempting to force a resolution to the dispute and the other withdrawing from any interaction. In short, as Kumar (2004: 104) says, '. . . emotions reflect who we are as individuals and within relationships'. Emotions, in short, can exacerbate the in-group/out-group distinction and make any resolution of the conflict even more difficult.

Nicotera (1993) sees the need for an emotion component in models of conflict styles such as the Thomas–Kilmann model referred to earlier, suggesting the inclusion of 'emotional intent' as a third dimension. This would, he argued, allow the model to take account of the basic mechanisms driving behaviour. Avoidance behaviour might therefore not just be to do with low concern for the other, but also because the person concerned is unwilling to deal with the emotional discomfort involved in the conflict. This suggested affective component is examined in Chapter 18.

Ting-Toomey et al (2000) advocate the inclusion of emotional expression. They recognize that a model such as Thomas–Kilmann's cannot account for the many subtleties in conflict management, particularly with regard to cultural and ethnic differences in conflict. The model Ting-Toomey and Oetzel (2002) propose is one based on their critical review of studies in the area of cultural conflict and includes emotional expression as well as neglect and third-party help. The model is given in Figure 17.2.

The inclusion of neglect accounts for responses that the authors call 'passive-aggressive' and which side-step the conflict at hand. Such responses receive an indirect reaction from the others in conflict. Another element proposed is third-party help, using an outsider who is acceptable to both sides to act as mediator. Use of mediation is not to be regarded as a form of avoidance, but rather a reflection of concern for both self and the other. Indeed, its employment is one possible way of overcoming the behavioural incompatibility referred to earlier.

The third-party conflict style is given more attention later on in this concept when examining the notion of conflict transformation as a radical way of resolving incompatibilities between those in conflict.

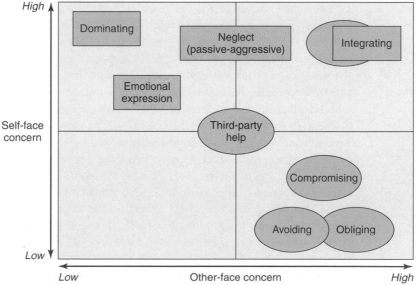

Figure 17.2 An eight-style conflict grid: an intercultural approach

Source: Ting-Toomey and Oetzel (2002): 160.

Management of conflict

Although a manager is expected to resolve conflicts as part of his general brief, the task is nevertheless a difficult one. When confronted with a conflict he has to make sure that a local dispute does not damage the whole organization. The importance of conflict management increases in an international context where organizations and people from different cultures are at work. Here, immense complications can arise whose knock-on effect can impinge severely on an organization's performance. If well managed, however, conflicts can improve relations between partners, customers and employees.

Having said that, attitudes towards conflicts can vary considerably from culture to culture, as can the ways in which conflicts are addressed. These differences relate to:

- The degree to which disagreement is acceptable and therefore the extent to which conflict is tolerated.
- The strategies to be adopted when dealing with conflicts.
- The moment when the manager needs to intervene and the way he intervenes.

The discussion below reflects considerations from Chapter 15 on the issue of distributive and integrative strategies in negotiating. The reader will recall that negotiating in Western management literature is often dealt with in terms of conflict management, that negotiating is essentially seen as a formalized way of resolving a conflict, a carefully managed problem-solving process whereby a number of techniques can be applied such as:

- Win-lose: the competitive approach, whereby the goals of one party are achieved at the expense of the other.
- Win-win: the co-operative approach, whereby the two parties collaborate to bring about a resolution to the conflict which is of benefit to both.

According to Covey (1989: 206), each of these approaches is 'a philosophy of human interaction', rather than being just a technique. Elaborating on these, he regards the 'win-lose' approach as an authoritarian one whereby people use their position, power, credentials or some other influence to get their way. The 'opposite' approach – 'lose-win' – is seen as total acquiescence to a situation, capitulation, doing anything to keep the peace. When two competitive – 'win-lose' – personalities interact, the outcome may well be a 'lose/lose' outcome. Both sides become so fixated by the behaviour of the other that all they want is for the other to lose, even if the result is that they lose as well. As Covey sees it, this is adversarial conflict, a war in which both sides can be annihilated.

When there is no context of competition, the 'win' approach is the most common. The only thing being considered here is the need to accomplish one's own goals. Nothing else is taken into account – others must look out for themselves.

The win-win approach is what Covey considers to be the healthiest form of interaction. A conflict is resolved with mutually beneficial outcomes for all parties. No one person or side needs to win or 'be right'. However, if a beneficial outcome cannot be achieved for both sides, there is 'no deal' and both can walk away.

As noted earlier, Ting-Toomey (1999) also considers such a win-win approach as being satisfactory, but only if the 'faces' of both parties have been saved in addition to a productive agreement. Unlike Covey, she explicitly addresses the culture-based factors in any intercultural conflict, including the perception of what is effective and what is appropriate in conflict resolution according to the self-construals of the individuals concerned.

Those with an independent sense of self will, she argues, consider a conflict effectively resolved if there has been a frank and open discussion of opinions, clarification of interests and goals reached or compromised – and plans for avoiding future conflict. The conflict will have been appropriately resolved if they have shown themselves to be sensitive towards the circumstances and causes of the conflict. Those with an interdependent sense of self will see the conflict as effectively resolved if faces have been saved and substantive consensus reached. For them, appropriate management involves meeting 'face' need during the conflict and settling any 'face' debts or obligations in the longer term.

When such different perceptions of effective and appropriate resolution are in play, any management of conflict involves each party making a great effort to bear in mind the cultural perspectives and personality factors. Ting-Toomey (1999) suggests a number of skills which can be developed to enhance conflict management, most of them linked to the idea of **mindfulness**, a concept described by Langer (1990), which involves being able to develop new categories (i.e. applying culturally-sensitive concepts such as high/low context communication styles) and being open to new information. One particular skill Ting-Toomey (1999: 221) refers to is **mindful reframing**. To manage conflict, those involved must 'learn how to "translate" each other's verbal and non-verbal messages from the context of the other's cultural viewpoint'. Furthermore, mindful reframing means also that those involved need to 'reprioritize their goals after mindfully observing and listening to the viewpoints and expectations of their opponents'.

One strategy which can be followed to facilitate this process is what Ting-Toomey calls **collaborative dialogue**. This is an inquiry process during which the parties try to grasp the cultural and personal elements involved in the conflict by inviting the other involved – either directly or through example – to tell their stories and talk in some way or other about their expectations and issues to do with face. Time and patience are of the essence, as well as the eventual willingness of the parties to suspend their own assumptions regarding the conflict.

Mindfulness is an approach not just to conflict management but to communicating generally. It involves monitoring the communication process, tailoring messages in line with the expectations of the receiver, finding the right wavelength on which to communicate. As such, mindfulness is relevant to effective and appropriate communication both within and between cultures. Chapter 18, which examines intercultural communicative competence, will examine this and other related skills.

Skills in the area of conflict management can be increased to some extent through developing cognitive awareness as to how other cultures perceive and manage conflict. To this end, this chapter will now examine how three countries in the Asia-Pacific region deal with conflict.

Managing conflict in the Asia-Pacific region

The people in the Asia-Pacific region, just as in other regions, often come into conflict in negotiations on issues ranging from the very specific to questions on setting up industries or working conditions. What interests Leung and Tjosvold (1998) is that those involved often have very different views as to how such conflicts should be managed. What seems reasonable to one group can appear strange to another. Methods of conflict management that appear natural and effective to an American can seem totally unproductive and inappropriate to a Japanese. On the other hand, although Koreans usually prefer to deal with conflicts outside the office during social events, Singaporeans will consider a formal discussion more appropriate. When divergent interests cause a conflict in Indonesia, social norms requires that an individual be prepared to take second place and, if necessary, leave aside personal interests and seek a common agreement to maintain harmony.

The contributors to Leung and Tjosvold's book (1998) reveal stereotypes they hold about their own and other countries concerning conflict management. Although conceding that their compatriots do not always manage conflicts effectively, the contributors explain how this is done. Their articles on three particular countries in the Asia Pacific region – Malaysia, Thailand and Korea – will be summarized below.

Malaysia

Malaysia is composed of several ethnic groups: 61 per cent of the population is Malays (and by constitutional definition Muslim), 27 per cent of Chinese origin and 8 per cent of Indian origin. There are also other Malaysians of European, Middle Eastern, Cambodian, Thai and Vietnamese origin. The presence of so many ethnic groups makes Malaysia a particularly interesting country in which to examine the management of conflict at an intracultural level.

The Muslim Malays are seen as being more pragmatic than Muslims in the Middle East and Pakistan. They have succeeded in maintaining their practice of Islam while being liberal and competitive in their commercial activities. They have managed to create their own economic system, which includes Islamic banks and insurance companies.

In his contribution to the book, Mansor (1998) mentions that the Chinese, who have come in large numbers to Malaysia, have developed social structures and values that in a broad sense have become an integral part of Malaysian society. Values such as 'hard work' and 'practical sense' have allowed them to succeed in business, to set up many family companies and keep control of them.

For historical reasons – both commercial and religious (Hinduism existed in Malaysia before Islam) – the Indians have been part of Malaysian culture for many centuries. Their respect for authority and hierarchy is reflected in the status they accord people working in government service and in the professions.

Mansor (1998) goes on to analyse certain core values of the aboriginal Malays that are applicable to Malaysian society generally:

- concern for face: this is of importance across all ethnic groups and is related to the notion of dignity, to how people see themselves as well as how they are seen by others.
- concern for others: this has to do with generosity, respect, honesty and sincerity, as well as being upright and caring. Malaysians hope these qualities will be reciprocated by their interlocutors.

Expectation of reciprocity brings these two elements together. Reciprocity is seen as a sign of respect towards others; not showing respect amounts to losing face. This in turn is regarded as being worse than physical maltreatment. What is more, no redemption is possible.

Respect for seniority, one of the principles of Confucianism, is another value embraced by all major ethnic groups – aboriginal Malaysian, Indians and Chinese. It plays an important role in the workplace. When a conflict breaks out in a Malaysian context, it is always important to know which of the two parties is older. In some conflicts a third person – preferably of a certain age – can serve as mediator: when two parties cannot come to an agreement, the only way to mediate, or at least to clarify the issues, is to call in a 'neutral senior', seniority being attributed either in terms of age or social status. That is why the intervention by the 'boss' is considered desirable, even when the conflict is seen as insignificant.

The core values outlined above explain, for example, why subordinates will never confront their superior, even if they do not appreciate his behaviour. Rather than disagreeing publicly, employees will behave in an unco-operative manner and eventually resign themselves to the way their boss behaves. The core values also account for the durability of personal relations: even if a strong divergence of opinion results in conflict, the confidence and loyalty developed between friends and colleagues will predominate. However, despite the importance given to friendship as a basis for business relations, the Malay businessman will still maintain a rational approach to his work.

Thailand

Thailand is relatively homogeneous compared with Malaysia, with 85 per cent of the population speaking Thai and sharing the same culture. According to Roongrengsuke and Chansuthus (1998), the name given to Thailand – 'The land of smiles' – faithfully reflects the social harmony in this country. They point out, however, that behind this collective smile hides a complex social web in which individualism is quite predominant. The result is behaviour which causes much confusion and disagreement among those non-Thais who have tried to do business in the country. Roongrengsuke and Chansuthus (1998: 168) give the following illustration:

> A British manager, upset about the continued unauthorised borrowing of equipment between departments, burst in on a meeting being held by his Thai subordinates and loudly berated the responsible person in front of his peers. Unwilling to dignify the insulting behaviour with a response, the Thais remained silent, smiling grimly, until the offending manager left. The incident was followed, however, by a work slowdown and a spate of resignations of key personnel.

When faced with such an unpleasant situation, a Thai smiles. He smiles not only in pleasant situations, but also in stress-filled situations that could be a source of considerable conflict.

When conflicts do erupt between Thais and non-Thais, the causes are often to do with lack of respect for deadlines, reluctance to take responsibility for a task, the imprecise – or tardy – nature of information delivered, the lack of service available, in short a lack of co-operation all round. These difficulties seem to be symptoms of a more profound problem. The Thais are basically more 'relationship-oriented' than 'results-oriented'. Therefore, to get results, non-Thais need to spend a lot of time creating strong and reciprocal relations with their protagonists at all levels of an organization. These relations will form the network on which the non-Thai will depend if he wishes to realize the objectives he has set himself. The Thais need to create an environment in their place of work that resembles the family circle.

Another aspect in the example given by Roongrengsuke and Chansuthus (1998) is the lack of emotion displayed by the Thai head of department. For a Thai to show his feelings in public would be the sign of a lack of self-discipline, which could in turn result in his losing status, prestige and, above all, face. Thais have been trained from childhood to avoid situations where they could lose face, by neutralizing their emotions and confining their problems to their private life.

This education reflects the teachings of Buddhism, the national religion of Thailand for more than seven hundred years. Its Karmic law is the origin of practices such as moderation, tolerance and compassion. Any behaviour shown in situations of conflict that does not reflect Karmic practices must be carefully avoided. If this is not possible, then a compromise is the preferred option. In fact, the values of the Thai culture encourage harmonious relations and discourage open conflict of any kind. The Thai concept of 'jai yen' (meaning literally 'cool heart') and one that emanates from Buddhism, is a very efficient mechanism for ensuring this social harmony while preserving an individual's 'face'.

According to the authors, the methods of conflict management such as those outlined earlier in the Thomas–Kilmann model could not be applied in Thailand. One fundamental reason for this is that conflict is rarely if ever regarded as either positive or negative, even by Thais who have taken management studies in Western countries. This accounts for why, if a conflict does arise, a third party – traditionally a respected elder – is called on to mediate.

Korea

Korea, with its very homogeneous population, reflects in a way the differences and similarities between Western and Eastern attitudes to conflict. On the basis of empirical research carried out by Cho and Park (1998: 31), four characteristics emerge with regard to South Korea:

- Koreans prefer a non-competitive (or non-dominating) strategy in face-to-face conflict.

- Koreans prefer resorting to a higher position or authoritarian personality to resolve conflict rather than trying to find an integrative solution.

- Koreans differentiate between in-group and out-group situations when handling conflict. When dealing with out-groups, their strategy is comparable to the competitive approach in Western culture.

- Koreans make efforts in managing conflict beyond those used in face-to-face conflict situations. This can be compared with what the authors call the Chinese 'self-confining' approach.

Mediation and conflict transformation

This brief survey of approaches to conflict in three countries in the Asia-Pacific area highlights the ways in which culture influences the perception and management of conflicting objectives and incompatible ideas. One similarity is the process of mediation by someone in the group concerned whose legitimacy rests on their social status within the group, knowledge of traditions, as well as personal characteristics. The mediation will be wide-ranging, encompassing issues for the group as a whole. This type of mediation is often contrasted with that used in Western cultures. Here, the authority of the mediator is seen as being defined more in terms of their expertise and experience, and frequently exercised within a legal framework. The process of mediation will be tightly focused and not pursue more general issues.

The skills involved in mediation include those already mentioned, particularly the idea of mindful reframing. By mindfully observing and listening to the viewpoints and expectations of the parties in dispute, the mediator can reframe the content and process issues of both parties and transform the whole conflict in terms of the attitudes and behaviour of those involved. If this is done, the conflict itself can be restructured to open space for cooperation.

This idea of **conflict transformation** is receiving much attention in relation to conflicts between countries. Its advocates see it as a more radical way of dealing with conflict and its long-term effects. The process involves first transforming attitudes, then transforming behaviour, then transforming the actual conflict in question by pinpointing incompatibilities and removing them (Augsburger, 1992).

As Botes (2003) indicates, conflict transformation is more concerned with the underlying causes of conflict and that this involves carrying out transformations at personal, social and structural level. Its proponents see conflict management or even conflict resolution as being more to do with putting out fires, which will come to life again after a short time. Conflict transformation, on the other hand, is a radical process that changes the whole nature of the relationship between warring parties.

Mediation is put forward as a possible instrument of transformation, but third-party intervention is not necessary if the parties involved are prepared to perceive the conflict process in terms of their own assumptions as well as in terms of those with whom they are in contention. This again brings up the notion of mindfulness, particularly mindful reframing whereby an integrated long-term perspective can be developed through collaborative dialogue.

This chapter has considered the notion of conflict and the role of culture in the perception and management thereof. Consideration has also been given to some of the skills involved, not only in conflict management but also in the notion of crisis transformation. This transformational approach prepares the ground for the notion of third-culture building, which is dealt with in Chapter 18.

As will be clear from the last part of this concept in particular, attention is moving away from relations between cultures and turning more towards the interaction between individuals involved in intercultural communication. This chapter's partial focus on the skills required for handling intercultural conflicts will be expanded upon in Chapter 18, which will deal with the skills individuals need to interact effectively and appropriately with people from other cultures. These are the skills required of anyone who wishes to be an effective intercultural communicator.

ACTIVITY 17.1

Crisis? What crisis?

During a visit to Japan, when the market was particularly bad, I was privileged to be witness to a peculiar incident that can only be explained in terms of cultural differences. The Japanese have a deserved reputation for being very tough negotiators. Our opposition on the occasion seemed to relish their position of strength and pummelled our suggested price down to a very low level indeed. The negotiations carried on for approximately an hour, when the Japanese gave us an ultimatum of either accepting their price or cancelling the deal.

My boss, a grey-haired British individual well-known and respected in the industry, is normally extremely polite when it comes to Japanese customers. The frustration of having a weak negotiation position, coupled with the pressure he felt at having to sell at a price that was hardly profitable, led to an uncharacteristic outburst. For a good fifteen minutes he harangued the Japanese team about their hypocrisy of criticizing white South Africans for exploiting blacks, while at the same time buying at prices that would lead to mine closures and the retrenchment of thousands of black workers. It was apparent from his demeanour that my boss was prepared to lose the customer rather than compromise on price.

After he concluded his monologue, a stunned silence followed. Our agent was aghast at the rudeness and started to apologize in Japanese. He was abruptly cut short by a few curt words from the Japanese lead negotiator.

The customer's team engaged in a whispered consultation. After a short time they asked us and our agent to leave the room, and wait outside in the passage. There we were left to cool our heels for an uncomfortable fifteen minutes, with our agent casting reproachful glances at my boss. At the end of the fifteen minutes we were summoned back into the room.

The Japanese team had recovered their composure, and regarded us with perfect inscrutability. Their chief negotiator, in a significant departure from protocol, dispensed with the traditional translator and addressed us in fluent English: 'Johnson, we appreciate your frankness in explaining the situation in South Africa to us for our better understanding. We have very seriously considered what you have said. We have therefore decided not to accept your offer.'

At this point we felt the tension really growing. We were after all going to lose this customer. Then the Japanese negotiator continued: 'We will however make you another offer. We have decided to offer you an additional fifty cents per tonne above the price that you originally asked for.'

This took a few moments to sink in. After insulting the Japanese, we were going to receive even more than we asked for. We accepted the offer with alacrity and good grace and returned to our hotel to celebrate and marvel at the strange course of events that had unfolded.

Sources: adapted from Browaeys and Trompenaars (2000): case 1.

Questions

1. Why did the Japanese offer a higher price than originally required?

2. What is the conflict-handling style chosen by each party? Give evidence from the case to support your answer.

3. Extract from the text those moments when emotions (do not) appear. Which are typically Japanese or British? Can you explain why?

Conclusion

This chapter has examined the way in which cultural values affect how we perceive and deal with conflicts. It presented two models to account for different conflict styles, which both essentially relate to the extent to which people are concerned about themselves and about those with whom they are in conflict. The way in which emotions are experienced and expressed according to cultural values was also explained.

The role of mediation as a way of resolving incompatibilities was considered and examples given of its use in the Asia-Pacific region. The chapter also showed how mediation-type behaviour, particularly 'mindfulness' (taking account of the different cultural perspectives and personalities involved), can promote conflict resolution without the intervention of a third party. The chapter also put forward the notion of cultural transformation whereby personal, social and structural factors can be transformed through mediation and/or collaborative dialogue.

Points for reflection

1. There are several strategies and methods for managing conflicts and each culture has its own preferences in this respect. The fundamental issue, however, is how each culture perceives the notion of conflict. For some, it can mean confrontation and hostility, for others it means no more than a difference of views. These differences are also reflected in the way people communicate in such situations: certain cultures create a tension, a climate of conflict during a discussion to force a debate on the issue in question.

   How do you perceive the notion of conflict?

2. When there are incompatible goals, practices and attitudes among the parts of an organization, conflicts can arise. There are many possible reasons for conflict.

   What, according to you, are the conflict sources within an organization?

3. The concept includes two proposed models (Figures 17.1 and 17.2) which account for different ways of handling conflict.

   What do you consider to be the essential similarities between the two models as well as the essential differences? How do you account for the positioning of the emotional component in Figure 17.2? Do you think this positioning applies to all cultures? If not, what change would you make to the model?

4. It is considered normal for a dynamic company to have conflicts between those working in a team, and for a manager to manage these tense situations and the resulting emotions (such as aggression). However, it is considered preferable not to wait till a conflict degenerates and becomes a real crisis but to intervene beforehand.

   How, in your opinion, can a manager prevent a crisis from happening?

Further reading

Leung, K. and Tjosvold, D. (eds) (1998) *Conflict Management in the Asia Pacific: Assumptions and approaches in diverse cultures.* **Singapore: John Wiley.** The book is about doing business globally and the chapters address not only the different ways in which nations manage domestic conflict but also how they manage conflict in international business. The authors of the chapters draw upon a range of disciplines to document the attitudes to conflict in Asia-Pacific countries. This can help business partners, managers and employees to appreciate and prepare for the variety of methods by which people in these countries manage conflict.

References

Augsburger, D.W. (1992) *Conflict Mediation across Cultures: Pathways and patterns* Louisville, KY: Westminster/John Knox Press.

Blake, R. and Mouton, J. (1964) *The Managerial Grid: The key to leadership excellence*, Houston: Gulf Publishing.

Botes, J. (2003) 'Conflict transformation: a debate over semantics or a crucial shift in the theory and practice of peace and conflict studies?' *The International Journal of Peace Studies*, 8 (2): 1-27.

Browaeys, M.-J., and Trompenaars, F. (eds) (2000) *Cases Studies on Cultural Dilemmas*, Breukelen, Netherlands: Nyenrode University Press.

Cho, Y.-H. and Park, H.-H. (1998) 'Conflict management in Korea: The wisdom of dynamic collectivism' in Leung, K. and Tjosvold, D. (eds) *Conflict Management in the Asia Pacific,* Singapore: John Wiley: 13–48.

Covey, S.R. (1989) *The 7 habits of highly effective people,* New York, NY: Free Press.

Hocker, J.L. and Wilmot, W.W. (1985) *Interpersonal Conflict,* Dubuque, IA: William C. Brown.

Kumar, E. (2004) 'Culture and emotions in intercultural negotiations' in Gelfand, M.J. and Brett, J.M. (eds), *The Handbook of Negotiation and Culture,* Stanford, CA: Stanford University Press: 95-113.

Langer, E.J. (1990) *Mindfulness*, Cambridge, MA: Da Capo Press.

Leung, K., Koch, P.T. and Lu, L. (2002) 'A dualistic model of harmony and its implications for conflict management in Asia', *Asia Pacific Journal of Management*, 19: 201-220.

Leung, K. and Tjosvold, D. (eds) (1998) *Conflict Management in the Asia Pacific,* Singapore: John Wiley.

Liu, J.H. (2004) *A Cultural Perspective on Inter-group Relations and Social Identity.* (www.wwu.edu/~culture), Washington, US: Western Washington University, Bellingham.

Mansor, N. (1998) 'Managing conflict in Malaysia: cultural and economics influences' in Leung, K. and Tjosvold, D. (eds), *Conflict Management in the Asia Pacific,* Singapore: John Wiley: 147-166.

Mitchell, C. (2002) 'Beyond resolution: what does conflict transformation actually transform?' *Peace and Conflict Studies*, 9 (1): 1-23.

Nicotera, A.M. (1993) 'Beyond two dimensions: a grounded theory model of conflict handling behavior', *Management Communication Quarterly,* 6: 282-306.

Roongrengsuke, R. and Chansuthus, D. (1998) 'Conflict management in Thailand' in Leung, K. and Tjosvold, D. (eds), *Conflict Management in the Asia Pacific,* Singapore: John Wiley: 167-221.

Saphiro, D.L. and Kulik, C.T. (2004) 'Resolving disputes between faceless disputants: new challenges for conflict management theory' in Gelfand, M.J. and Brett, J.M. (eds), *The handbook of negotiation and culture,* Stanford, CA: Stanford Business Books: 177-192.

Thomas, K.W. and Kilmann, R.H. (1974) *Thomas–Kilmann Conflict Mode Instrument,* Tuxedo, NY: Xicom.

Thomas, K.W. (1992) 'Conflict and conflict management: Reflections and update', *Journal of Organizational Behavior,* 13: 265-274.

Ting-Toomey, S. (1999) *Communicating Across Cultures*, New York, NY: Guildford.

Ting-Toomey, S. and Oetzel, J.G. (2002) 'Cross-cultural face concerns and conflict styles: current status and future directions' in Gudykunst, W. and Mody B. (eds), *Handbook of International and Intercultural Communication,* Thousand Oaks, CA: Sage: 127-147.

Ting-Toomey, S., Yee-Jung, K., Shapiro, R., Garcia, W., Wright T. and Oetzel, J.G. (2000) 'Cultural/ethnic identity salience and conflict styles,' *International Journal of Intercultural Relations,* 23: 47-81.

Chapter 18

Developing intercultural relationships

Other chapters in Part Three have put forward factors to do with interacting effectively and appropriately with members of different cultures. This final chapter will address the concept of intercultural communication competence (ICC) and so bring together the factors referred to earlier and add other features seen as fundamental to the concept.

The definition of ICC by Kim (1991) can serve as a starting point:

> ...the overall internal ability of an individual to manage key challenging features of intercultural communication: namely cultural differences and unfamiliarity, inter-group posture, and the accompanying experience of stress.

Such competence is not something people are born with, nor is it something that occurs by chance. People need to have an understanding of the information and actions necessary, the motivation to engage in the communication process, and also the skills to perform effectively and appropriately.

This chapter will examine the main components of ICC, addressing in particular the notions of empathy and uncertainty management, as well as the role of ethics in intercultural communication.

Learning outcomes

After reading this chapter you will:

- Gain further understanding of the difficulties inherent in intercultural communication.
- Be critically aware of the prerequisites of successful intercultural communication.
- Be able to reflect on the knowledge, motivation and skills required to become a competent intercultural communicator.

Concept 18.1 Becoming a competent intercultural communicator

Developing competence in international communication can be hard work. The process requires following many paths of investigation through other cultures, as well as one's own. It involves acquiring, analysing, sifting and interpreting considerable amounts of information from all manner of sources, including oneself. This information is not just to do with facts but also with perceptions and behaviours. Such interpretation demands both an insider's

Table 18.1 A developmental model of intercultural sensitivity

Ethnocentric stages			Ethnorelative stages		
Denial	Defence	Minimization	Acceptance	Adaptation	Integration
• Isolation • Separation	• Denigration • Superiority • Reversal	• Physical universalism • Transcendent universalism	• Respect for behavioural difference • Respect for value difference	• Empathy • Pluralism	• Contextual evaluation • Constructive marginality

Source: Bennett (1993): 29.

view of the values and beliefs underlying the behaviour of a culture (the so-called **emic** approach), as well as an external view (the **etic** approach) whereby such values and beliefs – and resulting behaviours – can be compared across cultures.

One way of conceptualizing this development of ICC is in terms of a progression through the stages outlined in Table 18.1. These stages suggest a logical, linear process towards a high degree of intercultural sensitivity. Bennett is anxious to emphasize, however, that this model is only a construct of reality, that having mastered these stages, 'the next task . . . is to construct new continua that stretch in directions beyond our current vision' (1993: 65).

Nevertheless, those involved in such a process see it much more as a series of trials and errors, a (life-) long chain of experiences during which insights are developed, hypotheses drawn and tested, fresh insights gained and new hypotheses developed that in turn require testing and assessment. The learning is more cyclical in nature, reflecting Kolb's model of experiential learning whereby 'knowledge is created through the transformation of experience' (1984: 38), as in Figure 18.1.

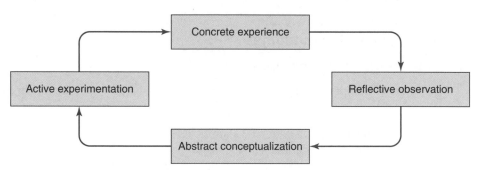

Figure 18.1 Kolb's learning cycle
Source: adapted from Kolb (1984): 33.

Components of intercultural communication competence (ICC)

By its very nature, communication generally, and intercultural communication in particular, involves people learning from interaction with others, seeking and developing ways of understanding, and responding to those around them. Three psychological components are involved in this process: cognitive, affective and behavioural. These will be reviewed and a fourth (ethical) component will be considered.

Cognitive

This is to do with knowledge about the people from the other culture(s) involved, their values, beliefs and expectations, knowledge of the language they use (even if the person in question is not fluent in that language) and the communicative strategies they tend to employ. Without this knowledge, the communicators in question may well make wrong assumptions, choose an inappropriate communication strategy and/or cause loss of face for themselves or the others. Obtaining the knowledge required has also to do with learning by doing, being open – or **cognitively flexible**, as Gudykunst (1992) calls it, to receiving and processing feedback. This flexibility also entails being able to take a perspective, to differentiate between describing, interpreting and evaluating behaviour. The skill of perspective-taking, according to Gudykunst and Kim (2003), reduces the possibility of attributing incorrect motives to another's behaviour, allowing instead a search for other interpretations, which may well allow a more accurate prediction of how others will behave. Linked to this is the notion of accumulating a repertoire of 'scripts' referred to in Chapter 15 for occasions when guidance is needed for communicative interaction. These scripts, which proved to be successful in other encounters in achieving certain goals, can be referred to, applied and/or adapted to cope with unfamiliar encounters.

The notion of **ethnocentrism** is often referred to in this context, a term meaning that one's own group or culture is at the centre of everything. Being ethnocentric entails the belief that one's own culture is the most important and that other cultures are judged in relation to one's own. Although ethnocentrism may be seen as an inherent part of any culture's make-up, the degree to which it colours an individual's view of other cultures can vary considerably. The more willing and able a person is to move beyond this ethnocentrism, the more capable that person is of assimilating the knowledge required to be a competent intercultural communicator.

Affective

This component relates to the feelings, needs and general motivation of an individual with regard to interacting with others from different cultures. If fears and prejudices cloud feelings about communicating with another, then a person's motivation will be negative and they may tend to avoid interaction, even though they have the knowledge and skills to communicate. The affective component is about applying the cognitive elements described earlier, having the motivation to interact with other cultures, the confidence to deal with any anxiety or stress involved in dealing with those from another culture.

Being able to **manage anxiety and uncertainty** is for Gudykunst (2002) the fundamental ability of an effective communicator. According to his anxiety and uncertainty management theory, there is a direct link between the anxiety and uncertainty of the communicators and the extent to which communicators experience their interaction as effective. An individual in a high state of anxiety tends to rely on simplistic information (by, for example, making excessive use of stereotypes) and cannot therefore communicate effectively. In a high state of uncertainty, the person may be unable to explain or predict the attitudes, behaviour or feelings of others. If, on the other hand, a person feels little anxiety, he may not be motivated to communicate and, if uncertainty is low, may feel confident enough to predict too eagerly – and inaccurately – the behaviour of others. Those, therefore, who engage in intercultural communication must consciously exercise anxiety and uncertainty management.

According to Gudykunst, one way to reduce anxiety and uncertainty is to minimize misunderstandings through effective communication. This involves employing mindfulness, a concept referred to in Chapter 17 when conflict management was being discussed. For Gudykunst, mindfulness entails people thinking about their communication and continually working at changing what they do to become more effective. Ellen Langer, who used the term to encapsulate a number of ways of thinking and behaving prevalent in Eastern cultures, identifies in her book on the subject (1990) a number of characteristics:

- making more categories and distinctions when categorizing others. As already noted, categorizing is a natural behaviour; effective intercultural communicators use more specific sub-categories and more personalized information to make predictions.

- being aware of more than one perspective. People cannot assume that their interlocutors interpret their messages the same way as they intended.

- focusing on the process of communication as it is happening – people being mindful of their own behaviour as well as the situation.

One aspect of the affective component is **empathy**, defined by Casse (1981: 139) as:

> ... the ability to see and understand how other people construct reality, or more specifically how they perceive, discover and invent the inner and outer worlds.

In a sense, empathy and perspective-taking ability are concepts that overlap: empathy has more to do with the emotional capacity to understand another's situation, while the latter is more to do with the cognitive skill of seeing the world from another's perspective.

When interacting with others, people are not only listening to what others say but also trying to work out what they are actually feeling and thinking. People naturally tend to think that what is going on in someone else's mind is the same as what is going on in theirs. However, the ability to put oneself in the shoes of the other, to try and discern the thoughts behind their words and actions is a major factor in ICC (Exhibit 18.1).

Exhibit 18.1

Empathic listening

Successful communication involves the parties listening actively and carefully to make sure they understand what the other person is meaning. This can be difficult because people are too busy planning a response to give active consideration to what the other is saying.

Klopf (1988) refers to active listening as empathic listening. This involves:

- Paraphrasing: rewording what the other person has said.

- Reflecting feelings: relating back to the other person those feelings that one thinks the other is experiencing.

- Reflecting meanings: restating what the other says to confirm its meaning.

- Summarizing: restating briefly the main points of the other person's message.

Table 18.2 Levels of awareness

Level	Information	Mode	Interpretation
Level I	Awareness of superficial or visible cultural traits – stereotypes	Tourism, textbooks	Unbelievable, i.e. exotic bizarre
Level II	Awareness of significant and subtle cultural traits that contrast markedly with one's own	Culture conflict situations	Unbelievable, i.e. frustrating irrational
Level III	Awareness of significant and subtle cultural traits that contrast markedly with one's own	Intellectual analysis	Believable, cognitively
Level IV	Awareness of how another culture feels from the standpoint of the insider	Cultural immersion: living the culture	Believable because of subjective familiarity

Source: Hanvey (1987): 20.

Having a high degree of empathy means that a person has attained a high degree of awareness. Hanvey's proposed levels of awareness (1987), as given in Table 18.2 in adapted form, highlights the levels of awareness that can be attained during the competence development process. Here again, be wary of the model's implication that someone can move logically from one level to another. Hanvey refers to four such levels of awareness, arguing that 'believability' is necessary if one group or individual is to accept the other. This believability can be achieved only at levels 3 and 4.

Reaching level 4, however, can be a lifetime's work. It may be possible for an 'expat' on a long assignment who becomes immersed in the culture where he is working to attain this degree of awareness. But what about a global manager who has to deal with a number of cultures? This problem was addressed earlier in Chapter 15. Can such a manager develop some of the aspects of awareness belonging to level 4 and so allow the manager, when necessary, to empathize with counterparts from another culture?

Hanvey (1987) refers to the very different nature of today's society: unlike just a generation ago, more and more of its members are engaged in all sorts of interaction across the world. It has become much more outward-looking, more ready for change, more mobile, more participative, more interdependent, and has developed a high empathic capacity. In his terms this means being able to imagine oneself in another role within the context of one's own culture. He suggests that such a society can go a step further and go beyond empathy by developing the capacity for **transspection**. This involves trying to share the beliefs, assumptions and feelings of the other, not within the context of one's own culture, but within the context of the other.

Behavioural

This third component is to do with how the knowledge and affective components described above are enacted, the actual *performance* of the behaviour felt to be effective and appropriate in the communication context. As Spitzberg (2000) sees it, competence in intercultural communication is not just a set of skilled behaviours, since any given behaviour may be seen as competent in one context, but incompetent in another. In other words, the competence does not lie in the behaviour itself but in the 'social evaluation of behaviour'. According to Spitzberg (2000: 347) this evaluation is made in terms of:

- appropriacy: does the behaviour meet the norms and expectations of the relationship?
- effectiveness: does the behaviour achieve 'valued goals or rewards relative to costs and alternatives'.

A person's behaviour that is considered to be competent may have been accidentally produced. If reproduced in a different context it may well be poorly evaluated. Equally, if the person has no clear and appropriate rationale behind the behaviour, the result might well be hit-or-miss, so the behaviour cannot be considered as competent. In short, Spitzberg maintains that communicative behaviour is only really skilled when it can be repeated and achieves a certain goal.

The many facets of intercultural communication behaviour have already been identified and commented on in Part Three. Worth mentioning again, however, are the following:

- The ability to effectively communicate: again, the idea that the cognitive and affective skills referred to earlier can be used effectively and appropriately. This includes entering into meaningful dialogue, initiating interaction, dealing with misunderstandings and interpersonal conflict and using different communication styles. These styles can relate, in particular, to an individual's position and role in the foreign culture, e.g. the expected behaviour in terms of their occupation and sex. The appropriate and effective use of a nonverbal repertoire must also be mentioned.
- The ability to establish meaningful relationships (Hammer et al, 1978). This has to do with being able to develop and maintain interpersonal relationships with those from other cultures. Such relationships require feelings to be accurately understood and any kind of collaboration to be effective and mutually satisfying. Empathy plays a vital role generally.

All these elements are an integral part of an individual's communication behaviour in dealing effectively and efficiently with the challenges of intercultural communication. However, a fourth component needs to be addressed, which concerns the way ethical issues are to be handled in one's dealings with other cultures and their members.

The ethical component

In examining intercultural communicative competence, the need has already been discussed to take a certain distance from one's own culture, to reduce one's ethnocentrism and be open to the norms and values of the culture whose representatives are being addressed. However, does the ability to describe, understand and judge any culture on the basis of its own values mean withholding criticism of practices in the culture that the communicator in question finds unacceptable? Although this sort of question raises many issues to do with morality and ethics, the concern here is whether it is possible to make moral judgements across cultures while being aware that moral principles of behaviour can be culture-bound and may vary across cultures.

Gudykunst and Kim (2003) make a distinction between two approaches to this issue: an analytical one (which involves being committed to a specific view of what morality is) and a normative one (i.e. knowing what should be done). The analytical approach does not allow ethical judgements whereas the normative approach does. Moreover, they argue, a distinction can be made between making moral judgements on the behaviour itself and on the person(s) displaying the behaviour.

As Gudykunst and Kim (2003) do, this normative approach can be applied to the question of making payments to company officials to ensure, for example, that a tender is accepted. This action or practice may well be regarded as unacceptable if the normative approach is taken. The people pursuing this practice, however, will not necessarily be 'blamed' since such an action is regarded as acceptable in the culture concerned. These people have not necessarily wandered off their own moral path: they may themselves regard their involvement in the payment of gratuities as morally wrong, but realize that this is a 'necessary evil' since those expecting gratuities do not know any better.

The conclusion made by Gudykunst and Kim (2003) is that people withhold any ethical judgements when interacting with those living in another culture until they have clearly described the behaviour and examined various interpretations. And this necessarily involves improving their ability to communicative effectively. Dealing with intercultural moral conflicts is, therefore, it can be argued, a necessary – if difficult – test of intercultural communication competence.

When confronted with behaviours that are considered unethical, Richard Gesteland (1996) advocates strategies which reflect the idea that the culture's norms and values must be carefully evaluated rather than immediate assumptions made and reactions taken accordingly. People should never, for example, assume that a 'bribe' of some sort is a prerequisite part of doing business. If it is hinted at or requested, they should say no, adding that corporate policy prohibits such payments. Gesteland acknowledges that this strategy appears to work best with companies which sell sought-after products or which are considered to have a strong influence in one form or another. The implication made here is that even if business is lost, moral courage should be shown. Gesteland's following strategy, however, implies that there may be other ethical ways of responding to unethical demands. Gesteland suggests, for example, making a public donation to a worthy cause in the country concerned, creating jobs locally in such a way that the honour falls on the decision-makers. Such (imaginative and necessarily legal) manoeuvres depend, however, on considerable knowledge of the way a culture 'works' and insights into the values reflected in the way it behaves.

In Case study 18.1, a manager is faced with an ethical dilemma, one to do with differing notions of fairness and loyalty. Should the manager concerned say no to the transaction proposed, simply accept the proposal, or devise a response that the manager considers ethical and which at the same time takes account of the fairness and loyalty issues involved?

When examining ethical aspects of interaction with other cultures, Gudykunst and Kim (2003) quote Barnlund (1980), who states that the cross-cultural arena is an 'ethical void'. In such an environment, he maintains, there is a 'meta-ethic' lacking, one that can be used or applied when ethical issues are being dealt with by people from different cultures. When making ethical judgements, people either use their own cultural standards as a framework of reference or those of the other culture. This means, however, that the ethical premises of one culture are necessarily subordinated to those of another. There is no meta-ethic to embrace both sets of premises.

Case study 18.1

Should I take the apartment?

My team and I were in Britain for a short stay because of business we were conducting for a client of ours based in the UK.

As a part of the contract with our client, my team was to be reimbursed for our living expenses in London. Our contract, however, specified that we needed to make every 'reasonable effort' to sign a short-term lease (13 weeks) and reduce costs related to this expense. The contract did, however, have a clause allocating sufficient funding for us to sign a lease for 26 weeks if necessary.

To assist us in finding housing, my Indian colleague offered to contact a 'friend'. This 'friend' failed to find us a short-term lease, and was only able to find us an apartment with a 26-week lease. Additionally, the lease cost $8,880 in total, the exact maximum amount of money the client had allotted us for housing expenses. My Indian colleague was very happy with the apartment and suggested we sign a lease form 'immediately.'

However, according to information I had received from other professionals who had travelled to London, it should have been possible to find a short-term lease for far less money. For this reason, I suspected that the apartment transaction might be taking advantage of my client.

My dilemma was whether I should risk insulting my Indian colleague by not accepting the apartment arranged by his 'friend' because I believed that the transaction did not seem 'fair'. If I failed to do this, it seemed likely that my client would question the legitimacy of such an odd transaction. I believed this could cause my own integrity to be put into doubt. Additionally, even if their auditors did not notice the 'coincidental' nature of the transaction, I could not help but feel it would be unethical if we did not abide by the contract and make 'every reasonable effort' to reduce costs.

Source: adapted from Browaeys and Trompenaars (2000): case 8.

Question

What do you think should be done?

There have been attempts to outline such a meta-ethic. Martin, Flores and Nakayama (2001), for example, use three principles to define a meta-ethic:

- The humanness principle, whereby peace is at the centre: respect for all, empathy and identification with others.

- The dialogic principle, which stresses the centrality of human relationships and the support people must give each other. It includes the principle of inclusion and mutual equality.

- The principle of speaking 'with' and 'to' instead of 'for' and 'about,' which usually reinforce oppression. Learning to understand oneself and others when engaging with others is a key principle. Engaging in a dialogue of any nature is being able to listen carefully as well as speaking.

This idea of a meta-ethic is indirectly approached in the following extract from question-and-answer session held on the *Financial Times* website. Two experts on business ethics, Avinash Persaud, chairman of Intelligence Capital Limited, and *Financial Times* columnist John Plender answered questions concerning the issues and pressures faced by all in business and finance. Exhibit 18.2 is one question they were asked, together with their responses.

Exhibit 18.2 FT

Ask the experts: Business ethics

Question from Arash Nazhad, Canada

What one person considers ethical another might not. Of course, there are certain issues that are clear cut. Other issues can create varying stances depending on an individual's culture and background. These two elements seem to have significant weight on people's opinion on what is ethical or not. As our economies become more and more inter-twined, how do you suppose we set ethical values or codes (whether internally or externally) to make sure diversity of cultures within an organization is represented?

Answer from John Plender

You are absolutely right that establishing ethical values or codes is a big challenge at companies operating in several different parts of the world. We argue in our book that there are nonetheless values to which people in all countries subscribe. For example, people virtually everywhere accept that bribery and corruption are wrong. The problem is one of definition – for example, the difference between a bribe and a gift differs in different cultures. It is for companies to work out what is workable for inclusion in an ethical code. That can only be done effectively through a group-wide process of consultation rather than by dropping tablets of stone from on high. Enforcement is an even bigger challenge than producing a code. In short, no simple solutions and a big learning process.

Answer from Avinash Persaud

I agree that ethics are not entirely objective and there are different perspectives. It is one of the reasons why we looked hard for examples of ethical abuses around the world and not just in Houston, Texas. We feel that there are a few objective building blocks however that can form the basis of ethical approach that is not culturally specific – we are particularly focused on conflicts of interest, secret contrivances to put yourself at an advantage and causing unmitigated harm to others.

Source: *Financial Times* website (www.ft.com/cms/s/2/6ad17f12-3110-11db-8c61-0000779e2340.html), 21 August 2006.

Question

To what extent do the building blocks mentioned reflect the meta-ethic described earlier?

A third culture?

Building blocks of this nature could, it is argued, be created through collaboration between the parties involved in the intercultural communication process. Casrnir (1999) proposes that building a third culture would allow a shared system of values or ethics to emerge. Cross-cultural encounters create a context where those involved are not only trying to achieve outcomes desired by all those involved, but also developing standards and methods for achieving those outcomes. The relationship developed during these encounters could enable a process by which mutuality evolves from which a third culture emerges – a framework designed by all those involved that ensures an enduring adaptation and survival. Value systems shared by the participants could emerge, as well as continuing personal relationships and an increasing interdependence. The third-culture building model he proposes represents:

> . . . a co-operative, communication, community building process which does not include the need for coercion by anyone, including outsiders.

Casrnir, 1999: 111

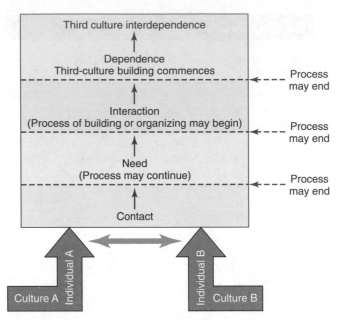

Figure 18.2 A dialogic communication model of third-culture building
Source: Casrnir (1999): 109.

The building process he describes takes account of the dynamic, changing, developing nature of the communication event. Figure 18.2 is the model devised by Casrnir to visualize the process.

A model such as this can account for the evolutionary nature of intercultural interaction. Rather than focus on culture A and B, using etic categories, i.e. generalizations about larger entities, the emphasis should be on what actually happens when individuals 'representing' these cultures come together.

As Figure 18.2 indicates, any initial contact between the people involved may not progress because of many possible reasons, including fear, lack of time, or simply lack of skills for dealing with 'outsiders'. If, however, a mutual need is perceived, communication may continue, but those involved may well stick to their own rules of engagement and cultural values for a number of reasons (anger towards the other participants, fear of the unfamiliar, reluctance to take risks, missing interactional skills). Eventually, however, as the interaction continues, the people concerned enter into deeper dialogue and realize that some sort of change is needed to encourage the developing relationship, which could be of benefit to all concerned. It is here that a process of building or organizing may well begin. Even here, though, the process may come to a halt when it eventually becomes clear to some or all those involved that a commitment to change is not really necessary, or that a meeting of minds is not possible. However, if the dialogue continues, the participants may show a dependence on each other to reach a goal that is mutually beneficial. If that happens, then the people can start developing the elements of a third culture, including their joint goals, interactional rules and their roles in the process. The final phase is based on interdependence: the groups and the individuals involved accept that cultural development depends on building mutual trust while constructing a third culture. While doing so, they need to develop their dialogic skills, these being a requisite for building the culture and maintaining it.

Casrnir's emphasis on the dialogic nature of third-culture building reflects ideas discussed elsewhere in this book:

- The notion of transcultural competence, described in Chapter 5, involves being able to reconcile seemingly opposing values and developing a dynamic equilibrium, an integration of values through synergy. The reconciliation approach opens the door to a third dimension.

- The nature of intercultural interaction, described in Chapter 13. Such interaction is not to be seen just in terms of a set of relations between the cultures, but also as a dynamic process whereby the cultures are defined both through their own characteristics as well as through their interaction with each other.

- The notion of crisis transformation described in Chapter 17 has to do with coming to terms with the underlying causes of cross-cultural conflict through collaborative dialogue, thereby enabling transformations to occur at personal, social and structural levels.

These ideas, including Casrnir's, focus less on static comparisons between cultures and more on dynamic interaction between individuals from different cultures; less on the categorizations of cultures and more on the process of cultural transformation among people in a collaborative dialogue. People coming together, entering into dialogue and creating a togetherness form the basis of Casrnir's concept of building a third culture. Rather than focusing on the dichotomies that come from the distinction between 'self' and 'other', he argues, people can build something that is eventually 'theirs':

> . . . something which sooner or later becomes part of the changes which help new or changed cultures and their societal structures to emerge from it. To put it in other words, such changes can help assure our survival as humans.
>
> Casrnir, 1999: 113

This exhortation is perhaps a suitable way of rounding off the discussion of third-culture building as well as of completing the final concept of this book. It also indicates the direction of much research into intercultural communication, one that fully recognizes the dynamic nature of all intercultural encounters.

ACTIVITY 18.1

Identifying assumptions

Casse (1981) developed an exercise to encourage his students to develop their empathic skills. He asked them to listen to a recording of a dialogue between John Miller (a US project manager in Kenya), and Costa Maniatis (a Greek agronomist involved in the same project managed by Miller, his boss). Below is a transcript of the dialogue and comments from the narrator.

Costa Maniatis: (knocking on door): Did you call me Mr Miller?

John Miller: Ah, Costa, yes . . . come in. (door shuts) It is about the report required by the Ministry of Agriculture. How long will it take you to finish it?

CM: (surprised) I don't know, Mr Miller . . . umm . . . Do you think . . .?

JM: No, Costa, no! You are in the best position to analyse time requirements.

CM: Well, let's say ten days.

JM: Ten days . . . OK . . . let's say fifteen – alright? Then . . . it is agreed you will do it in fifteen days.

CM: Yes, Mr Miller.

Narrator: In fact, the report needed thirty days of regular work. So the Greek worked day and night, but at the end of fifteen days he still needed one more day's work. The following dialogue took place fifteen days later in Costa Maniatis' office:

JM: Well, Costa, where is the report?

CM: It will be ready tomorrow.

JM: But we agreed it would be ready today.

Narrator: From that day the relationship between Costa Maniatis and Miller became more and more difficult, and three months later, Costa asked for his transfer to another project. **Why did Maniatis leave?**

To find an answer to this last question, the students were then asked to identify as many cultural assumptions as possible, assumptions underlying the words of Miller and Maniatis. These assumptions were to be based on the cultural frame of each protagonist, not of the students themselves. **Which assumptions do you consider to be the most appropriate? Write down the assumptions against each part of the dialogue given in the table below. You can give several answers against each.**

To help you determine the cultural profile of Miller and Maniatis, look at the following websites:

- http://international-business-center.com/geert-hofstede/index.shtml
- www.kwintessential.co.uk/intercultural-business-communication/tool.php

The first assumptions are suggested in Table 18.3.

Table 18.3

Who said	What	Meaning what? (cultural assumption)
Miller	How long will it take you to finish this?	I'm asking him to participate.
Maniatis	I do not know. Do you think . . . ?	His behaviour makes no sense. He is the boss; why doesn't he tell me? I'm going to ask for instructions.
Miller	You are in the best position to analyse time requirements.	
Maniatis	Ten days.	
Miller	Take fifteen. It is agreed you will do it in fifteen days.	
Maniatis	Yes, Mr Miller	
Narrator: In fact, the report needed thirty days of regular work, so the Greek worked day and night, but at the end of the fifteenth day, he still needed one more day's work.		
Miller	Where is the report?	
Maniatis	It will be ready tomorrow.	
Miller	But we had agreed it would be ready today.	
Miller	(The American is surprised)	
Maniatis	(The Greek is angry)	

Source: Adapted from Casse (1981): 140–141.

Table 18.4 gives the assumptions suggested by Casse (1981). **Compare his answers with yours and tick if you gave a correct assumption.**

Table 18.4

Who said	What	Meaning what? (cultural assumptions)	Tick here if correct
Miller	*How long will it take you to finish the report?*	(1) Employees should be involved in the decision-making process.	
		(2) Employees are accountable.	
		(3) Planning is important.	
Maniatis	*I do not know.*	(4) The question does not make any sense. The manager is accountable. To recognize that one does not know is OK.	
		(5) It is the responsibility of the manager to tell the employee what to do and how.	
Maniatis	*Do you think ..?*	(6) The manager is the one who is supposed to know. He should provide some instructions to the employee.	
Miller	*No, Costa . . .*	(7) The employee should take responsibility.	
Miller	*You are in the best position to analyse time*	(8) Delegation of responsibility to those who know.	
		(9) It is the role of the manager to press the team member to take responsibility for his/her own actions.	
Maniatis	*Well, ten days.*	(10) Since the boss insists, an answer has to be given. After all, he is the 'authority'.	
Miller	*Ten days OK. . . .*	(11) The problem has to be assessed. In this case, it is the team member's lack of ability to estimate time. (Problem orientation)	
Miller	*Take 15. It is agreed you will do it in 15 days.*	(12) A contract is offered.	
		(13) Instructions are received.	
Maniatis	*Yes . . .*		
Miller	*Where is the report?*	(14) Part of a manager's role is to make sure that the contract is fulfilled.	
Maniatis	*It will be ready tomorrow.*	(15) Today or tomorrow is all right. Besides, the report needed 30 days and it will be done in 16.	
Miller	*But we had agreed that it would be ready today!*	(16) Importance of deadlines. A manager should teach his employees to respect deadlines.	
Maniatis		(17) The wrong instructions were given, so the boss is incompetent.	
		(18) The boss is insensitive. (He does not appreciate that the job was done in 16 days instead of 30.)	
		(19) One cannot work with someone who is incompetent and insensitive.	
		(20) No further discussion with the boss is possible. The only option left is to leave.	

Source: Casse (1981): 143–144.

The key put forward by Casse is given in Table 18.5. **Add up the ticks according to your empathy for the two protagonists.**

Table 18.5 Calculate your score

	Number of correct assumptions given per protagonist
Empathy 1 (for Miller) = 1-2-3-7-8-9-11-12-14-16	
Empathy 2 (for Maniatis) = 4-5-6-10-13-15-17-18-19-20	
Total (Empathy 1 + 2) = 20	

Casse then illuminates the score, as in Table 18.6.

Table 18.6 Interpret your score

Empathy 1 (for Miller):
• A score between 7 and 10 shows that you understand some of the characteristics of US culture (managerial) quite well. • A score of 4–6 shows an average empathic ability regarding US managerial culture. • A score of 0–3 characterizes a lack of empathic ability regarding US managerial culture.
Empathy 2 (for Maniatis):
• A score of 7–10 shows a good understanding of the Greek culture. • A score of 4–6 shows an average empathic ability (could be improved). • A score of 0–3 shows a need to improve one's own empathic ability.
Overall empathic ability:
• A score of 14–20 shows you are able to put yourself into someone else's shoes. • A score of 9–13 means your empathic ability could be improved. • A score of 0–8 characterizes a lack of empathic ability.

Source: Casse (1981): 144-145.

When you have finished scoring your results, discuss with your colleagues the results and the validity of the exercise.

ACTIVITY 18.2

Corruption in business

After you have read Exhibit 18.3 on the results of a survey concerning corruption in business, read the letter sent to the editor in response (Exhibit 18.4).

Exhibit 18.3

Third of companies think they have been hit by bribery

By Michael Peel

A third of international companies think they failed to win new business over the past year because of bribery by their competitors. Half claim to be 'totally ignorant' of their countries' laws on foreign corruption.

A survey published today by Control Risks and Simmons & Simmons, the law firm, of 350 companies from Britain, the US, Germany, France, the Netherlands, Brazil and Hong Kong echoes the doubts many executives and anti-corruption campaigners have about the effectiveness of the international crackdown on bribery.

Nick Benwell, a Simmons & Simmons partner, said the survey suggested the Organisation for Economic Co-operation and Development anti-bribery convention of 1999 still had a 'long way to go in terms of making an impact on levels of corruption'.

He said: 'There still appears to be a fairly widely held belief that companies try to get round laws by using agents and intermediaries.'

The report says 43 per cent of the companies – ranging from a quarter in Britain to three-quarters in Hong Kong – claim to have lost out on business over the past five years because of bribery by competitors.

The number of countries that said bribery had cost them business in the past twelve months was higher in each of the five jurisdictions covered in a previous survey in 2002 – Hong Kong, the Netherlands, the US, Germany and Britain.

About three-quarters of the companies, including 94 per cent in Germany and 90 per cent in Britain, think businesses from their countries use agents to circumvent anti-corruption laws.

The report says two-thirds of the companies are either ignorant of their national anti-corruption laws or only vaguely aware of them, even though the six countries surveyed signed the OECD anti-bribery convention.

Source: *Financial Times*, 9 October 2006.

Exhibit 18.4

Globalised nature of business corruption needs to be taken into account

By Peter Fleming and Stelios Zyglidopoulos

Sir, Michael Peel's salutary article 'Third of companies think they have been hit by bribery' (October 9) strongly resonates with our research project at the Judge Business School, University of Cambridge. The article reported on a survey published by Control Risks and Simmons & Simmons showing how many companies felt they had lost business due to bribery by competitors.

We especially found interesting the suggestion that companies in Germany, Britain and the Netherlands among others use intermediates or agents to bribe local officials in host countries in order to secure a favourable business relationship. Our research project looks at how complex business networks are used to spread and conceal corruption. In relation to that project, the article is indicative of the growing use of outsourcing by certain companies to conduct morally questionable activities.

Just as the US government subcontracts the interrogation of suspected terrorists to countries with lax human rights regulations, some companies outsource the business of corruption to local agents and intermediaries. This makes it difficult to trace or formally connect the corruption to the company in question. Our project suggests that to ensure a more level playing field regarding competition for contracts, national-based corruption mechanisms need to take into account the increasingly globalised nature of such illegal transactions.

The article also revealed a striking lack of knowledge among many business managers with respect to national corruption legislation. While there are probably many causes for this ignorance, business schools must take some responsibility for it. Business ethics classes are still marginal within the MBA and general management training curriculum, and even these often lack precise details regarding legislative and moral obligations at home and abroad.

An upside to this story, however, is the increasing prominence of corporate governance issues in management education. The message we attempt to impart in our teaching and research at Cambridge is that ethical business does not have to undermine the competitive performance of a company. The two, more often than not, go hand-in-hand.

Peter Fleming and Stelios Zyglidopoulos, Judge Business School, University of Cambridge, Cambridge CB2 1AG.

Source: *Financial Times,* 16 October 2006: 31

Questions

1. The article reports that about three-quarters of the companies think businesses from their countries use agents to circumvent anti-corruption laws.

   ● **Who are these agents, according to the letter, and how do they go to work?**

2. The writers of the letter maintain that ethical business and competitive performance go hand in hand - more often than not.

   ● **What do you think the writers are implying with his statement?**

   ● **What terms of reference do you think they are using when talking of 'ethical business'?**

Conclusion

Chapter 18 has examined the main elements of intercultural communicative competence (ICC). Developing ICC involves not only a lot of hard work on the cognitive and affective level, but also being able to perform appropriately and effectively. This chapter has highlighted the importance of (self-) reflection and cognitive flexibility, of being able to manage anxiety and uncertainty, and the need to develop empathy and mindfulness. It has also raised the question of dealing with intercultural moral conflicts, where all ICC skills are put to the test, and it has given readers a chance to apply their insights to an ethical dilemma in business.

The final section has focused on the concept of building a third culture whereby those interacting apply their ICC skills in such a way that they can develop a mutually beneficial interdependence. This notion echoes similar ideas referred to earlier in this book, including reconciliation between seemingly opposing values, the dynamic nature of interaction and the notion of crisis transformation through mediation and/or collaborative dialogue.

Points for reflection

1. Empathy is put forward in the concept as a component of intercultural communication competence.

   To what extent do you think similarity among individuals is necessary to achieve empathy?

2. Casrnir proposes a model of third-culture building to account for the evolutionary nature of intercultural dialogue.

   What role do you think the many studies on cultural dimensions can play in the application of this model? Is it possible to anticipate how, for example, the interaction could evolve between individuals from a 'low-context' culture and individuals from a 'high-context' culture?

3. **If you were asked to design a training programme whose goal was to develop competence in intercultural communication, which of these components would you include? Explain your choice.**

   - Lectures with discussion on cross-cultural differences.
   - Case studies dealing with (mis)communication.
   - Simulations and role-plays (e.g. meetings or negotiations with participants from different cultures).
   - Self-assessment instruments (e.g. questionnaires that allow participants to evaluate their skills in intercultural communication).

   What other elements would you incorporate into an ICC development programme – and why?

4. **If you incorporated an element on ethics into such a programme, what would it look like and what would be its main objective?**

Further reading

Gudykunst, W.B. and Mody B. (eds) (2001) *Handbook of International and Intercultural Communication*, 2nd edn, Thousand Oaks, CA: Sage. Gives a clear overview of the many aspects of this field. The authors examine cross-cultural communication, intercultural communication, international communication and development communication. They describe theories in each of these areas before dealing with detailed elements and current issues.

References

Barnlund, D. (1980) 'The cross-cultural arena: An ethical void' in Asuncion-Lande (ed.) *Ethical Perspectives and Critical Issues in Intercultural Communication,* Falls Church, VA: Speech Communication Association.

Barnlund, D. (1985) 'The cross-cultural arena: an ethical void' in Samovar L. and Porter R. (eds), *Intercultural Communication: A reader,* 4th edn, Belmont, CA: Wadsworth: 394–399.

Bennett, M.J. (1993) 'Towards Ethnorelativism: A developmental model of intercultural sensitivity' in Paige, R.M. (ed) *Education for the Intercultural Experience,* 2nd edn, Yarmouth, ME: Intercultural: 21–71.

Browaeys, M.-J. and Trompenaars, F. (eds) (2000) *Cases Studies on Cultural Dilemmas,* Breukelen, Netherlands: Nyenrode University Press.

Casrnir, F.L. (1999) 'Foundations for the study of intercultural communication based on a third-culture model', *International Journal of Intercultural Relations,* 23 (1): 91–116.

Casse, P. (1981) *Training for the Cross-Cultural Mind,* 2nd edn, Washington DC: SIETAR.

Gesteland, R. (1996) *Cross Cultural Business Behavior: Marketing, negotiating and managing across cultures,* Copenhagen: Handelshojskolens Forlag.

Gudykunst, W.B. (1992) 'Being perceived as a competent communicator' in Gudykunst, W.B. and Kim, Y. (eds), *Readings on Communicating with Strangers,* New York, NY: McGraw-Hill: 382–392.

Gudykunst, W.B. (2002) 'Intercultural communication theories' in Gudykunst, W.B. and Mody, B. (eds), *Handbook of International and Intercultural Communication,* 2nd edn, Thousand Oaks, CA: Sage: 183–205.

Gudykunst, W.B. and Kim, Y. (2003) *Communicating with Strangers,* 4th edn, New York, NY: McGraw-Hill.

Hammer, M., Gudykunst, W. and Wiseman, R. (1978) 'Dimensions of intercultural Effectiveness,' *International Journal of Intercultural Relations,* 2 (Winter): 382–93.

Hanvey, R.G. (1987) 'Cross-cultural awareness' in Luce, L.F. and Smith, E.C. (eds), *Toward Internationalism,* 2nd edn, Cambridge, MA: Newbury House: 13–23.

Kim, Y.Y. (1991) 'Intercultural communicative competence' in Ting-Toomey, S. and Korzenny, F., *Cross-cultural Interpersonal Communication,* Thousand Oaks, CA: Sage: 259–275.

Klopf, D.W. (1988) *Intercultural Encounters: The fundamentals of intercultural communication,* Eaglewood, CO: Morton.

Kolb, D.A. (1984) *Experiential Learning: Experience as the source of learning and development,* Englewood Cliffs, NJ: Prentice-Hall.

Langer, E.J. (1990) *Mindfulness,* Cambridge, MA: Da Capo.

Martin, J.N., Flores, L. and Nakayama, T.K. (2001) 'Principles for a meta-ethic' in Martin, J.N. and Nakayama, T.K. (eds), *Experiencing Intercultural Communication,* Mountain View, CA: Mayfield.

Spitzberg, B.H. (2000) 'A model of intercultural communication competence' in Samovar, L. and Porter, R. (eds) *Intercultural Communication: A reader,* 9th edn, Belmont, CA: Wadsworth: 375–87.

Simulation – working internationally

This simulation is best performed with the assistance of an instructor. However, the material can be adapted and/or extended in accordance with the reader's learning situation.

You will be taking part in a simulation of a meeting involving two teams of department heads within a company that was formed as the result of a very recent merger between two companies from different continents. The aim of the meeting is to decide on company policy and work out how best to implement the decisions made.

Some of you will be playing a role as department head in one or other of the teams; some of you will be acting as observers. If you are playing a role in the meeting, you are expected to identify with the points of view given in your brief. These should be supplemented during a preparatory meeting by other information and opinions that support your team brief. This meeting will allow the team to develop its standpoints and the arguments needed to support them, as well as to devise negotiating tactics. If you are observing, you will be expected to report your observations to the teams on how the preparation for the meeting went as well as the actual simulation. Your report will be based on the questions given in your own brief.

Your instructor will explain the exact procedure and any time limitations involved.

All those involved in the simulation should read the introduction below. The teams appointed to participate in the meeting should then study their particular brief before preparing for the meeting; those appointed to observe should read their own brief to determine exactly what their task involves.

The value of this simulation – and any other simulation of its kind – depends on:

- the effort put into its preparation;
- the ability of team members to embrace the roles they are playing;
- the extent to which the observers are able to detect and describe behaviours that help or hinder effective interaction.

You are encouraged to apply, in a manner appropriate to the situation, those skills discussed in Part Three, particularly with regard to negotiating, conflict management and intercultural communicative competence generally. These factors should also form the framework for a post-simulation discussion, between the participants and observers, on the effectiveness of the interaction. Other concepts in the book could also prove to be relevant.

Learning objectives

After you have either performed the simulation and discussed the comments of the observers, or observed the simulation and discussed your comments with the performers, you should:

- Be more aware of the skills required to interact effectively, particularly with individuals from other cultures.
- Have a clearer insight into what it takes to be an effective team-member in such a situation.
- Have a deeper awareness of what intercultural communicative competence entails.

Introduction

MHC is a North American manufacturer of household equipment. It has recently merged with another production company. This company is referred to below as MHC Europe, although your instructor may decide that another company, such as MHC India or MHC Australia is more appropriate to your learning needs. If that is the case, your instructor will issue a different brief to the team negotiating with MHC America.

- MHC America would prefer to keep control over the production of all products sold in the US, because of the specific characteristics of the home market. In this respect, the company opposes a policy drawn up by MHC Europe to market its products globally.

- MHC Europe believes in developing an international image for MHC in Europe. It argues that because the MHC brand has an international appeal, the company must adopt a global marketing approach, particularly on account of the financial benefits this could bring. It proposes that MHC America should only be involved with the production of kitchen equipment and that MHC Europe should take care of larger household products such as washing machines.

MHC Europe has organized a meeting to discuss future company policy and to come to some working agreements. Two teams of division heads are meeting, one from MHC Europe and one from MHC America. Each team comprises the heads of (all or some of) the following divisions:

- production
- marketing
- sales
- finance
- public relations
- human resources

Briefing for the representatives of MHC America

- You are a US national and you work at MHC America.
- MHC America wants its products to correspond to the needs of the North American consumer. MHC Europe's intention to switch from a local to a global marketing strategy could result in MHC America losing an important share of its own market in North America.
- The North American market for household equipment has particular characteristics:

  - The consumer may prefer to cook traditional dishes but wishes to use a very broad range of modern appliances that offers maximum convenience and versatility.
  - Storage is a concern: Americans tend to buy in bulk and so need large cupboards, refrigerators and freezers for storage.
  - Consumers prefer the washing machine/dryer combi-model (because there is always a lack of space in the bathroom) and top-loading machines (because they are safer).
  - Advertising pays less attention to the purchasing price and more attention to the specific features of household equipment.
  - Distribution channels: MHC America sells more of its equipment through hypermarkets and department stores than through specialist household appliance stores.

Your counterparts at MHC Europe have proposed that MHC should adopt a global marketing approach. Using the above information and other information or opinions you consider to be relevant, prepare arguments to put forward at your meeting with the representatives of MHC Europe. As a team, draw up negotiating strategies to help you and your counterparts to come to an agreement on MHC's future marketing policy.

Briefing for the representatives of MHC Europe

- You are a European national (i.e. you come from a European country of your choice) and you work at MHC Europe.
- Although MHC Europe is smaller than MHC America in terms of turnover, you believe that the Americans will ultimately have to accept your proposal to switch from a local to a global marketing approach. The arguments you intend to put forward include:

  - MHC Europe has coped very well with the many changes in the European market and has pursued a successful integration of its various national operations there;
  - MHC Europe has considerable know-how in terms of the specifications needed for international products;
  - The strategy used in Europe should be pursued on a global scale, bringing even more substantial cost reductions, particularly through the use of internationally oriented advertising and other marketing channels;
  - The quality of MHC products in the global market will be enhanced through the incorporation of MHC America's prestigious brands;
  - Changes are taking place in consumers' purchasing patterns. Consumers are showing increasing preference for international rather than national products. Global consumers are emerging, characterized by their preference for similar kitchens with the same sort of appliances, such as microwave ovens, cookers, washing machines, all of a standard design. The quality and the safety of these appliances satisfy more or less the same standards.

Using the above considerations, as well as any other information or opinions you consider relevant, prepare your argumentation for a global marketing approach. As a team, draw up negotiating strategies to help you and your counterparts to come to an agreement on MHC's future marketing policy.

Briefing for the observers

Your goal is to prepare an account of your team's performance during the meeting, with particular focus on the verbal and non-verbal behaviour used towards the other team. The questions below are intended to guide you in your observations as well as to help you draw conclusions about your team's effectiveness during the interaction.

During preparation

- How did the team make its preparations?
- How would you describe the team's attitude towards the other team? Note any relevant remarks made, particularly those you think reflect certain prejudices.
- How would you describe the negotiating strategy drawn up? Is it, for example, competitive or co-operative in nature?
- To what extent did the members of the team show willingness to work together and suppress or adapt their individual wishes?

During the meeting

- Watch how the interaction between your team and the other proceeds. Note examples of your team's behaviour that you felt helped or hindered the meeting to reach its goal.
- Pinpoint, in particular, a key moment where the interests of both parties came into conflict. Follow the interaction closely and describe as best you can the behaviour (verbal and non-verbal) of the group and/or

individuals concerned. How effectively do you think your team handled that moment? What was the outcome?

- Note any examples from your team of empathy and/or mindfulness (see Chapter 18). What effect do you think they had on the proceedings?
- How closely did the group follow the negotiating strategy prepared beforehand? How do you account for any changes made to the strategy?
- To what extent do you think the goal of the meeting was reached by the end? What issues are still outstanding? How would you describe the relations between the two teams at the end of the meeting?
- What do you think should be the next step in the deliberations between the two parties? Explain why.

After the meeting

- Present a summary of your observations to both teams and add your comments on the general effectiveness of the teams in terms of their communication skills.
- Use this summary as the starting-point for a discussion with the participants.

The Vechtel case study deals with the cross-cultural problems experienced by a Dutch brewery's takeover of French breweries. The events described are based on the actual experiences of a Dutch brewer's endeavours to gain a foothold in the French brewing industry.

This case does not present a problem with the expectation that those studying it will come up with a solution. What the case does instead is to present events from the recent past and to describe the perceptions of those involved. By doing so, the case embraces many of the topics dealt with in this book, including:

- international takeovers
- leadership in an international environment
- cross-cultural communication
- company cultures
- stereotyping.

Learning objectives

After reading this case study and answering the questions, you should:

- Be in a position to identify typical cultural issues that companies and their managers can encounter when involved in an international take-over.
- Understand how such cultural issues can be effectively and appropriately managed.
- Be aware of how all the factors in this book relating to culture and management, culture and organization as well as culture and communication can be present in one particular international takeover scenario.

Vechtel – a case study

Adapting an international approach to the local market

1. BEFORE THE MEETING

The morning commuter traffic crawled through the suburbs of Lyons. Jean-Pierre Courbet sat at the wheel of his Renault, on his way to a meeting at Vechtel's headquarters. He had time, as usual, to contemplate his present situation. While doing so, he looked around at the name displays in the street and was encouraged by the ever-increasing presence of the Vechtel name amongst the myriad signs.

He had an urgent meeting with Jaap Harmelen, Vechtel France's chief executive. The meeting had been hastily planned the evening before and the agenda was not too clear – Harmelen's secretary had been vague when questioned. Courbet thought he got on well with Harmelen, despite a feeling that Vechtel headquarters in Rotterdam was always looking over Harmelen's shoulder. For Vechtel had recently taken over the ramshackle group of breweries that Courbet himself had been trying to manage. Now the group was in the middle of a radical restructuring and it was causing him and many of the old guard considerable pain.

From time to time Courbet wondered whether he had made right decision to stay on and help Vechtel in its mammoth task. Events in Spain were giving him doubts. For it was there that Vechtel had bought its way into a huge brewery and, from what he had heard, read and seen, the takeover was not going well. For a start there was a basic communication problem at local headquarters: key figures did not share the same language and were using interpreters a lot of the time. Some local managers had been fired, including a key marketing executive, and they had been replaced by Dutch expatriates. This was, in Courbet's eyes, a recipe for possible disaster.

There were not too many communication problems in Lyons at least, thought Courbet. He himself could manage English, and his skills were improving by the day through contact with Rotterdam HQ. The younger managers were better trained and could more than cope. Harmelen himself was proficient in English and, perhaps more importantly, he could speak fluent French. On top of that he seemed to be a real Francophile, one who particularly relished France's dedication to food and drink.

As for the present organizational upheavals, Harmelen seemed to be doing his best in a very difficult situation. There had been dismissals of some of Courbet's French colleagues, but Courbet thought this was inevitable in a reorganization where there were many overlapping parts – a consequence of previous mergers between rival breweries who had been thrown into each other's arms. Technical and financial experts had been called in from other operating companies belonging to Vechtel, but some key positions were still held by the French. Jean-Pierre Courbet was still there, advising the chief executive and helping to keep the train running while the rails were being changed. But what was going to happen next?

After taking over in Lyons, Vechtel had talked with great relish and persuasion about the power of Vechtel's brand name and the need to exploit this power as much as possible. This inevitably put a question mark over the future of some of the French brands the company was still promoting. Courbet realized there were too many of them and some rationalization would eventually be necessary. So far, however, he knew of no concrete plans.

There was one component in the French acquisition that Vechtel seemed to have problems with – Inter-HRC, the distribution company. As director of Inter-HRC, Courbet had spent a lot of time justifying the way it operated, particularly since the company was distributing its rivals' products as well as those of Vechtel. Up to now Vechtel had been persuaded to keep its hands off Inter-HRC, but Jean-Pierre was not optimistic. After all, Vechtel had been quick to sell off the distribution arm of the brewery it had bought in Spain.

Jean-Pierre Courbet could not help feeling that eventually things would go the way they had gone in Spain. Although he had heard that the Spanish operation was supposed to become the jewel in the Vechtel crown, he could not help feeling that the ruthless approach being taken there was a recipe for disaster. Would Vechtel make the same mistakes in France?

Jean-Pierre had no illusions. Although the board of directors had expressed confidence in the future of its French operation, Jean-Pierre knew the venture was a risky one. He had heard that Arie van der Vecht himself, the son of the founder of the Vechtel brewery, had pushed for the takeover in France. This was seen as one of Arie's many whims – a capricious addition to Vechtel's portfolio of companies, one resulting from Arie's strong emotional attachment to France. In fact, Jean-Pierre had the feeling that Vechtel believed the venture in Spain would be more successful than the one he was helping to run in France.

Courbet was now queuing to turn right into the street where the headquarters stood. Which direction, he thought, would his career take? Would he continue to have a role to play in reviving the breweries' fortunes? Or was he going to be set aside along with other relics of the old breweries?

Jean-Pierre looked at his reflection in the rear-view mirror. 'You're not easy to get on with, are you?' he said to himself. 'The trouble with you is you're not afraid to speak your mind. Why don't you blah-blah like those other polished executives you've met?'

Jean-Pierre cringed at the thought. He wasn't ever going to be like those graduates from exclusive top business schools (the 'Grandes Ecoles') who, as managers, still behaved as if they were analysing a business strategy case study. But he wasn't the blustering, domineering sort of old-style manager either: he simply saw no point in obsequious behaviour towards his new bosses. If he didn't agree, he said so. He wasn't looking for trouble; all that he wanted was the best for the company.

And the first signs were very encouraging. Since taking over, Vechtel seemed ready to learn, dynamic, open, willing to take the long-term view. But did they want Courbet to stay on? He had been the key instigator in their taking over the company, but he knew that sentimentality or gratitude for past good deeds was not necessarily a reason for keeping him on. Spain had showed how mercilessly Vechtel could act.

Why did Jaap Harmelen want to see him so urgently? Had the time had come for Vechtel and Jean-Pierre Courbet to go their different ways?

2. FROM VECHTEL FRANCE TO BRASSERIES VECHTEL

France: a beer-drinking country

France may still have the image of being a country of heavy wine-drinkers, but beer has come to play an increasingly important role in French drinking-habits. During the 1950s and 1960s there was a considerable increase in beer consumption and these years were the hey-day of the many small breweries scattered throughout France. From the mid-1970s, however, the increase in beer consumption levelled off and started declining. From then on many of the small breweries were forced to merge and some even had to close. By the mid-1980s two brewery groups dominated the market: together they accounted for over three quarters of all beer production.

The majority of the breweries in France are to be found in two regions – Alsace and le Nord. As any visitor to Alsace will discover, the region enjoys a long history of beer making – there were already nine brewers established in Strasbourg in the fourteenth century. Nowadays it accounts for about half of all beer consumed in France. The region Nord – with the city of Lille at its centre – is equally proud of its brewing skills. It dominated the brewing industry until after the Second World War, but now its position has gradually become less prominent. Together with all the other regional breweries outside Alsace, the region Nord accounts for only about one third of French beer production, despite the fact that it still contains a large number of breweries.

Vechtel to the rescue

As Figure A3.1 shows, Union du Nord, one of the three companies forming Groupe du Nord, was itself a collection of smaller breweries. It was Jean-Pierre Courbet who, as Union du Nord's general manager, had pulled the company out of an extremely precarious financial situation. Without any well-crafted strategy or other sophisticated means at his disposal, he had cajoled and bullied the breweries into grasping whatever opportunities they could find to increase sales. As part of the consolidation process within the industry, Union du Nord had been compelled to merge with its main rival, Brasseries Lilloises, to form Groupe du Nord. Despite this, survival was by no means assured. Courbet often talked about how everyone had used their bare hands to dig their way out of the red.

It was Courbet who saw that outside intervention was necessary to pull together the motley bunch forming Groupe du Nord and to give it financial strength. He approached Vechtel in the Netherlands, as well as a Danish brewery, to discuss possible co-operation. The Danes appeared to be interested in a licensing agreement only, but Vechtel was ready to go further, particularly as Vechtel saw its increased involvement in France as a step to reaching its goal – to become a dominant company in the European beer market.

Vechtel BV took over Groupe du Nord and merged it with Vechtel France to form Brasseries Unies. This company therefore comprised three components: Brasseries Lilloises, Union du Nord and Vechtel France. Relations between the three were strained: Brasseries Lilloises and Vechtel France were both full of resentment about being managed by the 'patron' of the third component of the new company, Union du Nord. Brasseries Lilloises took great pride in its very rigorous approach to the brewing of its beer, and was proud of its hard-working approach to the *métier*. Now it saw itself being run by the mercenary manager of the Union du Nord, who had fought tooth and nail to keep his own company afloat. Vechtel France, on the other hand, was proud of its role in developing the cult of the Vechtel brand in France and saw itself as Vechtel's torchbearer.

The original division between Vechtel France and Groupe du Nord soon showed itself to be unworkable. There were conflicting interests, particularly with regard to long-term plans: Vechtel wanted a freer rein and so, in 1997, it bought out the rest of Brasseries Unies' shareholding.

Apart from having to contend with internal friction, Vechtel also had to deal with a deplorable set of financial figures, an excessive number of breweries and an overloaded portfolio of brands. Restructuring was badly needed: several breweries would have to be closed, people laid off and the brand range revised to ensure that those brands remaining could be given sufficient support.

There was, however, one profitable company in the holding – the distribution company Inter-HRC. It was a major wholesale distributor in France and had around 70 subsidiaries scattered throughout the country. Despite it being a Vechtel company as well as an active promoter of Vechtel products, it also distributed the products of its competitors.

Although the French were naturally suspicious of their new owners, they soon discovered that Vechtel's approach to the company was intelligent and not too interventionist. A Dutch manager, Jaap Harmelen, was brought in by the corporate headquarters in Rotterdam to run Brasseries Unies. He turned out to be a considerate director, one who displayed dignity and sagacity, someone who respected the various brewery cultures within the company despite the friction they

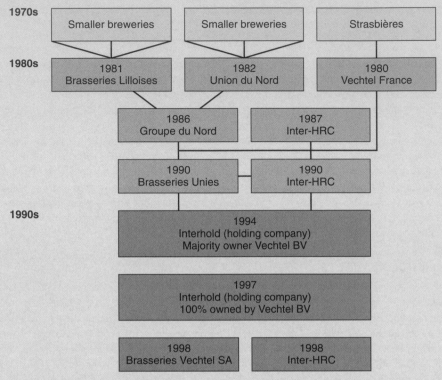

Figure A3.2.1 The path to Brasseries Vechtel

Notes: **Brasseries Unies** was formed in 1990, the result of a merger between Groupe du Nord and Vechtel France. Groupe du Nord itself had been the product of an earlier merger between Union du Nord and Brasseries Lilloises (based in Lille). The distribution arms of both groups were brought together to form a separate operating company, Inter-HRC.

    Vechtel France was the name given to an Alsatian brewery (Strasbières), which Vechtel BV had bought in 1980. Wanting to gain a larger share of a very competitive market, Vechtel France had decided to join together with Groupe du Nord to form Brasseries Unies. Vechtel France had a majority of the share equity, Groupe du Nord the rest.

were causing. He trod carefully, slowly creating confidence among employees as to the future of the company, despite the urgent restructuring now being planned.

    Harmelen was blown off course for a while, however, when in 1998 it was decided to change the company's name – from 'Brasseries Unies' to 'Brasseries Vechtel'. The idea behind the change was to accelerate the integration of the loose elements in the company by creating a clear identity, a Vechtel identity, both within and to the world outside. There was a lingering resistance to the change at all levels of the work force, and Jaap Harmelen was told on many occasions, in very clear terms, what his employees thought of the new name. He could not expect an overnight change of name to create an immediate change of attitude.

    It was Mr Harmelen with whom Jean-Pierre Courbet had his urgent appointment.

3. THE MEETING

Jean-Pierre Courbet walked quickly towards Jaap Harmelen's office. He was ten minutes late, but Harmelen's secretary offered him a cup of coffee while Harmelen was finishing a phone call. Jean-Pierre was eventually shown in, cup in hand, to be confronted by his very agitated boss.

    'Have you heard the news?' asked Harmelen as he firmly shook Courbet's hand and showed him a chair at the same time. Before Jean-Pierre could answer, Harmelen exclaimed, 'The management team at the Spanish brewery has been sent back to the Netherlands!'

Jean-Pierre was not surprised. He said nothing, but sipped his coffee. Staring into his cup he said, 'I suppose we sort of saw it coming. After all, they had sold their distribution network – you don't just sell an invaluable asset like that. If you do, you're bound to lose market share.'

'Come on,' said Harmelen impatiently, 'You know they had a great range of beer brands – that should have been enough, shouldn't it?'

Jean-Pierre looked at the clutch of beer bottles at the centre of the table. 'OK,' he agreed reluctantly, 'they had the Vechtel brands. But what about the local brands, Jaap? What did they do with them?'

Harmelen got up slowly from the table and walked to his secretary's office, deep in thought. He returned with a jug of coffee. 'Vechtel's approach was all wrong,' he said while topping up their cups. 'The company didn't understand the way the country was going. It wasn't up to the task. The management simply made too many mistakes. If the management is good, it will always find its way out of trouble.'

Jean-Pierre looked him in the eye. 'You know,' Jean-Pierre said scornfully, 'they didn't have a single Spaniard in the management team. What's more, not one manager could put together more than three words of Spanish. They had no idea about the way the Spanish do things. No idea about their feelings of pride! You've got to show that you at least have some idea about Spanish culture when you're taking over a local brewery!'

'You're right,' sighed Harmelen.

'We're lucky here, you know,' added Jean-Pierre before Harmelen could continue. 'The management here takes us seriously – you listen to us!'

'You're referring to Inter-HRC, the distribution company! Well, you were shouting so loud, we had no alternative but to keep it running! After all, as you say, the Horeca industry ('Horeca' being the Dutch abbreviation for the Hotel, Restaurant and Catering sector) is so difficult to segment – but the people running it do make up a considerable number of our customers in France – about 40,000 in all.'

'But that's not the only reason for keeping the distribution network,' Jean-Pierre responded. 'It's more complicated than that. You've got to go along to these pubs and bistros, chat up the people running them, shake hands with the new boss, get to know everyone personally. That's the way to get your beer sold in this country!'

'That's what we should have done in Spain,' said Harmelen, clearly annoyed. 'After all, they're the same sort of people as in France. They expect the personal touch, good contacts with the brewery.'

Harmelen pushed his coffee cup away and brought a smile to his face. 'Anyway,' he said cheerfully, 'that's not really why I called you in, Jean-Pierre. I know we've got a pile of things to do on the restructuring, but first I want to talk about you!'

Jean-Pierre felt his heart thumping fiercely. He gripped his coffee cup while Harmelen continued.

'You know all about the bottom line, don't you, Jean-Pierre? Rotterdam wants as quick a turnaround as possible. We're still too top-heavy. We've still got to rationalize further. We can't just stop here.'

After a long pause, he continued. 'There is, however, another, more important consideration: our market share. Rotterdam agrees with me that we've got to do everything to push it up. What's the point of it all if we start losing our customers? We've got to keep them and find new ones. That's our priority number one.'

Jean-Pierre shuffled in his chair. He felt anxious and relieved at the same time.

'I want you to go after that market share,' continued Harmelen. 'Yes, you! I'm going back to Rotterdam soon, to sit on the board, and I want you to take over here!'

Two hours later, after both had gone through the immense task that Jean-Pierre had been set, Harmelen and Courbet were walking to the café opposite the company's headquarters. They'd been talking beer all morning and now it was time to remind themselves of that Vechtel taste – and to celebrate Jean-Pierre's appointment to the position of chief at Vechtel's French operation.

4. SCHAEFFER FOR SALE

Expansion

After taking over Harmelen's position, Jean-Pierre Courbet had quickly established his position. He had managed to calm the waters after the change of company name from Brasseries Unies to Brasseries Vechtel. This was essentially due to the immense respect he had already acquired within Vechtel.

Vechtel was now in full control of Interhold, the holding company, and had successfully introduced its main brands into France. The country had become a strategic market for Vechtel, one in which the Vechtel Group had become a dominant player.

By 1997, Vechtel's expansion plans in Europe were well on course. The strategy of strengthening the Vechtel brand through buying local brewers with a strong local distribution network was still being followed. Vechtel had moved into Eastern Europe, and had strengthened its position in Western Europe by increasing its participation in companies it had bought stakes in during the 1990s.

Jean-Pierre Courbet was ever mindful of the question of Vechtel's market share in France and the need to improve it. Vechtel was doing well despite the tough competition. It was not yet market leader, but was rapidly improving its position, and was in fact beating its rivals in the Horeca sector. The own-brand beers sold by the large supermarkets were increasing in popularity and this was putting pressure on all branded beers. How could Vechtel improve its position in the French market?

The Schaeffer brewery, together with its subsidiary, Société Mundolsheim, came into the picture. Schaeffer, a family-controlled company, was quoted on the French stock exchange. It was one of the top five French brewers and was based in Alsace, where Vechtel had made its entry into the French market. Schaeffer was renowned for its speciality Alsatian beers, which sold well in the premium sector. Schaeffer's Mundolsheim subsidiary had built up its business by brewing *premier prix* beers – made for supermarkets to sell under their own name.

Long before the news reached the business press, Jean-Pierre Courbet had discovered that all was not well with the management of the company. Through his contacts in the brewery world he learnt that there were two factions within the management who were at each other's throats. As someone who had experienced similar boardroom battles when trying to manage an alliance of very different small breweries, he knew that this might be the moment for Vechtel to strike. If his company was to increase its market share in one fell swoop, a takeover of a strife-ridden company such as Schaeffer might be the answer.

Jean-Pierre realized that Vechtel had the power to manoeuvre. The mother company had plenty of cash in the bank as well as willing lenders. Moreover, it would be willing to invest the time needed to make the takeover a success. The other possible contenders in such a takeover would, he felt, be reluctant to pay what was sure to be a high price. They were so obsessed by the stock market that they would be unwilling to put their profitability at risk in the short-term.

Key to Jean-Pierre's plans was the future status of Schaeffer. Although the takeover was intended to strengthen the Vechtel brand, he did not want to see Schaeffer absorbed into Brasseries Vechtel, but to survive as a separate operating company within the Interhold holding. He advocated this step not just to allow the families running the brewery to keep some control after the takeover – a demand they would certainly put forward in the negotiations – but also to acknowledge in organizational terms the ever-increasing importance of speciality beers. Schaeffer was, after all, renowned as a brewer of special Alsatian beers.

Jean-Pierre also believed that Schaeffer's Mundolsheim subsidiary – which had built up its business by brewing *premier prix* beers for supermarkets to sell under their own name – should be hived off and designated as a further operating company under the Interhold umbrella. Again, this was the organization taking account of an area of the beer market – own-label beers – that was developing at a fast rate and putting the sales of national and international beer brands under pressure. The operating company he was proposing would also include another brewery that Vechtel was in the middle of taking over. This was the Noyelles brewery, based in Northern France, another brewer of own-label beers, which had its own distribution arm.

Deliberation

As he put together this detailed strategy, Jean-Pierre knew that its realization depended on his ability to convince the board in Rotterdam. He knew that the members had confidence in his judgement, but would still need to be presented with a solid case for the take-over.

Courbet raised the matter with the board at one of their frequent and regular meetings. Their initial reaction was luke-warm, to say the least. The questions and comments were many and Courbet had to explain in great detail the context in which the takeover was happening and the need for creating separate operating companies. One member of that board was his old sparring-partner, Jaap Harmelen, the previous chief of Brasseries Unies. Harmelen, who frequently confessed to one and all that he had become a real Francophile, gave gentle backing to Jean-Pierre's plans, adding supportive points of information where needed. Harmelen eventually called upon the members of the board to give Courbet the green light and to allow him to prepare detailed plans for the takeover. The board agreed.

Jean-Pierre set to work on the dossiers. Not only would they have to stand up to Rotterdam's critical scrutiny, they would also have to go as far as possible towards meeting Schaeffer's financial demands. On top of all that, the dossiers would need to deal with the other concerns of the Schaeffer management and its employees. Schaeffer's family managers would be reluctant not only to lose control but also to see the Schaeffer tradition jeopardized. The unions who would doubtless be involved in negotiations would do everything to prevent redundancies. Unemployment was their greatest fear: the number of unemployed in France was high and rising. In this respect Vechtel was generally regarded as a good employer: it knew a chequebook in such a situation was not the only answer. Its approach was more philanthropic and long-term.

There was also the possibility that the French government might throw a spanner in the works by raising objections. It might regard the move as one leading to an unhealthy domination of the market and use this as a reason for applying its anti-monopoly legislation.

Jean-Pierre set to work using not only his own vast experience but also that of the Vechtel group: Vechtel had recently created working groups relating to key areas of the business: logistics, purchasing, marketing – where the expertise of the various Vechtel companies were brought together. The resulting synergy helped to create various initiatives across the Vechtel group.

Despite initial resistance to Courbet's plans, the board gradually warmed to them. The weight of Jean-Pierre's experience in the French market and the tenacity of his conviction that the Vechtel organization in France must develop in line with the market it was serving, made the directors think again.

Courbet presented his finalized dossiers to the board in Rotterdam and, once it had given its approval, the talks with Schaeffer could begin. The negotiation team consisted of Harmelen, Vechtel's lawyer and a Dutch banker. These were to be supplemented at certain stages of the talks by experts to discuss nitty-gritty details. Courbet himself did not want to participate actively in the process: he had no wish to get caught up in the intensive day-to-day, hour-by-hour negotiations. He wanted to keep a clear head and a clear overview of progress, so preferred instead to stay behind the scenes, discussing progress with his team during the many adjournments as well as talking informally to the other side.

EPILOGUE

Jean-Pierre was quietly sitting in his office. He had spent much of the last couple of days hovering around as the final round of negotiations took place. They had reached the finishing-line, almost. He looked nervously at the phone. Why were they taking so long? The agreement was all but signed anyway!

He picked up a sheet of paper from one of the many piles on his desk. It was the organizational chart of the holding company Interhold, new-style. He drew a ring round the Schaeffer box, the one standing proudly between the Brasseries Vechtel and the other newly created company – Noyelles/Mundolsheim.

Figure A3.2.2 Organizational chart for Interhold

And there was also Inter-HRC – the grand survivor. In Spain, the company Vechtel had taken over had got rid of its distribution arm, and Jean-Pierre had felt under pressure to do the same in France. He had resisted. If he had not been able to make Vechtel understand the need to respect the French way of doing things, heaven knows what would have happened. In Spain, the Dutch managers had not taken account of the Spanish context and of the dominant Horeca sector. Fortunately, he had been more persuasive, perhaps more credible as well. In the end they had listened to him, otherwise things would have gone the Spanish way.

Schaeffer had to be bought, he mused, not just to increase market share but also to develop synergies, reduce costs and improve productivity. But there was another important factors: the people involved. Large brewers, he thought to himself, couldn't really handle specialty beers. A key for success was not only the ability to adapt to the market but also to adapt to a state of mind. Why not allow beer brands their independence? Certain schools of thought advocated mergers and acquisitions because they allowed for all kinds of economies of operation. But what was often lost in the process was that vital commodity – innovation. The people working in companies that had been taken over should be allowed to give full rein to their creativity and not just follow the corporate line.

He thought back to that meeting with Harmelen where he had been told his fate. How time had flown by since then! Time, he thought to himself, is the essential component of management. It proves whether you're right or wrong. You can imagine what things will be like in ten years' time, you can set your goal. But how can you reach it? It's not strategy that can make or break a company, it's the speed and manner of its implementation.

Absorbed in his thoughts, Courbet jumps when the phone rings. As he listens to Jaap Harmelen at the other end, a broad smile spreads across his face. Mission accomplished! After putting down the phone a few minutes later, Jean-Pierre mutters to himself: 'Well, the only real way to get results is to use us locals!'

The denouement

The outcome was successful, if expensive, for Vechtel. The acquisition of a majority of the shares held by the families involved was agreed on, and Schaeffer agreed to recommend to its remaining (public) shareholders that they accept Vechtel's offer to buy the remaining shares. So Interhold acquired a majority of the shares held by the family and made an offer to purchase shares held by the public. The same procedure was used for shares held by the public in Société Mundolsheim.

Questions

1. (Overview) Define the three phases of internationalization that occurred after Vechtel took over the French company.

2. (Concept of stereotypes) To what extent is stereotyping evident in the thoughts and words of the two protagonists (Courbet and Harmelen)?

3. (Classification of cultures) What sort of effect do you think the culture of each protagonist (Courbet, Harmelen) had on the success of the takeover by Vechtel of the French company?

4. (The cultures of the companies concerned) What are the strategies of Vechtel (Rotterdam HQ) and of Brasseries Vechtel (Paris) with regard to internationalization? In what ways are they similar/different?

5. (The way the cultures concerned behave in a cross-cultural situation) How are the two internationalization strategies you have described in question 4 reconciled?

   How did the two companies arrive at a common goal, despite the differences in their respective national cultures?

6. (Conclusion) Could the internationalization process have been improved in any way?
   a) What still has to be done to make Brasseries Vechtel/Vechtel (Rotterdam) more international?
   b) Could the first phase have been shortened and/or improved?
   c) Could the takeover of Schaeffer have been realized in a better way?
   d) Which elements, on the cultural level, do you consider to be the most influential in the success of takeovers such as those described here?

Further reading

Those who wish to gain further insight into aspects of the takeover process described in the case are advised to read the following articles:

Trompenaars, F. (1996) 'Resolving international conflict: culture and business strategy' *in Business Strategy Review*, **London Business School, 7(3): 51–68.** This article forms a basis for case analysis by giving an overview of seven dimensions by which cultures can be identified. The author also focuses on the question of reconciling cultural differences as an essential component of effective strategic management.

Morden, T. (1995) 'Management in France', *Cross Cultural Management: An International Journal*, **3(3): 31–38.** This article examines the nature of work relations in France before giving particular attention to the character and role of the *cadre* (the manager) and the professional status such people enjoy.

Dijk van, N. and Punch M. (1993) 'Open borders, closed circles: management and organization in the Netherlands' in **Hickson, D. (ed.),** *Management in Western Europe*, **Berlin/New York: Walter de Gruyter.** This chapter examines Dutch society and Dutch business, and attempts to find the source of what the authors call the mechanism of pragmatic accommodation, which permeates so many of the country's institutional arrangements.

Index